I0820971

JAN DVOŘÁK
ADAM HRADILEK

CZECHOSLOVAK JEWISH REFUGEES IN THE GULAG

SOVIET LABOUR AND POW CAMPS DURING WORLD WAR II AS RECOLLECTED BY JEWISH REFUGEES FROM CZECHOSLOVAKIA

CHARLES UNIVERSITY
KAROLINUM PRESS

INSTITUTE FOR THE STUDY
OF TOTALITARIAN REGIMES

PRAGUE 2025

KAROLINUM PRESS is a publishing department of Charles University
Ovocný trh 560/5, 116 36 Prague 1, Czech Republic
www.karolinum.cz

Originally published in Czech as *Židé v gulagu. Sovětské pracovní a zajatecké tábory za druhé světové války ve vzpomínkách židovských uprchlíků z Československa* by the Institute for the Study of Totalitarian Regimes in 2017 within the project Czechoslovaks in The Gulag https://cechoslovacivgulagu.cz/en/index.html.

The original manuscript was reviewed by PhDr. Lukáš Babka (Slavonic Library in Prague), and PhDr. Zdeněk Vališ

This publication is made possible thanks to a contribution from the Foundation for Holocaust Victims, funded by a Czech Ministry of Culture grant.

Cover and graphic design Jan Šerých
Copyediting Megan A. Bedell
Set and printed in the Czech Republic by Karolinum Press
First English edition

Cataloguing-in-Publication Data is available from the National Library of the Czech Republic

© Charles University, Karolinum Press, 2025
© Institute for the Study of Totalitarian Regimes, 2025
Translation © Mike Allen, 2025

ISBN 978-80-246-5926-8 (Karolinum Press)
ISBN 978-80-7516-062-1 (Institute for the Study of Totalitarian Regimes)
ISBN 978-80-246-5927-5 (pdf, Karolinum Press)

CONTENTS

In the gulags people were not systematically killed because they belonged to a particular race. On the other hand, membership of a certain class was there, too, something like a sentence of death. In all other respects, gulags and concentration camps were totally the same: here as well as there, detainees were used as slave labour. Here as well as there, was the kind of nutrition that must have been known to result in starvation. Here as well as there, were the same atrocious hygienic conditions, with epidemics causing men to die like flies. [...] Though Stalin might have argued that he had dispensed with systematic murder, nevertheless, in his unsystematic manner, he was responsible for the deaths of even more people than lost their lives in Hitler's concentration camps.

Simon Wiesenthal: Justice, not Vengeance: Recollections

I think with horror and shame of a Europe divided into two parts by the line of the Bug, on one side of which millions of Soviet slaves prayed for liberation by the armies of Hitler, and on the other millions of victims of German concentration camps awaited deliverance by the Red Army as their last hope.

Gustaw Herling-Grudziński: A World Apart

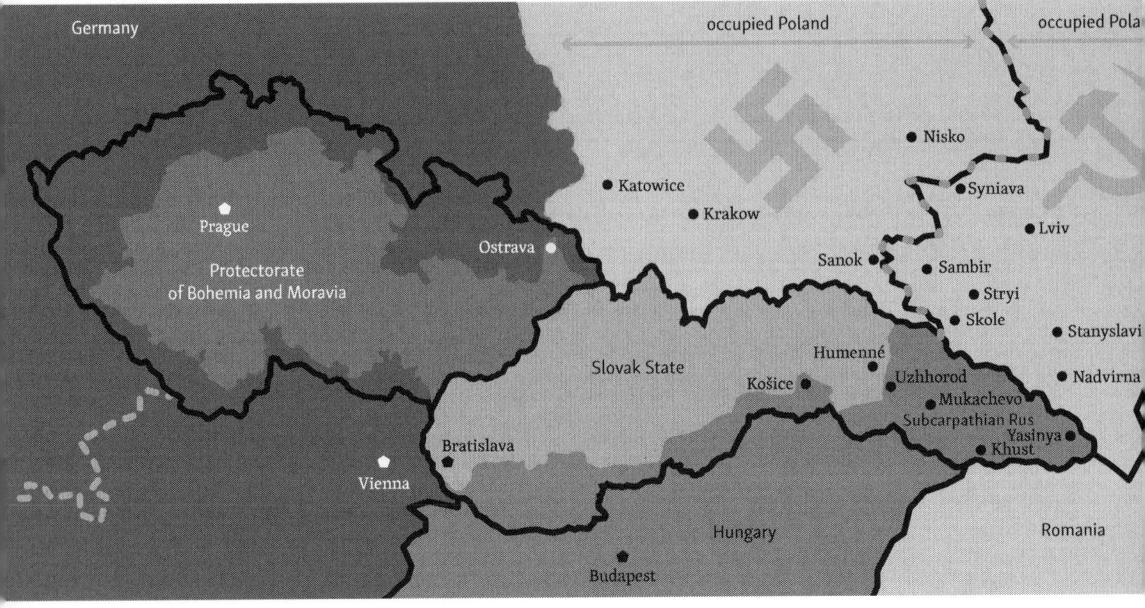

The former Czechoslovakia and part of occupied Poland, marking the places associated with the wave of refugees to the Soviet Union in the years 1939–1941. *Tomáš Říha*

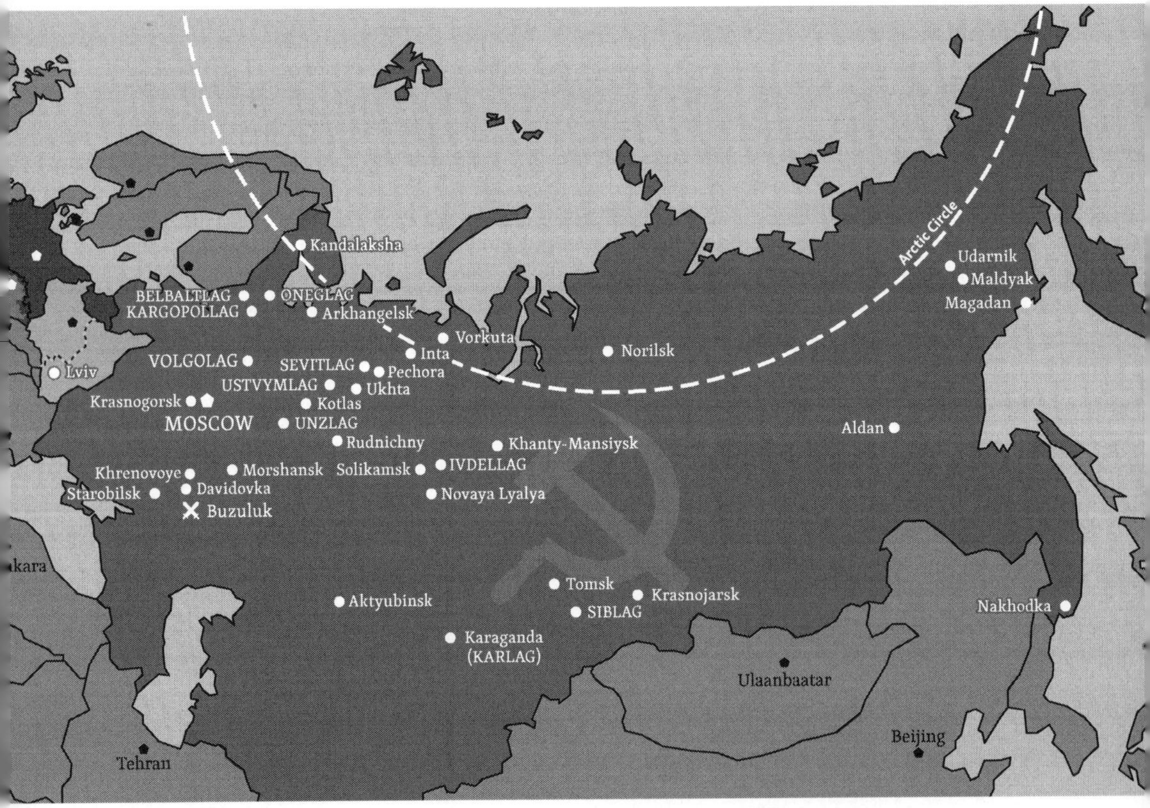

Soviet labour and POW camps (or the places they were close to) in which the refugees from Czechoslovakia whose stories are published in this book were imprisoned. *Tomáš Říha*

INTRODUCTION

Historical research on political repression in the Soviet Union to date has shown that in the period from the 1920s to 1950s, this repression affected around 15,000 Czechoslovak citizens and Czech nationals settled in Soviet territory in various forms.[1] Much like the local population, so did both Czechs and members of ethnic minorities originally from Czechoslovakia become victims of the various forms of persecution and terror that flared up at various times with varying intensity over the existence of the USSR. Be it the fight against the anti-Bolshevik opposition during the Civil War, the subsequent Sovietisation of society, the forced collectivisation of the countryside, or the obsession with espionage, this repression always paralysed the whole of society for years at a time. To date it remains a little-known fact that the greatest rise in Soviet repression against Czechoslovaks occurred during World War II, when a considerable portion of the Czechoslovak population was severely affected by persecution from the Nazi occupiers, with its Jewish population even facing the threat of extermination. The tragedy of the war-time fate of the local Jews is amplified by the fact that they were the second largest group of Czechoslovak citizens affected by the repressive Soviet regime in the years 1939–1945. A large number of studies have been published on this topic, among them several scholarly publications.[2] This book aims to

---

1 This approximate number of victims is based primarily on the research done by Professor Mečislav Borák and his colleagues from the Silesian University in Opava and the research team of the Institute for the Study of Totalitarian Regimes. More on this topic BORÁK, Mečislav: *České stopy v Gulagu. Z výzkumu perzekuce Čechů a občanů ČSR v Sovětském svazu* [Czech Traces in the Gulag. From Research on the Persecution of Czechs and Czechoslovak Citizens in the Soviet Union]. Silesian Museum, Opava 2003; idem (ed.): *Perzekuce československých občanů v Sovětském svazu (1918–1956). Sborník studií. Část 1. Vězni a popravení* [Persecution of Czechoslovak Citizens in the Soviet Union (1918–1956). Collection of Studies. Part 1. Prisoners and Executees.]. Silesian Museum – Silesian University in Opava, Opava 2007; DVOŘÁK, Jan – FORMÁNEK, Jaroslav – HRADILEK, Adam: *Čechoslováci v Gulagu* [Czechoslovaks in the Gulag]. Czech Television – Institute for the Study of Totalitarian Regimes, Prague 2017.

2 E.g. KULKA, Erich: *Židé v československé Svobodově armádě* [Jews in the Czechoslovak Svoboda's Army]. Naše vojsko, Prague 1990; BORÁK, Mečislav: "Českoslovenští Židé – oběti gulagů a popravišť v Sovětském svazu" [Czechoslovak Jews – Victims of Gulags and Execution Centres in the Soviet Union]. In: MACHAČOVÁ, Helena (ed.): *První pražský seminář. Dopady holocaustu na českou a slovenskou společnost ve druhé polovině 20. století* [First Prague Seminar. The Impact of the Holocaust on Czech and Slovak Society in the Second Half of the 20th Century]. Varius Praha – Spolek akademiků Židů, Prague 2008, p. 97–110; idem: *První deportace evropských Židů. Transporty do Niska nad Sanem (1939–1945)* [First Deportations of European Jews. Transports to Nisko

add to the existing findings with a collection of personal testimonies from those who experienced the events directly that were collected from various national and international archives.

IN THE CROSSHAIRS OF THE GESTAPO AND THE NKVD

At the end of the 1930s, refugees from many European countries threatened or occupied by the Nazis or their allies were seeking refuge in various countries around the world, where they met with varying degrees of sympathy and receptiveness. They encountered rather specific treatment in the Soviet Union, where society was paralysed by fear in the aftermath of the Great Terror.[3] In the years 1939–1941, the focal point of Soviet repression shifted from the interior to the newly occupied regions of Poland, the Baltics and Romania that the USSR had acquired on the basis of its agreement with Nazi Germany, the Molotov-Ribbentrop Pact. The main task of the Soviet security forces was to ensure the rapid Sovietisation of these territories. Repression not only targeted all opponents to the Soviet regime, "class enemies", and ethnic minorities, but also the hundreds of thousands of refugees that had found temporary refuge there from the oppression of authoritarian regimes, racial persecution and the advancing German army. Among these were refugees from Czechoslovakia, who came to the territory of the USSR in the years 1939–1941 in two main waves – from the Protectorate and from Hungarian-occupied Subcarpathian Rus. This totalled approximately ten thousand people, with the second largest group after the Ruthenians being Jews. According to current research, these numbered two thousand.[4] In comparison, refugees from the Slovak State only chose the Soviet Union as a destination in isolated cases (see the fate of Ernest Breiner on p. 210). Though these refugees escaped persecution by the Nazi and Hungarian occupiers or Slovak fascists by

(1939–1945)]. 2nd revised edition. Český svaz bojovníků za svobodu, Ostrava 2009; DVOŘÁK, Jan – HRADILEK, Adam: "Perzekuce československých Židů v Sovětském svazu za druhé světové války" [Persecution of Czechoslovak Jews in the Soviet Union in World War II]. In: *Historie – Otázky – Problémy* [History – Questions – Problems], 2013, No. 1, p. 105–120.

3 The Great Terror – one of the phases of political repression in the USSR in the years 1936–1938, during which some 700,000 innocent people were shot and hundreds of thousands more incarcerated in work camps and prisons. For more see e.g., CONQUEST, Robert: *The Great Terror: A Reassessment*. Oxford University Press, Oxford 1991; on the statistics of the Great Terror see ZEMSKOV, Viktor N.: K voprosu o masshtabakh represiy v SSSR. *Sociologicheskie issledovania*, 1995, no. 9, p. 123.

4 In his studies, E. Kulka estimates the number of Jewish refugees at five thousand, of which at least four thousand were taken to NKVD camps. Research at the archives of the former NKVD suggests however that the number was likely about half that. Cf. KULKA, Erich: *Židé v československé Svobodově armádě* [Jews in the Czechoslovak Svoboda's Army], p. 132.

In the years 1939–1945, the Soviets used thousands of refugees fleeing Nazism for slave labour in the Gulag. Construction of the Kotlas–Vorkuta railway, with the labour camp in the background. *Komi Republic National Archives*

fleeing to the east, most of them were sentenced to years of forced labour in the Gulag[5] camps for illegally crossing the border, espionage and other fabricated criminal offences. A specific group was those Jews who had either deserted or been captured by the Soviets as members of the Hungarian army's labour units.[6]

Refugee's sentences were to be served at camps and work colonies run by the Soviet secret police, the NKVD,[7] all over the Soviet Union, but especially in the polar regions of northern Russia, the Urals, the Volga, Kazakhstan and Siberia. All these areas were home to large-scale extraction of mineral resources – lumber, coal, crude oil and gold – or camp complexes tied to the

5 Gulag – short for the Russian title Glavnoe upravlenie lagerei, in English Chief Administration for Camps, which fell under the NKVD (see footnote 7) and ran the hundreds of labour complexes through which millions of prisoners passed in the years 1930–1960.

6 A separate chapter is dedicated to this issue, *Deserters from the Auxiliary Labour Units of the Hungarian Army and Prisoners of War in Internment Camps.*

7 NKVD – short for Narodny komissariat vnutrennih del, in English the People's Commissariat for Internal Affairs, from 1934 the name for the central security service of the Soviet Union and the main instrument of repression, dealing with such things as internal security, intelligence and counterintelligence activities, guarding the borders, and running prisons and labour camps.

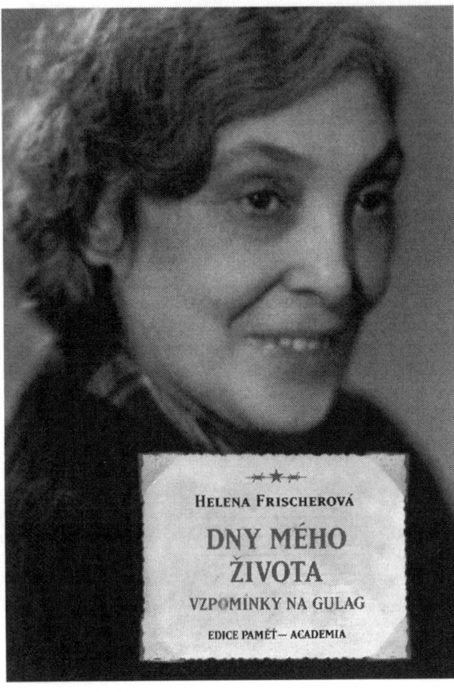

The written memoirs of Helena Frischer, born in Prostějov, a victim of the Great Terror and Gulag prisoner in the years 1937–1947, were not published in Czech Republic until 2017. *Reproduction by ÚSTR*

construction of railways or other gigantic industrial structures that required labour.[8]

At the site of their sentences, the incarcerated refugees usually encountered a broad range of other prisoners – real and imagined opponents of the Bolshevik regime, criminals, Soviet soldiers returning from Finnish captivity, or communist immigrants from Europe who had survived the Great Terror, but had been sentenced to long prison terms.[9]

Given that Jewish refugees were far from the only victims of the system of forced labour, the question arises as to whether and in what way their experience differed from that of others. Longtime Gulag prisoner and one of the icons of the Soviet dissident movement Alexandr Solzhenitsyn claims in his book *Two Hundred Years Together* that Jews lived better than the other

---

8 See KHLEVNIUK, Oleg Vitalyevich: *Historie gulagu. Od kolektivizace do „velkého teroru"* [History of the Gulag. From Collectivisation to the "Great Terror"]. BB/art, Prague 2008, p. 288–291. (English edition: *The History of the Gulag: From Collectivization to the Great Terror.* Yale University Press, New Haven & London 2004).

9 Among these were many Czechoslovaks. In 1937, for example, Helena Fischerová of Prostějov was arrested along with her husband Abraham, with whom she had lived in Moscow since 1935. While Abraham was executed not long after being arrested, Helena spent ten years in Gulag camps. She was not released until 1947. See FRISCHEROVÁ, Helena: *Dny mého života. Vzpomínky na Gulag* [Days of My Life. Memories of the Gulag]. Academia -Institute for the Study of Totalitarian Regimes, Prague 2017.

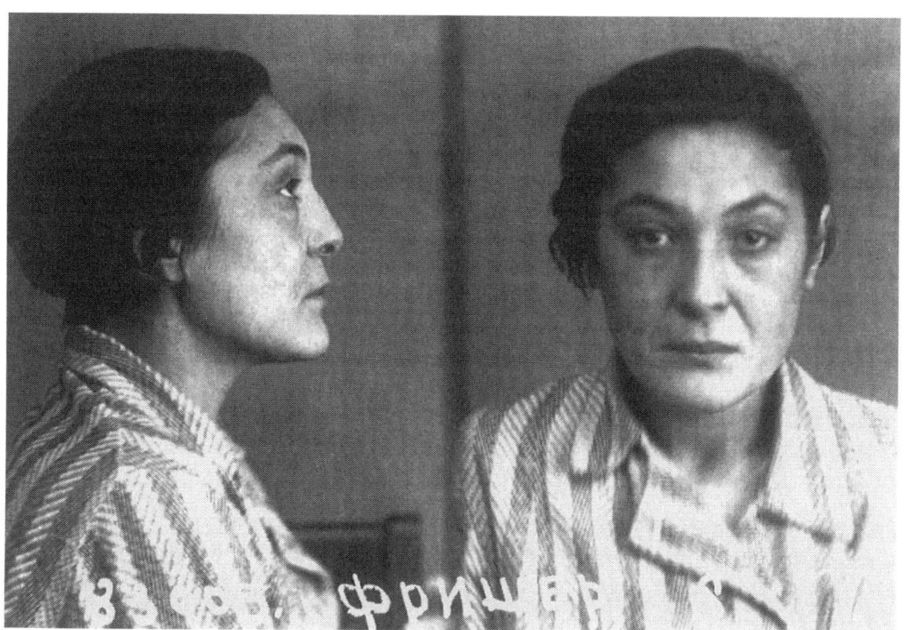
Prison photograph of Helena Frischer. *Estate of Miroslav Kryl*

prisoners in the camps.[10] Vladimír Levora (1920–1999) from the village of Křížovice near Klatovy came to a similar conclusion, having also fled Gestapo persecution to the Soviet Union as a student. There he was sentenced to the Vorkutlag camp. In his autobiographical book *Ze stalinských gulagů do československého vojska [From Stalin's Gulags to the Czechoslovak Army]*, he writes: *"Jew – that word was an insult; you had to say Hebrew. Because they occupied the cushiest jobs, no one liked them, but everyone licked their boots."*[11]

Drawing on the available archival materials and the testimony of those who were there, however, it follows that Soviet security authorities and management of the individual camps generally treated the Jewish refugees from Czechoslovakia the same as other prisoners. One proof of this is the case of two Jewish defectors from Subcarpathian Rus, who received the highest known sentence of all – 15 years of forced labour in the Gulag for alleged espionage (see p. 135). How can Solzhenitsyn and Levora's claims be explained then?

---

10 SOLZHENITSYN, Alexander Isayevich: *Dvě stě let pospolu. Dějiny rusko-židovských vztahů v letech 1795–1995* [Two Hundred Years Together. The History of Russian-Jewish Relations in 1795–1995]. Academia, Prague 2005, p. 261–270. In original: Dvesti let vmeste (1795–1995). Ruskii puť, Moscow 2001–2002.

11 LEVORA, Vladimír: *Ze stalinských gulagů do československého vojska* [From Stalin's Gulags to the Czechoslovak Army]. Organised by Zora Dvořáková. Nakl. Josef Hříbal, Plzeň 1993, p. 96.

Undoubtedly, the ability to get by in the struggle with both the criminal prisoners and other internees was important for one's position in the camp and survival. They competed with each other for a place to sleep as close to the stove as possible, for higher food rations, for favourable work assignments, a spot in the infirmary, etc. As an individual, no prisoner could have much hope of success, which amounted to survival. It is evident from the testimony of those who were there that a vital role in successfully surviving the camp was played by friends, in particular fellow countrymen. Cooperation with others meant for example helping to fill another's quota if they were sick, sharing food, protecting one another from criminals, but also providing psychological support. Just like the Poles, Finns, Latvians, Estonians and Ruthenians, so too did the Jews manage to stick together and help each other in camps. Compared to other religious and certain ethnic groups, the Jews had the advantage that, during their internment, they could run into a Soviet official, NKVD investigator or guard who were of Jewish origin, who would certainly have had more empathy and understanding for Jews fleeing the Nazis than for, say, Poles or others whom the Soviets considered enemies.

Another advantage that led to a better standing was any special skill or profession that could be utilised in the camp. This was traditionally true of physicians, but also medical students, who obtained positions as camp doctors or nurses. Beyond that, those who knew foreign languages, accountants, musicians, engineers, mechanics, watchmakers and other specialists could be useful to the camp administration in helping to run the camp, repair equipment, translate, write up reports, etc. As the prisoners often mentioned in their recollections, even a short-term special task meant breaking out of the monotonous drudgery and allowed the prisoners to regain their strength. In this regard, the more educated urban Jews, or those who knew multiple languages or trades, had a clear advantage for example over the young, strong Ruthenian refugees from the poor agricultural regions of Subcarpathian Rus, whom the camp leadership tasked with the hardest jobs. This was naturally not just true of Jews. For example, even V. Levora himself obtained the "cushy job" of painting propaganda banners for a time. On the other hand, the prisoners used to doing farm work from an early age, such as the aforementioned young Ruthenians, or the Finns used to a harsh climate, these endured the rough conditions of internment much better than people from the cities or those who had made a living other than by manual labour when they suddenly had to work hard for days on end with minimal food.

There was no official distinction between Jews and non-Jews at Soviet correctional labour camps the way there was at Nazi camps. According to the recollections of some, however, anti-Semitic insinuations and verbal attacks of an anti-Semitic nature were not uncommon on the part of investigators, guards or fellow prisoners, in particular if they were easily identifiable pious Jews. These were nevertheless more manifestations of "traditional" anti-Semitism stemming from the stereotypical prejudices about Jews or Soviet aversion to religion as such, rather than the racial version known from areas under Nazi rule. The Soviets often even punished expressions of anti-Semitism at the camps. Any religious ceremonies were prohibited, yet some prisoners still tried to secretly observe at least the most important holidays, and at some camps they even tried to uphold basic religious rituals.

Regardless of their origin, all those held at Soviet prisons and camps struggled to survive and faced essentially the same conditions.[12] The chances of surviving, however, whether at a camp or a labour colony, depended on a range of other circumstances as well – for example its geographical position, the organisational abilities of the camp leadership, the camp regime, the living and working conditions, the health care, the period of internment, and the willingness of the camp leadership to release amnestied prisoners. The death rates at camps were high. In this respect, the period from 1941 to 1942 was the most tragic in the history of the Gulag; during that time, approximately 25% of the total number of prisoners died.[13] Based on current research on refugees from Czechoslovakia that were sentenced to the Gulag in the years 1940–1942, we can speak of a mortality rate of roughly 20%. There would undoubtedly have been many more deaths, however, had the prisoners stayed at the internment camps longer. Paradoxically, many of them were saved by war breaking out between Germany and the USSR.

The German attack on the unprepared Soviet Union in June of 1941 forced the Soviet leadership to release a considerable portion of the able-bodied convicts from the camps and prisons. Some Czechoslovaks attempted to get out of internment immediately by applying to join the Red Army, but few were successful.[14] Mass releases only began after the creation of national military formations in the Soviet Union. The Polish were the first to start organising their international troops, in the second half of 1941. Many Czechoslovak prisoners (in particular those from the Ostrava and Těšín regions) took advantage of this and volunteered for what was called Anders' Army[15] due to the opportunity to earn release. The Poles often rejected them, however, much like Polish Jews, and for this reason amnesty for the imprisoned

12 ADLER, Eliyana R.: "Crossing Over. Exploring the Borders of Holocaust Testimony". In: *Yad Vashem Studies*, 2015, vol. 43, n. 2, p. 87.

13 BORÁK, Mečislav: *České stopy v Gulagu* [Czech Traces in the Gulag], p. 81.

14 idem: "Z nacistického koncentračního tábora do sovětských gulagů. Osudy ostravských Židů z transportů do Niska nad Sanem" [From Nazi Concentration Camp to Soviet Gulag. Fates of Ostrava Jews from the Transports to Nisko]. In: *Ostrava. Příspěvky k dějinám a současnosti Ostravy a Ostravska, sv. 25* [Ostrava. Contributions on the History and Present of Ostrava and the Ostrava region, Vol. 25]. Tilia, Ostrava 2011, p. 128–129.

15 Anders' Army – the informal name for Polish military units formed in 1941 and 1942 in the USSR,

Czechoslovaks was crucial, being successfully negotiated only at the start of 1942. At the same time, voluntary enlistment for a Czechoslovak military formation in the USSR began, both for Czechoslovak nationals and for Soviet citizens of "Czechoslovak" ethnicity. Enlistment was essentially viewed as a prerequisite for release.[16] Thanks to the amnesty, most Czechoslovaks earned their freedom, but by no means all those to whom it applied. To a considerable extent it depended on the whim of the commander for the particular camp. Thus many were still dying in Gulag camps at a time when their released compatriots were already fighting on the front, or even after the war was already over (see the case of G. Edelstein on p. 135). For many prisoners, the amnesty came too late. Sick and exhausted releasees died on the way to reach the Czechoslovak unit, or after arriving. "They arrived in Buzuluk and we were forced to immediately transport them to the hospital. Often there was nothing we could do for them though. They were in terrible shape. They arrived starved, careworn, emaciated. They had lived in horrible conditions. Every night shift I had, many of them died."[17]

Unlike the Jewish and non-Jewish refugees from Subcarpathian Rus, often considered by the Soviet authorities to be Hungarian citizens, Jews from the Czech lands tended to have the fortune that no one questioned their nationality. For this reason, at first Jewish prisoners originally from the Czech lands made up a significant portion (as much as 70%) of the 1st battalion of the Czechoslovak military formation in the USSR. Despite the fact that, over the following years of the war, the ethnic breakdown of the Czechoslovak military formation in the East changed considerably, the proportion of Jewish soldiers remained quite significant after the defeat of Nazi Germany and liberation of Czechoslovakia.[18] Many of those who survived the escape from Nazism and the hardships of the Gulag or incarceration then laid down their lives in the bloody fighting on the Eastern Front.

---

primarily made up of released Polish Gulag prisoners. The name was in recognition of its commander, General Władysław Anders.

16 BORÁK, Mečislav: *Z nacistického koncentračního tábora do sovětských gulagů* [From Nazi Concentration Camp to Soviet Gulag], p. 48.

17 *Yad Vashem Archive*, interview with Chana Nagel recorded 3 January 1969 by Erich Kulka.

18 VALIŠ, Zdeněk: Ze sovětských gulagů do československé armády. Heliodor Píka v boji za životy Podkarpatorusů [From the Soviet Gulags to the Czechoslovak Army. Heliodor Píka in the Fight for the Lives of Subcarpathians]. *Historie a vojenství. Časopis Vojenského historického ústavu*, 2008, vol. 57, no. 1, p. 57–58. As of 5 February 1943, of 1,892 enlisted persons in the Czechoslovak military unit, there were 141 volunteers that declared Jewish ethnicity – of those 105 in the 1st field battalion, 3 in the reserve regiment and 33 in the reserve company. According to the statistics of 1 November 1944, 16,444 volunteers had signed up for the Czechoslovak military unit, of those 1,040 Jews (though not all Jews declared their Jewish ethnicity).

FORBIDDEN MEMORY

After the defeat of Nazi Germany, most Jews in the reconstituted Czechoslovakia did not have any space for public reflection of their war traumas. Not only was there no demand for it in the euphoric time of victory, but the Jewish war survivors themselves had to deal with a whole range of pressing issues stemming from the loss of relatives, often entire families, homes and property, and from the complicated post-war situation in Czechoslovakia. Those who came from Subcarpathian Rus, which was occupied by the Soviets at the end of the war, had to decide whether to accept Soviet citizenship or to move to Czechoslovakia. Some of them left to build a new home in Palestine, many participated with revolutionary fervour in building the communist establishment in Czechoslovakia, while others still emigrated to the West or tried to assimilate with majority society and forget about everything that had happened to them. What little was published on the topic of Nazi persecution of Jews in the post-war years[19] was gradually overshadowed by the communist interpretation of the events of the war. Remembrance of the war and the Nazi crimes was gradually stripped of its Jewish dimension and emphasis of the communist victims of Nazism and fascism and the resistance of the Communist Party predominated.

It is logical that these conditions in no way provided Jews returning from the Soviet Union with the opportunity to publish their recollections of what they experienced. Unless of course they were free of any information that cast a negative light on the "fraternal" USSR.[20] Sharing one's experience with Soviet reality, including Gulag camps, during conversations with co-workers at the workplace or lending friends one's unpublished memoirs could have serious consequences for returning prisoners in communist Czechoslovakia.[21] Gulag survivors could thus only share their repressed memories of Soviet interment publicly in exile. The same was true of survivors originally from other countries of the Soviet bloc. Many of their memoirs received international attention,[22] but those penned by Czech authors fell by the wayside. What did come out in print was the memoirs of Prague lawyer of Jewish origin and Gulag prisoner in the years 1939–1947 František Polák

19 E.g., the works of authors František R. Kraus, Erich Kulka, Ota Kraus, and Jiří Weil.

20 See the recollections of L. Kellner on p. 266.

21 See the cases of D. Matik and V. Levora in: HRADILEK, Adam: *Perzekuce uprchlíků z Podkarpatské Rusi do SSSR v letech 1939–1945* [Persecution of Refugees from Subcarpathian Rus in the Years 1939–1945]. Thesis. Technical University of Liberec, 2017, p. 79—80.

22 E.g. GLIKSMAN, Jerzy G.: *Tell the West.* Gresham Press, New York 1948; MARGOLINE, Jules: *La condition inhumaine. Cinq ans dans les camps de concentration sovietiques.* Traduit par N. Berberova & Mina Journot. Calmann-Levi Editeurs, Paris 1949 or HERLING-GRUDZIŃSKI, Gustaw: *A World Apart.* Heinemann, London 1951.

František Polák published his memories of the Soviet camps at his own expense in three volumes in the years 1955–1960 during his exile in the USA. *ÚSTR / Adam Hradilek, copy from ÚSTR*

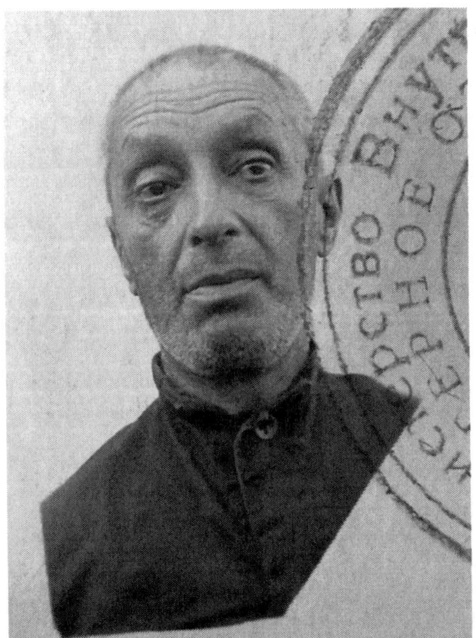

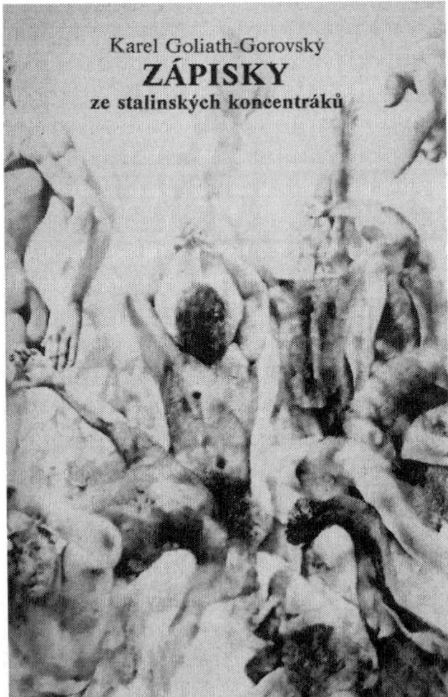

In 1986, Karel Goliath's *Zápisky ze stalinských koncentráků* was published by the exile publishing house Index. Goliath was a Gulag prisoner in the years 1939–1955. On the left is his photograph from his Gulag release form. *Archives of National Museum in Prague, copy from ÚSTR*

During the recording of the interview with Eugen Libermann in 2012, handwritten memoirs of his time in a Soviet labour camp were found in his home in Tel Aviv, having been written for posterity in the 1960s in Czechoslovakia and then taken to Israel. On the right Libermann's photograph from his Gulag release form. *Czechoslovaks in the Gulag project collection (CVG collection) / Adam Hradilek*

(*Zrcadlo sovětského žaláře* [Mirror of a Soviet Jail], 1955, *Cestou ze sovětského koncentráku* [On the Way from a Soviet Concentration Camp], 1959, *Jak žili a umírali sovětští otroci* [How Soviet Slaves Lived and Died], 1960),[23] and many years later the memoirs of Jewish lawyer from Ostrava and Gulag prisoner in 1939–1955 Karel Goliath (*Zápisky ze stalinských koncentráků* [Notes from the Stalinist Concentration Camps], 1986).[24] In the meantime, Czech-Israeli historian Erich Kulka gave room for dozens of former prisoners to provide testimony on the Soviet camps at the end of the 60s and in the 70s, conducting personal correspondence interviews with them as an employee of the Hebrew University in Jerusalem as part of a research project focused on Jewish participation in the anti-Nazi resistance. Kulka used the testimony collected in Israel from Czechoslovak immigrants with Soviet experience to compile the publication *Jews in Svoboda's Army in the Soviet Union*, which first came

---

23 All these works were published by F. Polák in Czech at his own expense in New York. Fifty years later, they came out in a collected edition POLÁK, František: *Sedm let v Gulagu. Vzpomínky pražského advokáta na sovětské pracovní tábory* [Seven Years in the Gulag. A Prague Attorney's Memories of Soviet Labour Camps] (eds. Adam Hradilek – Zdeněk Vališ). Institute for the Study of Totalitarian Regimes, Prague 2015.

24 GOLIATH-GOROVSKÝ, Karel: *Zápisky ze stalinských koncentráků* [Notes from Stalinist Concentration Camps], Index, Köln 1986.

out in 1977 in Jerusalem.[25] Aside from a detailed analysis of the participation of Czechoslovak Jewry in the fight against Nazism, the book also contains a chapter dedicated to the repression against refugees in the USSR and the conditions at labour and prison camps. The original audio recordings of the interviews, transcripts, and correspondence with witnesses and other documents are stored in the archives of the Hebrew University in Jerusalem and the Yad Vashem archives.[26]

After the fall of the communist regime in 1989, Anna Hyndráková and Anna Lorencová from the Jewish Museum in Prague could record recollections of Soviet persecution as part of an extensive oral history project by the museum, with nine of these stored in the archives of the Shoah Documentation Department of the Jewish Museum. The most extensive oral history project focused on memories of the Holocaust is the Shoah Foundation project[27], initiated by US director Steven Spielberg, which managed to procure nearly 52,000 recordings with witnesses from 56 countries in 32 languages in the years 1994–1999. Of these, 4,613 were conducted with people originally from Czechoslovakia. These include 31 interviews with survivors of Soviet repression, in particular prisoners of the Gulag and internment camps. Thematic recollections are also found in the archives of the Czech association Post Bellum (or rather its Memory of Nations archive) and the Institute for the Study of Totalitarian Regimes. In addition to unique interviews, in the years 2006–2015, employees of these institutions (among them the authors of this publication) conducted interviews with the people already interviewed by E. Kulka, but several decades later.

The presented publication contains twenty-one interviews obtained from the aforementioned collections. These represent a significant portion of Czechoslovak memories of both the Holocaust and political repression in the USSR. They supplement the already published memoirs of Czech and Czechoslovak nationals of Jewish origin affected by repression in the USSR in the pre-war period (e.g., the already mentioned memoirs of H. Frischer, see p. 12) and the post-war period (e.g., those by F. Polák, K. Goliath, see p. 18,

25 The first incomplete Czech edition came out in 1979 under the exile publishing house Sixty-Eight Publishers in Toronto. In Czechoslovakia the book was published shortly after the fall of the communist regime, in 1990, by the publishing house Naše vojsko.

26 *Yad Vashem Archives*, f. P 25 – Erich Kulka Archive. Testimonies collected by Erich Kulka regarding the war period; *Hebrew University in Jerusalem*, f. Holocaust Oral History Collection, "Jews in the Czechoslovak Army in World War II" (Project 72). Some of the interviews from the collection are available in audio recording and print form on the internet: https://www.youtube.com/playlist?list=PLZEGL2eD5gA1q Ozp2EotujkmZzjgrAoIf (accessed 25 November 2017).

27 Today the archive of recordings is cared for by the USC Shoah Foundation at the University of Southern California in the USA. Popularisation of the archives and access to them in the Czech Republic is provided by the Malach Centre.

or Blanka Rubinová,[28] as well as those by other Czechoslovaks, e.g. V. Levora, see p. 13, in particular Carpathian Ruthenians).[29]

In most cases, research on Soviet repression was not the primary objective of the aforementioned oral history projects under which the interviews took place. These were predominantly recorded with the goal of studying another historical topic or period, moreover by people who did not know a lot about the Gulag and the whole Soviet repressive apparatus. Erich Kulka, for example, focused primarily on the topic of the resistance, while the Shoah Foundation editors were collecting the memories of Holocaust survivors. Experiences from the Gulag were recorded as a kind of by-product. Some interviews thus only touch on the topic and hurry along to another, while others, generally where the survivor had a particular rhetorical talent or the interviewer's curiosity was piqued, delve into the issue of Soviet repression in detail. This disparity of resources was a particularly limiting factor in assembling this publication. Given the dearth of not only personal testimonies but also other historical sources, all of them nevertheless constitute a significant contribution to learning about Soviet repression against Czechoslovak citizens. Despite the fact that we can today reconstruct some life stories in quite some detail on the basis of declassified and accessible NKVD documents, the preserved testimonies of the survivors remain highly valuable for the study of the issue in question, as they provide a different, personal perspective on the subject, in contrast to the impersonal, cold and machine-generated investigation files of the Soviet security forces.

The interviews were selected based on several criteria. The main concern was their informative value, the details in their description of events, and the scope. Another determining criterion was the manner in which the person had found themselves in Soviet territory, with the goal of balancing as much as possible the main routes by which Czechoslovak Jews fled to the Soviet Union, according to which the book is divided into chapters.

---

28 See the chapter "Race and Class Enemies. The Story of Blanka Rubinová and Other Czechoslovak Jews Taken to the USSR After the War", in: DVOŘÁK, Jan – FORMÁNEK, Jaroslav – HRADILEK, Adam: *Čechoslováci v Gulagu* [Czechoslovaks in the Gulag], p. 152–166.

29 E.g. DEMČÍK, Jan: *Můj útěk do gulagu* [My Escape to the Gulag]. Literary adaptation by Karel Richter based on memoirs. Česká expedice, Prague 1995, 2nd edition Cody Print, Prague 2001; LUŤANSKÝ, Štěpán: *Pečorlag. Útěk do ráje (1939–1942)* [Pechorlag. Escape to Paradise (1939–1942)]. Argo, Prague 1999; PAVLIČ, Jiří: *Přežil jsem Gulag. Vyprávění po padesáti letech* [I Survived the Gulag. The Story Fifty Years Later]. MNP, Kruh v Podbezdězí 2000; KRIČFALUŠI, Michal: *Účtování s časem. Díl první – V náručí gulagu* [Settling Accounts with Time. Part One – In the Arms of the Gulag]. Literary adaptation by Karel Richter. Česká expedice, Prague 2004; IZAJ, Michal: *Příběhy mého života* [Stories of My Life]. Československá obec legionářská, Prague 2011; HAJDUR, Vasil: *Z gulagu přes Buzuluk do Prahy. Vzpomínky frontového vojáka*[From the Gulag via Buzuluk to Prague. Memoirs of a Frontline Soldier]. Futura, Prague 2011.

Due to the limited scope of the publication and its narrow focus, the interviews are not published in full here. Only passages that describe the circumstances of leaving for the USSR and the repression on the part of the Soviet security authorities, from arrest to interrogation and internment at camps through to release were chosen. The interviews are however presented in biographical vignettes summarising the life journey of the interviewees. These were drawn up on the basis of the information contained in the interviews and, where possible, with the help of findings obtained from surviving relatives or other sources. In particular the recently declassified documents and photographs made available from the NKVD archives are a source of important information and also supplement the interviews with images.

I.
REFUGEES FROM THE PROTECTORATE OF BOHEMIA AND MORAVIA

ROBERT SYLTEN (b. 1902 in Orlová), arrested in 1939 during an attempt to illegally cross the Soviet-Romanian border. Sentenced to five years in the Gulag. Interned at the Knyazhpogost camp (Sevzheldorlag) in 1940–1942. *DAZO* ▶

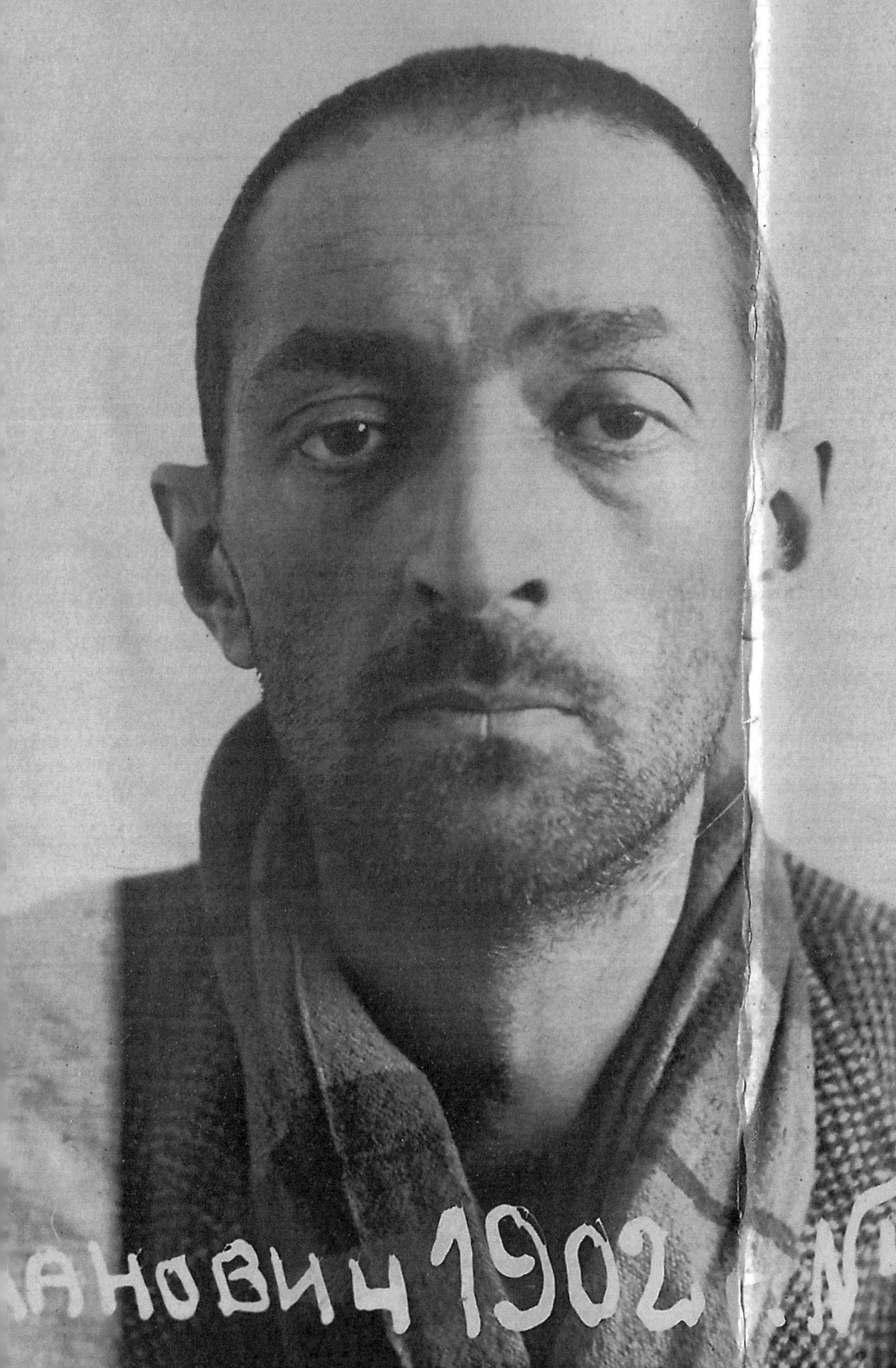
АНОВИЧ 1902

Up until 1938, Czechoslovakia was seen as a country in which, unlike many other countries of central and eastern Europe, anti-Semitism was not particularly prominent. The events of the following months would however show how quickly the situation could change.

The Munich Agreement came as a huge shock for all democratically minded citizens of the Czechoslovak Republic. It not only precipitated a deep domestic political crisis, but also indignation, disappointment and apathy. Proportionately to the deepening problems in society, nationalism and chauvinism began to flourish, with anger being increasingly directed against the Jewish refugees that were primarily coming in from the German-occupied border region, but also from Austria and Germany. Yet even local Jews, including those who had declared Czechoslovak nationality and been loyal to the republic, could no longer be sure of a carefree existence. The deepening sense of hopelessness forced many to consider the option of fleeing before the mounting threat. In light of the ever-deteriorating social climate in the Second Republic, emigrating to safety abroad was an increasingly relevant draw for Jews of all segments of society.

Jewish emigration posed a major problem for the already weakened state however. The number of refugees was considerable, while the options for emigration limited. Legal emigration abroad was hindered in general by the averse stance of most European countries, who gave priority to political refugees, with only a predetermined, limited number of Jewish immigrants accepted. Emigration to more exotic destinations, particularly South America or Africa, required significant financial resources that most lacked. Moreover, the preparations and formalities for Jewish refugees being accepted were generally quite lengthy. The departure date was therefore often repeatedly postponed and so most Jews did not manage to leave before the Nazi occupation in March.[30]

Due to these aforementioned problems with emigrating legally, illegal emigration began to intensify as early as October 1938. The main refugee routes led via Slovakia, Hungary and Romania to Palestine, and more notably through the newly delineated border region of Czech Silesia[31] to Poland. Over

---

30 For more on Jewish emigration and organisational issues of emigration, see e.g. BENDA, Jan: *Útěky a vyhánění z pohraničí českých zemí 1938–1939* [Escapes and Expulsions from the Czech Borderlands 1938–1939]. Karolinum, Prague 2013, p. 399–419; PRZYBYLOVÁ, Blažena: "Emigrace ostravského židovského obyvatelstva ve 30. a 40. letech 20. století" [Emigration of Ostrava Jewish population in the 1930s and 40s]. In: *Sborník prací Filozofické fakulty Ostravské univerzity – Historie/Historica* [Collection of Works of the Ostrava University Faculty of Arts – History/Historica], 1995, No. 153, p. 63–65.

31 On the day the Munich Agreement was signed, 30 September 1938, Poland gave the Czechoslovak government an ultimatum demanding a significant portion of the Czechoslovak Těšín region (known as Záolží – Zaolzie, in English Trans-Olza). The Czechoslovak government gave its consent the following day. In the first days of October, Poland took over the majority of the eas-

EGON MORGENSTERN (1914), a native of Fryštát, fled to Poland in June 1939 with his brother and sister. During a Polish police raid against illegal refugees however, he was arrested and jailed at a Krakow prison. He was only released when the war broke out in autumn 1939. He had been left without documents though, and thus decided to go to Lithuania with the goal of getting to Sweden. In the city of Dvinsk (today Daugavpils), he was detained by the Latvian gendarmes and didn't get out of prison until the Soviet occupation of the Baltics. Later he was transferred to a prison in Vilnius, where he was sentenced to 5 years. He served his sentence at one of the Pechorlag camps in northern Russia, being transferred to Karlag in Kazahkstan in 1943. He was only liberated in 1945. He never returned to Czechoslovakia and lived in Vilnius, Lithuania until his death in 2016.

CVG collection of interviews, interview with Egon Morgenstern recorded 20 February 2011 by Jan Dvořák; POSKOČIL, Stanislav: Egon Morgenstern. Přežil jsem peklo gulagu [Egon Morgenstern. I Survived the Hell of the Gulag]. Nakladatelství P3K, Prague 2015.

the several following months, hundreds managed to flee Czecho-Slovakia, and not only Jews.

The tendency to leave logically rose manyfold after the Nazis occupied the rest of the Czech lands in March 1939. After this, the largest wave of emigration the country had seen arose, with Jews, who were rightly afraid of the occupiers' anti-Jewish policies, clearly predominating. At the start of the occupation, the option for Jews to emigrate abroad through official channels was still open, but after Poland was attacked and World War II broke out in September 1939, legal Jewish emigration from the Protectorate ceased to be pertinent.[32] Most of those interested in emigrating thus had practically no option other than choosing illegal emigration. The illegal routes that refugees

tern territory – i.e., the Czechoslovak part of Těšín Silesia. Czechoslovakia retained the smallest part of the Silesian territory – a truncated Frýdek region and part of Silesian Ostrava.

32 KREJČOVÁ, Helena – BEDNAŘÍK, Petr: "Emigration after the Munich Agreement". In: *Exil v Praze a v Československu 1918–1938/Exile in Prague and Czechoslovakia 1918–1938*. Pražská edice, Prague 2005, p. 206—207; ROTHKIRCHENOVÁ, Livie: *Osud Židů v Čechách a na Moravě v letech 1938–1945 [The fate of Jews in Bohemia and Moravia in 1938-1945]*. In: ROTHKIRCHENOVÁ, Livie – SCHMIDTOVÁ-HARTMANNOVÁ, Eva -DAGAN, Avigdor (eds.): *Osud Židů v Protektorátu 1939–1945* [The Fate of Jews in the Protectorate 1939–1945]. Trizonia, Prague 1991, p. 61.

had been taking in the previous months did not change after the Protectorate was established. There was still the option of fleeing via Slovakia and then by the Balkan route to Palestine, but most refugees once again chose the relatively simplest route to neighbouring Poland, this despite the fact that the Polish state had long not been providing any refugees, let alone Jewish ones, almost any possibilities for long-term stay and livelihood. The maximum concession was a short transit stay with the condition that the emigrant would soon depart for another country. Yet nor did the Jewish refugees from occupied Czechoslovakia generally plan to connect their future with Poland. They themselves also believed that it would be but a mere transfer station on their way to the West, particularly to the USA or UK, or potentially Palestine. The activity of support organisations in Katowice, Krakow and Warsaw ended up facilitating emigration for a small number of Jews, but most of them did not manage to obtain the required departure permit in time.[33]

There were no longer many options for them other than emigrating to the West: one of these was voluntarily entering the Czechoslovak military unit that started being formed at the end of April 1939 in Krakow (only officially recognised as the Czechoslovak Legion after the invasion of Poland). This variant could really only be considered by young men however. Despite the initial reluctance of the Czechoslovak military authorities to admit Jews, in the end Jewish volunteers made up a significant portion of the formation.[34]

The option of leaving for the countries neighbouring Poland was also still in play however: south to Romania, north to the Baltic countries, or east to the Soviet Union. The willingness of Soviet authorities to admit Jewish refugees at that time was not strong though. On the contrary, the immigration policy of the USSR was highly restrictive. At the end of the 1930s, the USSR was the only major power to refuse Jewish refugees threatened by Hitler, on the grounds that they were primarily representatives of the middle class who would have a hard time adapting to Soviet society and for whose critical situation the Soviet Union bears no responsibility, as it was a conflict amongst capitalist states.[35] This was also reflected in the Soviets' negative attitude towards the League of Nations High Commission for Refugees, underpinned by concerns that the activities thereof could include support for anti-Soviet refugees.

---

33 KULKA, Erich: *Židé v československé Svobodově armádě* [Jews in Svoboda's Army in the Soviet Union], p. 18–31; BORÁK, Mečislav: *První deportace evropských Židů* [First Deportations of European Jews], p. 38–39.

34 KULKA, Erich.: *Židé v československé Svobodově armádě* [Jews in Svoboda's Army in the Soviet Union], p. 35–38. Members of the Czechoslovak military group in Poland later became members of three Czechoslovak foreign military units (in France, in the Middle East and in the USSR). Czechoslovak Jews played a major role in all of these.

35 BORÁK, Mečislav: *Z nacistického koncentračního tábora do sovětských gulagů* [From Nazi Concentration Camp to Soviet Gulag], p. 110–111.

It also adopted a negative stance on the international conference in Évian, France that took place in July 1938, where there was discussion of the fate of the persecuted European Jews and Jewish emigrants. It called the conference a conspiracy to encourage sabotage activities by "Trotskyist" emigrants.[36]

For refugees from Czechoslovakia, the conditions for emigrating to the USSR were further complicated after the definitive collapse of Czechoslovakia in March 1939. The privilege of legal emigration and admittance to the USSR continued to only apply for a limited circle of selected communists, pre-selected in Moscow. Even more significant complications arose after the signing of the German-Soviet Treaty of Non-Aggression in August of 1939 (known as the Molotov-Ribbentrop Pact), one of the results of which was limitation of the diplomatic relations between the Czechoslovak government-in-exile and Soviet representatives.[37]

Getting into the USSR legally was thus nearly impossible after 1939, not only for Jews but also for the majority of Czechoslovak citizens. For this reason they had to resort to illegally crossing the state border. Up until the war broke out, however, this was mostly just individuals or small groups, generally left-wing people influenced by Soviet propaganda. Others were hardly interested in emigrating to the USSR, but in several months they would no longer have a choice.

When the Soviet-German coalition was formed at the end of summer 1939, Poland ceased to be taken as an independent state. On 1 September 1939, Nazi Germany invaded Poland from the west, and seventeen days later the Soviets would enter Poland from the east. The partitioning of Poland between the Third Reich and USSR was soon complete.

Even though no one could yet imagine in 1939 how far the Nazis would go in their terror against the racially and ideologically "unsuitable" population, the question of fleeing from further persecution became pressing, especially for Jews. In autumn of 1939, however, both the locals and the refugees still lingering in the western parts of Nazi-occupied Poland (including Czechoslovak Jews) suddenly found themselves at a dead end. The option of leaving for the West became essentially unrealistic, and thus the only viable solution seemed to be going east – meaning to the areas controlled by the Soviets.[38] Though there was still the option of going south to Romania or north to the Baltics, as

---

36 POLONSKY, Antony: *The Jews in Poland and Russia. Volume III: 1914 to 2008*. The Littman Library of Jewish Civilization, Oxford – Portland, Oregon 2012, p. 396.

37 BORÁK, Mečislav: *České stopy v Gulagu* [Czech Traces in the Gulag], p. 78.

38 From the first days of the German invasion of Poland, hundreds of thousands of Jews (estimates range around 300,000) began to flee the Nazi-occupied zone, rightly fearing possible arrest, anti-Jewish attacks or other persecution. After the German-Soviet demarcation line was established 28 September 1939, the wave of refugees was further fuelled by the Jews driven out of the border areas by the Germans.

HEINRICH BACHNER (1907), a clock repairman from Orlová, left for Krakow on 1 October 1939 to visit his cousin. At the latter's advice, he crossed the German-Soviet border near Przemyśl on 2 November 1939 and was arrested straightaway. Because he was carrying a pass from the Krakow Gestapo, he was taken into custody. He was imprisoned in Dnepropetrovsk, where he was sentenced to 5 years on 10 August 1940. He served his sentence at Ustvymlag in Komi Republic, from which he was released 8 October 1941 under the amnesty for Polish citizens. The town of Kirov in the central Urals was designated as his next place of residence. Here he was arrested again by the Kirov NKVD on 31 August 1943. On 23 November 1943 he was sentenced to another 10 years for anti-Soviet propaganda. He was not released until 3 October 1944, after which he was to settle in the village of Darnica (today part of Kyiv) in the Kyiv region. His subsequent fate is unknown.

DALO, f. R-3258 (1939–1950), vol. no. 14296.

later events clearly showed, this was not a better choice. As early as autumn of 1939, the Soviets took "control" of all the Baltic states, with their territories definitively absorbed into the USSR in June 1940. At that time it also annexed the Romanian territories of Bessarabia and Northern Bukovina.[39]

Not all the refugees who ended up in the USSR were eager to get there, however. Many of them found themselves in Soviet territory involuntarily upon the Soviet occupation of eastern Poland or several months later of

39 E.g. *Dějiny Ruska 20. století* [History of Russia. XX Century]. Part II. Ed. Andrey B. Zubov. Argo, Prague 2015, p. 15. In original: *Istorija Rossiji v XX. veke*. Vol. II. Ed. Andrej B. Zubov. Eksmo, Moscow 2017.

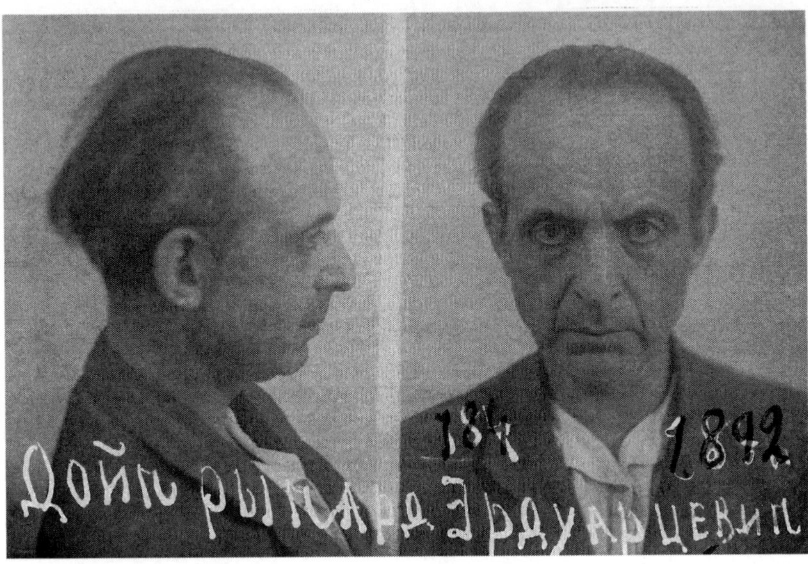

RICHARD DEUTSCH (1892), born in Moravský Krumlov, made his living as a clerk. Soon after the Nazi occupation of Czechoslovakia, he was arrested by the Gestapo, but was released in June of 1939. After this he decided to flee to Poland. The Polish authorities, however, immediately returned him to the Protectorate, where he was arrested by the Gestapo a second time. He was released again and sent back to Poland by the Germans. Up until the start of the war, he resided in Katowice, then he decided to flee to the USSR. After several weeks' travel, he arrived in Zhytomyr, where he began working in Stalin's factories as an accountant. He was arrested on 20 June 1940 and subsequently charged with planning to leave the USSR illegally and anti-Soviet agitation. After passing through several transit prisons, he arrived at the NKVD prison in the Rostov region, where he died on 10 September 1942.

HAD SBU, f. Criminal Files (1939–1994), vol. no. 6573.

the Baltics and northern Romania. It is still difficult to establish how many Czechoslovak refugees from the Protectorate this affected. Research to date indicates that it was approximately two thousand people from 1939 to 1941, predominantly of Jewish origin. This number also includes those deported to Nisko in October 1939, who entered the USSR in a quite specific manner (see the chapter on p. 57). Stalin's main concern in the newly acquired territories of Poland and later the Baltic states and Romania was their rapid "cleansing" and immediate Sovietisation. The whole situation was complicated, however, not only by the resistance of the local population, but also by the massive influx of refugees from the Nazi-occupied western parts of Poland. The Soviets, though they bore much of the blame for destabilising the region,

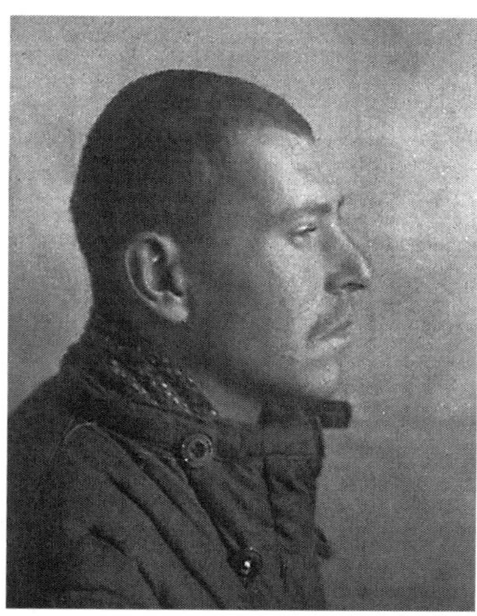

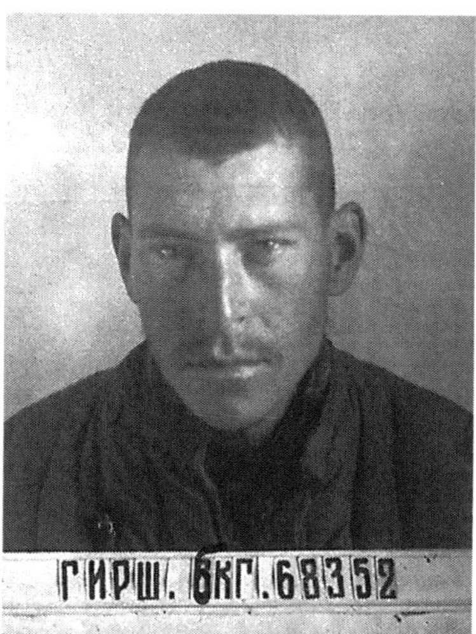

BRUNO HIRSCH (1907), a chauffeur from Ústí nad Labem, first fled from the Nazis from Prague to Katowice, then in September 1939 to Kovel, which had however been occupied by the Red Army in the meantime. At the end of October, he arrived in Lviv. On 27 June 1940, he was arrested and more than a year later, on 3 July 1941, sentenced to three years for illegally crossing the border. He died on 22 March 1942 at Oneglag.

HDA SBU Lviv, f. Jewish Files (1939–1941), vol. no. 355.

did not want the refugee problem to disrupt the integration of the annexed territories into the USSR. Moreover, from the perspective of Soviet security interests, the presence of any foreigners near the Soviet-German border was unacceptable. This was reflected in the repressive measures adopted by the Soviet occupation administration in the very first weeks of the occupation, which were meant to prevent the influx of further refugees. These included heightened border surveillance and later also directives seeking to cleanse the western border areas (of what were now already the Ukrainian and Byelorussian SSRs) of all "hostile elements".

Thus it was that one-time Czechoslovak citizens also found themselves wanted by the NKVD. Like others, they had almost no chance of avoiding Soviet repression, regardless of whether the NKVD arrested them while crossing the border (crossing legally was possible up until October 1939, but afterwards only illegally) or several months later, during the major crackdowns on refugees in the spring and summer of 1940. The tens of thousands of detained refugees (predominantly Jews) also included hundreds of Czechoslovak Jews, primarily arrested in Lviv and its surroundings. Similar sweeps over the coming months also affected the other annexed areas.

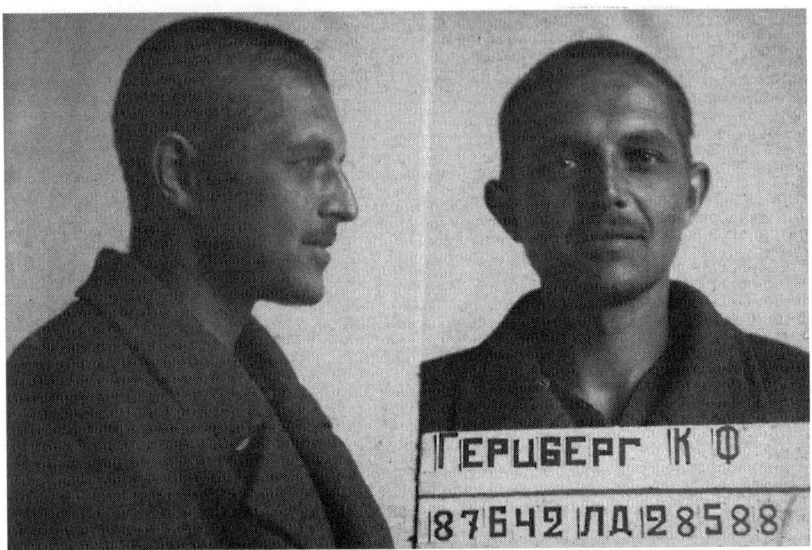

KARL HERZBERG (1914) was born in Ivančice, Moravia. For a long time, however, he lived in Poland, working as a foreman in a leather factory in Żywiec. Later he adopted Polish citizenship. After the Nazi attack on Poland, he was mobilised into the Polish army as a driver. He arrived in the Soviet-occupied Polish territory on 17 September 1939 with the retreating units of the Polish army. At the end of November, he set out for Lviv. Here he was arrested by the Lviv NKVD on 29 June 1940. He was imprisoned without trial at Kargopollag in the Arkhangelsk Oblast. He got out of prison with the amnesty for Polish citizens on 20 January 1942. He was assigned to live in Verkhny Ufaley in the Chelyabinsk Oblast. His further fate is not known.

HDA SBU Lviv, f. Jewish Files (1939–1941), vol. no. 285.

Many of the detainees faced imprisonment in the overcrowded holding prisons of the NKVD, where they remained for several months of investigation. Due to the huge number of detainees, however, these investigations were largely formal in nature. The Soviets were mainly interested in removing these "spies" and other "enemies of the state" from everyday society and using them for forced labour. The most frequent sentence imposed by the NKVD Special Council for illegally crossing the border was three years of forced labour in the Gulag, and for more serious offences such as espionage, five or more years. In particular in the later years of the war, however, there was the threat of even higher penalties.[40]

40 *State Archives of Lviv Oblast* (Derzhavnyy arkhiv Lvivskoyi Oblasti – DALO), f. Criminal Files R-3258 (1939–1950); *Sectoral State Archive of the Security Services of Ukraine* (Haluzevyy derzhav-

Criminal proceedings were not undertaken in all cases though. It was not possible due to the enormous number of detained refugees which the NKVD had to process in those years. The prisons were constantly overcrowded and there was nowhere to place the detainees. Less dangerous refugees (often whole families) were therefore deported as "special displaced persons" without trial to forced labour in special labour colonies or kolkhoz collective farms set up and run by the NKVD.

Not all refugees were necessarily subjected to repression. In particular those who voluntarily accepted Soviet citizenship avoided it. Most Czechoslovak Jewish refugees however did not react to the call to register with Soviet authorities. They often considered themselves patriots and believed that Czechoslovak passports provided them with sufficient protection. The Soviets on the other hand considered this stance a clear expression of disloyalty and proceeded to treat them accordingly.

Still, there were other ways of avoiding arrest and deportation. Even the all-powerful NKVD was not able to catch all the "hostile elements". Some refugees managed to gain official work and were thus covered for a certain period by their employer. Others managed to get to areas (e.g., Central Asia) where they later got involved in wartime production and moreover where the situation was quite messy. Some refugees managed to slip away from NKVD surveillance for a time, but the Soviet repressionary machinery did not let up in the following years. The German invasion of the USSR in June 1941 set the stage for further mass persecution, not just in the western border regions, but over the whole Soviet Union.

With the rapid advancement of German troops, the Soviet authorities did not have time to sentence the detainees, yet "evacuation" to the east did not cease even after this. Though we know today what this "evacuation" usually meant, a paradox of the time remains the fact that the prisoners and other people transported east, usually to Gulag camps, ended up often having a greater chance of survival than those who somehow managed to avoid deportation and remained in the western part of the Soviet Union when the German troops were arriving. Only very few managed to escape in time, many more fell when the front moved in, were murdered in pogroms often perpetrated by the local population, or died in the Nazi extermination and concentration camps.[41]

nyy arkhiv Sluzhby bezpeky Ukrainy – HDA SBU) *Kyiv*, f. Criminal Files (1939–1994); *Sectoral State Archive of the Security Services of Ukraine Lviv* (HDA SBU Lviv), f. Jewish Files (1939–1941).

41 BORÁK, Mečislav: *Z nacistického koncentračního tábora do sovětských gulagů* [From Nazi Concentration Camp to Soviet Gulag], p. 117.

SIGMUND HLADÍK

Born 1 March 1927 in Mainz into a mixed Czech-Jewish family – his father was Czech, his mother from Latvia. Both parents worked as circus performers and were constantly travelling, not only around Czechoslovakia, but also all of Europe. In the years 1938–1939, the family was residing in Prague, but as soon as Czechoslovakia was occupied by Nazi troops in March 1939, they decided to flee abroad, leaving for fictitious employment in the Baltics right at the start of April 1939. After various trials and tribulations, they reached Sigmund's mother's family in Latvia, soon thereafter finding a gig with the Estonian circus Krone. For two years, they worked in the circus in Latvia and Estonia. On 22 June 1941, however, the day the Soviet Union was attacked by Nazi Germany, the family was detained by Soviet soldiers and transferred to an internment camp near Tallinn, where foreign nationals "hostile" to the Soviet regime were being held. After roughly two weeks, they were to be deported from there further east, however the railway transport was attacked by German planes not far from the Estonian town of Oru. Of the whole carriage (about 40 people), only little Sigmund and his father survived the bombing. All the surviving prisoners were then loaded onto another transport and taken to the internment camp in Oranki.[42] Here the Hladíks met with other detained and interned Czechs and Czechoslovak citizens. In the adjacent camp section were interned soldiers from the Eastern Group of the Czechoslovak Army Abroad (formerly the Czechoslovak Legion). After three months in Oranki, the Hladíks were deported along with other selected prisoners to Kazakhstan, specifically to a labour colony, a fenced-off camp near Aktyubinsk.[43] Some eight hundred people were crammed together here in harsh hygienic conditions, of those roughly fifty Czechoslovaks. Sigmund Hladík was hospitalised in the local infirmary a few days after arriving at the camp – at first roll call his feet had become frostbitten and he soon fell ill with jaundice. Thanks to the help of his father and other detainees, however, he recovered in a month. At that time, it was common for several people to die every day. They were only freed with the amnesty for Czechoslovak citizens in 1942. The Czechoslovaks were released from the Aktyubinsk camp on 10 February 1942, and eleven days later Sigmund Hladík was enlisted in Buzuluk. At first he served as a cadet, then later he was posted to the Army Artistic Ensemble as a musician. During the war, he worked in supply and as a liaison officer. He was at the battles for Kyiv, Vasylkiv, Krosno and the Carapathian-Dukla Operation. From February 1944, he was a member of the musical troupe, among other things playing on the occasion of the proclamation

42 Oranki – a village not far from Nizhny Novgorod in the central part of European Russia.
43 Aktyubinsk (today Aktobe) – a city in north-western Kazakhstan.

of what was called the Košice Government Programme. After the war, he was demobilised and began once again making a living as a circus performer.[44]

— — —

You were arrested on 22 June 1941. What happened?
It was actually right after the Soviet Union was attacked. We'd spent a year with the circus in Estonia and another in Latvia, and we had just returned to Estonia. That day we were sitting in this kind of circus performer café in Tallinn and discussing the situation. It was already known that war had broken out, and so we were discussing what we were going to do next... We were living on the street Pärli tee, in English that means Pearl Street, where it was all wood buildings at that time. So you could see the situation very clearly: as soon as the Germans started bombing the city, the wood would fly everywhere and nothing would be left of the houses. Sitting with us in the café were some Estonian circus performers who proposed that we go with them to some house about ten kilometres outside of Tallinn, where the Germans hopefully wouldn't be bombing. Dad agreed, so we arranged that we would just go home and get our things and then set out with them. But when we got to Pearl Street, there was a truck parked outside our house that wasn't normally there. A Russian soldier with a rifle was walking by outside, but he let us go inside. At home, mum said that she'd make fried eggs for dinner, I can see and hear it like it was in a movie, when suddenly there was a knocking at the door. When we opened it there was a soldier standing there with some civilian holding some papers. He informed us that we were being arrested as suspect foreigners and that we were to grab our essentials and go with them. Dad objected that we were protected by Czech Protectorate passports and valid visas. The civilian replied, "Then we'll let you go after. Don't worry, we just need to check everything out." They loaded us into the truck and took us out of Tallinn to an area fenced off with barbed wire. We were one of the first to get there, but it soon filled up with other nationalities as well. I remember there were a lot of Norwegians, but no Germans at all. We spent fourteen days at that internment camp. Then they carted us all to the train station and loaded us on a train, forty to a car. In the car with us were all Estonians.

Where were they taking you?
Nobody knew. The Russians just always said: "Line up, move out, let's go." It could've been a few kilometres or across the whole Soviet Union to somewhere in Siberia. That's what the Russians are like. During that transport to God-knows-where, though, we were attacked by German fighters. Our car

44 *CVG collection of interviews*, interview with Sigmund Hladík recorded 30 May 2012 by Jan Dvořák.

was hit, and of forty people, only me and dad survived. He was very resourceful, you see. When he heard the sound of the approaching planes, he pulled me down from the upper bunk to his lower one, where we huddled into a corner and he covered the both of us with a basin of some sort. All that was left of the carriage after the strike was a platform with no walls, full of torn apart bodies. That's what became of my mother as well. It tore her into pieces, as the bomb fell on the part of the carriage where she was lying. When we recovered from the initial shock, father had a bump on his head, and I had a bruised arm. He shouted at me that we needed to run away and hide in the nearby forest, which we managed to do. As soon as the air raid was over, our guards ran into the forest with rifles and started chasing out everyone who had hidden in there. Then they loaded us onto another car and took us past Leningrad and Gorky[45] to the town of Oranki. There was a former monastery in the middle of a forest, where they washed us, shaved our heads and shut us up in the church. There were maybe a thousand of us crammed inside.

Where were the prisoners from?
All over. There were Estonians and also lots of Czechs. By the way, one of the prisoners was communist Bedřcih Reicin[46] and there was the complete crew of a Danish merchant ship, from the captain to the lifeguard, Spanish anti-Franco fighters, Yugoslavs and so on. It was just a mishmash of European nations, other than Germans.

Do you remember Bedřich Reicin?
Of course, he was constantly organising something there. For example he had the idea that we needed some military training, that we should do exercises. Then he went off on raising awareness and started selling the works of Marx and Engels. Dad had some money with him, rubles we'd made at the circus. Because he was a smoker, he'd bought a pack of *makhorka*, tobacco, but he didn't have anything to roll it in. When he found out the Marxist books had good quality paper, he bought them and made his rollies out of the pages. Reicin saw it and scolded him something awful, saying, "What are you doing, Hladík?! Is that any way to treat the wisest books in the world?" But dad, God rest his soul, was an impertinent one and had no problem telling him to go fuck himself.

---

45 Gorky (today Nizhny Novgorod) – a city in the central part of European Russia.

46 Bedřich Reicin – an official of the Czechoslovak Communist Party, Czechoslovak solider, NKVD agent, after the war the head of the Defence Intelligence, after February 1948 the deputy defence minister, promoted to the rank of brigadier general on 1 December 1949. Sentenced to death as part of Slánský's Trial of the Anti-State Conspiratorial Centre and executed on 3 December 1952.

Sigmund Hladík (left) as a cadet in the Czechoslovak Army Corps in the USSR, Buzuluk 1942. *CVG collection*

So the regime at that camp was more relaxed?
Yes. Then in the autumn, some Czechoslovak volunteers came with Lieutenant Colonel Svoboda. They went around and called through the fence to the prisoners that anyone who's a Czech should come forward. Then they told us through the barbed-wire fence that we shouldn't be afraid, that a Czechoslovak unit would be formed and they'd get us out of there.

Can you estimate how many Czechoslovaks there were?
Something like forty, fifty. But there were Russian Czechs there too, for example one family from Voronezh. Then one day they loaded us all into wagons and we moved on again. Winter was starting then and the conditions in the transport were getting worse from day to day. Paradoxically, there was a stove and a bucket of coal in the wagon, but no chimney, no pipe for the smoke to get out. So the Yugoslavs constructed a kind of make-shift chimney out of boards and sheet metal they tore off the roof of the wagon. The Czechs sang

while they did it so the guards wouldn't hear the noise and come investigate. Then we could heat it a bit, but we had to sit on the floor, because we gradually burned all the bunk beds.

Again you had no idea where you were going?
We didn't know anything at all. The trip took about a week. Here and there we got three hundred grams of bread per person and a bit of tea. And then they suddenly announced: Aktyubinsk. From the train we walked. At the camp there were three wooden huts for about four hundred people. There were eight hundred of us, but they crammed us all in anyway. We sat on the bunks next to each other, no one could lie down, and instead of a floor there was just frozen mud. They were always hounding us out into the yard to do a count. Russians are quite illiterate or semi-literate, so some of the guards could barely count to twenty, most of them couldn't read or write. So you can imagine what it looked like during those counts. Once we were standing in the cold for eleven hours, they just couldn't get the count done. Suddenly I said, "Dad, I can't feel my feet." Father started protesting until they carried me off and took off my shoes. Both feet were completely white, so they quickly rubbed snow on them. Thank God I didn't lose them.

What did they feed you?
Two hundred grams of bread a day, one spoonful of porridge for lunch and for dinner soup, which was just murky water with some shreds of cabbage and leaves floating in it. For Christmas we got dried fish. It was tough as an old boot, but at the camp you didn't see meat the whole year long, so everyone hungrily fell upon that fish and tried to chew it up. Then people started dying from it. For example, there was an old man that sat on the bunk next to me, originally French. Once he said something and then suddenly went silent. I look at him and he's just sitting there dead. We went to the bathroom outside in the snow, peeing and pooing, there was nowhere else. So I'm peeing and I see my urine is completely red. I told dad straight away and he took a good look and he and says, "Jesus, Mary and Joseph, you're as yellow as a Chinaman." I'd got hepatitis from the fish. Luckily there was a stove in the building and my dad would regularly toast my bread on it. I didn't eat anything else the whole month, which was an absolute diet, and that saved me.

Are you able to describe what the camp looked like?
A few wooden buildings, a fence and barbed wire around them, watchtowers. To be exact it was a classic concentration camp, just without the gas and crematoriums. But people were dying anyways, all the time. When someone died, they didn't burn them, they just buried them in a hole. Eight hundred of us came, two hundred survived.

In the Army Artistic Ensemble, the leader of which was Vít Nejedlý, son of historian and communist politician Zdeněk Nejedlý. Sigmund Hladík is first on the left, 1944. *CVG collection*

How did the guards treat you?
They were completely indifferent to our fate. On the other hand, I can't say that they beat us, kicked us in the ass or anything. Often they couldn't, because there tended to be really wild snowstorms. Lots of times we couldn't even get out of our quarters because the building was up to the roof in snow. The guards were glad when they could at least be holed up in the watchtower or in their house, where it was nice and warm. There weren't any forests nearby either, so they didn't have to take us to work and watch over us there. There was nothing but steppe in all directions. I liked to watch the caravans with camels that would sometimes pass by.

And what kind of work did you do?
None, there was no work there. The unit I was assigned to was called a labour unit, but we didn't do anything. After a time they released the Danish ship crew. The prison grapevine then started claiming that they were going to release the Czechoslovaks too. One fine day, people from the NKVD really did come and summoned us. They told us we were being released and that we were going to Buzuluk, where a Czechoslovak military unit was being formed. They also wanted us to sign something saying the Soviet government treated us decently, that we weren't in any prison camp, just temporarily interned in the Aktyubinsk region.

Sigmund Hladík during the recording of the interview, Prague 2012. *ÚSTR/Jan Dvořák*

And did you sign it?
Of course we did. Everyone wanted to get out of there as quick as possible, so why make waves, right?

When exactly did they release you?
We were in Oranki from July to October 1941. Then we went to Aktyubinsk and stayed there until February. They released us 10 February 1942. Each of us got two loaves of bread and two bottles of sunflower oil for the trip. We all gorged ourselves on the bread, and we had soup at the train station as well, so we were all constantly passing gas on the way to Buzuluk. You know, black bread, oil, soup, long-term empty bowels, it does a number on you.

How was the welcome in Buzuluk?
A Czechoslovak patrol was waiting for us at the train station. They took us to the headquarters, where Lieutenant Colonel Svoboda came out and spoke to us: "Well, folks, we welcome you here. You can be at ease, nobody will hurt you anymore. I will personally see to it that you are well taken care of, here and after returning to Czechoslovakia. Each of you is under my protection." Then he told us that joining the army was voluntary and anyone who didn't want to would be offered work in the Soviet Union. Only one old violinist took that offer, the rest of us joined the unit.

What condition were you in?
Mostly malnourished and terribly infested with lice. They examined us, bathed us, and we got clean uniforms, underclothes, and a backpack. All the things were from the UK, new and immaculate. We also got a toothbrush and toothpaste, and shoe polish. It was like we were suddenly in a different world.

You were fifteen at the time. Was there anyone at the camp or in the Czechoslovak military formation the same age as you?
Definitely not at the camp. When we arrived in Buzuluk, I was the first underage soldier. Two days later though, Petr Tokanovič from Subcarpathian Rus showed up, who was fourteen. We immediately became friends. You know, two boys among adults tend to hit it off quickly. Then Pavelko came, he was fifteen, and then others, so in the end there were twenty of us. We had our own separate quarters, commanded by this one officer, unfortunately I can't remember his name anymore. He supervised us, organised our schooling, mostly reading and writing, but also drill and military training. Otherwise we did auxiliary work there. Of course they didn't send us to the fight for Sokolovo, minors were not allowed to participate in combat operations. But after Sokolovo we started doing regular services, say with the signalmen in the rear. Then when taking Kyiv and then at Dukla, we were indirectly involved in the fighting as well. For instance, we transported the wounded, guarded temporary storehouses, supplied ammunition to the troops. By then, grenades and bullets were whizzing around us and exploding like on the front line.

ALICE SALAMON KUPFERMAN

Born 21 May 1920 in Brno as the only daughter of Abraham Kupferman, a sales representative for Syneberger, a leather processing company. Her mother Käthe (Kateřina, née Růžičková) ran a bridal shop in the city. Alice spent her childhood in the relative prosperity of the Jewish middle class in pre-war Brno. Like her three brothers, she attended a private secondary school, where aside from German and Czech she also learned English and Hebrew so she would be ready for life in Palestine, where her Zionist-leaning parents were preparing to go. As early as 1936, the family moved to Krakow, where one of the Syneberger factories was located. Her father died of cancer soon thereafter however, and the family was supported only by her widowed mother. In the meantime, Alice was taking active part in the social life of the large local Jewish community, swam competitively and attended business school. After Krakow was occupied by the Nazis in September 1939, she fled to her brother in Lviv, which was occupied by the Red Army. Her brother soon returned to his fiancée in Krakow, however, and his tracks were lost somewhere in the Krakow ghetto. In Lviv, Alice found accommodation thanks to a local Jewish organisation, sold soda at a kiosk, and soon met her future husband – a Polish Jew. They lived there until June of 1940, when mass arrests and deportations of refugees took place in Lviv. Alice and her fiancé met the same fate, along with his family. They spent eleven days travelling in a livestock car before arriving at the end of the line, from whence they marched to the Novaya Lyalya labour colony[47] in the Sverdlovsk Oblast. From there the prisoners were sent to individual work sites in the woods, where they primarily harvested lumber, even in the harsh arctic freezing weather. While still at the labour colony, Alice got married to her fiancé, being secretly wed by one of the prisoners, a rabbi. She and her husband survived at the camp up until they were released as Polish citizens on the basis of an agreement between Poland and the USSR. They then went to Samarkand,[48] where her husband's brother was residing, having also gone through the camps, and lived there in relative peace until the end of the war. After a short stay in Krakow, they left for Sweden, and from there to Boston, USA in 1951, where they became successful entrepreneurs.[49]

— — —

How did you get from Lviv to the labour colony?
My future husband Moritz managed to escape from the transport at the Lviv railway station. I don't know how he managed, but he came for me. He told me that his whole family was on that train and that we have to go with them. I tried to convince him we should hide in the city somewhere instead. But he didn't want to leave his brothers. So I followed him, without my things, with nothing. My only possessions were the clothes I happened to be wearing. We got to the train station, but the NKVD officers didn't want to let us on. Moritz pleaded that he had just run away from it to pick me up and now he wanted back on. We argued with them for a bit and then they did end up letting us on. I think they'd never seen anything like it. I mean, someone trying to convince them to put them on a transport. Then we travelled for eleven days in wagons originally meant for transporting horses, thirty-five people in each. There were bunk beds. Some slept up top, some on the floor. Sometimes at a stop we would get soup, though it would be more accurate to call it hot water. Eleven days later we arrived at our destination.

---

47 Novaya Lyalya – today a town of the same name 300 km north of Yekaterinburg on the river Lyalya.

48 Samarkand – a city in the south-east of Uzbekistan.

49 *Collection of interviews USC Shoah Foundation*, interview with Alice Salamon Kupferman recorded 27 September 1997 by Renee Hecht, translated from English by Štěpán Hlavsa.

What were the hygienic conditions like on the train?
Bad. There was no hygiene to speak of. We went to the bathroom outside. It was dirty all over. When we got there, we were all infested with lice. As soon as we got off the train, I immediately started looking for kerosene to get rid of the lice. Luckily I found some.

Do you remember the name of the camp you reached?
They called it Novaya Lyalya. It was somewhere in the Sverdlovsk Oblast.

Were you allowed to leave the camp?
Not a chance. When my husband got pneumonia, they sent him to a hospital in some bigger city nearby. They wouldn't let me accompany him and stay with him. So I tried to go there by foot anyway, but they caught me. They locked me in the barracks and wouldn't let me out.

What work did you do?
We worked in the forest and chopped trees. As soon as the work was done in one section, they moved us somewhere else, to untouched forest. Sometimes we'd walk eight kilometres to work. In the winter along the frozen river, which tended to be easier than wading through the snow. The winters there were really tough. We needed warm clothes, which surprisingly we got. The ordinary Russians that lived nearby got mad that we were getting warm clothes and they got nothing.

The men and women lived in shared barracks?
Yes. Mostly it was only young and able-bodied people there. Some of them didn't go to work though, and then they didn't get any food, that was the unwritten law. So sooner or later they'd die of hunger. For example I remember these two brothers from a very rich family, who never left the barracks. Until one day we found out they were dead. Things like that happened a lot there.

Was there an infirmary there?
No, nothing of the sort. In the case of serious illness they'd just take you to the hospital. Luckily the climate there was very healthy. It usually wasn't windy, and it was below freezing in the winter, so the air was dry and healthy. Even those who had tuberculosis praised how well the climate suited them.

What was the regime at the camp like?
The conditions were hard, every day we had to go to work. Six days a week we supposedly worked for money, then the seventh day for free, which was supposed to be a gift to the Soviet government. Of course no one ever paid us any money. Those who worked got bread as payment. Sometimes you could

get a couple of potatoes from the locals too. The next spring we even planted potatoes, but when they released us, we left them in the ground. Otherwise you had to fend for yourself. The same was true of clothing. We were afraid of lice, which spread typhus, so we made a kind of makeshift laundry outside the camp. There was enough wood, so we'd heat up water and boil the clothes in it. We also set up simple showers in one room, divided into men's and women's sections, where we washed thoroughly.

Was there some kind of daily schedule there?
We had to get up very early. Then we'd go to work and we didn't get back until late in the evening. Then we'd cook, say cabbage if we had any. There was never much food, you see. They'd give us bread, about half a kilo a day. It was heavy and rectangular like a brick, but we liked it a lot, we were always really hungry. In the summer we'd pick mushrooms and various berries, which added some variety to our diet. Then we'd surreptitiously trade with the local Russian population. They mostly wanted clothes, say warm socks, which they'd pay for with flour or eggs.

Were there any cultural activities at the camp?
Not officially, but we discussed various things like in any human community. Say politics, we'd argue about what was going to happen next. Once I got a letter from my uncle advising us to go to the American consulate in Moscow and apply for a visa there. He had no idea what our lives were like, that we couldn't even go a kilometre from camp, let alone to Moscow. But there were lots of intellectuals, and lawyers, who tried to think about our future, and there were long debates and disputes about it. We didn't have any news from outside though. There was no radio and the Russians didn't tell us anything. How the war was going and all that.

Did you experience any anti-Semitism there? Did you encounter any references to your Jewish origin?
Sometimes the Poles were anti-Semitic. They'd call us "kikes", which the Russians would lock them up for 24 hours for. We were all in the same boat though, so we tended to stick together. People tried to help one another. For example, my husband's cousin would share flour with us, even though she had two kids herself.

Did any religious ceremonies take place?
Any religious ceremonies were forbidden. But on holidays, say on Yom Kippur, we would fast, even though we'd walked eight kilometres to work and then worked hard all day. Later in Samarkand, things were better, and we could celebrate holidays normally.

At the start you mentioned you got married at the camp. How was that possible?
We arrived in July and I got married in August. There was a rabbi that came on the same train as us. As it turned out, in Czechoslovakia he had buried my grandma and uncle in one of the camps. Then he ran away and ended up in the same train as us. And he married us. Ritual weddings were banned in Russia at that time, so it was better that no one knew about it.

How did that secret ceremony take place?
The cousin, the one who gave us the flour, had a fairly large family. So they were assigned one little separate room. During the wedding, two men watched the door. Inside there was a canopy tied to four posts and the ceremony took place under it.

Did you have a ring?
I did. My husband was always good at business, even in Lviv. He worked the black market there for gold, dollars, everything there was a shortage of. So he also had a ring from Lviv. To confirm our marriage.

How did you get out of the camp?
The Polish government made a deal with the Soviet Union, and one of the conditions of the agreement was that the Russians would release all the Polish refugees they were holding in the camps. As soon as the deal was enacted, we could choose from a few cities we wanted to live in. Everyone wanted to go to Moscow, but we were told only high-ranking people and officers could go there. We chose Samarkand, because we'd had enough of the cold and we wanted to go somewhere warm. The trip itself took about a week. Of course that's not counting waiting at the train station until we could get tickets. The train stopped a lot, for example in Tashkent we got stuck completely and slept outside on the street. But in the end we got to our destination and lived in Samarkand another four years.

Did you have any money?
We always managed to take care of ourselves. We gradually sold off what my husband had left from Lviv, dollars for instance. For one dollar you could live for a month there, it was worth a thousand rubles, which was a lot of money. But you had to be constantly on your toes and carefully hide and guard your money, because otherwise they'd steal it or just confiscate it.

What were your plans when you got to Samarkand?
We hoped we could somehow get across the border and head for Palestine. But as soon as we got there they told us that such an attempt was punishable by death, so we didn't even try. We thought we'd go home after the war and

everything would be like before. Four years in Samarkand wasn't bad in the end, because you were more free there than in the Russian part of the Soviet Union. In Russia everyone was constantly afraid of the government, but the Muslims in Samarkand didn't care about the government and did what they wanted. They were born speculators, actually criminals according to Soviet laws, but they were good for trading with.

What did you trade with them?
At first we dealt everything possible. Then we made cotton fabrics and ended up making candy. We were allowed to do business, but we couldn't employ anyone. So our whole family made candy and sold it in a little kiosk. For example on May Day we sold four thousand pieces of candy, a ruble each. We couldn't complain. Life in Samarkand was also peaceful during the war, no bombing or military operations. The locals were nice and very kind. We learned a lot there, say how to cook various foods and other things useful in life.

HANAN RON (HANUŠ ROSENBAUM)

Born 6 February 1928 as Hanuš Rosenbaum in Moravian Ostrava, where his father Eliáš ran a wholesale sewing machine and bicycle shop. In the 1930s, his father became actively involved in assisting Jewish refugees fleeing Nazi persecution in Germany. In part due to this, he was among the first on the Gestapo's radar in March 1939. For this reason he fled to his brother in Krakow almost immediately, followed by his wife and two children in April 1939. There he tried to get an exit permit to the United Kingdom at the British consulate, but unsuccessfully. Because the Germans quickly occupied the western part of Poland after World War II broke out in September 1939, the Rosenbaums continued east, to the land occupied starting in September 1939 by the Soviet Union. In the end they reached Lviv, where they remained for eight months. In July 1940, however, the whole family was arrested by the NKVD with no reason provided. Along with other prisoners, they were loaded onto freight wagons and sent to a labour colony falling under the NKVD industrial facility Yakutstroj near Aldan[50]. At the camp, his family mostly worked harvesting lumber, while the children were placed in the camp boarding school at the settlement of Orochen II. Though the Rosenbaums were officially freed in September 1941, they had to remain there. Hanuš's father, who suffered from serious health problems as a result of imprisonment, died in July 1943. After

50 Aldan – a town in the Yakutsk Autonomous Republic in eastern Siberia.

Hanuš Rosenbaum (left) with a friend, 1938. *CVG collection*

his death, the family decided to leave for Buzuluk, where the fifteen-year-old Hanuš immediately volunteered for the Czechoslovak military unit. He was enlisted on 26 August 1943. Over the rest of the war, he served as a liaison officer with the artillery. After the war, he returned to Ostrava. As early as April 1948, he emigrated to Israel and fought on the Jerusalem front in the First War of Independence. In 1950 he became a civilian, and seven years later applied for the position of liaison officer in the services of the Israeli Foreign Ministry. He served in various places, among them in Bucharest, at the trade representative office in Cologne, in the African Congo and lastly, at the end of the sixties, in Rome. From the Foreign Ministry he transferred to the services of the Israeli secret service, Mossad.[51]

— — —

51 *CVG collection of interviews*, interview with Hanan Ron (Hanuš Rosenbaum) recorded 2 November 2011 by Jan Dvořák.

Hanuš Rosenbaum with his family, Krakow 1939. *CVG collection*

How did you get to Soviet territory?
We were hiding on a farm near a Polish town. We stayed in the attic for several days there. Through a little window we could see the Germans from the surroundings taking away the local Jews to fix roads and various similar work, of course accompanied by beatings, kicking and slaps. Then the good man who was hiding us there said, "Stay here a bit longer, the Russians are going to come." And so it was, after five or six days Soviet soldiers arrived. Of course we left the farmer's place and continued on to the town. I can't remember what is was called, but there were lots of Jews there. At that time, the Soviets wanted to take more than they'd agreed with the Nazis in the Molotov-Ribbentrop Pact, which the Germans naturally did not agree with, and so the Soviets had to give the area around that town back to them. My father decided that he would choose the lesser of two evils. We got on some train that took us to Lviv. We spent about ten days there. At first we had no choice but to sleep in various public places, in parks and the like, then we met the owner of this one café, who let us sleep in his establishment. In the end, dad did manage to rent us a room at 14 Reymonta Street. That was very fortunate, because at that time Lviv was full of refugees and there was no accommodation.

What did you live off in Lviv?
I don't exactly know what we lived off. I know mum cooked for some people, and that made a little money, but where the rest came from, I don't know.

I think in part we sold off jewellery and other valuables. That lasted until May 1940.

Who were you in contact with there?
We found some relatives there that were also refugees and dad got them a flat in the same building.

When were you arrested?
One night, it was in July 1940, the NKVD came. They had some papers with names on them, we weren't the only case. They knew exactly where everyone was. It was an operation targeting refugees. So we ended up at Lviv railway station, they loaded us into a livestock wagon, there were at least twenty, twenty-five of us there, and then we slowly started our new "journey" east.

Did they actually tell you the reason for the arrest?
Not at all, they just said, "You're coming with us." Then in Siberia they explained to us that we were unreliable elements. I was thirteen years old, how could I possibly have been an "undercover spy"?

Who all were the Soviets deporting?
In our wagon everyone was a Jewish refugee, just one was a Polish officer, of course without a uniform. He begged us to also pass him off as a Jewish refugee, as he knew what would happen to him if they found out he was a Polish officer. His name was Kochanowski. You couldn't help but notice him. He was almost two metres tall, a handsome man. He didn't look Jewish at all, but of course we did it for him and somehow it worked.

Did you know where they were taking you?
No. We asked the guards, but they wouldn't talk to us. They gave us a bare minimum of food, only the essentials. There was bread, and sometimes soup. Occasionally, when we'd reach a small station and the train would stop, they'd allow us to take some *kipyatok*[52] and go to the bathroom, then we'd move on. I have to say, we were unfair to Stalin on that one. I mean, he gave us a free trip – six weeks, free of charge, food included, gave us the opportunity to see the Russian countryside. I never would've got to see Baikal, say, if it weren't for Stalin...

How long was the trip?
Six weeks, and unless I'm mistaken, it was the Trans-Siberian Railway. The last station was, I think, Skovorodino[53] or maybe one past that. I can't recall

52 *Kipyatok* – boiling water.
53 Skovorodino – a town in the Amur Oblast in south-eastern Siberia.

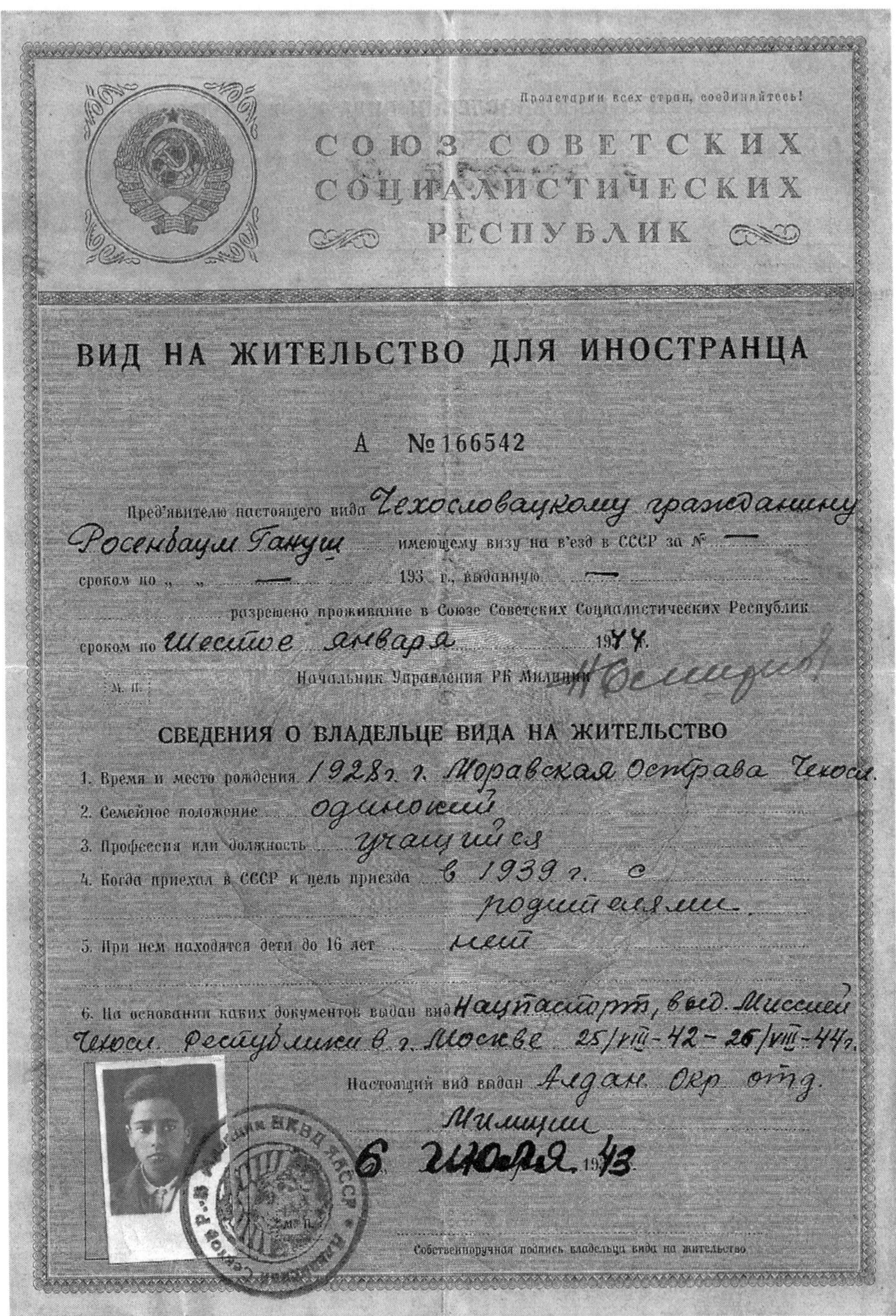

Пролетарии всех стран, соединяйтесь!

СОЮЗ СОВЕТСКИХ
СОЦИАЛИСТИЧЕСКИХ
РЕСПУБЛИК

ВИД НА ЖИТЕЛЬСТВО ДЛЯ ИНОСТРАНЦА

А №166542

Пред'явителю настоящего вида Чехословацкому гражданину Росенбаум Ганущ имеющему визу на в'езд в СССР за № —
сроком по „ „ — 193 г., выданную —
разрешено проживание в Союзе Советских Социалистических Республик
сроком по шестое января 1944.

М. П. Начальник Управления РК Милиции

СВЕДЕНИЯ О ВЛАДЕЛЬЦЕ ВИДА НА ЖИТЕЛЬСТВО

1. Время и место рождения 1928 г. г. Моравская Острава Чехосл.
2. Семейное положение одинокий
3. Профессия или должность учащийся
4. Когда приехал в СССР и цель приезда в 1939 г. с родителями.
5. При нем находятся дети до 16 лет нет
6. На основании каких документов выдан вид Нацпаспорт, выд. Миссией Чехосл. Республики в г. Москве 25/VIII-42 – 26/VIII-44 г.

Настоящий вид выдан Алдан. Окр. отд. Милиции
6 июля 1943

Собственноручная подпись владельца вида на жительство

Residence permit for foreigners in the USSR granted to Hanuš Rosenbaum by the local militia unit in Aldan, East Siberia in July 1943. *CVG collection*

Временное воинское удостоверение

Настоящим удостоверяется, что

строевой №

год и место рождения

является военнослужащим чехословацкой воинской части.

Prozatímní vojenská legitimace

Potvrzuji, že slob.
Rosenbaum Hanus
kmenové číslo 3736
narozen 6.2.1928 v
Mor. Ostrava
jest příslušníkem československé vojenské jednotky.

razítko

печать

podpis velitele

Ztráta legitimace se trestá!

Temporary military identification from 1944. *CVG collection*

the name right now. There they transferred us to open-bed trucks and we drove some six or seven hundred kilometres, that was in Yakutia, and we ended up in the town of Aldan. Today it's already a fairly large and well-known town. There were several barracks on the outskirts of town that were separated from the town by a barbed-wire fence, and that's where they sent us. When we drove into the town, the locals were standing on either side of the road and were all yelling, "The spies have arrived!" There were even little kids among them and we were all spies!

How did the camp guards treat you?
I have to say, decently – no torture or beatings. There were relatively few guards, after all there was nowhere to run. The closest railway station was six hundred, seven hundred kilometres away. Nothing in between, just taiga. Only once every few weeks, trucks with provisions came and carted away the wood cut there, and that was the only connection to the outside world. So the guards were pointless. They just made sure all the adults went to work. There was no distinction made between the sick and the healthy. In the morning you went into the taiga, in the afternoon back.

What kind of work was it?
Cutting wood. There was also gold being mined in the whole area, but prisoners didn't do that, they only harvested lumber. Sometimes it was a bit

ridiculous. My mother was 148 centimetres tall, skinny, and her partner in tree-cutting was perhaps a bit older than her, half-blind, sickly, and that was a team that cut wood in the taiga. There was no differentiation in what or how much you could do, you just had to do it.

How many hours a day did you work?
In summer, which was only like two months, it was around seven hours. Then, when the days got shorter, it depended on how long the day was and how cold it was. We even worked at minus thirty-eight, and that was fairly common, because in the winter the temperature could often fall as low as forty-two, forty-five. The advantage of the harsh cold was that there was no wind. We couldn't stay outside long though, and we had to have these kind of scarves over our noses and mouths. But the conditions there were overall better than at ordinary prison camps. We didn't have any convicts, just unreliable elements they had to cart away.

I hear you saw two suns.
The natural phenomena in Siberia, that was something else. The moon, that was something incredible. But something altogether was when there were suddenly even three suns in the sky. The middle one was probably the real one, but next to it were two more, completely identical. In general, the nature there was beautiful, in the winter, when the Yakuts came in with their deer and so on.

Did the locals try to help you at all?
No. We were of no interest to them. The only people who had a bit of contact with us were the local children.

What nationalities were the prisoners? Did you meet any other Czechs?
I think we were the only ones. They were all Jews from Poland, mostly from eastern Poland. There were around three hundred fifty, four hundred of us, including the children. There could've been eighty to a hundred children.

What did you do during the day when the parents were working?
We didn't have school, we didn't have any job, so we helped collect wood for heating at home, and in the summer, rhubarb. Then there was the river Aldan, so we fished, but no one was very good at it.

How did the adults handle the working conditions?
The conditions were very harsh and people soon started dying. There were weak people, there were strong people, but everyone had to work. When the amnesty came in summer of 1942, there were maybe one hundred fifty fewer of us.

Hanuš Rosenbaum served in the Czechoslovak military unit as a liaison officer with the artillery, 1944. *CVG collection*

What did people die of most frequently?
Most often of frailty, of vitamin deficiency. There was hunger there the whole time. Once a month they gave us a bit of sugar, a bit of flour, and we had to live off that.

Was there any kind of doctor at the camp?
There was no one like that at the camp. In town there was someone they called the barber surgeon. He wasn't a real doctor, but someone who understood medicine. But people were dying like flies there. Dad couldn't take it and died in May of 1943, that was already after the amnesty.

Was there any kind of storehouse there that they gave you food from, or a dining hall, a communal kitchen?
There was no dining hall. We lived in long barracks, where every family would hang up a rag of some sort on one side to separate them from the others, and on the other side were these kind of iron ovens where they'd cook. The bit of flour and sugar we got would be eaten in two, three days, then cooking was no longer an issue.

What did the barracks look like?
They were massive wooden buildings. Eight to twelve families lived in each of them. The conditions there were dismal. We slept on these kind of two-storey bunks. The hygiene was terrible. Picking out lice was almost a whole day's work. This was after the amnesty, when I got very sick – I had a high fever and was even unconscious for a day or two. When I had recovered, my parents asked if I could change my environment, and even allowed me to move to the local boarding school. It was about eight kilometres from our camp and the conditions were better there.

What boarding school was it?
The boarding school in the Orochen II settlement, as I said about eight kilometres from our labour camp. It was mostly Russian kids there and a few children of prisoners. Of course they were constantly indoctrinating us there, but we also learned things. After all, I hadn't seen a school since 1939.

Was life at the boarding school better than life in the camp?
Much better. First of all, we had normal rooms, big rooms, like auditoriums. Ten to twelve children in one, guaranteed food at least twice a day, morning and noon, not in the evening. Before noon we studied and after noon we worked. It was work for the boarding school. Overall it was a big leap for me. I think it was the only time in elementary school where I was happy to learn, where I wanted to learn. I'd always been too lazy to study. We had general education, mathematics, Russian literature, science and so on. And there were several teachers there, even Jewish ones.

How did you learn about the amnesty?
One day, the camp commander told us that an amnesty had been declared for all the dangerous elements imprisoned there. Not just for the Czechs. This was almost a year after the USSR was attacked. But where was one to suddenly go? At that point someone proposed that the best place to go was Uzbekistan. Most of the people were in favour, I don't even know why. At any rate Uzbekistan, that was heaven on earth.

What did the camp commander have to say about that?
He gave us the option of applying to leave. Of course we had to state exactly where to... It was a good decision. Dad died of exhaustion in May 1943 and about a month later mum found out the Czech army was forming...

Where did you end up heading?
We ended up setting out for Kuybyshev. But that was no journey of a day or two. There were no trains, and when there were, they were packed, so some-

Hanan Ron during the interview, Tel Aviv 2013. *ÚSTR / Jan Dvořák*

times we had to wait whole days before we could move on. In the end we arrived in Kuybyshev, got to the embassy, and they told us we could continue to Buzuluk. Mum asked them what they'd do with me. And one accountant took a look at me and said, that boy could be a cadet. And so I became a soldier. We got there in July 1943.

II.
DEPORTEES AND REFUGEES FROM THE NAZI CAMP IN ZARZECZE NEAR NISKO

RUDOLF GOLDFLAM (b. 1906 in Brno), deported to Nisko in October 1939. Arrested in Lviv in May 1940. Sentenced to three years in the Gulag. Imprisoned at Volgolag in the years 1940–1942. *HDA SBU* ▶

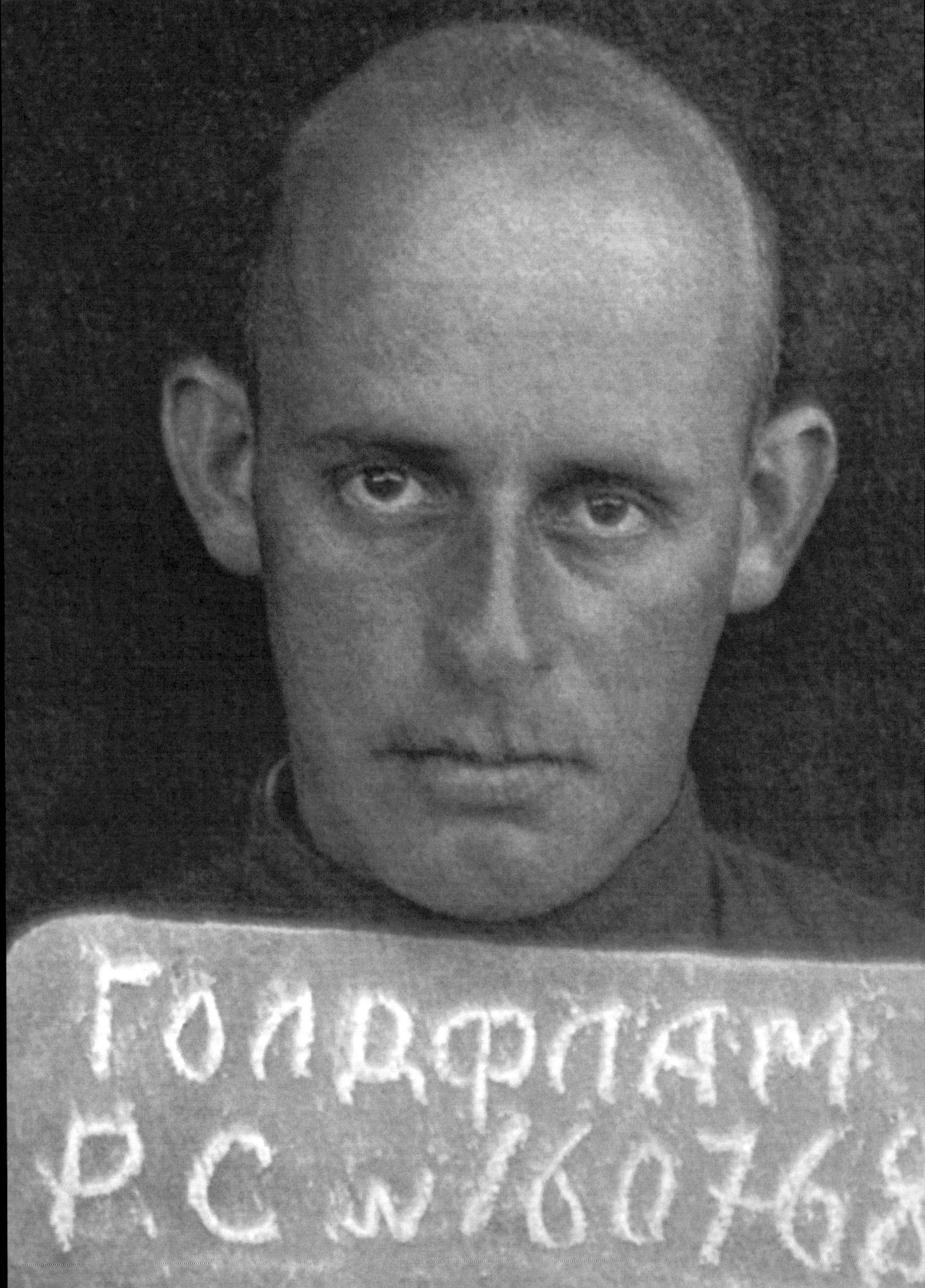
ГОЛДФЛАМ

The occupation of western Poland essentially meant the first step towards implementing the Nazi's territorial plans to Germanise and colonise the newly occupied eastern regions. Their idea was that only Germans would live in the territory annexed to the German Reich[54] and thus it should be "cleansed" of non-German "elements" in as short a time as possible. This was closely tied to the solving of the "Jewish question".

One of the first plans slated for implementation was the Nisko Plan, based on the Nazi leadership's intent to concentrate all Jews in a single large "ghetto" or "reservation" in the eastern parts of occupied Poland, then already the General Governorate. Although the Nazi occupiers were primarily concerned with expelling the Jews from the conquered Polish territories, this also affected nearly 1500 Czechoslovak Jews. Most of them, however, ended up in Soviet prisons and Gulag labour camps instead of the Nazi "ghetto".

The organisational preparations for expelling the Jews from the western provinces to the swampy areas around Lublin got fully underway as early as the start of October 1939. According to the original plan of Gestapo chief Heinrich Müller, the territory of the Katowice government district was to be cleansed first, but the opportunity soon arose to also resettle the Jews from around Moravian Ostrava.[55] In the end, evidently at the express wish of Hitler himself, it was decided that Vienna would also be added to the first transports.[56]

Organisation of the transports was provided by the Gestapo in cooperation with employees of the Centre for Jewish Emigration in Vienna and in Prague. Coordination of the whole operation was entrusted to Adolf Eichmann, then already a leading Nazi expert on the "solution to the Jewish Question", who also personally chose the site for the first camp several days later – a hill by the village of Zarzecze near Nisko. The whole operation was presented to the public however as a voluntary initiative of the respective Jewish communities.[57] All men of Jewish background over the age of 14 were

54 The final decision on the administration of the occupied Polish territory was ultimately made by Hitler himself – the "Decree of the Fuehrer and Reich Chancellor concerning the Incorporation and Administration of Eastern Regions" of 8 October, which came into effect 26 October, ended the period of military administration in the occupied territory. The new provinces of West Prussia (later Danzig-West Prussia) and Posen (Warthegau) were formed as part of the German Reich, while the province of Silesia was formed out of Upper and Lower Silesia. The remainder of Poland became the General Governorate.

55 BORÁK, Mečislav: *První deportace evropských Židů* [First Deportations of European Jews], p. 48–49.

56 For more on the Vienna transports, see MOSER, Jonny: "Nisko. Ein geplantes Judenreservat in Polen". In: *Das Jüdische Echo*, Bd. 120, Nr. 36. Verein zur Herausgabe der Zeitschrift „Das Jüdische Echo", Vienna 1989, p. 118–122; DVOŘÁK, Jan: "Směr Nisko nad Sanem. První organizované deportace Židů z Vídně" [Destination Nisko. The First Organised Deportations of Jews from Vienna]. *Historica. Revue pro historii a příbuzné vědy*, 2012, vol. 3, no. 1, p. 44–57.

57 BORÁK, Mečislav: Příprava a průběh niských transportů [Preparation and Implementation of the Nisko Transports]. In: NESLÁDKOVÁ, Ludmila (ed.): *Akce Nisko v historii „konečného řešení ži-*

One of the oldest deportees from Ostrava to Nisko was mine inspector MAX BACHRACH (1887). He reached Soviet territory on 25 October 1939 near the village of Dachnów. He lived in Lviv up until 16 November 1939, then left for the city of Buchach, where he remained until he was arrested by the local NKVD authorities on 17 June 1940. He was subsequently charged with illegally crossing the border and sent to one of the Unzhlag corrective labour camps in the Volga region. He was liberated by the amnesty for Czechoslovak citizens 21 January 1942. After the war he lived in Ostrava.

HDA SBU, f. Criminal Files (1939–1994), vol. no. 3598.

to board the transport to the eastern Polish regions for "re-education", otherwise they faced severe punishment.

Despite some difficulties putting together the transports – some individuals decided to hide or flee from the impending deportations – in the end two transports each from Ostrava, Vienna and Katowice were dispatched between 17 and 26 October, carrying more than five thousand deportees.[58] It remains

dovské otázky". K 55. výročí první deportace evropských Židů. Mezinárodní vědecká konference. Sborník referátů [The Nisko Plan in the History of the "Final Solution to the Jewish Question". On the 55th Anniversary of the First Deportation of European Jews. International Academic Conference. Collection of Papers]. Rondo, Ostrava 1995, p. 100.

58 A third transport with over three hundred persons was dispatched on 1 November 1939 only from Ostrava. In the end it did not reach its destination in Nisko because of a collapsed bridge over the flooded San River near Zarzecze and had to be re-routed to Sosnowiec in Upper Silesia. The fate of those on the third Ostrava transport therefore differed from those that reached Nis-

One of the youngest deportees to Nisko was 16-year-old student KURT ROSENZWEIG (1923) of Těšín. He crossed the German-Soviet border in a group of prisoners expelled from Nisko on 2 November 1939 by the village of Rudka. Though the border guards apprehended him, he was released following registration and could continue to Lviv. He was arrested again by the NKVD 27 June 1940 and sent to Belbaltlag in the Arkhangelsk Oblast. In June 1941 he was relocated to the nearby Kargopollag. Only in 1942 was he informed that he had been sentenced to 3 years in the Gulag for illegally crossing the border. He was released in June 1944. From that time, he lived in the town of Bugulma in Tatarstan. In the year 1947 he was granted Soviet citizenship at his own request.

DALO, f. R-3258 (1939–1950), vol. no. 8823.

a paradox of the whole operation, however, that by the time the first transport was departing, the Nazi leadership had already decided to stop these deportations, as on 17 October 1939, Hitler had decided that the Wartheland and West Prussia provinces were to be "de-Jewified" first. The departure of the remaining, already prepared and announced transports to Nisko was primarily approved so as to preserve the integrity of the state police.[59]

ko. For more on the third Ostrava transport, see PŘIBYL, Lukáš: "Osud třetího protektorátního transportu do Niska" [The Fate of the Third Protectorate Transport to Nisko]. In: KÁRNÝ, Miroslav – LORENCOVÁ, Eva (eds.): *Terezínské studie a dokumenty* [Terezín Studies and Documents]. Academia, Prague 2000,

59 BORÁK, Mečislav: *Příprava a průběh niských transportů* [Preparation and Implementation of the Nisko Transports], p. 103.

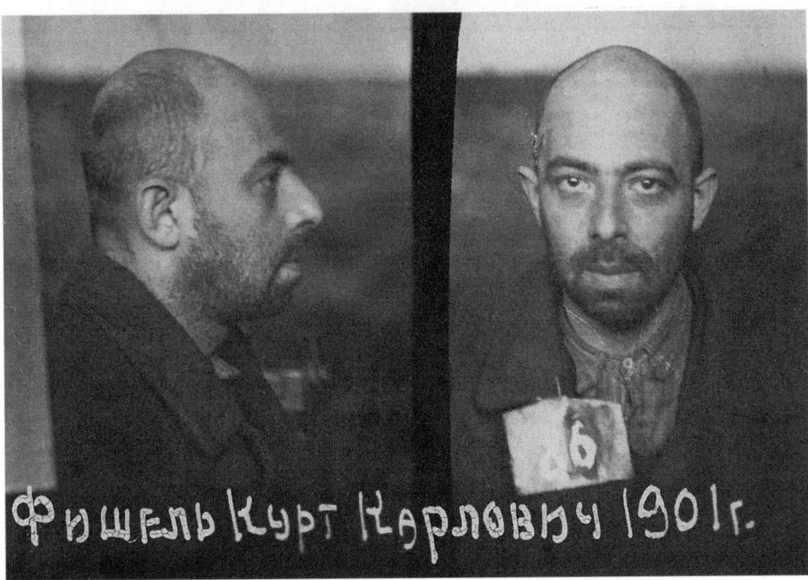

KURT FISCHL (1901) was another included in the first Ostrava transport, having worked as an accountant for various companies in Ostrava up until 1939. On 25 October 1939, during a mass crossing of the German-Soviet border, he was arrested near Syniava by Soviet border guards. He was taken to Lviv for further investigation, then transferred to the NKVD prison in Nikolayev (today Mykolaiv) at the start of 1940. On 25 October 1940, he was sentenced to 5 years in the Gulag for illegally crossing the border. He served his sentence at one of the Ivdellag camps in the northern Urals in the Sverdlovsk Oblast, where he died 8 December 1941.

DALO, f. R-3258 (1939–1950), vol. no. 18990.

The cancellation of the Nisko Plan at its very outset also significantly impacted the fates of the deportees. Only around one in nine of the transported prisoners could stay at the temporary concentration camp on the hill by the San River (tradespeople and experts to construct the camp were chosen), while all the others, i.e., over four and a half thousand deportees, were driven east by SS guards to the nearby German-Soviet demarcation line immediately after arriving in Nisko. There they were forced to cross over into Soviet territory under threat of being shot.

Of course even those that could temporarily stay at the camp started fleeing it over the course of the following days, weeks and months. Their escape was greatly facilitated by the lack of security at the camp itself and its

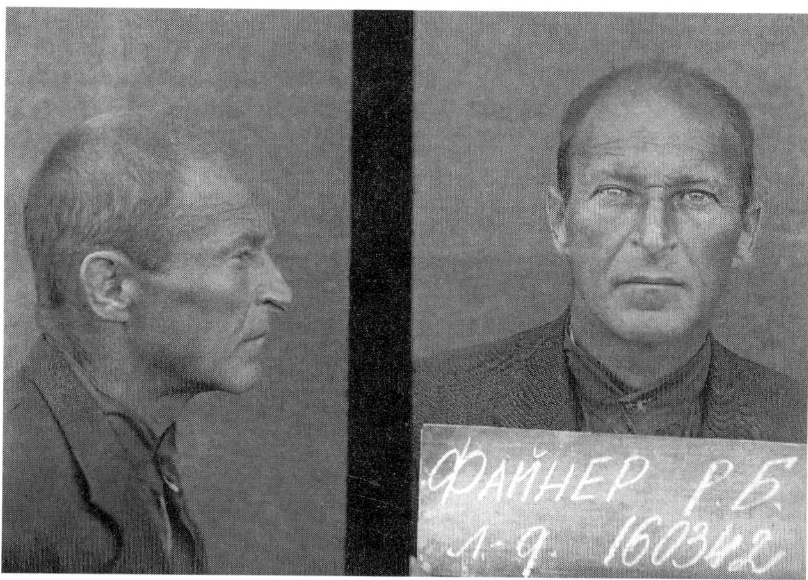

Accountant ROBERT FEINER (1893) of Ostrava was one of the few prisoners deported to Nisko who were selected by the Nazis for the temporary camp near the village of Zarzecze after arrival. He remained there until 5 December 1939, when he was released along with other prisoners. After crossing into Soviet territory, he was arrested by Soviet border guards near Syniava on 14 December 1939. The following day he was released and went to Lviv, where he was arrested by the NKVD 28 June 1940. From September 1940 he was imprisoned at Volgolag (Volgostroi) near the city of Rybinsk in the Yaroslavl Oblast. Only subsequently was he sentenced to 3 years for illegally crossing the border by a judgment of 2 May 1942. He was released on 15 August 1942, and 27 August 1942 he was drafted into the Czechoslovak Army Corps at Buzuluk. He fought in its ranks on the Eastern Front until the end of the war, reaching the rank of lieutenant.

DALO, f. R-3258 (1939–1950), vol. no. 10015.

outposts scattered around the vicinity. The paths of these refugees also led predominantly to Soviet territory.[60]

Around a thousand Czechoslovak Jews deported to Nisko successfully managed to cross to the Soviet side from the end of October until the end of 1939. From the moment they entered Soviet territory, they essentially shared the fates of the other refugees from Czechoslovakia.[61]

60 idem: *První deportace evropských Židů* [First Deportations of European Jews], p. 107–122.

61 On the issue of the transports to Nisko and repression against deportees in the USSR, see DVOŘÁK, Jan – HORNÍK, Jan – HRADILEK, Adam: První transporty evropských Židů v dějinách holo-

KAREL BORSKÝ (KURT BIHELLER)

Born on 13 May 1921 as Kurt Biheller in Silesian Fryštát (today part of Karviná) to the family of merchant Adolf Biheller. Despite the fact that he grew up in a multi-ethnic city and most Silesian Jews tended towards German culture, his parents raised him in the Czech spirit. First he attended the Czech Alois Jirásek School in Fryštát, then he continued his studies at the Czech grammar school in Orlová. In the second half of the 1930s, his family moved to Moravian Ostrava, where he once again studied at the Czech grammar school. Soon after the Protectorate of Bohemia and Moravia was established, however, he had to leave school due to his Jewish background. At that time, his father was already in Gestapo custody. In October 1939, Kurt was assigned to the first Ostrava transport heading for Nisko. Almost immediately after arriving, he and the other prisoners were herded to the German-Soviet demarcation line, which he crossed along with a small group of deportees at the end of October 1939. At the start of November they reached Lviv, where he supported himself for several months in all sorts of ways. He was living there without the proper papers however (a Soviet residency permit), and thus was arrested by NKVD officers on 4 July 1940 and subsequently sentenced to three years at corrective labour camps. He was deported to the Volgolag (Volgostroi) camp complex in central Russia in the Yaroslavl Oblast.[62] Here the prisoners worked building the individual parts of the Volga-Don Canal. He himself ended up in the camp by the village of Parsovo and was assigned to the logging squad. As a Polish citizen, he was released on 21 October 1941. Instead of joining the Polish army, he and his friend from Ostrava, Bruno Finger, headed to Makhachkala[63]. There he worked for several months in the tanning chemical plant Promkhimkombinat before he found out about the formation of a Czechoslovak military unit in Buzuluk, which he decided to join. He was enlisted on 29 June 1942. He took part in the entire adventures of the Czechoslovak Army Corps in the USSR, ending the war as lieutenant-commander of the artillery battery of the 5th artillery regiment in the USSR. He also acted as the brigade photographer. He was seriously wounded several times during the fighting. While still on the front, he married unit member Anna Graplová. After returning home, he learned that twenty-two members of his family (including his father, mother and younger brother) had been killed in the Nazi extermination camps. He remained in the Czechoslovak Army after the

---

caustu [First Transports of European Jews in the History of the Holocaust]. *Paměť a dějiny*, 2014, vol. 8, no. 4, p. 101–119.

62 Volgolag (Volgostroi) – the camp administration was based in the city of Rybinsk. Prisoners mostly worked here on waterway construction projects and associated works. BYSTROV, Vladimír: *Průvodce říší zla* [Guide To the Realm of Evil]. Academia, Prague 2006, p. 698–699.

63 Makhachkala – the capital of the autonomous Republic of Dagestan in the Russian Federation.

war, changing his name to Karel Borský in 1946, which among other things facilitated being accepted to the Czechoslovak Communist Party. In the army, he served as an education officer and at the end of 1948 he was transferred to the headquarters of the 1st military circuit in Prague and soon thereafter to the Ministry of National Defence. From October 1949 he worked as a military and aviation attaché in Budapest. In connection with the intensifying campaign against Zionism launched by the Party at the start of the 50s, however, he was dismissed from this function in April 1951 and discharged from the army. He worked briefly in construction, but as soon as 4 April 1951 he was arrested on suspicion of espionage against the Hungarian People's Democratic Republic. He spent four months in pre-trial detention before he was released in April 1952 for insufficient evidence. Subsequently he worked at the national enterprise Hydraulic Works as an editor of the plant magazine and head of the cultural department. In 1956, he was rehabilitated and summoned back to the Czechoslovak army. He was assigned to the combat training department of the 30th Fighter and Bomber Air Division in Čáslav. As he could speak several languages, he worked from March 1965 until December 1966 as the head of the Czechoslovak delegation on the Neutral Nations Supervisory Commission in Korea. After returning to Czechoslovakia, he worked in the foreign affairs department of the General Staff, holding less important functions in the army from the 1970s until his retirement. He was active in the ranks of the Czech Union of Anti-Fascist Fighters, and after 1989 became the deputy chairman of the restored Czechoslovak Legionnaires. He published several works on the topic of World War II. In the year 2000, Václav Havel promoted him to the rank of retired brigadier general. He died on 9 August 2001 in Prague.[64]

— — —

When did you arrive in Nisko?
In October 1939. The Germans transported us to that utterly unknown town under terrible conditions by train. We were crammed into a wagon in which you couldn't even breathe and it wasn't possible to open a window. They didn't give us any water, the hygienic conditions were horrible, and the old people couldn't endure such a journey and fainted. That was the first time I experienced the Nazi terror firsthand. Once we got to Nisko, we managed to get from the train station to the closest village. The situation was complicated however by the fact that there were Ukrainian nationalists at the station and they were attacking various groups of refugees and robbing them. There wasn't much they could take from us though. They were mainly after money and none of us had any. In the end it turned out all right, they let us go and we reached the

64 *Collection of interviews USC Shoah Foundation*, interview with Karel Borský (Kurt Biheller) recorded 9 March 1996 by Eva Benešová.

Photograph of Kurt Biheller taken a few days before leaving for Nisko, October 1939.
CVG collection

San River.[65] There a local farmer took us in, even then there were good people. He hid us in a barn, which was a fairly safe hiding place. German soldiers were patrolling the village, but they had little interest in chasing after refugees. They walked around the village in patrols and if they got their hands on someone, it would certainly turn out badly. But it wasn't like they were systematically searching houses or barns. They didn't feel like doing that.

How many of you fled?
Four guys.

What was your plan after that?
The farmer was the first to tell us that the Soviets were across the river. He also warned us not to have any illusions about them. If we got across the river and fell into the hands of the Red Army border guards, he said they wouldn't welcome us with open arms, but we'd go right to court and then to a work camp. Which was important information. At the same time, he explained to us that the best thing would be to get to Lviv or another largish city, where

65 In all likelihood it was not the San, but one of its tributaries, most likely Tanew.

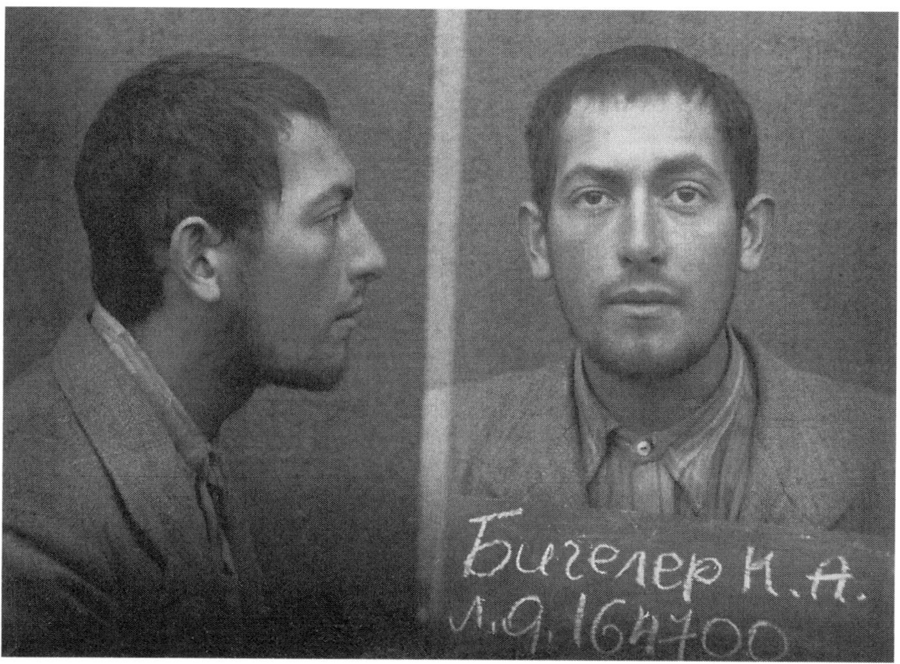

Kurt Biheller after arrest by the NKVD. *HDA SBU*

we could disappear. He was absolutely right. In the morning he took us to a place from where we could see the river and the Soviet guards, who changed every two hours. It was this changing of the guard that was the best moment for crossing to the other side. The San wasn't too deep, you could cross it with the water up to your waist at most.

So the crossing went off without any problem?
What's interesting is that at that time, we met a lot of people like us, refugees from the transports or from the places they took them but hadn't managed to build the camps for them yet. Eichmann's pupils really miscalculated, because they weren't able to build camps with barbed wires for that many people that fast. Some of the refugees headed across the San, where they immediately surrendered to the Soviets. As we later found out, that automatically meant imprisonment and then internment. We followed the farmer's instructions, however, and headed for Lviv. Life in Lviv was a chapter in itself because Czech refugees, usually Jews, who had fled the Protectorate and were looking for a way out of Europe would meet at the local Café de la Paix[66]. It was still quiet in the city then, so we found work.

66 Café de la Paix – in the years 1939–1941 one of the largest refugee centres in Lviv.

What kind of work was it?
At first I was employed at a mill. Carrying fifty-kilo sacks was hard work. I couldn't handle it, so I switched to the *artel*. That was a kind of cooperative of photographers, where I worked in the lab, but I didn't like it there either. Eventually I settled on being a *khudozhnik*, a painter. My "studio" was in a big pub, named Polyanka, where I made various slogans of the sort "Long Live Stalin", or other times I painted benches. It wasn't bad. At the pub I had access to food, so I had enough to eat. Plus I could bring some to my friend Arnošt Foltýn, another guy from Ostrava I met in Lviv. To give you an idea of the conditions at the time, I have to mention that Lviv had a population of around half a million at the time, and there were another half million emigrants crammed in every which way. The city suddenly had twice the population. The situation was untenable. The Soviets knew how to deal with it very quickly though. One night, trucks rolled in and started carting away the emigrants living in various buildings there.

How did they know who was a refugee? How did they look for them?
They had it all planned out. In that regard the NKVD was perfect. They went according to exact lists, including addresses. They'd just ring the bell downstairs, the caretaker would come answer, they'd push him aside mercilessly with no explanation, and armed soldiers would enter the building. They'd burst into the individual flats and shout, "Where are the foreigners?!" They drove the detainees out uncompromisingly and without delay. At that time, me and Arnošt Foltýn were living in a sublet. They didn't let us take anything with us but personal effects, so a towel and a toothbrush. They were decent about it though, no beating or other violence. Outside there were trucks waiting that took us to some barracks. There I saw that most of my buddies, friends, classmates who were in Lviv at that time had ended up like me. Indeed, other cities where emigrants were concentrated, for example the former Stanyslaviv[67], encountered the same fate.

What happened to you next?
We spent one or two nights at the barracks. Then they loaded us like cattle onto livestock wagons and we headed out who knows where. They didn't talk to us, didn't answer any questions about where we were going, moreover with no trial, no nothing. In this manner they took us to various places. I have no clue on what basis they divided us up. So it was I had to soon say goodbye to my friend Foltýn, who by the way had been a soldier in the pre-war Czechoslovak army. I ended up as a builder of the Volga-Don Canal, which meant

67 Stanyslaviv – today Ivano-Frankivsk, a city in western Ukraine.

travelling to Parsovo in the Ivanovo Oblast, where there were two camps: Parsovo and Turgenovo. There we worked at what was called *lesopoval*, i.e., clearing the forest. The young people could just barely manage the hard work, but the older generation suffered cruelly. I remember a Mr Langfelder, for example, who had a stationery shop near us in Ostrava. As a student, I used to buy my pencils and notebooks from him. Imagine, they sent this old man into the forest to fell six- to eight-metre long tree trunks. He was working with an equally old café owner from Ostrava. Unfortunately, they didn't last long, and both died. Lots of people died there in that way. In short, us young lads had a better chance of surviving, and then... Czech wits always find a way to make life easier.

Can you specify in what way easier?
Like you could get around the work quotas. At the end of every shift, the standards guy would take the cut planks and put a stamp on each of them – the board was accepted and according to quality was placed in the first or second category. One morning, after we got to work, we distracted the guard and some other lads went over to the stamped planks and cut off the piece of wood with the stamp on it. Normally they'd stamp them on the end, you see. Then we took the planks to the place where we were working, so first thing in the morning we had four to five boards we could meet the quota with. That was incredibly important, because if we met the quota, we'd get more bread, more food.

What was your living situation?
We lived in barracks of a hundred or more people with a minimum of sanitary facilities. In order to make our lives more "pleasant", before we got to the camp from work, a band would play for us outside, which was utter cynicism. The band included famous Czech musicians. For example Bedřich Scharf, who played in a café in Ostrava. There was Erich Trautman, or Toman, who later wrote the well-known song Směr Praha.[68] They were truly elite musicians. They had to play even in the bitter cold, with the temperature sometimes falling tens of degrees below zero. They stood in front of the camp and played us Strauss or other pieces before they finished counting us and let us in.

68 Směr Praha [Destination Prague] – a song written by Ervín Toman, after the death of Vít Nejedlý the commander of the Army Artistic Ensemble of the 1st Czechoslovak Army Corps in the USSR. This successful military song became a prototype for the later production of not only battle songs, but also post-war socialism-building songs.

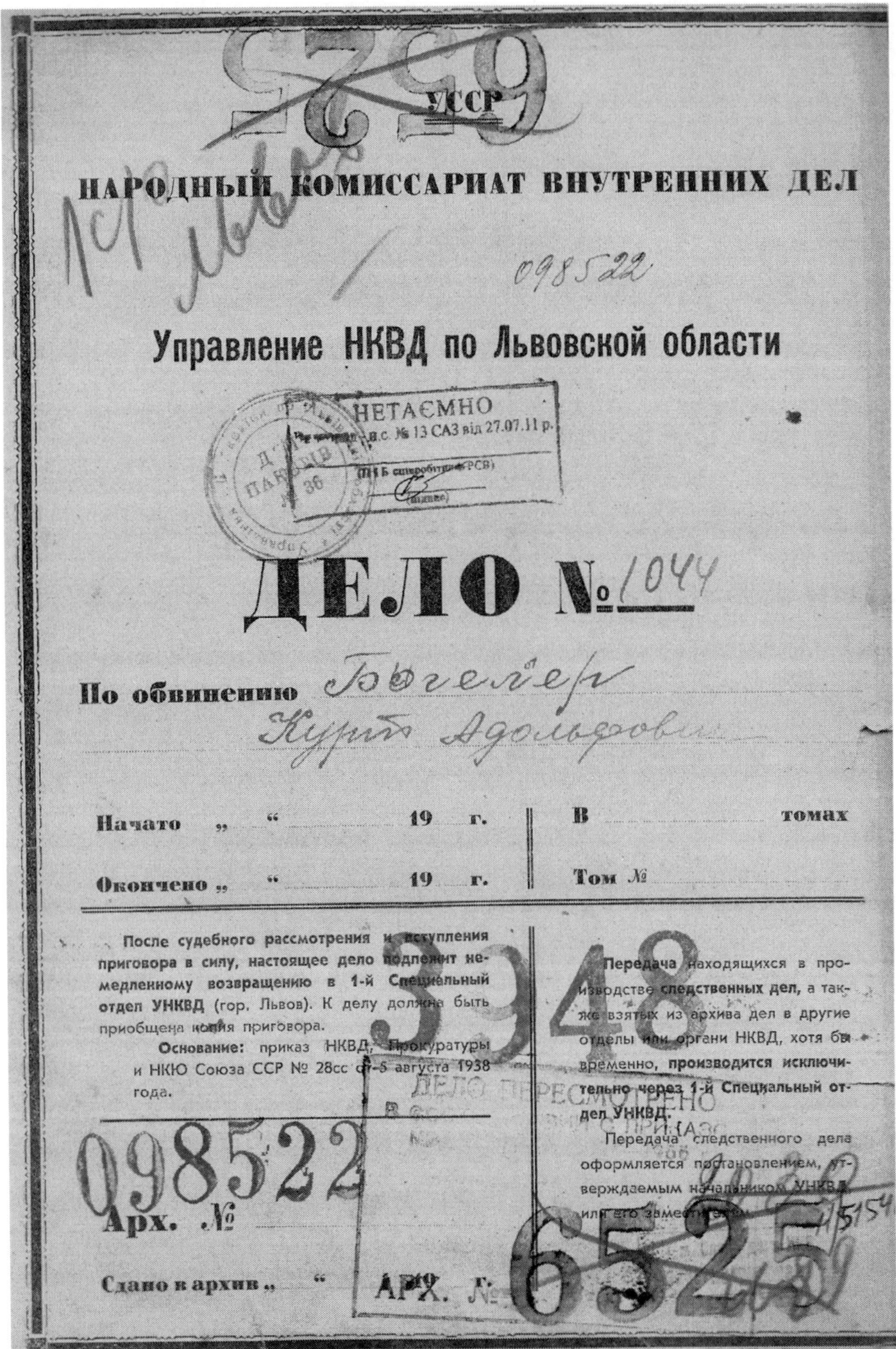

УССР

НАРОДНЫЙ КОМИССАРИАТ ВНУТРЕННИХ ДЕЛ

098522

Управление НКВД по Львовской области

НЕТАЄМНО

ДЕЛО № 1044

По обвинению Бигелер Курт Адольфович

Начато „ “ 19 г. | В томах

Окончено „ “ 19 г. | Том №

После судебного рассмотрения и вступления приговора в силу, настоящее дело подлежит немедленному возвращению в 1-й Специальный отдел УНКВД (гор. Львов). К делу должна быть приобщена копия приговора.

Основание: приказ НКВД, Прокуратуры и НКЮ Союза ССР № 28сс от 5 августа 1938 года.

Передача находящихся в производстве **следственных дел,** а также взятых из архива дел в другие отделы или органи НКВД, хотя бы временно, **производится исключительно через 1-й Специальный отдел УНКВД.**

Передача следственного дела оформляется постановлением, утверждаемым начальником УНКВД или его заместителем.

3948

098522

Арх. №

Сдано в архив „ “ 19 г.

6525

Title page of the investigation file on Kurt Biheller. *HDA SBU*

44 от 164700 Форма № 2

Пол муж

Фамилия Бичеллер дакт. форм. 1044

Имя Курт

Отчество Адольфович

Год рождения 1921 Место рождения Фриштат Чехословакия

Правая рука

1. Большой	2. Указательный	3. Средний	4. Безымянный	5. Мизинец
	16		8	

Линия 16 перегиба 8 4

Левая рука

6. Большой	7. Указательный	8. Средний	9. Безымянный	10. Мизинец
4		2		1

Линия перегиба 2 1

Контрольный оттиск

Левой рукой	Правой рукой

Карта заполнена „26" Августа 1940 г. в Уп. Тарсова Поленовский уч. Вологлага НКВД.
(указать где и в каком органе НКВД)

Карту составил Ст. нарядчик Антонов А. К.
(должность и подпись)

Проверил
(должность и подпись)

Подпись зарегистрированного Бичеллер Курт Адольфович

В карте должны быть четко заполнены:
1) Фамилия, имя, отчество, установочные данные регистрируемого и его подпись. 2) Когда, где и в каком аппарате НКВД кем карта составлена и кем проверена. 3) В квадратиках каждый палец прокатать на своем месте полностью и ясно. 4) В контрольных оттисках левой и правой руки сделать оттиски 4-х пальцев каждой руки без большого.

Т. им. Воровского.

After his arrest, Kurt Biheller's fingerprints were taken. *HDA SBU*

СССР
Народный Комиссариат Внутренних Дел
Волжский

СПРАВКА

Дана в том, что при мед. освидетельствовании з/к Бигеллера Курта Адольфовича обнаружено:

ДИАГНОЗ: Здоров

Начальник санчасти Поленовского участка Волголага НКВД (ГЕНКИН)

„14" Сентября 1940 г. Врач

The record of the doctor's examination upon admission to Volgolag (Volgostroi). Kurt Biheller was found healthy. *HDA SBU*

Did they single you out as Jews at the camp? Did you profess Judaism?
I wouldn't say so. A substantial portion of the prisoners were former Polish officers. We Jews were a minority and we just kind of got lost among the others. Sometimes we'd hear some of the Russian prisoners say: "Eto yevrey" – "It's a Jew", but it didn't come across as anti-Semitic. As Jews we stuck together, we knew each other and helped each other out. There were also older Jews there, and when someone died, we could give them the kind of final Jewish ritual farewell. On the other hand, lots of people died there and were buried without those things. We were basically lucky that the majority of prisoners were Polish, because the Polish government eventually achieved amnesty for its imprisoned citizens.[69]

How did that relate to you?
It was our good fortune that there were few of us Jews and our jailers did not abound in geographical or linguistic knowledge. So when they were carrying out the registration, they confused us for Poles. We of course made no attempt to correct them and were released as well. The camp was essentially disbanded. The Poles joined the army and we could choose our next destination outside the first category cities. That meant major cities, important cultural centres and so on. I had another friend from Ostrava at the camp, the tailor Bruno Finger. He made out fairly well at the camp because he would repair the prison apparel and sew European suits for the commanders. He helped me out a lot, particularly with food, always bringing some extra bread,

69 See Introduction, p. 16 (Anders' Army).

СССР

Народный Комиссариат Внутренних Дел

Строительство гидротехнических узлов на р. Волге

Рыбинск—Углич

„ВОЛГОСТРОЙ"

ОТДЕЛ ___

22 - X 1942 г.

№ 164700

Адрес: г. Рыбинск—Переборы „ВОЛГОСТРОЙ"

Литер „___"

Вх. № ___ от ___ 19 г. получено ___ 19 г.

На № ___ от ___ 19 г.

При ответах ссылаться на №, число и отдел

Копия

УДОСТОВЕРЕНИЕ.

Предъявитель сего гр-н Бигеллер Курта Адольдоовича

родился 1921 года в г. Фриштат Чехословакия

На основании решения Государственного Комитета Обороны от 3 января 1942 года освобожден из заключения, как чехословацкий гр-н, имеет право свободного проживания на территории СССР, за исключением пограничных районов, запретных зон, местностей объявленных на военном положении и режимных городов 1 и II категории.

Гр-н Бигеллер Курт Адольфович направляется к избранному им месту жительства в г. Махач-Кала Дагест. АССР

Удостоверение действительно на три месяца и подлежит обмену на паспорт.

Изложенное удостоверяется подписью и печатью.

ПОМ.НАЧ.ВОЛГОЛАГА НКВД
КАПИТАН ГОСБЕЗОПАСНОСТИ. (КЕММЕР).

ЗАМ.НАЧ.ОУРЗ ВОЛГОЛАГА. (КЕЛЛЕР).

Отдел учета и распределения заключенных

Kurt Biheller's release form from Volgostroi. His designated place of further residence was the city of Makhachkala. *HDA SBU*

or onion, which was the main source of vitamins. So Finger and I chose Makhachkala, the capital of the Dagestan Soviet Socialist Republic.

Did they make out any documents when they released you?
We got some release papers from the camp, saying we were only allowed to be there and there. When we got to Makhachkala, though, as fate would have it, Finger and I accidentally split up. Or rather, we lost each other at the train station. I was eighteen years old and found myself with no knowledge of the local language alone in a foreign city full of minarets by the sea. Out of desperation, the first thing that occurred to me was to drown myself. In the end I headed to a restaurant, where I had some tea. After life in the camp and in my old clothes I looked like an emaciated beggar, so no one took any notice of me. Not until a very pretty girl, evidently a student, came over to me. She was sitting nearby with some company and eating fish. There was lots of fish in Makhachkala. Well, so this girl brings over a plate with two buns and piece of fish and says, "Young man, eat, you must be hungry." I was so deeply moved that it occurred to me again to go drown myself. But by the sea I met a Dagestani Jew. He advised me to go to the militia, announce myself and ask for work. He said they'd definitely give me a job, that there was work enough. So I headed to the militia, where I encountered a captain in polished boots. When I told him I was originally from Czechoslovakia and that I'd been in a labour camp, he became visibly nervous.

But you had your release papers...
But the whole story didn't sit with him somehow. He kept examining my documents, asking questions, but in the end it worked out. He gave me a referral to a factory with a terribly complicated name: Narkomprokhimkombinat. I have to acknowledge that they let me spend the night at the militia in something almost like a cell and gave me something to eat. The next day I came up to the gatehouse of the factory and told them I'd like to see the director. The porter haughtily replied, why do you of all people need to see the director... But when I showed him the *bumazhka* from the militia, he softened up straightaway and took me to the director himself. Fortunately he turned out to be a decent man.

What was your position there?
That first job wasn't exactly pleasant, we were processing sheep and goat leather, which for a young student from Ostrava was something completely new. But I learned it, and moreover I met a whole bunch of Jews there. For one thing emigrants from Poland, but also locals, who by their physiognomy were from some branch of Tatars. They wore fur coats and sheepskin hats, in the summer with the fur out and in the winter with the fur in, and would

often invite me into their homes. They even had their own synagogue there, but it was closed. Actually they were keeping up their religion illegally. It was in Makhachkala in 1942 that I learned a Czechoslovak military unit was being formed on the boundary of the Kazakh steppe and the Ural foothills.

So did you sign up as a Czechoslovak?
It wasn't that simple. I didn't have any concrete proof that I was a citizen of Czechoslovakia. They didn't believe me again and asked all sorts of questions. I remember one absurd scene from the military office. The war between the Germans and Soviets was in full swing, and the head of the military administration asked me, if I couldn't prove my Czechoslovak nationality, whether I'd go fight in the Red Army... I responded that against Nazi Germany I'd go fight with anyone and anywhere. He nodded his head and after that initial distrust and interrogation he said, "All right. In that case you go fight in your Czechoslovak army."

What was the farewell in Makhachkala like? After all, you had a lot of friends there...
The farewell was incredible. Almost the whole plant came to say goodbye at the boat sailing to Astrakhan[70]. Sure, I had a lot of friends there. On the other hand I knew that as a foreigner and a prison camp releasee, I was under constant surveillance. So I actually let out a sigh of relief once I was on the boat. In the end I was in for one of the happiest moments of my life. It was in Buzuluk, where for the first time in many years I saw the Czechoslovak colours flying at the train station as a symbol of our independence, as a symbol of the fact that our state, our nation, still existed. That's why I was proud I was becoming a soldier in the Czechoslovak army. To my great surprise, I also found there a considerable portion of my friends with whom I had shared the same fate after the fall of Czechoslovakia. From them I learned that, paradoxically, we had been saved by being taken by the NKVD from Lviv to the prison camps. The lads who weren't home back then, either sleeping at a friend's place or a girl's place, they had stayed in Lviv. But that was fatal for them. When the Germans came to Lviv, they shot them all.

70 Astrakhan – a city in the south of the European part of the Russian Federation near the Caspian Sea.

MORITZ (MOSHE) FRIEDNER

Born 11 April 1896 in Moravian Ostrava. There he graduated from grammar school, then from a business academy in Vienna. He fought in World War I in the Austro-Hungarian army on the Russian and Italian fronts. After his return, he worked as a travelling salesman. He lived with his wife and daughter in his birthplace up until October 1939, when they were taken to Nisko with the first Ostrava transport. Like most of the deportees, they were not selected for the camp. They crossed the German-Soviet demarcation line with a group of prisoners on 23 October 1939 and were arrested by the Soviet border guards immediately after crossing the river. The guards first took them to the border town of Syniava for the first interrogations, then the next day to Przemyśl and finally to Lviv. After two months, Moritz was transported from Lviv to a jail in Dnepropetrovsk, where the NKVD authorities sentenced him to five years of forced labour for illegally crossing the border 5 August 1940. With a transport of prisoners he travelled by train, boat and then by foot to arrive in very poor shape at the basin of the river Pechora – at one of the Pechlag camps by the settlement of Abez[71]. After recovering, he was assigned to a work commando clearing the railway line from Vorkuta to Kotlas. Due to a serious leg injury, however, he spent most of his time lying in a hospital instead of working. After the Nazi attack on the USSR in June 1941 and the declared amnesty for Polish citizens, he applied as a Pole to the Polish units forming in the USSR. At one of the gathering places however, the competent authorities exposed him along with other foreigners and in October 1941 he was sent back to the camp, where he once again spent most of his time in hospital. He was only released on 25 March 1942 with the amnesty for Czechoslovak citizens. He subsequently travelled to Buzuluk, where he was enlisted on 5 May 1942. There he travelled to the hospital again, where he underwent another operation. He could not enter active service until mid-June 1942. Due to his age and health, he worked as a staff sergeant and accountant, later in the rear with the reserve battalion. With the 1st Czechoslovak Army Corps, he went all the way to Czechoslovakia. He was demobilised 1 June 1945 and started working as a weaving shop manager. After six months he began working in Prague as a representative of the Textile Factory and later ran the enterprise's records office as an auditor. At the end of December 1948, he emigrated to Israel, where he lived until his death.[72]

— — —

71 Abez – a railway station and settlement in the north-east of the European part of Russia in the Komi Autonomous Soviet Socialist Republic (today Komi Republic in the Russian Federation) on the Arctic Circle about 100 km east of Inta.

72 *Yad Vashem Archive*, interview with Moritz (Moshe) Friedner recorded 28 April 1973 by Erich Kulka, translated from German by Jan Horník.

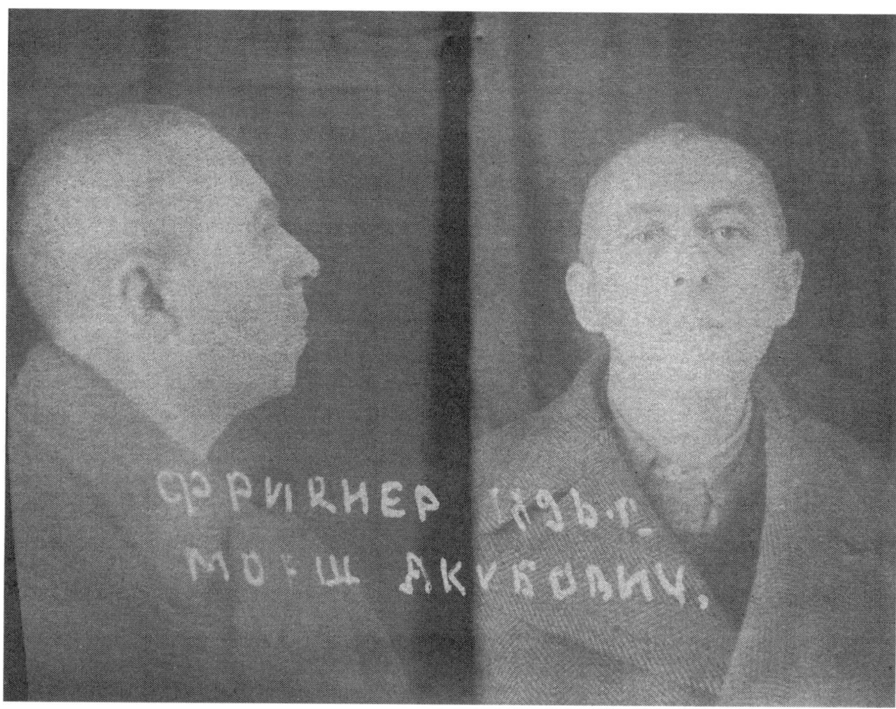

A photograph of Moritz Friedner taken after his arrest in Soviet territory. *DALO*

How did you get out of the camp at Nisko?
We actually went over to the Russians with the consent of the Germans. The SS guards accompanied us to a Polish village ten kilometres away, where we were however ambushed by Ukrainians. They shot at us and took all our luggage. We had two dead and several wounded. After the attack, we split up into groups and fled to the Soviet border. Myself, I was in a group of about ten fellow countrymen and we reached the San River. There were German soldiers patrolling on one side and Soviet soldiers on the other. A German soldier, he was Austrian, asked us where we want to go. We said to the Russians, that we can't stay there as Jews. He recommended that we would do better to return to Slovakia and offered to show us a safe route. When we told him we couldn't go there, he let us go to the other side.

And the reception on the other side?
Three Soviet soldiers led us along the bank of the San to a village, where the command centre was. The commander, who looked like a Jew, assured us that nothing would happen to us, that we'd go to Syniava, where everyone would get a passport, be registered, and we'd be free. We believed him. When we got to Syniava though, the guards took us to be interrogated to the chateau, where

Выписка из протокола № 72

ГП.
Особого Совещания при Народном Комиссаре Внутренних Дел СССР

от „23" июля 1940 г.

СЛУШАЛИ	ПОСТАНОВИЛИ
94. Дело № 1734/УНКВД Днепропетровской обл. по обв. ЛАУФЕР Отто Якубовича, 1898 г.р. ур. гор. Слезка-Острова/Чехословакия/, еврей, чешско-подданный, из семьи кулака, поручик чешской армии, учетчик.	ЛАУФЕР Отто Якубовича, за нелегальный переход госграницы – заключить в исправительно-трудовой лагерь сроком на ПЯТЬ лет считая срок с 25 октября 1939 года.

Нач. Секретариата Особого Совещания при Народном Комиссаре Внутренних Дел СССР

OTTO LAUFER (1898), an accountant from Moravian Ostrava, was deported to Nisko on the first Ostrava transport. He was arrested by Soviet border guards during a mass crossing of the German-Soviet border near Syniava on 25 October 1939. He was taken to Lviv for further investigation, then to the NKVD prison in Dnetropetrovsk. Because he had served in the Czechoslovak Army before the war, the Soviet authorities suspected him of espionage. On 23 July 1940, he was sentenced to 5 years for illegally crossing the border. He was imprisoned at Sevpechlag. His fate thereafter is unknown.

DALO, f. R-3258 (1939–1950), vol. no. 16756.

the NKVD headquarters was. I had all my personal documents with me. As soon as the Soviet investigator found out I was a reserve officer, he called me a Gestapo spy. I responded that, on the contrary, the Nazis were persecuting me for my Jewish origin. He replied, “We know you flat-footed kikes, you’re a rat, *davay*.” The guards approached me, patted me down, emptied out all my personal effects and took them. All they left me was food. They treated all my companions the same. We spent the night in a cell and the next day they took us to Lviv. There they imprisoned us for two months. With me in the prison was Otto Laufer from Ostrava. Then they sent us to Dnepropetrovsk, where I was imprisoned about five months, when suddenly they summoned me one day and read me my sentence: five years of forced labour in a camp in Siberia.

АНКЕТА

1. Фамилия: Фриднер
2. Имя и отчество: Морис Яковлевич
3. Дата рождения: 1896г.
4. Место рождения: м. Моравска Острава - Чехословакия
5. Место жительство: м. Моравска Остраве „ — „
6. Нац. и гражд. (подданство): еврей
7. Паспорт: 23.X.39г. перешел из Чехословакии на Советскую сторону потому, что меня немцы прогнали.
(когда и каким органом выдан, номер, категор. и место приписки)
8. Род занятий: бухгалтер фирмы текстиля м. Моравска Остраве Чехословакии.
(место службы и должность)
9. Социальное происхождение: Отец был купцом, сейчас его нет помер. С имущества имел дом.
(род занятий родителей и их имущественное положение)
10. Состав семьи (где проживает): матка, жена, 1 дитятя, 2е сестры которые проживают в м. Моравска Острава Чехословакии.
11. Образование (общее, специальное): высшее — академию купцов.
12. Партийность (в прошлом и настоящем): —
13. Категория воинского учета запаса и где состоит на учете: Служил в Австрийской армии 30 пех. полку с 1915–1918г. офицером. В Чехословацкой армии служил офицером-резервистом, командовал ротой, ежегодно на уч. сборах с 1921–25г.

подпись: Moric Friedner

Сотруд. след. группы — мл. лейтенант

The form from the first interrogation of Moritz Friedner. *DALO*

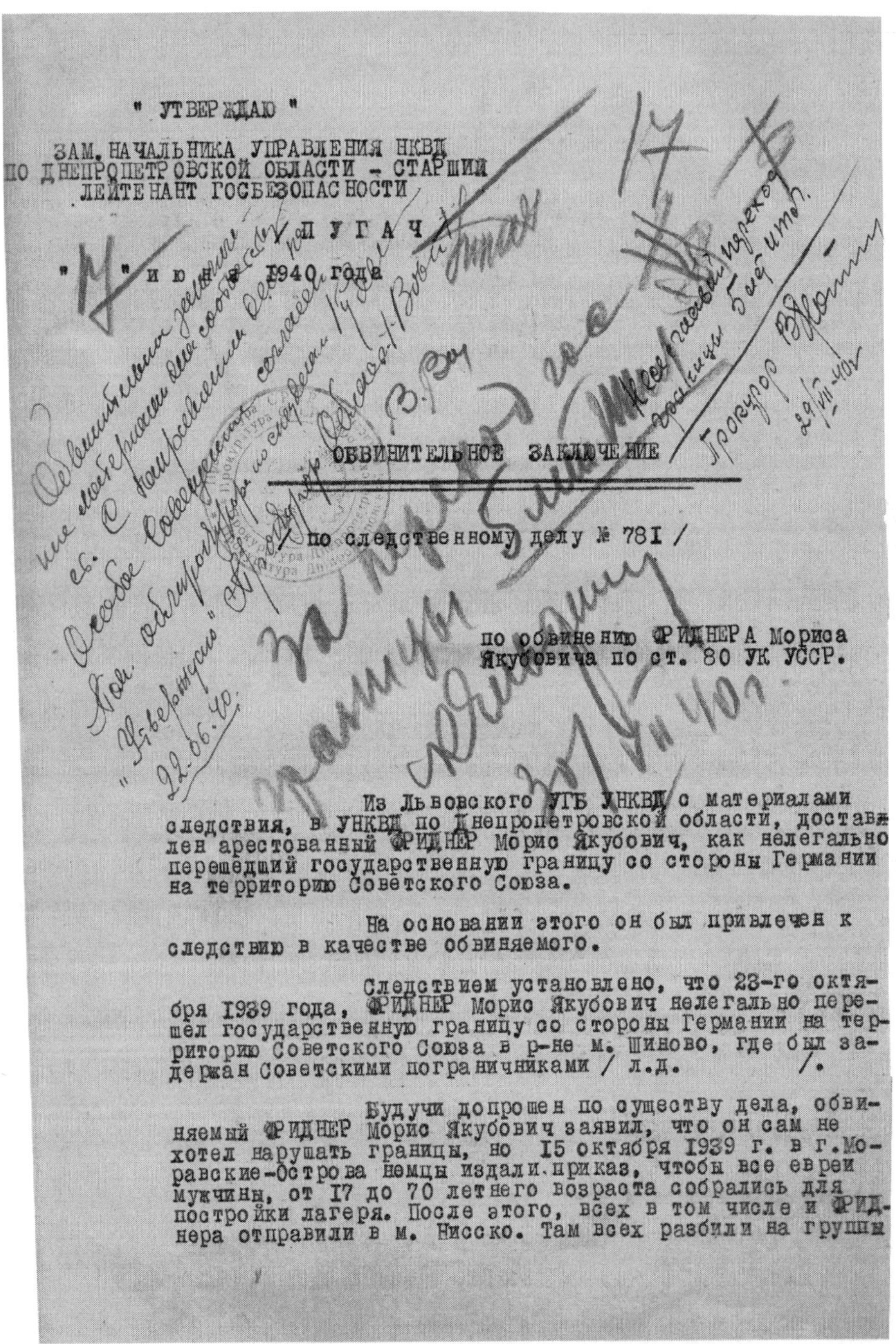

" УТВЕРЖДАЮ "

ЗАМ. НАЧАЛЬНИКА УПРАВЛЕНИЯ НКВД
ПО ДНЕПРОПЕТРОВСКОЙ ОБЛАСТИ - СТАРШИЙ
ЛЕЙТЕНАНТ ГОСБЕЗОПАСНОСТИ

/ ПУГАЧ /

" 17 " июня 1940 года

ОБВИНИТЕЛЬНОЕ ЗАКЛЮЧЕНИЕ

/ по следственному делу № 781 /

по обвинению ФРИДНЕРА Мориса Якубовича по ст. 80 УК УССР.

Из Львовского УГБ УНКВД с материалами следствия, в УНКВД по Днепропетровской области, доставлен арестованный ФРИДНЕР Морис Якубович, как нелегально перешедший государственную границу со стороны Германии на территорию Советского Союза.

На основании этого он был привлечен к следствию в качестве обвиняемого.

Следствием установлено, что 23-го октября 1939 года, ФРИДНЕР Морис Якубович нелегально перешел государственную границу со стороны Германии на территорию Советского Союза в р-не м. Шиново, где был задержан Советскими пограничниками / л.д. /.

Будучи допрошен по существу дела, обвиняемый ФРИДНЕР Морис Якубович заявил, что он сам не хотел нарушать границы, но 15 октября 1939 г. в г. Моравские-Острова немцы издали приказ, чтобы все евреи мужчины, от 17 до 70 летнего возраста собрались для постройки лагеря. После этого, всех в том числе и ФРИДНЕРА отправили в м. Нисско. Там всех разбили на группы

The first page of the indictment against Moritz Friedner, 17 June 1940. *DALO*

Where did they send you?
I travelled by railway transport with about eighteen hundred convicts via Kharkiv and Moscow to Arkhangelsk. From there, on Chinese barges across the White Sea and then along the river Pechora. On the boat we sailed under unbelievably wretched conditions. There were criminals, thieves and rapists on board. They robbed me of my last things and my clothing. I remember it was just 10 October 1940, but the cold was already so strong that our boat froze on the Pechora.

So you carried on by foot?
They ordered us to get off the ship and checked everyone to see if they could walk. After a month sailing on the Chinese barge, we were all dirty, louse-ridden and hungry. Many had died along the way. At least fifteen corpses were thrown overboard daily. People mainly died of typhus and dysentery. There was no medical assistance on board, nor any treatment. The worst was the dysentery epidemic. I was lucky I didn't catch it. During the check by the frozen Pechora, which was essentially a triage, they divided the prisoners into two groups. It was obvious that the group they sent left were write-offs and wouldn't live long. Those who ended up on the right, on the other hand, set off marching. Those who couldn't walk, they left on the boat to die without any assistance. I was sent left too. But I quickly understood the danger I was in. That's why I crept over to the right side. I found myself a walking stick, and so equipped, I walked three days and three nights, during which we covered sixty kilometres. To this day I marvel at where I found the strength to endure such a march. We only got food once in some poor fishing village: a piece of bread and dried fish.

Where were they taking you?
After three days we reached the gathering point. That's where I learned that of the original transport numbering eighteen hundred men, after three months there were twelve hundred left, meaning six hundred were missing. You see, they called out the names according to the transport list at the gathering point. Anyone who didn't report was declared dead. There were only Jews on the transport, mostly from the Polish lands; there could've been about two hundred from Czechoslovakia. Then they carried out another selection at the gathering place. I lay there on the ground with swollen feet, utterly exhausted and completely without hope. A man named Tuchmann, from Krakow, lay next to me, and he advised me to give something to the Russian guard who was looking for men still capable of recovery. I had one pair of good quality breeches left, albeit lice-ridden, but the Russian took them and sent me along with twenty-three other prisoners to the hospital.

What condition were you in?
It's hard to describe. They carried me to the hospital on my back. When the doctor saw me, he wrung his hands and asked how they could bring a man into such a wretched state. I lay at the camp hospital for two months. Aside from me, there was no other Jew from Czechoslovakia there. After two months, they sent me to work. I got warm clothes and felted boots. There were twenty Polish Jews working in my group. As part of a large work commando of about a thousand men, we were clearing the railway track from Vorkuta to Kotlas. It could've been about mid-December 1940 and the average temperature fell to fifty degrees below zero. After work I didn't dare put my soaked boots by the stove for the night, because they warned me someone would steal them. In the morning I put the wet boots back on and by evening my heels were frostbitten and swollen. The next day I couldn't get up and I crawled to the infirmary. While I was waiting for the doctor, a man standing nearby spoke to me. It turned out he was a German communist who had been sentenced to fifteen years' forced labour because he fled from Germany to the Soviet Union. He recommended that I tell the medic, whose civilian profession had

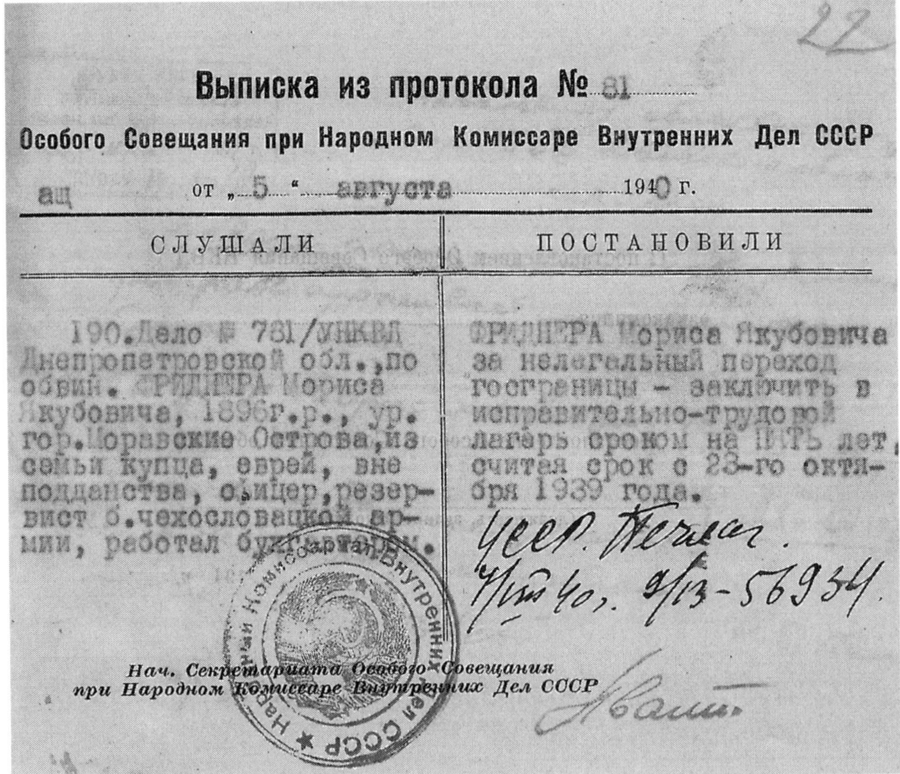

Выписка из протокола № 81

Особого Совещания при Народном Комиссаре Внутренних Дел СССР

от „5" августа 1940 г.

СЛУШАЛИ	ПОСТАНОВИЛИ
190. Дело № 781/УНКВД Днепропетровской обл., по обвин. ФРИДНЕРА Мориса Якубовича, 1896 г.р., ур. гор. Моравские Острова, из семьи купца, еврей, вне подданства, офицер, резервист б. чехословацкой армии, работал бухгалтером.	ФРИДНЕРА Мориса Якубовича за нелегальный переход госграницы – заключить в исправительно-трудовой лагерь сроком на ПЯТЬ лет, считая срок с 23-го октября 1939 года.

Нач. Секретариата Особого Совещания при Народном Комиссаре Внутренних Дел СССР

Moritz Friedner was sentenced to five years in the Gulag on 5 August 1940. *DALO*

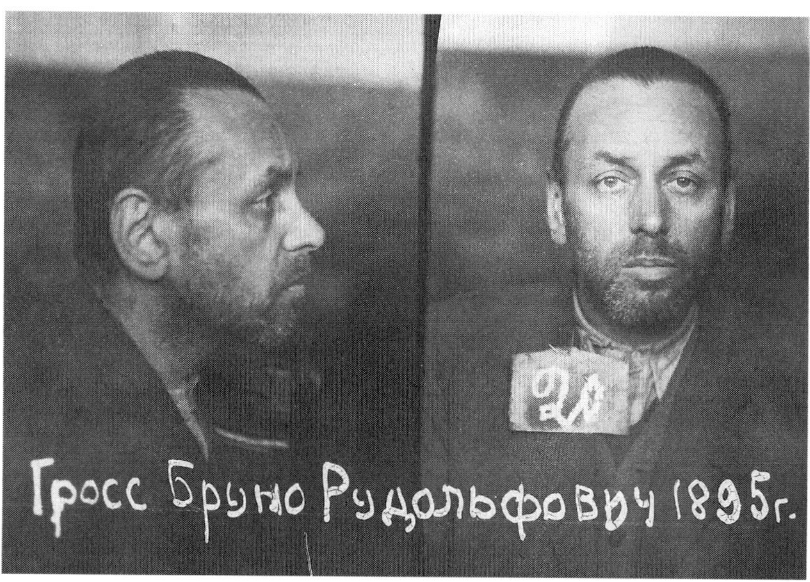

BRUNO GROSS (1895), a merchant from Hrabůvka near Moravian Ostrava, was also included in the first Ostrava transport. He crossed into Soviet territory on 22 October 1939 near the village of Lesko, and was immediately arrested by the Soviet border guard. Imprisoned at first in Przemyśl and Lviv, by February 1940 he was in the prison in Nikolayev. On 27 June 1940 he was sentenced to 5 years for illegally crossing the border. He was interned at one of the Sevzheldorlag camps in the Komi Republic. Like Friedner, he was not released in summer of 1941 as a Polish citizen, but only in May 1942 in the amnesty for Czechoslovak citizens. On 22 June 1942, he was enlisted in the Czechoslovak military unit in Buzuluk. He then fought in its ranks on the Eastern Front.

DALO, f. R-3258 (1939–1950), vol. no. 14481.

been a pharmacist and who was sentenced to twenty-five years in prison, that I'm not a Russian, but a Czechoslovak Jew. And that I should tell him my whole tale. The former pharmacist really did hear me out and granted my request to be sent to the hospital. He had me hitched to a sleigh and took me there himself. At the hospital, the doctors cut open my boots. The left foot was nearly healthy, but the right had become a lump of swollen flesh and I could only walk on crutches.

How long did you remain in hospital?
After six months, a medical commission came from Moscow to see me. You see, a patient could only stay in hospital for three months at most. After that,

they were to be treated as a malingerer, and either they were to be punished, or the doctor was. The commission included a German doctor, Becker was his name. When he examined me, he ordered them to put a lapis compress on my foot three times a day. After three weeks, it really was almost cured. In the meantime, the German-Soviet war broke out. The Polish prisoners were amnestied in summer 1941 and could sign up for the army. After I was well, the hospital doctor sent me to the light labour unit. When he was saying goodbye, he recommended I join the Poles so I could be free. Thus I enlisted in the army as a Polish national. In the army, the Poles quickly forgot their anti-Semitism and accepted my request. That was also the first time after several years I met a prisoner from Czechoslovakia – Bruno Gross of Ostrava. On my advice, he also declared himself a Pole and almost immediately thereafter we left for the gathering point, where the Poles were gradually being released under the amnesty. There I met other compatriots from Czechoslovakia, among them my son-in-law Ervín Frischer, who later became a captain in Svoboda's Army. We stayed at the gathering point about eight weeks. Every day, several hundred Poles were being released and things looked hopeful.

The Soviets didn't check whether you were really Polish?
That's just the thing. It was already October 1941 by then, with cold and snow again. One day they summoned us all and called out individuals. I didn't think the Russians had files on everyone. That's why I was surprised when they called out Moritz Friedner, a Czechoslovak national born in Ostrava. In the same way they identified all the others, not just Czechoslovaks, but also Ruthenians, Latvians and others pretending to be Poles. They transported us all back. The march on foot took five days and we got rusks and dried fish for the journey. At the camp, we were brought before a committee. They interrogated me and when I told them my foot was injured, the doctor responded, "Here you'll be healthy soon!" And they gave me a grade of A, which meant I'd either meet the quota or die. I knew I wouldn't be able to handle the hard work, so I went back to the end of the queue. The whole situation made me furious, my heart started pounding and gave out. When the doctor examined me with a stethoscope, he declared, "You'll be given light work for a fortnight, but if it turns out you're faking, you're going in a penal cell." Luckily, the wounds on my foot reopened after a few days and I couldn't walk. So I remained behind in the barracks, where the head of the camp found me. I explained to him that the commander of our squad had left me behind for the day as indisposed. The superintendent thus ordered the commander to take me to the hospital for examination. If they found out I was faking, I'd go to jail. But if it turned out I'm truly sick, the squad commander would be the one going into a cell.

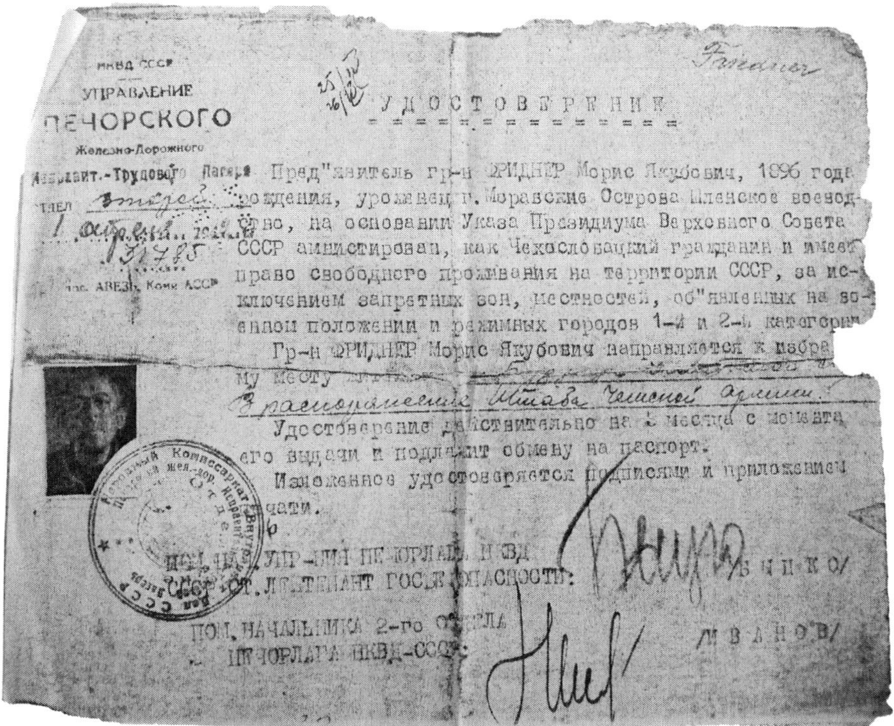

НКВД СССР
УПРАВЛЕНИЕ
ПЕЧОРСКОГО
Железно-Дорожного
Исправит.-Трудового Лагеря
Отдел [illegible]
Пос. АБЕЗЬ, Коми АССР

УДОСТОВЕРЕНИЕ

Пред"явитель гр-н ФРИДНЕР Морис Якубович, 1896 года рождения, уроженец г. Моравские Острова Шленское воеводство, на основании Указа Президиума Верховного Совета СССР амнистирован, как Чехословацкий гражданин и имеет право свободного проживания на территории СССР, за исключением запретных зон, местностей, об"явленных на военном положении и режимных городов 1-й и 2-й категории.

Гр-н ФРИДНЕР Морис Якубович направляется к избранному месту [illegible] В распоряжение Штаба Чешской армии.

Удостоверение действительно на [illegible] месяца с момента его выдачи и подлежит обмену на паспорт.

Изложенное удостоверяется подписями и приложением печати.

НАЧ. УПР-НИЯ ПЕЧОРЛАГА НКВД СССР СТ. ЛЕЙТЕНАНТ ГОСБЕЗОПАСНОСТИ: /[illegible]ЧЕНКО/

ПОМ. НАЧАЛЬНИКА 2-го ОТДЕЛА ПЕЧОРЛАГА НКВД-СССР: /ИВАНОВ/

Moritz Friedner's release papers from Pechorlag. *Yad Vashem Archives – E. Kulka Collection*

That must've been a tough situation for you both...
Of course. Moreover, the squad commander was Ukrainian and an anti-Semite. He had to take me on a sleigh to the hospital seven kilometres away and he spent the whole trip cursing me as a dirty, stinking Jew. At the hospital, the doctor examined me and immediately sent me to the surgical ward and the commander back to the camp. What happened to him, I don't know. I was at that hospital for three months.

How did you end up getting released?
On the twenty-eighth of March 1942, the deputy superintendent came, called out my name, and informed me: "You are to be released." Even though I wasn't fully recovered yet, I begged the doctor to bandage up my feet and release me. I took the first train. It was still freezing and I remember spending the night sleeping on the coal behind the locomotive. When I was in front of the committee again at the gathering point, they asked whether I wanted to live and work in the Soviet Union or enter the Czechoslovak army... Of course I chose the latter. They immediately issued me my call-up papers and paid me 248 rubles as my wages for two years of work. I then set out on foot back to the train station. When the train arrived, I boarded a wagon where there

were some sixty men, a few Slovaks and the rest Poles. I was the only Jew among them and the Poles immediately showed their anti-Semitism. I wasn't allowed to sleep on a bunk like the others and they didn't want to give me any food. After four days, the train arrived at Kotlas, where I got off. The station master was standing on the platform and I went up to him and said, "Sir, I cannot ride on this train anymore. I'm a Czechoslovak officer and I won't be treated like this." Then I told him about my four days' experience with the Poles. He called his adjutant and ordered him to give me boots, provisions and a hundred rubles. Then he put me on a train to Buzuluk.

BEDŘICH (FRED) MORGENSTERN

Born 2 January 1922 in Brno to the family of Jakub Morgenstern, a former colonel in the Austro-Hungarian army who became the head of a textile factory in Brno after the creation of Czechoslovakia. He first attended a Jewish school, then continued with his studies at a Czech secondary school. After the Protectorate was established, however, as a Jew he had to leave his studies in his fourth year. He thus found a spot as an auto mechanic at an auto repair shop. When the occupation security authorities started arresting members of Jewish youth organisations however, he and his brother Leopold took refuge in the countryside, where they went into hiding with his father's former employees. This did not last long – when their father was arrested in their place, they turned themselves in to the Gestapo. Nevertheless, this was of no help to their father, and all three of them ended up in the Brno prison in Špilberk, where they were exposed to very harsh and indiscriminate treatment by their jailers. While their father was soon released, being still needed for the textile factory to operate – only later were he and his wife and only daughter taken to Terezín and then to Auschwitz – his two sons were slotted for deportation to Nisko in October 1939. Like many others, upon arrival they were driven by the German guards to the newly established German-Soviet demarcation line, which they crossed at the start of November 1939 near Syniava. They reached Lviv, where they found lodging at a refugee shelter in the municipal theatre. After several days, they decided to leave for the town of Monastyryska[73] near the Romanian border, where their grandparents and other relatives lived. Up until the Soviet authorities started registering refugees, they worked at a tobacco-processing factory. On 17 June 1940, he and his brother were arrested and subsequently transported to Buchach[74], where they were interrogated by the NKVD. Here Bedřich and Leopold were both sentenced to five years in

73 Monastyryska – a town 15 km from the city of Buchach.
74 Buchach – a city in the Ternopil Oblast in the south-west of Ukraine.

corrective labour camps. Later, they were transported in livestock wagons to the camp in Starobilsk, where they spent another three months. From there, they were sent on an eighteen-day trip along the Trans-Siberian Railway all the way to Vladivostok. Immediately upon arrival, he and his brother were moved to the transit camp at Bukhta Nakhodka[75]. Here their ways parted forever. After several more months, Bedřich and other prisoners were deported to Magadan in the Kolyma region and sent to one of the many labour camps of the Sevvostlag[76] on the Orotukan River. He was assigned to a work squad for mining ore. Due to insufficient food and tough working conditions, one day the prisoners there decided to go on strike. On the orders of the investigating NKVD officer, Bedřich was then transferred to the transit camp in Nakhodka, where he was assigned to work in the auto repair shop. In addition to that, he became the personal driver of the officer that arranged his transfer. He was released as a Czechoslovak national on 21 January 1942 and subsequently sent to the Czechoslovak military formation in Buzuluk, where he was enlisted 16 February 1942. His brother never awaited release, dying 12 December 1941, a few days before the amnesty was declared, at one of the Sevvostlag camps in north-eastern Siberia in the Far Eastern District.[77] After completing his infantry training, Bedřich participated in the Battle of Sokolovo and then the other battles of the Czechoslovak military formation. He ended the war with the rank of sergeant. After returning to Czechoslovakia, the only person he met from his whole family was his sister, who had survived imprisonment at the Auschwitz concentration camp. He soon moved to Karlovy Vary, where he opened a shop selling automotive parts and where he was married. Soon after February 1948, however, his shop was nationalised by the Communists. In the same year, he trained with the Haganah[78] brigade in Czechoslovakia, and in 1949 he went to Israel with his family, where he briefly served in the Israeli air force. In 1956, he moved to the United States of America and settled in Rochester, New York. He started working as a maintenance worker at a bowling alley and over time worked his way up to running a whole chain of bowling alleys.[79]

— — —

75 Bukhta Nakhodka (aka Building 213 with corrective labour camp) – a camp in the Far East in the south of the Primorsky Krai. The administration was based on the coast of the Sea of Japan, 85 km south-east of Vladivostok in the Nakhodka Bay.

76 Sevvostlag (in English North-Eastern Corrective Labour Camp) – the administration was initially located on the Kolyma River in the settlement of Srednikan (today the village of Ust-Srednekan), later on Nagayev Bay within Taui Bay near Magadan, and eventually directly in Magadan.

77 *HDA SBU*, f. Criminal Files (1939–1950), vol. no. 12982.

78 Haganah – Hebrew for "the defence", an illegal Jewish paramilitary organisation that operated in Palestine in 1920–1948. After the creation of Israel in 1948, it formed the basis for its army.

79 *Collection of interviews USC Shoah Foundation*, interview with Bedřich (Fred) Morgenstern recorded 25 April 1996 by Barbara Appelbaum, translated from English by Štěpán Hlavsa.

How did you end up getting arrested in the Soviet Union?
We were awoken by a pounding at the door. They told us, "Get your things, you're coming with us." They took us to a prison in the nearby town of Buchach. I was in a cell with many people, mostly priests and officers from the Polish army. There was only one Jew there. His name was Roth and he was from Łódź. He was very religious and would stand in the corner and pray every evening. The others wouldn't leave him alone though, mocking him and beating him, so I tried to help him any way I could. What happened to him after they took us away, I don't know.

Was there any trial?
They gave us all forms, saying we had to sign them because we'd been convicted of illegally crossing the Soviet border. I told them I would do no such thing. We hadn't come illegally, they'd let us cross the border normally. They responded that nothing could be done about it now, whether I liked it or not I'd been sentenced to eight years of hard labour. When I continued to insist I wouldn't sign it, they took me to the *kartser*, which is what they called solitary. That was a space of around 4 × 4 metres with a single open window. It was already November, pretty cold. Plus I had to give them all my clothes other than my underwear. And so I sat there and sat there. Every day they'd only give me hot water and a tiny slice of bread. And every day they'd bring the paper and demand a signature. I refused for a long time, until one day

The staircase in the NKVD prison no. 1 on Loncky Street in Lviv. *ÚSTR / Adam Hradilek*

I looked at my feet and they were already swollen, puffed up like balloons. I told them to bring the paper, I didn't care anymore. So I signed the sentence and in a few weeks I was sitting in a transport to a work camp. They said we'd be happy at the camp, because we'd be building the Soviet Union and getting good food for it. We almost started to be glad. Then they crammed us into livestock cars, the train had about forty of them, and this train of human cargo set off to build the Soviet Union.

How many people were placed in one car?
Like fifty, sixty. The cars weren't very big, we were packed together like sardines. We had to stand the whole time. Sometimes you could sit down for a while and fall asleep for a few minutes, but soon your surroundings forced you to wake up and stand up again. It also stank something awful there, because the toilet was a hole in the floor everyone went to the bathroom in. It was a pretty traumatic experience.

Was your brother still with you? Did he have to sign the form like you?
My brother was in the transport too. He signed the verdict form right away. He said there was no point in resisting them. He was smarter than me. They took us to Starobilsk[80]. This was a fairly small town in Ukraine, where there was however a big, really huge church, which they had made into a prison. We stayed there for three months. Living on bread and water in the company of an unbelievable number of rats. All we could do was wait until they transferred us somewhere where we could work and build the Soviet Union, as they kept saying.

A prison in a church, that sounds really strange...
It wasn't really a church anymore. The gorgeous building was only reminiscent of its former function from the outside, inside there was nothing that evoked a church. All the furnishings and decorations had been destroyed or taken away. Most churches and places of worship in the Soviet Union met a similar fate under the Communist regime.

80 Starobilsk camp of the People's Commissariat for Internal Affairs for POWs – established in September 1939 in the eastern part of the Ukrainian SSR in the Voroshilovgrad (today Luhansk) Oblast and originally intended for interning members of the Polish army captured by the Soviets following the Soviet occupation of eastern Poland in September and October 1939, who were then executed in spring 1940 as part of the Katyn massacre. The camp was located three kilometres from the Starobilsk railway station in the former Holy Trinity convent and the internees were housed in two churches. In May 1940, the camp was transformed into the Starobilsk Sorting Camp of the People's Commissariat for Internal Affairs for POWs. In the following months, thousands of refugees arrested by the NKVD were interned here.

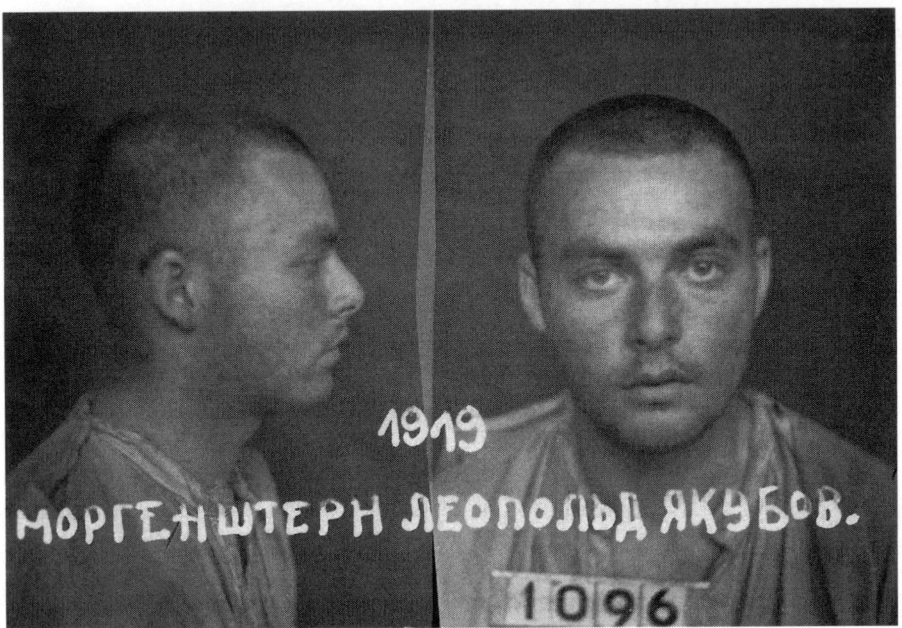

Bedřich's brother Leopold after arrest by the NKVD. *HDA SBU*

What nationality were the guards?
Russian soldiers that belonged to the NKVD.

Were they anti-Semites?
Yes. But most of the prisoners weren't Jews, there were only a few. At the church they were mostly holding Polish officers, intellectuals and priests that had fled the Germans. In the part where I was, there might've been like four or five Jews.

How long were you imprisoned in Starobilsk?
After about three months, they herded us once again onto a train convoy, as they called it, and sent us along the Trans-Siberian Railway east. The train line ended in Vladivostok. We passed through a number of places, Novosibirsk, Alma-Ata, past Baikal, which is a beautiful lake by the way. There were no windows in the car, but there were holes and gaps in the walls, so if you were standing nearby you could see something. We reached a very interesting place, the Jewish Autonomous Oblast[81] in southern Siberia not far

81 Jewish Autonomous Oblast – the Jewish National Raion was formed in 1928 in southern Siberia. Under Stalin's rule it was to stand in contrast to the newly forming Jewish state in Palestine. The emigration of Jews did not meet expectations, however. In 1934, the Soviet government esta-

from the Chinese border, the capital of which was Birobidzhan. When the Bolsheviks took power in Russia, they wanted to found an independent Jewish state, so they sent lots of Jews there. Over time though, people started to leave, because the climate was very unpleasant there. Nothing but swamps, mosquitoes, really miserable. We passed through there, too, and saw a few bearded Jews with their heads wrapped in nets so the mosquitoes wouldn't eat them so much.

What were the conditions in the train like then? Could you ever leave the train during the transport?
Our train didn't stop at stations, but always before them or after them. Sometimes we'd stop for say four days like that, because there were constantly military trains passing by that had priority. Even when the train was stopped, we were constantly shut up inside. In the whole eighteen days we were travelling, we could at least rinse ourselves off maybe twice. In terms of food, they'd give us a piece of bread and what was supposed to be soup – ordinary hot water.

Where did you end up?
We got off the wagons in Vladivostok, where they divided us up into several sections and sent us to the transit camp Nakhodka, which was a terrible place. A few barracks surrounded by barbed wire where the guards didn't even go and left running the camp to the rabble, in other words the murderers and criminals. For example I saw a Polish officer passing by a group of those "camp leaders" and they noticed he was wearing a ring. They immediately started shouting they'd play cards with him for it, and since the officer resisted and didn't want to give up the ring voluntarily, they just cut off the finger with the ring on it. Plus people were dying there by the hundreds, mostly of dysentery. Nakhodka, that basically meant zero hygiene, a lack of food, cold and terror, in other words a nightmare that drove you mad. And people really did go crazy there, if they didn't die. One time for example I woke up and this naked guy was running around completely blue from the cold, talking to himself.

And your brother?
I didn't know anything about that. They split us up as soon as we got to Nakhodka and got off the train. From that time, I never saw him again.

---

blished the Jewish Autonomous Oblast. The whole project of a Soviet "new Zion" started to falter as early as the mid-1930s, and completely collapsed after World War II.

How long were you at Nakhodka?
A few months. From there they sent people to various places, to Okhotsk, to Kolyma or to other places in the Far East. When they finally decided what to do with us, they sent us to Kolyma. Compared to the transport by land, only the means of transport changed. It was some old ship, but the conditions were still awful. Hundreds of prisoners crammed in the hold, again lots of rats and no food, no toilets, just horrible. We sailed four days like that across the Sea of Japan to Magadan, where they sent us to what they called "kilometres". Those were camps that were approximately ten kilometres apart. I ended up in one of those camps and finally started building the Soviet Union. To be more specific, every day we had to dig nine cubic metres of dirt out of the frozen ground and transport it about ten metres away. We only had picks and shovels, nothing more. It was horrible work, plus most of us weren't used to hard work like that.

What kind of clothes did you have?
Well, I can't say we were well-dressed, but we had *telogreikas*, so clothing stuffed with cotton. It really kept you quite warm. Instead of socks we would wrap rags around our feet. For footwear we had what they called *valenki*, which were boots made and fashioned from a single piece of thick felt. They kept you fairly warm, so it wasn't so bad.

How did you personally manage the work?
The terrible thing was that we didn't have the slightest hope of ever meeting the quota. My brigade had about twenty people, all intellectuals. I was basically the only one that had ever worked with their hands before. That meant we didn't meet the quota and got less food. They simply reduced the ration that was already quite small. I was eighteen at the time, but I looked fourteen, because I only weighed some forty kilos. When you're hungry, your desperation gets crazier every day. You think to yourself: What am I doing here? What's the point? In the end we called a meeting in the building we slept in. We all agreed that if we were going to die, then it should be quick. Thus we decided to stop working. The next morning, as soon as we reached the site where we were supposed to work, one of our leaders, he was a colonel in the Polish army, went up to the NKVD guards and told them: "Gentlemen, look, we're not going to work anymore. Go ahead and shoot us." They said OK, but that we should sit for a bit. We sat there for several days. Here and there they gave us a bit of food, the bare minimum. In a few days, two men on horses came. The commander of our camp and an NKVD colonel we didn't know. He took a look at us and wanted to know what was going on. We explained to him the situation we were in, that we just couldn't work like that when we don't have enough to eat. He ordered them to take us to the camp, where he

called each of us separately into his office and asked us where we were from and so on.

Before the NKVD colonel came, you were sitting outside in the woods the whole time?
During the day we sat at the work site, at night they would lead us back to the barracks at the camp, where we would repeat that we weren't going to work.

The colonel interrogated you personally too?
Of course. When I told him I was from Czechoslovakia, he asked what I was doing there. I responded that I'd like to know that too. Suddenly he started speaking Yiddish to me, asking where my mother and father were. At that moment I completely broke down and that was basically the end of the conversation. I burst out crying and told him I weighed maybe forty kilos and instead of waiting until I weighed ten and was dying of hunger, they should just shoot me. It really got to him. I could see that he was very upset, because he ordered me out of his office. The next day though he gave me bread and some fish and sent me back to the transit camp in Nakhodka. There I got into the workshop with the auto mechanics, where I felt like I was in paradise. I fixed cars and had enough food. I often drove the colonel around as well, because he was in charge of the camp and arranged everything. After work I could also go out whenever I wanted, suddenly everything was just unbelievable.

Did you have the chance to talk to the colonel more? How did he treat you?
When I was driving him somewhere, we'd chat a bit, but I wouldn't say we became friends. His wife was also nice, a stocky Jewish woman, and when I'd go pick him up at home sometimes, she'd always give me a bit of food and coffee. Basically the previous suffering was suddenly a bad dream and I was fine.

That didn't last forever though, did it?
After a time living in the "paradise" of auto mechanics and drivers, out of nowhere they called me into the office and sent me to a camp where they were again dividing people among different work camps. I was shaking with fear that I'd done something wrong and was going back to Kolyma. After about three days, though, another guy from Czechoslovakia turned up at the camp. In a month, approximately twelve Czechoslovaks had arrived. By that time we could tell that something was happening and that we weren't going to Kolyma, they were simply gathering us together. And then one day they called us into the office, where they gave us temporary documents and tickets to Buzuluk. The building of the Soviet Union was over for me.

MAREK (MORDECHAI) NEUER

Born 24 September 1904 in the village of Rymanova Vola (Wola Romanova)[82] in what was then Austro-Hungarian Galicia. Before World War I, the Neuers lived near the town of Ustrzyki Dolne[83], but in 1914 they fled from pogroms and war to Michalovce, Slovakia. Here, Marek attended a Slovak elementary school and eight grades of grammar school. Subsequently, he studied at the Masaryk University Faculty of Medicine in Brno, where he was later employed as a physician. Up until the Nazi occupation, he was the chairman of the Society for the Support of Jewish University Students in Brno. By order of the Nazi occupiers, however, this organisation had to be disbanded. As early as 12 September 1939, the Gestapo arrested Marek as a Polish national, imprisoning him along with other detained Jews in the prison at Špilberk. From there they took them to work at the local barracks or to the Brno Gestapo headquarters. He only spent a short time at the Brno prison, however, being deported to Ostrava at the end of October along with other Jewish prisoners, where they were put on the second Ostrava transport to Nisko. As a doctor, he was not driven to the German-Soviet border immediately upon arrival like most prisoners, but could stay near the camp for the meantime. On 8 December 1939, however, he fled the camp along with a large group of other prisoners and tried to cross into the USSR. He was however detained by the Soviet border guards and subsequently charged with illegally crossing the border. He reached the prison in Chernihiv[84], where he was sentenced to three years at forced labour camps on 13 July 1940. Via prisons in Poltava and Kharkiv, he travelled first by train and then by boat to one of the subcamps of Kandalakshlag near Kandalaksha[85] in the Murmansk Oblast on the Kola Peninsula. In light of his profession, he was made the prison doctor. There were two thousand prisoners at the camp at that time, five of them doctors. After the Germans attacked the USSR, the camp was evacuated in July 1941. Neuer was relocated to a camp with a less harsh regime by the town of Solikamsk[86] in the central Urals in the Perm Oblast, where he again worked as a physician. He was released from there on 29 August 1942 under the amnesty as a Polish citizen. On the way to Tashkent, however, he fell ill with typhus, and for this reason was taken to Bukhara[87], where he was treated for over two months.

82 Wola Romanowa – a village in south-eastern Poland.
83 Ustrzyki Dolne – a town in south-eastern Poland.
84 Chernigov/Chernihiv – a city in the north of Ukraine.
85 Kandalakshlag (in English the Kandalaksha Corrective Labour Camp) – the administration was based in the town of Kandalaksha on the banks of the Kandalaksha Gulf on the White Sea.
86 Solikamlag (in English the Solikamsk Corrective Labour Camp) – the administration was based in the village of Borovska and later in the town of Solikamsk.
87 Bukhara – a historical and the fifth biggest city in Uzbekistan.

After his recovery, he worked briefly as a doctor at the local hospital, then he continued to Qarshi[88], where he once again worked as a doctor in a nursing home. His main goal was to get to Palestine. After Polish-Soviet relations deteriorated in connection with the discovery of the Katyn Massacre, he gave up on that journey, leaving to Buzuluk where he volunteered for the emerging Czechoslovak military unit. He was enlisted 31 January 1943. He was a physician in the unit with the rank of lieutenant. He reached Czechoslovakia with the 1st Czechoslovak Army Corps and after the war became the head of the military hospital in Slaný and after that he led the internal medicine section of Masaryk Hospital in Ústí nad Labem. In the autumn of 1948, he signed up for the Jewish paramilitary organisation Haganah. He left for Israel at the start of 1949 and later worked there once again as a physician. He died in 1972.[89]

— — —

What happened to you when you were detained by the Soviet border guards?
I remember the trip… There were as many as sixteen prisoners crammed into small sections in railway wagons. After travelling for a whole day, we arrived completely exhausted in Chernihiv, in Ukraine. There was an endless investigation. The prisoners were divided into cells and completely isolated, so we couldn't find out what was happening in the other cells. We went to the bathroom by cell and under supervision. After that, the guards would search the toilets so prisoners couldn't hide a message or write something on the wall. Walks in the yard were also done by each cell separately. Fifteen-minute walks took place once every three days. Interrogations always took place at night, from midnight on.

Everyone was nervous because it would often happen that people didn't come back from the interrogations and we never learned anything more about what happened to them. Everything took place as follows: a guard dressed in a *rubashka* would open the door and first ask for the prisoners' names. When I responded, "Marek Neuer Ben Yaatzov", he shouted in German, "Die, scum!" In great fear, I went with him and his big dog along winding corridors and staircases. The whole time I was afraid it was the end of me. In the end we reached a large, gloomy courtyard, where there was a strong blinding light shining right at us. Every prisoner who came to that yard had to stand facing the wall. I could hear my heart pounding and I thought they were going to shoot me then and there. After a while though they took me to the investigator. They accused me of espionage and kept posing the same questions over and over. After several nights like that, I told the investigator

88 Qarshi – a city in southern Uzbekistan.

89 *Yad Vashem Archive*, interview with Marek (Mordechai) Neuer recorded 19 December 1969 and 4 January 1970 by Erich Kulka, translated from German by Jan Horník.

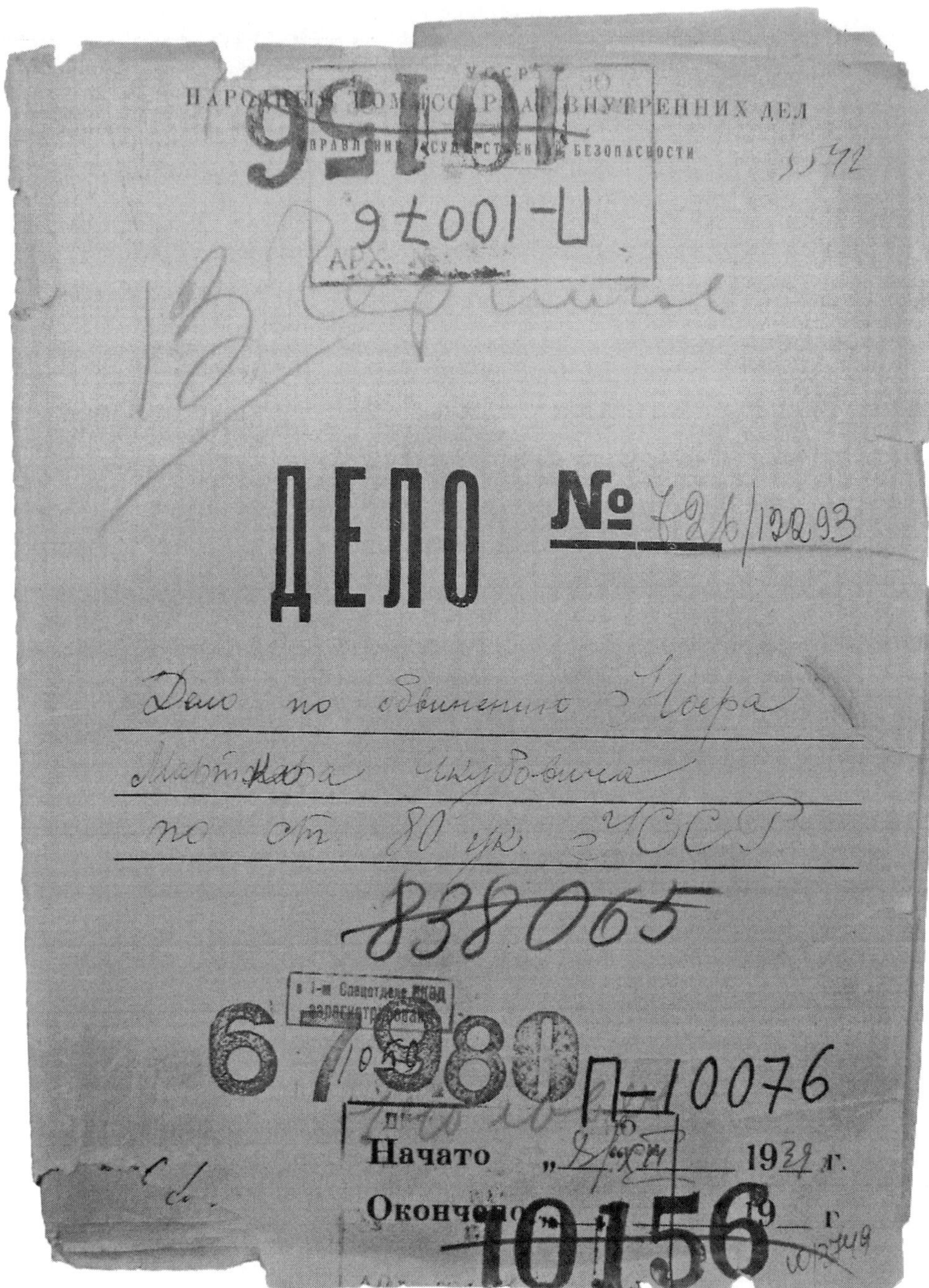

НАРОДНЫЙ КОМИССАРИАТ ВНУТРЕННИХ ДЕЛ

УПРАВЛЕНИЕ ГОСУДАРСТВЕННОЙ БЕЗОПАСНОСТИ

П-10076

10156

ДЕЛО № 726/12293

по ст. 80 УК УССР

838065

67980

П-10076

Начато 19 г.

Окончено 19 г.

10156

The cover of the investigation file against Marek Neuer. *HDA SBU*

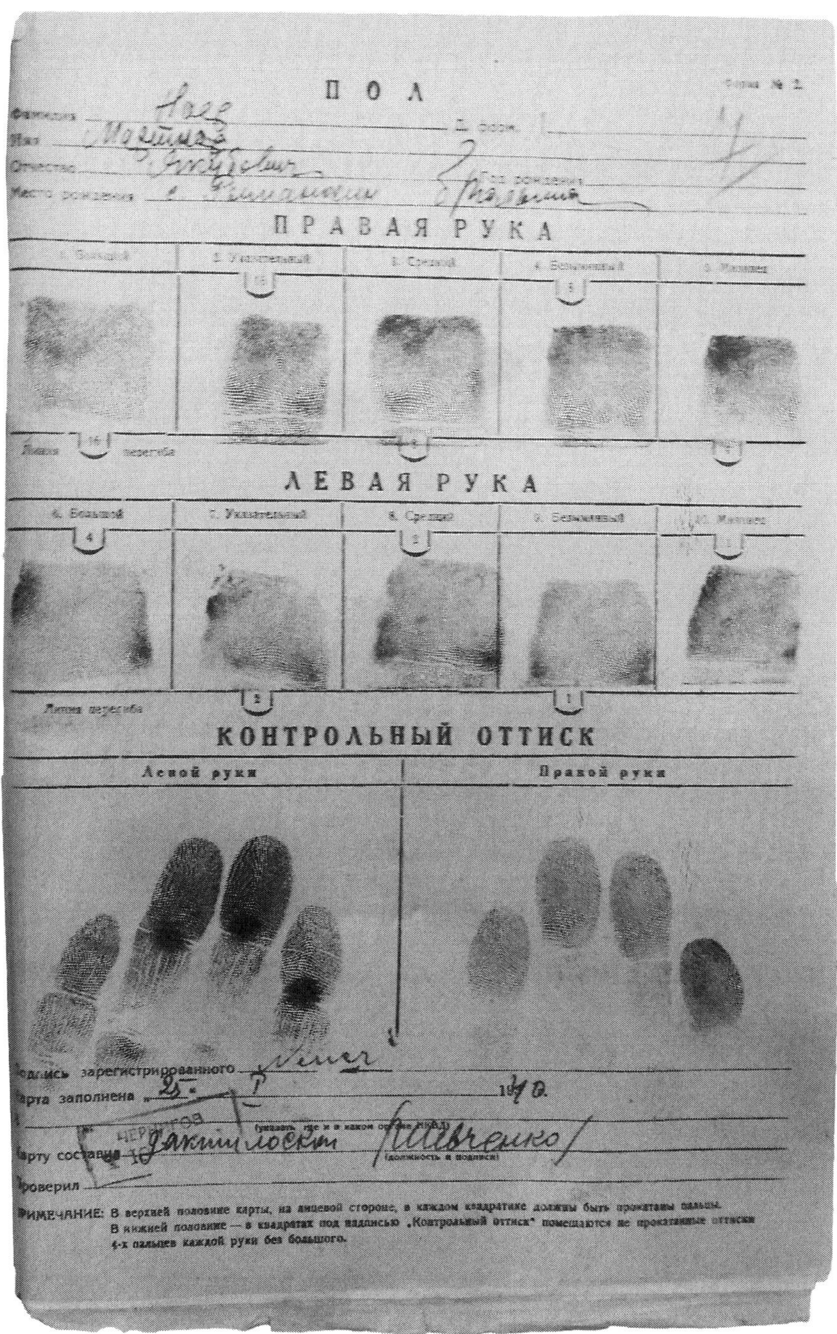

ПОЛ

Форма № 2

Фамилия

Имя

Отчество

Место рождения

Год рождения

ПРАВАЯ РУКА

1. Большой	2. Указательный	3. Средний	4. Безымянный	5. Мизинец

Линия перегиба

ЛЕВАЯ РУКА

6. Большой	7. Указательный	8. Средний	9. Безымянный	10. Мизинец

Линия перегиба

КОНТРОЛЬНЫЙ ОТТИСК

Левой руки	Правой руки

Подпись зарегистрированного Neuer

Карта заполнена „25“ I 19

(указать где и в каком органе НКВД)

Карту составил Закипоск

(должность и подпись)

Проверил

ПРИМЕЧАНИЕ: В верхней половине карты, на лицевой стороне, в каждом квадратике должны быть прокатаны пальцы. В нижней половине — в квадратах под надписью „Контрольный оттиск“ помещаются не прокатанные оттиски 4-х пальцев каждой руки без большого.

The fingerprints taken from Marek Neuer shortly after his arrest by the NKVD. *HDA SBU*

that they already knew everything about me anyway and I'm willing to sign anything if they'd just leave me alone.

So you signed the espionage accusations?
I didn't sign anything because out of nowhere they replaced the investigator. The new officer overturned all the accusations of espionage and gave me paragraph 80 – illegally crossing the border. In a few months I was transported by freight train to the city of Gomel[90] with about three hundred prisoners.

A bizarre thing happened there. The conditions were approximately the same as in the previous prison, but they were constantly pulling people out of their cells who never came back. We were very worried about what was happening to them. Thus we agreed that everyone they took away would break a match and throw it on the ground. If they broke it in two pieces, it would mean they stayed in the prison, if it was three, then they were being taken away. You had to do it with the utmost care because there were guards everywhere. Sometimes I had to take a rag and bucket and clean the corridor where the guards would clear their noses and spit on the ground. But even then I didn't find a single sign. Then came my turn. At one in the morning they took me to a large room with tables and weak light from oil lamps. I was alone in the room and was terribly afraid. There were huge rats like I'd never seen running around there. I crawled up on one of the tables and awaited my fate. Suddenly I heard the door open and a guard ordered me to follow him. We went to the office of the prison warden, who showed me the decision of the troika:[91] three years in a labour camp with particularly harsh conditions. They took me to another room, where I found the friends and cellmates that had disappeared before. They had also been sentenced to labour camps.

Where did they take you?
Once everyone had received their verdicts from the troika, they crammed us back in a freight train. Via Poltava[92] we got to a transit prison in Kharkiv and then to Kandalaksha by the White Sea Channel on the Kola Peninsula by the Arctic Circle. The trip took four weeks. The transport from Kharkiv to Kandalaksha had about fifteen hundred to two thousand prisoners on it.

90 Gomel – a city in south-eastern Belarus.
91 Troika – a three-member extrajudicial body entrusted with extraordinary judicial powers, including the right to sentence the accused to being shot. Rulings against the accused were made in a simplified, expedited investigation and without a proper trial. The composition of the troikas changed over the years. Most frequently they consisted of two employees of the Soviet security authorities (of which one was the chair) and a prosecutor. The troikas officially functioned until 1938, but the name remained in use for the future extrajudicial bodies of the Soviet security services afterwards as well.
92 Poltava – a city in north-eastern Ukraine.

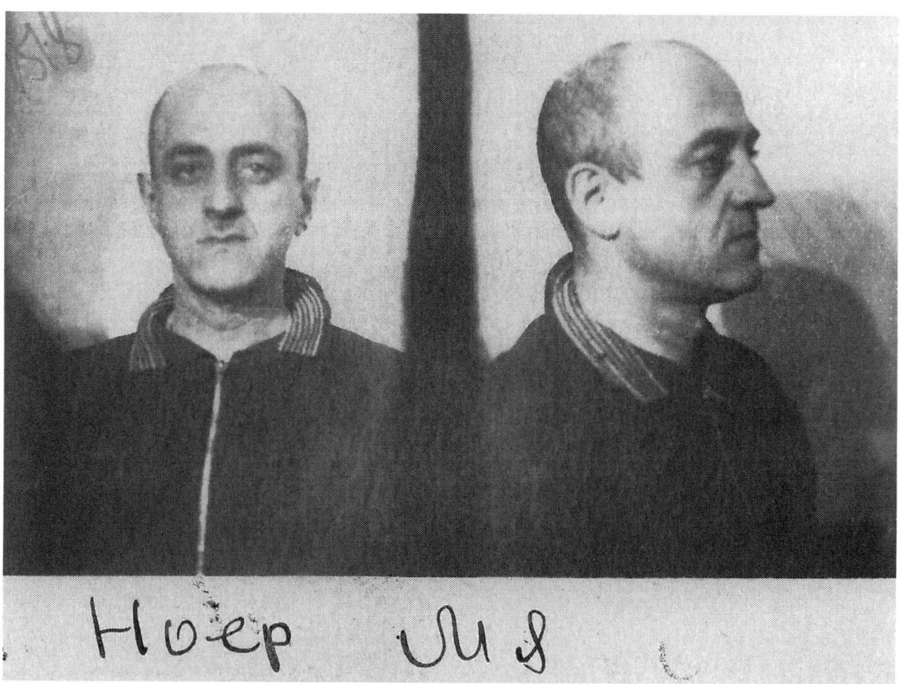

Marek Neuer after being arrested in Soviet territory. *HDA SBU*

The medical exam we had to undergo before entering the Article Circle was purely formal. Three doctors examined us in as short a time as possible. They put a stethoscope to our chests and signed a paper saying we were completely healthy and fit to work in the area. Once we reached the camp, my mental health improved. I stopped being afraid because here there finally wasn't any "Gestapo".[93] Even though secret executions occurred and they would eliminate undesirable elements whom they had allegedly shot while trying to escape, there was no collective death penalty or collective retribution on others. I saw and felt that, given my knowledge, it was my duty to help others. Regardless of the wishes of the NKVD.

If I had to die, it would be with honour and a clear conscience while performing my medical duties. At the camp I became a doctor.

What did the camp look like?

It was surrounded by three rows of barbed wire. Each row was separated by a narrow patch of soil. Outside the third outer fence, the camp was guarded by armed guards with dogs. The inner side of the four-metre-high second fence

93 Here M. Neuer meant agents of the Soviet NKVD.

was topped with an inwardly slanted grille with barbed wire mesh. Inside the inner fence stretched a six-metre-wide empty swath marked as a no-go zone, with guard towers with lights placed around it. There were guards with machine guns aimed at the camp on the towers. Prisoners that entered the no-go zone were shot without warning. The no-go zone was separated from the camp area with its wooden prison barracks by a wire fence a metre and a half tall with warning signs on it. Close to it, right next to a guard tower, was the prison hospital – not a very good position.

How do you mean?
There was a fellow named Blechin in the second hospital ward. He was a boy of fifteen or sixteen who had contracted typhus. His bed was next to a window that opened onto the no-go zone. Because of his high fever, he wasn't fully conscious and he started yelling about how the NKVD had arrested and interrogated him. I asked the attendants to stay by his bed all the time and if he started to go amok they should bind him with sheets and call me immediately. One attendant, Mr Moser, left him alone for a minute and at

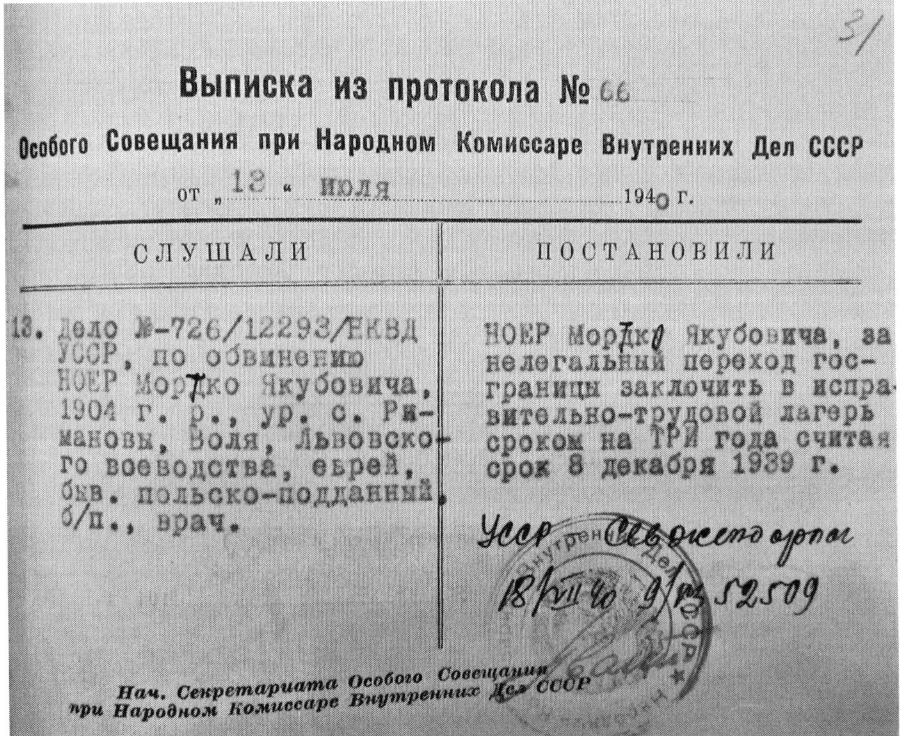

Выписка из протокола № 66

Особого Совещания при Народном Комиссаре Внутренних Дел СССР

от „13" июля 1940 г.

СЛУШАЛИ	ПОСТАНОВИЛИ
13. Дело №-726/12293/НКВД УССР, по обвинению НОЕР Мордко Якубовича, 1904 г. р., ур. с. Римановы, Воля, Львовского воеводства, еврей, бкв. польско-подданный, б/п., врач.	НОЕР Мордко Якубовича, за нелегальный переход госграницы заключить в исправительно-трудовой лагерь сроком на ТРИ года считая срок 8 декабря 1939 г.

Нач. Секретариата Особого Совещания при Народном Комиссаре Внутренних Дел СССР

Extract from the ruling sentencing Marek Neuer to three years at corrective labour camps on 13 July 1940. *HDA SBU*

Gulag prisoners were taken to remote places where no railroads or roads led on cargo ships.
CVG collection

that moment he leapt out of the window into the no-go zone. When I saw it from the next room over, I ran up to the bars and begged the guards not to shoot him. Nearby stood these big latrines, from which the waste flowed into the no-go zone. The lad jumped into the pit and disappeared, with only bubbles coming up. Wasting no time, me and another prisoner pulled the guy out using a metal hook. After a long treatment, he eventually recovered.

Could you describe an average day of prison life?
The prisoners lived in wooden barracks where they slept on bare pallets. There was one stove for heating, which someone was always in charge of. At four in the morning came the wake-up call and roll call. After all the prisoners had all been counted, every group went with their capo to get soup and then to work. In the evening we got bread. The capo would divvy it up based on our work performance. For example, a group of thirty men got 25 kilos of bread. When the capo determined that ten people had worked above the quota, each of them got 900 grams. Another fifteen, who worked to the quota, got 700 grams. The rest, who didn't meet the quota, had to make do with 500 grams each. The capo always got the same share as the best workers. That's why he also had an interest in having "Stakhanovites"[94] on his squad.

94 Stakhanovite – a worker striving to achieve exceptional work goals. The movement is named after the Ukrainian miner Alexei Stakhanov.

What happened to sick prisoners?
For a camp of that size, there were five doctors, of those three Russians, Dr Larinov, Dr Denisov and Dr Lensky. Then there was one attendant and one orderly. Sick people could only report for a medical exam in the morning. Meaning at the time when food was being served. Which presented a certain risk. A sick person whom the physician did not find unfit for work would not have managed to get soup and so had to work all day without food. What's more, in extremely harsh climatic conditions. In winter it was always night-time, in the summer always day. In the winter the temperatures fell as low as minus 45, but the nearby sea meant that it was wet under the snow. The *valenki* would get wet, and so the feet as well, and then they froze. Pathological changes to the extremities were irreversible. Amputation had to be performed, but most of the patients died during treatment anyhow. Prisoners would commit suicide in that way. I witnessed this, for example, when they failed in an escape attempt.

There certainly must have been many other health problems at the camp...
Of course. Malnourishment was rampant. Hunger caused some people to completely shrivel up, others to swell up. They were always searching for food in their spare time as well, say in the trash, where with a bit of luck you could sometimes dig out herring heads and quickly wolf them down or save some for later. The most frequent afflictions were dermatitis[95], diarrhoea[96] and dystrophy[97]. The latter meant certain death, which occurs from the breakdown of electrolytes due to changes in the kidneys and liver. As soon as the kidneys break down and no longer fulfil their function, the person drinks endless amounts of water. When those poor souls got to the hospital, they'd even drink the urine of other patients, but they still died like flies.

Did the camp administration force you as doctors to declare the prisoners fit at all costs?
One time at the camp entrance examination, I was to check the health of two Russians. They must have been part of some kind of cult, because they'd only speak to me, nobody else. They said they don't want to let me examine them. We could do what we wanted with them, even shoot them if we liked, but they wouldn't be examined. The camp elder stated, there's only two of them, no point in pussyfooting. So I was supposed to examine them despite their protests and declare them fit. I objected that a doctor can only examine a patient with their consent and cooperation. It was a very dangerous situ-

95 Dermatitis – inflammation of the skin.
96 Diarrhoea – indigestion, loose bowels.
97 Dystrophy – degenerative changes to the body due to malnutrition.

ation because the commander could accuse me of sabotage. I put it down to their rather mentally abnormal state and said I couldn't make any decisions in such a case.

The administration dealt with it in a different way. They called me and the Russian doctor Denisov to the NKVD to sign off that the two were fit. The NKVD was holding a report from some informant saying there was nothing wrong with them and that they were avoiding work as saboteurs and counter-revolutionaries. I responded that I would never break my medical oath. They could do with me as they willed, but I wouldn't sign anything until I examined them, which I couldn't if they wouldn't cooperate. To my surprise, the Russian doctor didn't sign it either. I was amazed that he managed to refuse. I was fully aware of what could happen. But above all, I wanted to help people, and if I couldn't, then to die with honour. The following day, there was a trial, I was also summoned. The prosecutor had an amputated arm and was armed with a pistol. A defence lawyer was also present. There was another young man on trial as well, who had deliberately swallowed glass. When they'd finished operating on him, he told them to shoot him. So they sentenced him to death by firing squad. Just like the two accused of being counter-revolutionaries. The defence in the young man's case objected that he had already been in prison once and maybe he hadn't been educated properly. The prosecutor replied that the point of the labour camp was to educate. The defence attorney immediately shut up. Everyone got 48 hours to apply for clemency. The other two didn't respond to anything in court and they took them away. I never saw either of them again.

What did the prisoners there do for work?
There were aluminium mines by the camp, plus cellulose was produced there. I saw them chopping down trees. There were also female prisoners in a separate camp. Contact with them, including sexual relations, was of course strictly forbidden. But I saw it happen sometimes, especially with the capos. They threatened to have me shot. But I pretended not to have seen anything or know anything.

What were the chances of surviving the harsh working and living conditions at the camp?
Only certain individuals had one, depending on their physical constitution and profession. In general, those who had done manual labour before being arrested had better prospects, as opposed to, for example, businesspeople, doctors or others not used to physical labour. For them it was really tough, and they also died quickly. I received many more prisoners from this group at the hospital, from the ranks of the intelligentsia. As the head physician, I was also accused of accepting more Central Europeans, primarily Poles, than

Russians. Over time, though, I established such a strong position with the Russian prisoners that they eventually recognised me as an objective doctor.

And the camp administration didn't criticise you for this objective approach?
The camp administration had to react to various allegations or provocations from the head nurse, who was an NKVD agent and had more influence than the camp commander Fedorovich. For example, one morning at roll call when I was checking the prisoners going to work, when I got back to the hospital I discovered that the morning rounds were already going on without me. She was conducting them, head nurse Anna Ivanovna, along with Dr Denisov, a Russian prisoner sentenced to ten years, and the Polish imprisoned physicians Gibel and Schneider. I didn't like that and I objected and we fought. In my anger I took off my doctor's coat and tossed it away and declared that if they didn't trust me, I wanted to go in the mineshaft and share the same fate as the other prisoners. I was summoned to commander Fedorovich, where I had to defend myself in the presence of the head nurse and doctors. The accusation was once again made that I had more Central Europeans in the hospital than Soviet nationals.

The head nurse and other doctors accused you of that?
Fedorovich said it, but he didn't state the source. A pleasant surprise for me was that all the doctors stood up for me. To the accusations I replied that according to Stalin's book, which I had read at the camp, prisoners and sick people from areas with warm climates should not be sent to the Arctic Circle. In other words, such people have no business being here. But they were, and here they are accusing me of admitting these poor souls to the hospital? I also said that I don't admit Russians, Czechs or Poles, but that I provide inpatient care to sick people who in my opinion require treatment. The commander replied that, according to his information, my patients didn't even have a fever. I responded that many such patients "without a temperature" had already died.

Wasn't it bold of you to defy the commander like that?
Look, I once took an oath to do my job honestly and fairly. Maybe they would have shot me straightaway somewhere else, but for some reason Fedorovich liked me. Maybe my self-confident manner impressed him, I don't know. In the end he only reproached me for one thing. "A doctor does not throw their coat on the ground, which you did. It looks like sabotage and the punishment for that is public execution by firing squad. Fortunately, you won't do it again, right?" I responded, "Either you have faith in me and I can continue to work as a doctor, or you can send me to the others because I'm no better than them." Fedorovich ordered me to return to the hospital because they needed me as a doctor.

There were no civilian doctors working at the camp?
No, only prisoners worked as doctors there. From time to time, one civilian doctor would turn up though. His name was Larimon, he had ultimate power over the hospitals and inspected all the camps. He also tested my knowledge, though his own was not that extensive. He was the one who recommended me when the camp commander's daughter fell ill. I would go to Fedorovich's home to treat her. He lived like a prince, in rooms with Persian rugs. He addressed me "zakluchony – prisoner". Indeed, every prisoner had to report with this title, adding their surname, patronymic, reason for conviction and sentence.

You worked as the head physician. What did that function entail aside from treatment at the camp hospital?
I assigned work to the other doctors. When new transports arrived, I received some of them and looked for the stronger, fitter prisoners. I remember they also brought two dead bodies on one of the transports. I ordered Moser to take them to the autopsy room. Ten minutes later, Moser came to report that one of the dead bodies had sat up on the table, looked around, then collapsed and died. Cases like that were common there. Everyone who died at the camp hospital had to undergo an autopsy. The NKVD demanded it. I usually performed the autopsy myself, because the other doctors weren't as good at it. An autopsy report was always drawn up on the findings in Russian, the written form of which I wasn't very good at, so I often didn't know what all was in the report. At any rate, I would sign it, aware of the risk that some kind of betrayal or trap might be in there. But I did it because I thought I'd never get out of the camp anyhow. It was common there for someone to be summoned and never come back. People just disappeared. We didn't know what'd happened to them.

Did the situation change for you when Germany attacked the Soviet Union?
Yes, there was the danger of the Germans occupying the area, as they were attacking from Finland by plane. For this reason, the camp in Kandalaksha was hastily evacuated. Some of the prisoners they took to Arkhangelsk, the rest, including me, to the northern Urals to Solikamsk. But before that, a strange thing occurred. The evacuation was already being prepared, when suddenly the camp administration led by Commander Fedorovich decided, I don't know why, that all the particularly cruel and hated capos and guards from the ranks of the prisoners would be rounded up into a guarded building and then sent to a harsh penal camp, where they would be watched over by a special security force. The terrified capos started giving themselves serious injuries, for example chopping off fingers and even hands, cutting themselves in the abdomen, so that we had to admit them to the hospital.

PRESIDENT

REPUBLIKY ČESKOSLOVENSKÉ

UDĚLIL

V UZNÁNÍ BOJOVÝCH ZÁSLUH, KTERÉ ZÍSKAL V BOJI

ZA OSVOBOZENÍ REPUBLIKY ČESKOSLOVENSKÉ

Z NEPŘÁTELSKÉHO OBSAZENÍ

Por. zdrav. v zál. MUDr NEUER Marek Jakub

přísl. 1. čs. arm. sboru SSSR.

D R U H Ý

ČESKOSLOVENSKÝ VÁLEČNÝ KŘÍŽ 1939

V Praze dne 20. června 1945.

Číslo matriky: 3511.

In June 1945, Marek Neuer was awarded the Czechoslovak War Cross 1939. *Yad Vasehm Archives – E. Kulka Collection*

I admitted them, but after the surgeon had sewed them up and bandaged them, they were sent to the transport. I remember two Jews, capo Artschuler from Odessa, he chopped off three fingers on his left hand, and assistant capo Orman from Kolomyia.[98] I met him some time later in Bukhara in Uzbekistan. The others I never saw again.

When the Germans were approaching, were you afraid you'd be captured by the Germans?
It might come as a surprise to you, but I was looking forward to it and wanted the Germans to come and liberate us. Of course I didn't know what they were doing to the Jews in Europe. No news of the extermination had reached us. So I hoped that the Germans would come from Finland and free us. The hope was all the greater the more anxious the Russian camp administration became. But it didn't happen and they hurriedly sent us away from Kandalaksha in groups.

How did the conditions in the camps you went through differ?
The camp in Solikamsk was more for political prisoners. Moreover, there was also a special camp there for women. Some even gave birth there. After a very short time, they took the children away from the mothers and sent them to be raised as what were called "Stalin's children". In Solikamsk I met truly good doctors. The camp was in the northern Urals. The conditions, particularly in terms of housing, were once again rough. The prisoners slept on bare pallets without mattresses or straw. A brick duct heating system ran through the whole building and the prisoners would dry their *valenki* on it overnight. The building manager watched over the fire and was also in charge of the *valenki* drying out. If they didn't, he couldn't let the prisoners go to work the next day, because their feet would freeze in the wet felt boots. If that happened, I could get a bullet in the head, because I was responsible for that along with the camp commander. My medical duties there also included checking up on the prisoners with disciplinary punishments. I often discovered dead bodies that the other prisoners had beaten to death. I had to perform autopsies on these corpses as well. But I never experienced cannibalism at that camp.

In terms of the conditions, it was still a fairly good camp. Important things were manufactured there and those who met the quotas could get by on the food. The prisoners that didn't meet the quotas were declared saboteurs. The old or feeble prisoners were sent away and replaced with new ones from the transports. Suddenly these exhausted people would just disappear, gone. I never found out what happened to them. I could only estimate the death

98 Kolomyia – a city in western Ukraine.

Photograph of Marek Neuer in the book of distinctions of the USSR, 1945. *Yad Vashem Archives – E. Kulka Collection*

count based on those that died at the hospital, which was a mere fraction of the dead.

What happened after you were finally freed?
Shortly after my release from the labour camp, I tried to get to Palestine. At that time I met another recently released prisoner Berger in Tashkent, who had had the same idea. We decided to cross the Soviet-Persian border and then head to Palestine. First we went to Bukhara and then travelled to the railway station in Kogon.[99] We watched the trains by which the Polish Anders' Army was leaving via Ashkhabad[100] to Persia. There were lots of them passing through, but foreigners weren't allowed to board. But one day we found a wagon where the people were speaking Yiddish. They let us in and there I met an acquaintance, Mr Klausner from Hodonín, who had also got out of the camp in the amnesty. At one stop, where the transport with about five hundred releasees stopped, I went to try to find water. Berger stayed on board. When I got back, the train was gone. I stared at the empty tracks, aban-

99 Kogon – a city in the Bukhara Region of Uzbekistan.
100 Ashkhabad – the capital of Turkmenistan.

doned, with none of my personal belongings. No one at the station could tell me where the train had gone. I walked along the rails until I got to the place where the line branched off to Ashkhabad. In desperation I hopped on an empty freight train that happened to be passing in that direction. I lay down on the floor and fell asleep. I woke up near the station of Parav, which was the border between Uzbekistan and Turkmenistan. When the train stopped, I hopped off. It was midnight, but there was a crowd of people waiting at the station, so I mingled with them and tried to find out what had happened to my transport, which was supposed to have arrived in the afternoon. They told me it had left for the port. From that station, the track headed to Ashkhabad. About three kilometres from Parav, one of the largest bridges in the Soviet Union crosses the river Amu Darya. Before it, the railway line turns to the port on the river bank, from where all the transports were to depart. They were waiting for the water level to rise enough. That same night I headed for the port, but there I found out my friends Berger and Klausner had stayed in Parav. When I wanted to go back, out of nowhere the Soviet secret police turned up. I managed to pass through and get back to the station, however, where I really did find both friends. Berger and I decided to return to Bukhara.

Was it the right decision?
Yes. I found work there at the hospital. Shortly thereafter, however, I fell ill with typhus and jaundice. Luckily I recovered. Then I tried to get to Palestine again. I tried to find the place where the Polish families of the soldiers in Anders' Army were gathering to go to Palestine. At the Polish mission in Bukhara I got the information that the place was located in G'uzor[101] in Tajikistan on the Afghan border. The leader of the Polish mission in G'uzor, Mr Wechsler, who was from Lviv, was sympathetic to my plan. While I was waiting to leave, I worked at the local old folks' home. Due to the massacre of the imprisoned Polish officers in Katyn, however, relations between the Polish government-in-exile in London and the Soviet government deteriorated. I therefore changed my plan and followed my friends. I headed to Buzuluk, and there I joined the Czechoslovak military unit.

101 G'uzor – a city in southern Uzbekistan.

YEHUDA PARMA (LEOPOLD PRESSER)

Born as Leopold Presser on 31 July 1922 in the Polish village of Jasienica not far from the Czech-Polish border, he grew up however in Český Těšín. He and his siblings attended the Czech primary and secondary school and he was involved in the activities of the Český Těšín youth organisations Maccabi[102] and Scouting. He continued his studies at the Český Těšín grammar school. During the Munich crisis in September 1938, when Poland lay claim to the Czechoslovak part of the Těšín region, the boys from several youth organisations in Český Těšín took part in putting together border patrols. Leopold also became a member of the patrol guarding the border by the river Olše. It was for this reason he was thrown out of school after the Polish occupation of the Czech part of Těšín in October. He thus decided to leave to join his older brother in Moravian Ostrava. There he joined the organisation Aliyat Hano'ar[103] as a volunteer, in the meantime working in the ironworks. After the German troops arrived in Ostrava, however, he was immediately fired as a Jew and with some difficulty returned to his parents in Těšín. Though he applied to the Czechoslovak conscription commission in Krakow in August 1939, he was not accepted due to his Jewish origin. In September 1939, World War II broke out and the western part of Poland including the Těšín region was rapidly occupied by German troops. Shortly thereafter, Leopold was put on the second Katowice transport to Nisko along with his father Artur and other Jews from the Těšín region. Most of the Jews from that transport never reached the camp, which was just starting to be built. Therefore the group in which Leopold and his father were in had to seek refuge in the nearby village of Jarocin. After several days, they decided to flee to the USSR across the nearby border. Immediately after crossing, however, the group of refugees was detained by a Soviet border patrol, taken to what was then the border town of Syniava and placed in classrooms at the local school, where there were already several dozen internees at that time. Among these was Leopold's older brother Egon, who had also managed to flee to the area occupied by the Soviet Union after arriving on the first Ostrava transport to Nisko. After the initial interrogations and registration, they were all transported to Lviv, where they could move about freely for a certain time. The Pressers were among those arrested in one of the NKVD raids against refugees in 1940. This was followed by deportation without trial via Sverdlovsk[104] to Tyumen[105]

102 Maccabi – a Jewish physical education and sports association.

103 Aliyat Hano'ar (in English Youth Aliyah) – a Jewish organisation founded in 1933, the main task of which was to resettle Jewish children and youth from countries at risk from Nazi Germany to Palestine.

104 Sverdlovsk (today Yekaterinburg) – a city in the Urals.

105 Tyumen – a city in the Tyumen Oblast in south-western Siberia.

on the river Irtysh. After three weeks travelling by train, they continued by steamer to Tobolsk[106] and from there on boats along the Irtysh all the way to the town of Khanty-Mansiysk[107] and then to the Soyma forced labour camp. The prisoners in the local camp primarily chopped down trees. What was surprising was that almost the whole Presser family ended up meeting at the camp, with Leopold's sister and cousin with their husbands arriving on the next transport. All Polish nationals were released from the camp as early as June 1941, including about three hundred Polish Jews, but the commander refused to release Czechoslovak citizens. For this reason, several men decided to flee during New Year's celebrations with the help of "kulak" farmers who were living in exile around the camp. They then reported to the local military headquarters in Khanty-Mansiysk. Other than Leopold's father, all were found fit to serve in the army and could travel to Buzuluk, where Leopold and his brother enlisted on 28 February 1942. It took a year for the brothers to get the rest of the family to Buzuluk. His father, however, died as a result of physical exhaustion shortly after arriving. As a member of the reconnaissance platoon of the second infantry company under First Lieutenant Jan Kudlič, Leopold Presser took part in the first action of the 1st Czechoslovak Independent Field Battalion in the USSR in March 1943 – the Battle of Sokolovo, where his older brother Egon fell. He then fought in the Czechoslovak unit as a scout up until the end of the war, being deployed in all major operations. At the end of war, he commanded the second company of the 2nd Infantry Battalion of the 1st Czechoslovak Independent Brigade with the rank of lieutenant. He remained in the Czechoslovak army after the war as an intelligence officer with the Provincial Military Headquarters in Bohemia, then serving in the 5th Division of the Defence Intelligence Crew Command of Great Prague. In July of 1948, he changed his surname to Parma. Starting in 1948, he was heavily involved in organising the training of Jewish volunteers, with whom he went to Israel in 1949. He never returned to Czechoslovakia. In Israel he worked briefly in the army, then joined the Israeli police force in 1953, where he remained in various posts until retirement. He retired with the rank of lieutenant colonel of the police. He died in Givatayim near Tel Aviv on 18 December 2016.[108]

— — —

106 Tobolsk – a city in the Tyumen Oblast in south-western Siberia.

107 Khanty-Mansiysk – the capital of the Khanty-Mansi Autonomous Okrug in south-western Siberia.

108 *CVG Collection of Interviews*, interview with Jehuda Parma (Leopold Presser) recorded 28 October 2011 by Jan Dvořák.

Leopold Presser (first from the right) with his friends, 1938. *CVG collection*

Could you describe the events that followed your arrival in Nisko?
When we arrived there, the barracks weren't ready, they were still being built. We saw there was a lot of disorder there, which was a bit strange for the Germans. That's why the group my father and I were in moved to the nearby village of Jarocin. We didn't do much at all there. The older ones of us, who had some experience, knew or learned from the locals or from refugees from the Polish army that we were near the Soviet border, that there was a river there and that the Soviet army was on the other side. We decided we wouldn't remain under the Germans and would try to escape.

How did you get to Soviet territory?
We formed a group, approximately fifty people. I was evidently the youngest. On the way we were stopped by a German patrol on horseback. There were a lot of people moving around at that time though, so they didn't check them that much. They only took some jewellery from us. With the help of locals, we crossed the river Tanew on a little boat. Thus we got to the other side,

where there were already Soviet border guards, who arrested us. Under the threat of being shot, we had to form a group and not fall out of line during the journey. After walking for several kilometres, we reached the district town of Syniava. They housed us in a school and gave us water and some soup. They suspected us of being spies or smugglers, however, so they started investigating each of us. The next day I saw my brother in the schoolyard. It was such a surprise that we had met! He had also heard they were planning to make a camp when he arrived in Nisko, so he fled with some others and reached Syniava. During the investigation, my father showed the investigators his Czechoslovak passport with the names of his children. The Soviet investigator treated Czechoslovaks differently and gave us permission to travel by train to Lviv.

Could you describe the situation in Lviv?
Lviv was a big city, but at that time it was completely overrun with refugees and fugitives. It wasn't easy to find a roof over one's head. What's more, it was extremely cold at the time, maybe 10 to 15 below zero, and we were exhausted. In the end we got to Rahodemitska Street, where there were accommodations

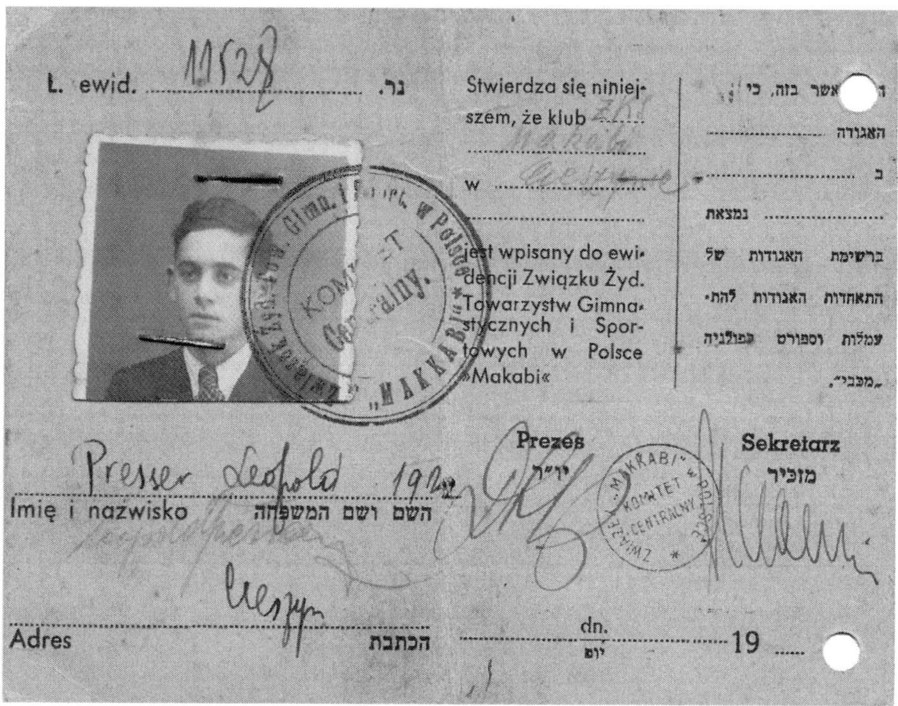
Ł. ewid. 11528 נר.

Stwierdza się niniejszem, że klub ...
w ...
jest wpisany do ewidencji Związku Żyd. Towarzystw Gimnastycznych i Sportowych w Polsce »Makabi«

מאשר בזה, כי ...
האגודה ...
ב ...
נמצאת ...
ברשימת האגודות של התאחדות האגודות להתעמלות וספורט בפולניה „מכבי".

Presser Leopold 192..
Imię i nazwisko השם ושם המשפחה

Prezes יו"ר
Sekretarz מזכיר

Adres הכתבת
dn. יום ... 19 ...

Leopold Presser's membership card as a member of the Těšín Maccabi gymnastic and sports club. *CVG collection*

for students and academics. Though the floor in the hall was full, we managed to find a spot to sleep. Me and my brother laid down under the piano and we stuck my father next to the wall behind us. Luckily it was warm there. When we got up though, we banged our head into the piano. We started looking for some work. There was a place there where the refugees congregated – the Café de la Paix passage. There were black marketeers there and you could buy or sell anything. Even get food. Since it was going to be very cold, we decided to go house to house and help with wood. We bought a saw and axe and did the rounds. We didn't get any money for it, but food. Since we didn't know Russian, we started learning, in the meantime communicating with our hands and feet. We fought our way through day after day. And then came another surprise! One day in the Café de la Paix passage we met my sister, who had fled with her boyfriend to Poland earlier. That changed our situation, because they had come to Lviv at the start of the war and had a room somewhere. We also started working in the house we lived in, helping with wood, mostly for Poles. Then as Czechoslovaks we got work permits and I could get a job as an apprentice at a bakery, even though I knew nothing about baking. So I had to learn the trade from scratch. My brother worked with a saw and then also at an alcohol factory, where he was a stockkeeper. We gradually got used to life in Lviv and the winter flew by. The spring was beautiful and we took advantage of it. We got to know the city in our free time. We had work permits and the Russians left us alone. Which cannot be said about the other emigrants, who they started taking away.

Were you in touch with the others from the group you fled to Soviet territory with?
As I said, Lviv was overcrowded and they continued to travel around Ukraine. Some headed for Stanyslaviv, others to other Ukrainian cities. We weren't in contact with them anymore. But we met some of the refugees from the transport in the Café de la Paix passage. For example a friend from Český Těšín, Josef Turs, who was a year younger. He was arrested as a spy though, and sentenced to prison in Lviv. But then he proved he was a refugee, Jew and Czechoslovak and they released him. When he came back, I couldn't recognise him – he was completely decimated, but he got out of it. I was an optimist and tried to take things positively despite everything.

How long did your optimism last?
Starting in the summer, the atmosphere in the city changed. The Soviets started suspecting every refugee of espionage. This meant our turn came as well. The militia came in the night and banged on the door. They ordered us to get dressed, take our things and go with them. We protested that we had permits to stay, to work, that we're Czechs, Czechoslovak nationals. They responded, "It's all right, we'll investigate everything there." Of course

Leopold Presser being drafted in Buzuluk, 28 February 1942. *CVG collection*

instead they loaded us, the whole family, onto trucks without any investigation and drove us to the train station and loaded us on a train. We travelled three weeks across the whole Soviet Union. The first stop where they gave us food, something soup-like, was in the Urals, in Sverdlovsk. Then we got some kind of lousy food every time the locomotive stopped to refill water. In that way we reached Tyumen, which was a railway hub on the Trans-Siberian. The river Irtysh ran through there and we transferred to a steamer.

How many of you were there on the transport?
I don't know exactly. At any rate there were Jews, Poles of varying fates and then a Czech, Leopold, from Bohumín. As I already said, they gave us food when they filled water in the locomotive. I don't know what, I guess soup. One time we learned we'd got lunch at midnight. But it was day, it wasn't dark. Then they transferred us onto boats, about thirty people on each. Then we spent the whole day continuing on to the forced labour camp, it was called Soyma, where there were three barracks. About fifty people fit in each – men and women, all together on bunks, three tall. The commander welcomed us: "You have arrived at the settlement, the worksite. Just as you will never see your ears, so you will never see your home. Here you will work the land and then build barracks and you will live here." Again we protested that we were Czechs, which was supposed to be checked back in Lviv. He didn't care at all.

Leopold Presser (bottom left) with other soldiers from the Czechoslovak military unit in the USSR, 30 January 1943. *CVG collection*

He informed us the railway was a thousand kilometres away and there was nothing but taiga and swamp around. Anyone attempting to flee would die.

And did anyone try to escape?
Running away meant deliberate suicide. They weren't afraid we'd flee. We could move around the camp and its surroundings more or less freely. I mean, there were also only three or four guards aside from the commander.

What did they feed you in that wasteland?
We started working and we got food based on how the quota was met. For example Russian soup with cabbage and sometimes dried fish as well. There was not sugar or tea. Just *kipyatok* – hot water. Food was brought in by boat in the summer. Then big pits were dug where it was stored. For example they brought in potatoes, which would freeze in the pits at the start of winter, so we got sweet potatoes.

How did the guards treat you?
The camp commander and the guards were Russians and had also been convicted for some offences in the army. But they weren't sadists.

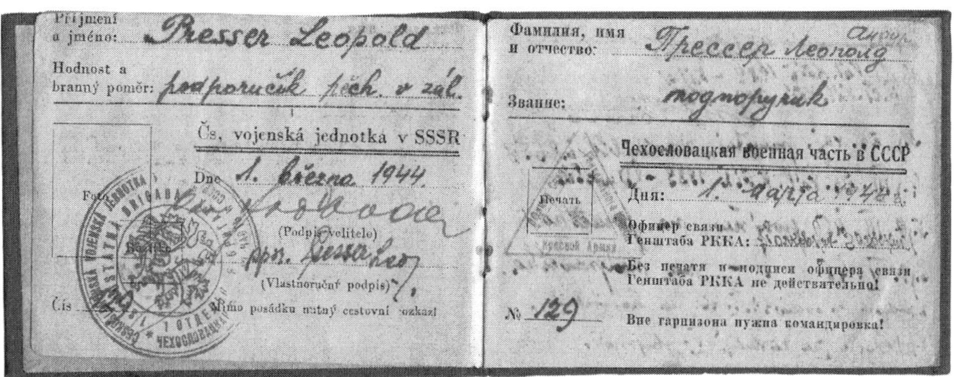

Příjmení a jméno: Presser Leopold
Hodnost a branný poměr: podporučík pěch. v zál.
Čs. vojenská jednotka v SSSR
Dne 1. března 1944
(Podpis velitele)
(Vlastnoruční podpis)
Čís.
Mimo posádku neplatný cestovní rozkaz!

Фамилия, имя и отчество: Прессер Леопольд
Звание: подпоручик
Чехословацкая военная часть в СССР
Печать
Дня: 1 марта 1944
Офицер связи Генштаба РККА:
Без печати и подписи офицера связи Генштаба РККА не действительно!
№ 129
Вне гарнизона нужна командировка!

Leopold Presser's military ID. *CVG collection*

And how about the work?
Work was mandatory every day. From morning to evening, Saturday and Sunday too, we had to meet the quota. In other words, log a cubic metre of wood in the forest. Our tools were an axe, saw and hammer. The trees were cut into seven-metre logs, which after lopping were tied with bast fibre into bundles, which were called rhapsodies. These were then lined up along the bank, and the when the ice broke and loosened up in the spring, which was deafening, because it could be as thick as a metre, the rhapsodies were put in the water and from May till the end of summer, we pushed them to the dam with large poles. There they were loaded on boats and sent for export. All the work was measured by quotas. Those who met them got a whole loaf of bread, soup, and sometimes fish.

Did you manage to meet the quota?
Yes, but my brother and father didn't. So my cousin and I helped them. When the supervisor went to make his big round, we gave them wood from our pile. Eventually, because we were good workers, they reassigned us to a different job, building additional barracks. But there weren't any nails, just a saw, axe and hammer. So wide grooves were carved into the beams and planks and then they were fit together, which was incredibly laborious. You have to realise, the trees there were the diameter of a man's outstretched arms. First they had to be cut into smaller pieces and then the necessary parts and beams had to be prepared for the future building. We did all of that by hand.

What did the buildings look like?
The floor plan was 6 × 4 metres and the walls were built to a height of approximately two metres sixty. The holes and gaps between the logs were sealed with moss from the bogs. Then came a wooden roof with a thirty-degree slope so

Leopold Presser (leaning over) with other members of his unit, 1945. *CVG collection*

Leopold Presser (seated in the middle) ended the war with the rank of infantry lieutenant of the 1st Czechoslovak Independent Brigade, 1945. *CVG collection*

water could run off it. Moss was laid in the top again for insulation. The beds inside were simple pallets. Every family then had a primitive shack like that.

How many of you were there in the camp?
About a hundred.

And how many of them were Czechs?
My family, meaning me, my father, brother, my sister with her husband and my cousin. And then one other family, the Löwenholzes. A total of twenty Czechs. The other prisoners were Jews from Poland. Among them was a doctor named Saksišovič. I met him later in Tel Aviv, but he's dead now... There was also one Austrian from Vienna there. He made himself out to be Czech, but he didn't speak Czech.

Could you hang out together freely, spend your free time?
After work we could talk to each other, move about freely. Only those who had done something wrong or disobeyed an order were punished with lock-up, which meant three days in the camp jail. They got a bit of food, but were cut off from society.

Did your situation change after the Soviet Union was attacked?
The situation changed immediately mainly for the Poles, who were all released from the camp as part of the international agreements. Only those who were in lock-up remained. Maybe ten, fifteen people. Then we learned that it wasn't just wasteland and taiga all around us, but that there was the city of Khanty-Mansiysk nearby. About ten kilometres from the camp was a settlement where former kulaks were living, and they owned horses and sleighs. We arranged with them to take us there. We took advantage of the 1941 New Year's celebrations, when there were almost no guards left in the camp. The journey took a whole day and night, but it worked. We reported to the military unit commander in the city that we wanted to fight against the Germans as Czechoslovaks because we knew a Czechoslovak army was being organised.

How did you find out about that?
In the summer of that year, a doctor came to the camp for an inspection. It was sweltering, almost forty degrees, and we were under constant attack by millions of mosquitoes from the swamps and the taiga. The doctor wanted to rest, so he lay down on the hay and covered himself with newspaper so the mosquitoes couldn't get him. Then he left the newspaper there. In it, we found a report that a Czechoslovak unit was being formed. That's why we went to sign up. The commander of the military unit made a condition, however, that he would only draft the able-bodied.

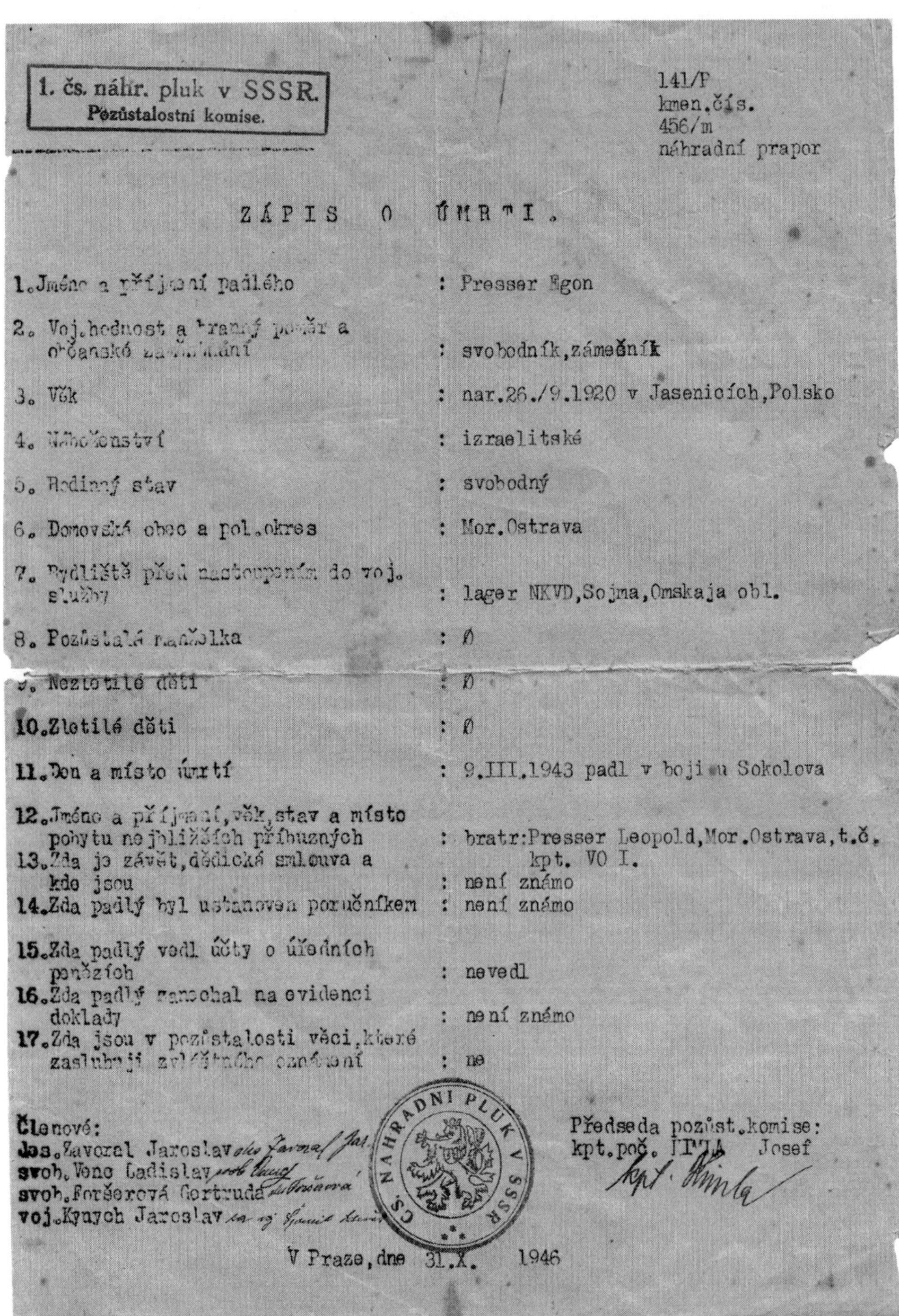

1. čs. náhr. pluk v SSSR.
Pozůstalostní komise.

141/P
kmen.čís.
456/m
náhradní prapor

ZÁPIS O ÚMRTÍ.

1. Jméno a příjmení padlého	: Presser Egon
2. Voj. hodnost a branný poměr a občanské zaměstnání	: svobodník, zámečník
3. Věk	: nar. 26./9.1920 v Jasenicích, Polsko
4. Náboženství	: izraelitské
5. Rodinný stav	: svobodný
6. Domovská obec a pol. okres	: Mor. Ostrava
7. Bydliště před nastoupením do voj. služby	: lager NKVD, Sojma, Omskaja obl.
8. Pozůstalá manželka	: Ø
9. Nezletilé děti	: Ø
10. Zletilé děti	: Ø
11. Den a místo úmrtí	: 9.III.1943 padl v boji u Sokolova
12. Jméno a příjmení, věk, stav a místo pobytu nejbližších příbuzných	: bratr: Presser Leopold, Mor. Ostrava, t.č. kpt. VO I.
13. Zda je závěť, dědická smlouva a kde jsou	: není známo
14. Zda padlý byl ustanoven poručníkem	: není známo
15. Zda padlý vedl účty o úředních penězích	: nevedl
16. Zda padlý zanechal na evidenci doklady	: není známo
17. Zda jsou v pozůstalosti věci, které zasluhují zvláštního oznámení	: ne

Členové:
jés. Zavoral Jaroslav
svob. Veno Ladislav
svob. Foršerová Gertruda
voj. Kynych Jaroslav

ČS. NÁHRADNÍ PLUK V SSSR

Předseda pozůst. komise:
kpt. pěch. HRMA Josef

V Praze, dne 31.X. 1946

Death certificate of Leopold's brother Egon. The NKVD camp Soyma is listed as his last place of residence before joining the unit. *CVG collection*

Yehuda Parma during the interview, Tel Aviv 2013. *ÚSTR / Jan Horník*

He didn't care you'd escaped from a camp?
Our camp was disbanded after the Poles left. Which we didn't know, because our commander didn't feel like going to war, he preferred to keep giving orders at the camp, so he kept it a secret. That's why the military commander in Khanty-Mansiysk admitted us. They drafted my brother, me, Löwenholz and the Austrian.

And what about your father and sister?
My father was sick, he had a heart defect. So my sister and her husband stayed with him and made do as best they could. We left with the plan that we could get them to Buzuluk later.

How did you travel to Buzuluk?
We travelled three weeks by various trains. It was January 1942, they were fighting for Moscow, and all the trains were packed with soldiers. For example, at the train station in Tyumen, we waited three days. In the end, we managed to get in one of the trains through the window. We made it to Chelyabinsk. That's a railway hub, so we got off, but they nabbed us right away. Everyone who got off the train had to undergo disinfection. They took us to a big room. Aside from us, it was all women, because the men were at war. They stripped us, put some kind of symbol on our clothes and we all went naked into the showers. While we were washing, they disinfected the clothes with steam. In the end we got different clothes anyhow, too long though. But that didn't matter. Then we continued on by train south to Kazakhstan. There things were good, no cold, but desert, warm wind and lots of sand. We arrived in Buzuluk after three weeks.

And the welcome?
The unit was already being formed, so they were awaiting the new arrivals at the train station. There they registered us, I got the number 457, my brother 456. I was quite weak after the camp and the three weeks of travel and I fell ill with louse-borne typhus with a fever of over forty degrees. They took me to the infirmary of the Czechoslovak formation. I was unconscious, my hair was completely falling out, but the Jewish doctors working at the infirmary cured me and got me back on my feet. In the meantime, they had assigned my brother to the reconnaissance platoon. Because I was a Scout and could read a map, they also assigned me to that platoon after I'd recovered. Our commander was Antonín Sochor. And so I began my training.

III.
REFUGEES FROM THE TERRITORY OF PRE-WAR CZECHOSLOVAKIA ANNEXED BY HUNGARY

FAJGA BERKOVIČOVÁ (b. 1918 in Vyšné Studené), arrested in July 1940 trying to illegally cross the Hungarian-Soviet border. Sentenced to three years in the Gulag, interned at Siblag. *DAZO* ▶

Беркович
Файга
1918

The territory of interwar Subcarpathian Rus was a cultural, religious and ethnic crossroads. According to the 1930 census, there were 725,357 inhabitants, of those 446,916 considered themselves Ruthenians, 109,472 Hungarians, 91,255 Jews, 33,961 Czechoslovaks, 13,249 Germans and 12,641 Romanians.[109] This diverse composition brought with it clashes between them, which escalated in the 1930s in connection with the growing tensions on the international scene. Aside from the Munich Agreement, another result of the Hungarian and German pressure on Czechoslovakia and the European powers' policy of appeasement was the Vienna Arbitration of 2 November 1938, which meant south-eastern Slovakia and the south-western part of Subcarpathian Rus being ceded to Hungary. The goal of the Hungarian politicians was, however, to further destabilise the area and thus lay the groundwork for the acquisition of additional territory. On 12 March 1939, Adolf Hitler approved the Hungarian occupation of the remainder of Subcarpathian Rus. Three days later, on 15 March, Hungarian troops launched an attack, which was defended by two regiments of the Czechoslovak army and divisions of the Carpathian Sich.[110] By 18 March, however, Budapest had already taken full control of Subcarpathian Rus after 21 years, and it became part of the Kingdom of Hungary under the name Kárpátaljai terület – Carpathian Territory, or Karpátálja for short.

Immediately after the annexation, the Magyarization of the area began, which meant the suppression of all non-Hungarian elements, in particular expressions of Ruthenian and Ukrainian nationalism and communism. Last but not least, the situation of the Jewish population began to deteriorate, gradually progressing from daily displays of anti-Semitism and deprivation of rights to organised violence and mass extermination several years later.

Yet just several months prior, when the Hungarian army took the south-western part of Subcarpathian Rus in autumn 1938, the majority of local Jews had welcomed the soldiers alongside the Hungarian minority. This was not solely due to linguistic, cultural, kinship and trade ties to Hungary, but also due to the distrust of the autonomous Carpathian Ukraine and the worsening relations between Ukrainian nationalists and the Jewish minority. Thus in many places, Jewish people welcomed the Hungarian soldiers with Hungarian flags. In Mukachevo, for example, the local Jews gave the commander of the Hungarian troops occupying the city a bouquet on behalf of

---

109 For more details, see ŠVORC, Peter: *Zakletá zem. Podkarpatská Rus 1918–1946* [Cursed Land. Subcarpathian Rus 1918–1946]. Nakladatelství Lidové noviny, Prague 2007, p. 124–125; RYCHLÍK, Jan – RYCHLÍKOVÁ, Magdaléna: *Podkarpatská Rus v dějinách Československa 1918–1946* [Subcarpathian Rus in the History of Czechoslovakia 1918–1946]. Vyšehrad, Prague 2016, p. 7.

110 Carpathian Sich – a paramilitary organisation of Ruthenians and Ukrainians formed in November 1938. For more on the struggle for Subcarpathian Rus, see e.g. LÁŠEK, Radan: "Obrana Podkarpatské Rusi" [The Defence of Subcarpathian Rus]. *Paměť a dějiny*, 2009, vol. 3, no. 1, p. 21–29.

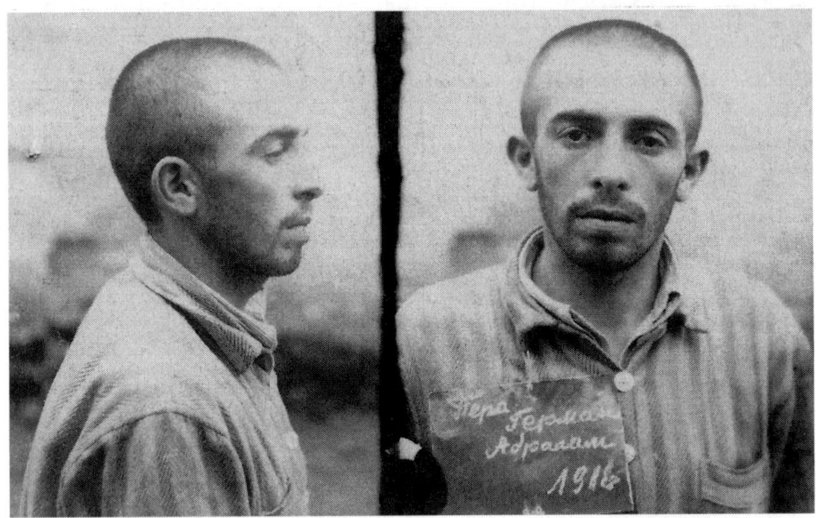

The refugees also included many married couples, for example HERMAN (1916) and SIMA (1923) PERL. Before the war, Herman Perl lived eight years in Brno, where he worked as a locksmith and a driver. After the German annexation of Bohemia and Moravia, he and his wife first went to Slovakia, and then to Subcarpathian Rus. They crossed the border on 18 July 1940 near the village of Lavochne, where they were also arrested. On 27 September 1940, they were sentenced to 3 years of labour in the Gulag. While Sima was sent to Siblag and her further fate is unknown, they transported Herman to Kargopollag, where he died on 8 March 1943.

DAZO, f. 2558 (1939–1993), vol. no. 4055.

The former Czechoslovak-Polish border, Hungarian-Soviet border during the war, was formed by the Carpathians, which refugees to the USSR had to cross. *ÚSTR / Adam Hradilek*

the whole city. Although there were attacks on the Jewish participants in the welcoming crowds in Berehove and other areas, in most places their sincere and pragmatic expressions of loyalty to the new government were received positively.[111]

In March 1939, the situation was repeated after the occupation of the remainder of Subcarpathian Rus by the Hungarian army and the introduction of temporary military rule. The initial hopes of the Jewish population placed on the "old-new" Hungarian rule of Subcarpathia was gradually dampened by the increasing pressure on the non-Hungarian population, the growing anti-Jewish sentiment and legislative measures, as well as manifestations of both random and organised violence.

Arrests, mistreatment in prisons, executions and forced deportation became an everyday reality in the annexed territory. The occupying power also proceeded to immediately Magyarize the school system. One of the main instruments of Hungarian indoctrination of youth aged twelve to twenty-three was compulsory service in the paramilitary organisation Levente. The primary objective was to teach the youth discipline and allegiance to Hungary

---

111 JELINEK, A. Yeshayahu – MAGOCSI, R. Paul: *The Carpathian Diaspora: The Jews of Subcarpathian Rus' and Mukachevo, 1848–1948*. East European Monographs, New York 2007, p. 233.

and prepare them for military service. Serving in Levente was unbearable for non-Hungarian youths due to the humiliation, bullying and violence on the part of the commanders.[112]

The occupation did not only have a negative impact in the school system and upbringing of youth, however, but also affected a number of work sectors and professions. Key positions at enterprises and self-governing units were taken over by Hungarians. The non-Hungarian population was relegated to the fringes of society.[113]

The life of Carpathian Jews was increasingly bound by anti-Semitic laws and regulations. Almost immediately, the already existing Hungarian discriminatory law, No. 15 of 29 May 1938, restricting the employment and education of Jews, began to be applied in the annexed territory, which meant the closure of most Hebrew schools and a loss of livelihood for the vast majority of smaller Jewish business owners. A year later, on 4 May 1939, the so-called "Second Law", No. 4, was adopted, considerably expanding the existing restrictions on Jewish civil rights. Among other things, it introduced quotas regulating the number of Jews at universities, in various sectors of business, and deprived a significant portion of the Jewish population both in the annexed territory of Subcarpathian Rus and in the south of Slovakia of their human rights, livelihood and citizenship.[114] Undue faith in the advantages of Hungarian rule, the political situation in Europe, the immigration policies of countries "safe" for Jewish populations, as well as the gradual escalation of repressive measures were the factors that prevented a mass exodus of Jews from Subcarpathia. Though thousands of young Zionists were preparing to leave for Palestine in numerous cells of Zionist organisations, only a fraction of them managed to do so after 1939. Zionist associations were banned and their representatives subjected to severe repression.[115] Given that legal departure was no longer an option for the Jews being persecuted by the Hungarians in Subcarpathian Rus, they had no choice but to resort to illegal emigration.

The annexing of the south-eastern part of Poland by the Soviet Union in September 1939 meant the borders of the USSR shifted to the west, all the way to the northern border of Hungarian Subcarpathia, which was formed by the

112 HORVATH, Attila: "War and Peace: The Effects of the World War II on Hungarian Education". In: LOWE, Roy (ed.): *Education & the Second World War: Studies in Schooling & Social Change*. Falmer Press, London 1992, p. 147.

113 ŠVORC, Peter: *Zakletá zem. Podkarpatská Rus 1918–1946* [Cursed land. Subcarpathian Rus 1918–1946], p. 253; cf. DOVHANICH Omelan: "Repressii uhors'koho okupatsiĭnoho rezhimu proty hromadian kraiu". In: *Reabilitovani istoriiu. Zakarpatska oblast* I. Uzhhorod: VAT "Vydavnytstvo 'Zakarpattia'", 2003, p. 21–38.

114 ROZZET, Robert: *Conscripted Slaves. Hungarian Jewish Forced Laborers on the Eastern Front During the Second World War*. Yad Vashem, Jerusalem 2013, p. 5.

115 JELINEK, A. Yeshayahu – MAGOCSI, R. Paul: *The Carpathian diaspora: The Jews of Subcarpathian Rus' and Mukachevo, 1848–1948*, p. 247.

ABRAM SINGER (1921) of Mukachevo was one of those who ended up in Soviet territory involuntarily. After the Hungarians annexed Subcarpathian Rus, he was denied Hungarian citizenship and subjected to repression. He was summoned to the police station three times to submit the necessary documents and for interrogation. The last time, on 24 July 1940, he spent three days in a cell. On 27 July, they put him on a train, escorted him to the station Uzhok and forced him to cross the nearby border with the USSR. Shortly thereafter he was arrested by the NKVD and imprisoned in Stryi. On 10 February 1941, he was sentenced to 3 years in Vorkutlag.

DAZO, f. 2558 (1939–1993), vol. no. 3674; cf. Memory of Nations archive, interview with Antonín Slavík (Abram Singer) conducted 9 May 2003 by Jiří Luděk.

Carpathian Mountains. This difficult-to-monitor, mountainous and forested terrain was, primarily for young refugees making use of local smugglers and a sympathetic population, a relatively easy obstacle to overcome and a tempting opportunity to escape the misery of life under Hungarian rule without much prospect. These factors were behind the rising of a massive wave of thousands of refugees – predominantly young Ruthenians, as well as persecuted communists, social democrats and Jews to the Soviet Union.

By no means were these only inhabitants of Subcarpathian Rus however. Hundreds of persecuted Jews from Romania, Hungary, Slovenia, and the Protectorate of Bohemia and Moravia also began fleeing en masse to the Soviet Union via its territory.

For decades, it remained for historians a matter of conjecture how many people fled Subcarpathian Rus to the Soviet Union between the Soviet invasion

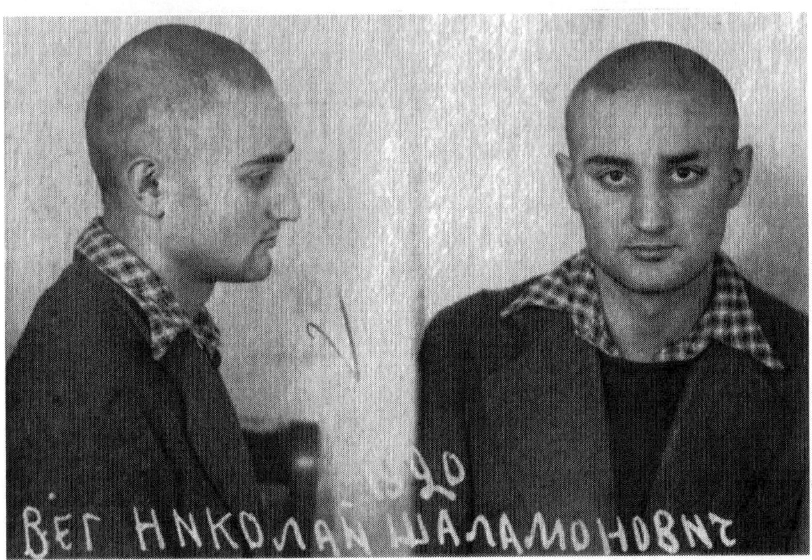

MIKULÁŠ VÉGH (1920), a student of civil engineering in Brno, had to end his studies on racial grounds in 1939 and left for his native Košice, occupied by the Hungarians. In September 1940, he went via Subcarpathian Rus to the USSR, where he was arrested. On 27 December 1941, he was sentenced to 5 years in labour camps for the crime of illegally crossing the state border and as a "socially dangerous element". An aggravating circumstance was that one of his uncles, Imrich Roth, a pre-war Communist Party official, was sentenced to eight years in the Gulag in 1938. Mikuláš died of pneumonia on 8 June 1942 at the Solikamsk transit prison of the Usollag camp complex, where prisoners awaited transfer to other camps.

DAZO, f. 2558 (1939–1993), vol. no. 4628.

of Poland and the German attack on the Soviet Union in June 1941. In the literature, Czech and Ukrainian experts put the numbers at between 5 and 105 thousand.[116] Concrete data could only be obtained after the fall of the Soviet Union, when some of the NKVD archives were declassified and gradually made available, in particular those in the Zakarpattia Oblast (formerly Subcarpathian Rus) in Ukraine. In the State Archives of the Zarkapattia Oblast in Uzhhorod, over five and a half thousand investigative files have been preserved concerning persons who crossed the Hungarian-Soviet border from Subcarpathia in 1939–1941 and were arrested and investigated by the NKVD border units.

116 For more detail, see e.g., OFICYNSKYJ, Roman: *Nelehalnyj perekhid uhorsko-radyanskoho kordonu v 1939–1941 rokakh. Studia Carpatica – Karpatoznavchi studii: specialnyj vypusk. Uzhorodskyj derzhavnyj universitet; Naukovo-doslidnyj instytut karpatoznavstva*, Uzhhorod 1993, p. 14–30.

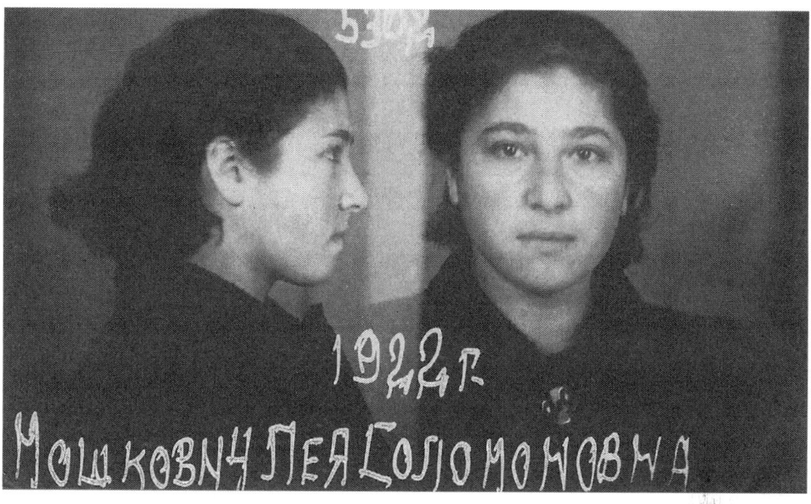

Among the first persecuted after the Hungarian annexation of Subcarpathian Rus to seek refuge in the USSR were members of Zionist organisations. LEIA MOSHKOVICH (1922) of Khust, a member of the Hashomer Hatzair movement, which promoted Zionist ideas among Jewish workers in the Rakhiv region, was arrested with her fiancé LEIB POLLAK (1918) by the Soviets on 21 September 1940. Their illegal association with the Budapest headquarters of Hashomer Hatzair aroused the distrust of the NKVD and influenced the further course of the investigation. Leia was sentenced to 3 years of work camps and sent to Karlag in eastern Kazakhstan; Leib to 5 years at the Sevitlag camp.

DAZO, f. 2558 (1939–1993), vol. no. 1491.

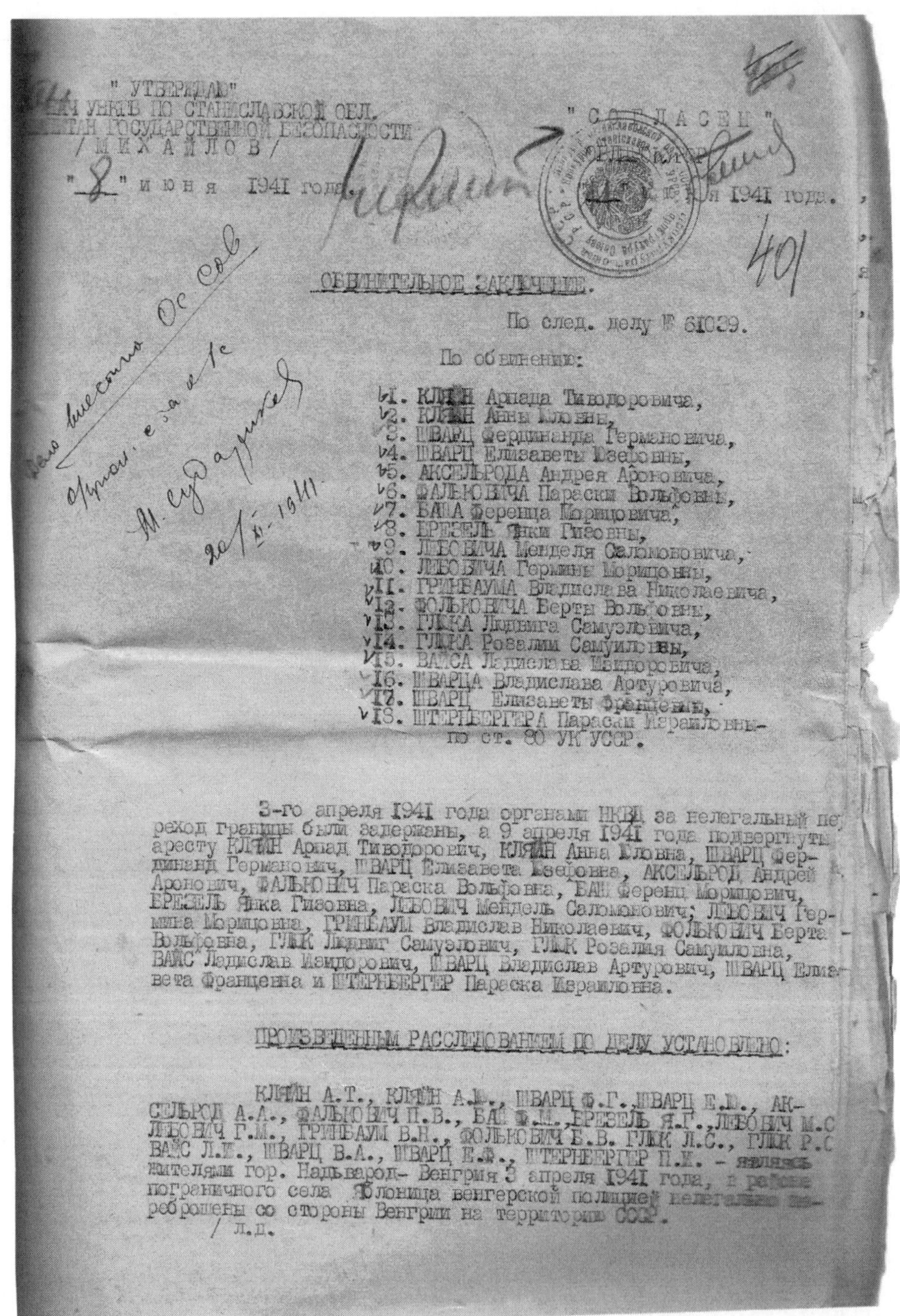

"УТВЕРЖДАЮ"
НАЧ УНКГБ ПО СТАНИСЛАВСКОЙ ОБЛ.
КАПИТАН ГОСУДАРСТВЕННОЙ БЕЗОПАСНОСТИ
/МИХАЙЛОВ/
"8" июня 1941 года.

"СОГЛАСЕН"
… июня 1941 года.

ОБВИНИТЕЛЬНОЕ ЗАКЛЮЧЕНИЕ.

По след. делу № 61039.

По обвинению:

1. КЛЯЙН Арпада Тиводоровича,
2. КЛЯЙН Анны Юловны,
3. ШВАРЦ Фердинанда Германовича,
4. ШВАРЦ Елизаветы Юзефовны,
5. АКСЕЛЬРОДА Андрея Ароновича,
6. ФАЛЬКОВИЧА Параски Вольфовны,
7. БАША Ференца Морицовича,
8. БРЕЗЕЛЬ Янки Гизовны,
9. ЛЕБОВИЧА Менделя Саломоновича,
10. ЛЕБОВИЧА Гермины Морицовны,
11. ГРИНБАУМА Владислава Николаевича,
12. ФОЛЬКОВИЧА Берты Вольфовны,
13. ГЛИКА Людвига Самуэловича,
14. ГЛИКА Розалии Самуиловны,
15. ВАЙСА Ладислава Изидоровича,
16. ШВАРЦА Владислава Артуровича,
17. ШВАРЦ Елизаветы Францевны,
18. ШТЕРНБЕРГЕРА Параски Израиловны-

по ст. 80 УК УССР.

3-го апреля 1941 года органами НКВД за нелегальный переход границы были задержаны, а 9 апреля 1941 года подвергнуты аресту КЛЯЙН Арпад Тиводорович, КЛЯЙН Анна Юловна, ШВАРЦ Фердинанд Германович, ШВАРЦ Елизавета Юзефовна, АКСЕЛЬРОД Андрей Аронович, ФАЛЬКОВИЧ Параска Вольфовна, БАШ Ференц Морицович, БРЕЗЕЛЬ Янка Гизовна, ЛЕБОВИЧ Мендель Саломонович, ЛЕБОВИЧ Гермина Морицовна, ГРИНБАУМ Владислав Николаевич, ФОЛЬКОВИЧ Берта Вольфовна, ГЛИК Людвиг Самуэлович, ГЛИК Розалия Самуиловна, ВАЙС Ладислав Изидорович, ШВАРЦ Владислав Артурович, ШВАРЦ Елизавета Францевна и ШТЕРНБЕРГЕР Параска Израиловна.

ПРОИЗВЕДЕННЫМ РАССЛЕДОВАНИЕМ ПО ДЕЛУ УСТАНОВЛЕНО:

КЛЯЙН А.Т., КЛЯЙН А.Ю., ШВАРЦ Ф.Г., ШВАРЦ Е.Ю., АКСЕЛЬРОД А.А., ФАЛЬКОВИЧ П.В., БАШ Ф.М., БРЕЗЕЛЬ Я.Г., ЛЕБОВИЧ М.С., ЛЕБОВИЧ Г.М., ГРИНБАУМ В.Н., ФОЛЬКОВИЧ Б.В. ГЛИК Л.С., ГЛИК Р.С., ВАЙС Л.И., ШВАРЦ В.А., ШВАРЦ Е.Ф., ШТЕРНБЕРГЕР П.И. - являясь жителями гор. Надьварод- Венгрия 3 апреля 1941 года, в районе пограничного села Яблоница венгерской полицией нелегально переброшены со стороны Венгрии на территорию СССР.
/ л.д.

Refugees most frequently fled racially motivated persecution to the Soviet Union as individuals or in pairs, but larger groups were not an exception. The group of refugees arrested on 3 April 1941 and investigated by the NKVD as "Klein et al." numbered eighteen people. *DAZO*

Analysis of the aforementioned fonds carried out by Ukrainian historians shows that of the overall number of five and a half thousand refugees, 1079 of them fled in 1939, 4037 in 1940 and 537 in 1941.[117] Another hundred people chose the route via the German-occupied part of Poland and were then apprehended by the Soviets in the Lviv Oblast after crossing the German-Soviet border. Altogether these were approximately six thousand persons.

The majority consisted of young Ruthenians. In addition to men, around 400 women also decided to flee. There were also 492 persons from the Hungarian midlands, 129 from the parts of Slovakia annexed by the Hungarians, and 119 from Romania that fled to the Soviet Union via the territory of Subcarpathia. Additionally, there were individuals from Bohemia, Poland and Yugoslavia.

Of those five and a half thousand refugees, 640 were of Jewish origin, i.e., around 11%. However just under half of them came from the territory of pre-war Subcarpathian Rus. More than a hundred of them had lived in pre-war Hungary, a similar amount had left the Hungarian-occupied part of Romania, fifty came from the annexed part of Slovakia, two from the Czech lands, two from Poland and one from Yugoslavia.[118] Among the refugees of all the aforementioned groups, there was a relatively large number of Communist Party members or communist activists. Among the Jewish refugees originally from Czechoslovakia, 23% were members of the Communist Party of Czechoslovakia. The considerably lower number of communists among the Carpathian Ruthenians (around 5%)[119] was in part due to the significantly lower average age of this group.

The refugees crossed the border either alone, more frequently in twos, threes or fours, or they fled with their whole families, siblings, schoolmates, friends, spouses or neighbours.

For most of them, the decision to flee to the Soviet Union was primarily due to the hopelessness of their personal situation and the geographic proximity of the USSR, whose borders became closer after the Soviet expansion at the expense of Poland. Undoubtedly, however, a role was also played by political sympathies and pro-Soviet propaganda, which found fertile soil in the poor Subcarpathian Rus.

Nevertheless, the vast majority of refugees hoping to find refuge from persecution on racial and political grounds and better living conditions in the

---

117 DOVHANICH, *Omelan: Peresliduvannia hromadian radyans'kym totalitarnym rezhymom u peredvoienni ta povoienni roky. In: Reabilitovani istoriiu. Zakarpatska oblast I. Uzhhorod: VAT "Vydavnytstvo 'Zakarpattia'"*, 2003, p. 39–56.

118 DVOŘÁK, Jan – HRADILEK, Adam: "Perzekuce československých Židů v Sovětském svazu za druhé světové války" [Persecution of Czechoslovak Jews in the Soviet Union in World War II]. In: *Historie – Otázky – Problémy* [History – Questions – Problems], 2013, no. 1, p. 109.

119 OFICYNSKYJ, Roman: *Nelehalnyj perekhid uhorsko-radyanskoho kordonu v 1939–1941 rokakh*, p. 47.

USSR were arrested immediately upon crossing the border by NKVD border patrols. The work of the guardians of the Soviet borders was made easier by the considerable naivety of most of the refugees. After the harrowing journey through the border regions of Hungary and Germany and hiding from their police and border forces, in Soviet territory they were suddenly carefree, relieved and expectant of a better future. Thus they either fell into the hands of the border patrols in the practically uninhabited swath of mountains on the border, or they reported themselves to the Soviet authorities at border stations or town halls in the first Soviet municipalities they encountered after crossing the border.

After being arrested, the refugees were placed in temporary prisons set up by the NKVD border units not far from the border. Usually these were stables and other utility buildings, basements of various farmhouses near the border guard buildings, or such buildings directly. Here they were held until there were enough of them to transfer by marching escort or automobile to the nearest NKVD prisons in the border region. Generally they remained in temporary cells overnight, but quite often even for several days. Those who crossed the Hungarian-Soviet border in its western part were often first escorted to the refugee holding camp in Skole, which had a capacity of several hundred. The camp served as a pre-entry station, primarily for the NKVD prison in Stryi, forty kilometres away, which could not handle the influx of refugees. For this reason, detained refugees were also sent from Skole to other prisons. According to an analysis of 1800 NKVD files kept on 3200 detainees, most refugees from Subcarpathian Rus were placed in the prisons in Stanyslaviv (38%), Stryi (37%), Ivanovo (10%), Poltava (5%), Mikolaiv (4.5%), Zhytomyr (2%) and Dnepropetrovsk (1.5%), as well as other cities.[120] Upon arrival at the detention centre, the refugees passed under the authority of the NKVD counterintelligence units, which took them over from the NKVD border units and launched investigations.

The subsequent fate of the refugees from Subcarpathian Rus was very similar to that of the refugees from the Protectorate that fled through Poland. Immediately after crossing the border they were charged and tried. They received sentences of 3 to 5 years in the Gulag, most frequently for illegally crossing the border. To a lesser extent, they were tried for espionage, or occasionally as "socially dangerous elements". In this category, the sentences mostly ranged from 5 to 8 years. The highest sentence handed down was 15 years of forced labour in the camps (see p. 135).

The difference in the approach of Soviet authorities to refugees from the Hungarian-occupied territory compared to refugees from the Czech lands

120 Ibid, p. 43

The highest sentence of all the refugees was given to GÁBOR EDELSTEIN (1901), a stonemason and Czechoslovak Communist Party member, and JOSEF REIS (1906), a pharmacist and lieutenant in the Czechoslovak army, both of Uzhhorod. On 23 December 1942, they were sentenced to 15 years of forced labour in the Gulag for espionage. Unlike other refugees investigated for the same matter, both of them admitted to espionage during interrogation. After the ruling they were transported to Ivdellag in the northern Urals in the Sverdlovsk Oblast, where they both died – J. Reis 27 March 1943, G. Edelstein 12 May 1945.

DAZO, f. 2558 (1939–1993), vol. no. 1458.

only became apparent in connection with the amnesty for Czechoslovak citizens in the USSR in 1942. The Soviets considered refugees from Hungarian territory to be Hungarian citizens and refused to release them on the basis of the amnesty. It took several months before the Czechoslovak authorities managed to negotiate their release.[121]

121 See VALIŠ, Zdeněk: "Ze sovětských gulagů do československé armády. Heliodor Píka v boji za životy Podkarpatorusů" [From the Soviet Gulags to the Czechoslovak Army. Heliodor Píka in the Fight for the Lives of Subcarpathians]. *Historie a vojenství*, 2008, no. 1, p. 43–58.

ERNEST VIDER

Ernest Vider at the end of the 1930s before fleeing to the USSR. *CVG collection*

Born 1 February 1922 in Mukachevo. His father Julius Vider (1892) came from Sziget, Hungary, and served in the Austro-Hungarian army in Mukachevo in World War I, where he met Ernest's secondary-school-educated mother Alena Wettenstein (1890). After they married, she remained a homemaker and raised five sons. The father worked in Mukachevo as a merchant, becoming at the start of the thirties the main distributor of a company that imported colonial goods from Prague and supplied the whole of Subcarpathian Rus. Ernest was born at his grandparent's house. They spoke Hungarian at home, only speaking Yiddish with the grandparents. The family observed Jewish holidays, but were not Orthodox. Ernest attended a Jewish school – a *cheder*. After 1938, when the anti-Jewish laws came into effect, relations between the city's inhabitants began to change. His father, who had been doing well and had built them a house, lost his job and the family experienced difficulties subsisting. They had to sell the house and move into a smaller flat. After the Hungarians came, they sent his father and other Jewish men to the auxiliary units of the Hungarian army. Ernest also paid the price for his background: they expelled him from school and he couldn't find a job. For this reason, he crossed into the Soviet Union in September 1940 along with three other young men in the same position as him. Shortly after crossing the border they were arrested by Soviet border guards and imprisoned in Nadvirna and then in Starobilsk. Here they were sentenced to three years of forced labour for illegally crossing the border. Ernest Vider served his sentence in the Pechorlag camps. Although he was sentenced to three years, he only awaited release in 1946, spending more than six years in camps. After returning to Mukachevo, he started working as a storekeeper at a department store. He gradually worked his way up to deputy storeroom manager and eventually department head. While working, he graduated from a technical school. Up until his retirement, he worked in the food industry at a mineral water plant. Though he was not a member of the Communist Party, he held high positions in the enterprise. He first married in 1949, to an eighteen-year-old girl who had survived the Holocaust. Shortly after their second child was born, his wife fell ill and died. His neighbour Maria Ivanovna took over care for the children and home, and Ernest later married her. After 1985, when the Sovi-

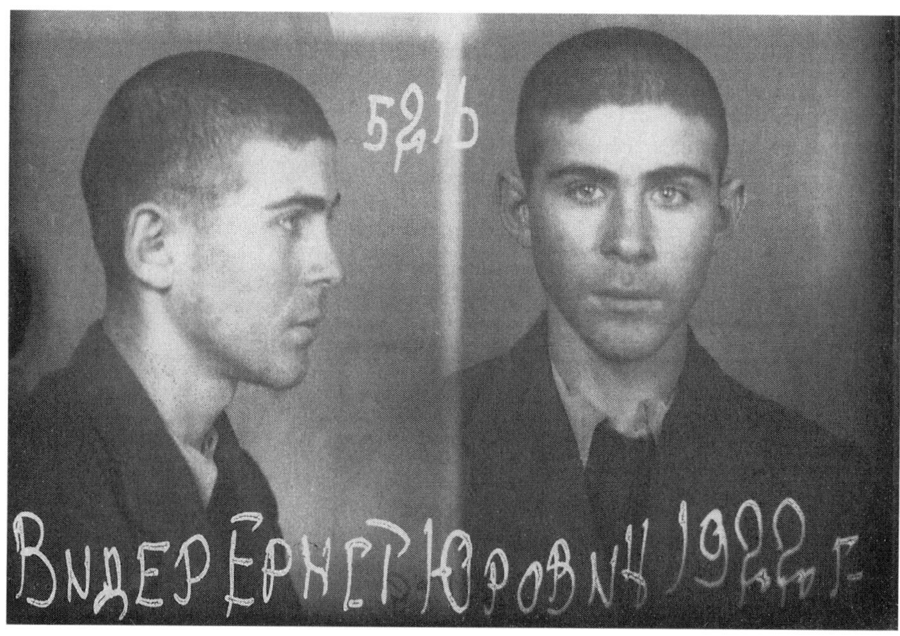

Ernest Vider after arrest by the NKVD in 1940. *DAZO*

ets returned the Mukachevo synagogue for religious purposes, Ernest Vider helped restore the Jewish community in Mukachevo.[122]

— — —

How did your life change after the Hungarian annexation of Subcarpathian Rus?
The dissolution of Czechoslovakia took place in two stages. The first started right after the Munich conference, when the Germans gained the Sudetenland, and southern Slovakia and the part of southern Subcarpathian Rus with Uzhhorod, Mukachevo and Berehove was annexed to Hungary. The Czechoslovak soldiers left these places peacefully and were replaced by the Hungarian army. Because my father, mother, grandmothers and grandfathers were born in Austria-Hungary, we all considered ourselves Hungarian Jews. So when the Hungarians arrived, at first we thought everything would be great. Unfortunately, this vision was not borne out. At first nothing happened and there was calm, other than a few skirmishes with the so-called Free Corps,[123] who caused provocations, here and there even shooting, but there were no

122 *Archive of USC Shoah Foundation*, interview with Ernest Vider recorded 12 September 1997 by Boris Timur, translated from Russian by Jiřina Dvořáková.

123 Szabadcsapatok – in English Free Corps or Freikorps, Hungarian paramilitary groups active within the territory of Czechoslovakia in 1939–1939 with the goal of destabilising the areas claimed by Hungary.

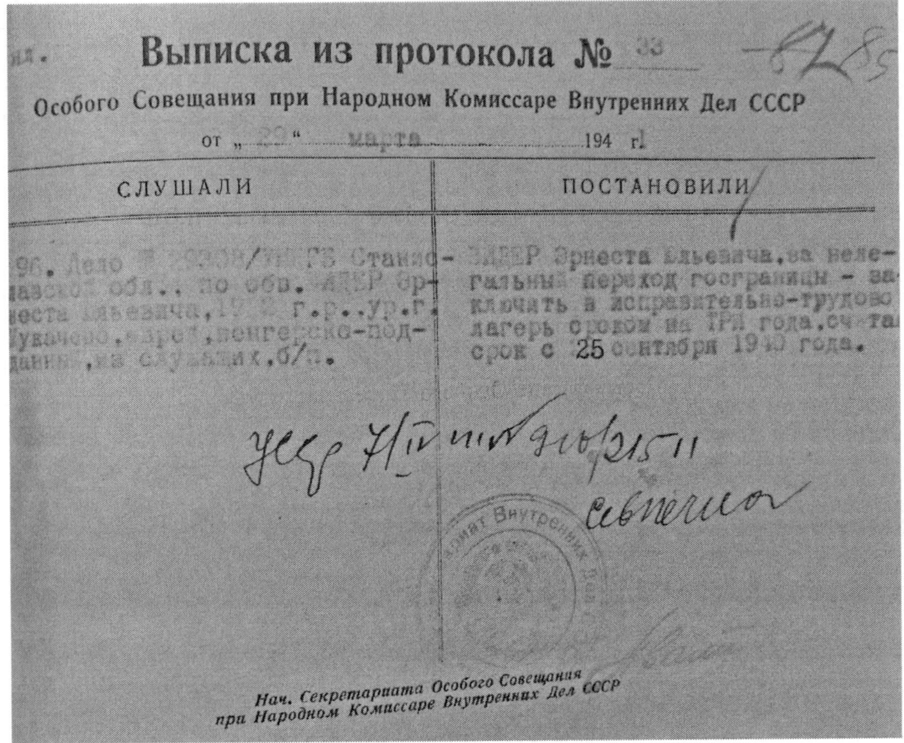

Выписка из протокола № [illegible]

Особого Совещания при Народном Комиссаре Внутренних Дел СССР

от „[illegible]" марта 194 г.

СЛУШАЛИ	ПОСТАНОВИЛИ
96. Дело № [illegible]/[illegible] Станиславской обл., по обв. [illegible]ЕР Эрнеста Ильевича, 19[illegible] г.р., ур. г. Мукачево, еврей, венгерско-подданный, из служащих, б/п.	[illegible]ЕР Эрнеста Ильевича, за нелегальный переход госграницы – заключить в исправительно-трудовой лагерь сроком на ТРИ года, считая срок с 25 сентября 1940 года.

Нач. Секретариата Особого Совещания при Народном Комиссаре Внутренних Дел СССР

Excerpt from the ruling with a handwritten destination of transport, which was Sevpechlag in the Komi Republic. *DAZO*

notable hostilities. We were wrong about the Hungarians however, and their government's next move disappointed us. The second and definitive stage of Czechoslovakia's demise was the occupation of the remaining areas by the Germans and Hungarians in March 1939. After this, the situation changed dramatically, especially for the Jews. The real oppression began. Jews gradually began losing the right to own shops, to work as civil servants, to study at universities, and so forth. The restrictions were vast. As a result of these measures, my father had to sell the house he had built himself a few years prior, but which he could not afford as he was unemployed. I wasn't around to see that though, as I fled across the border before the house was sold.

What was the catalyst for your escape?

Mostly the aforementioned oppression by the Hungarians. A great number of people were fleeing at that time. Lots of people I knew had fled before me. You heard people saying, "Look, Ivan left," "You know that Moishe fled...," "Vasya and Chaim are gone," and so on. It was just tempting. And I dreamt of a world where I could study and work, because at that time I had already

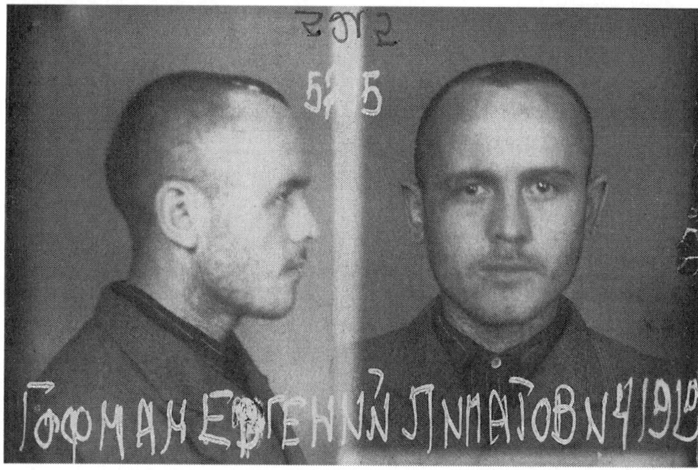

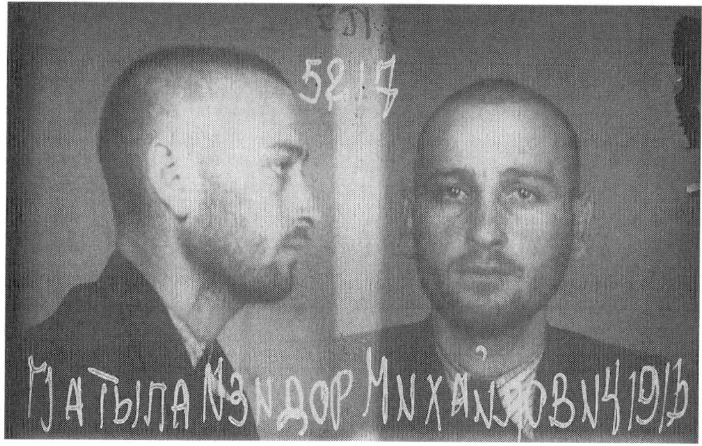

Ignat Klein, Eugen Hofmann and Izidor Potipa, who fled along with Ernest Vider to the Soviet Union, shortly after being arrested by the NKVD in 1940. *DAZO*

-36-

УТВЕРЖДАЮ:
ЗАМ НАЧ 95 ПО НКВД
КАПИТАН

АРЕСТ САНКЦИОНИРУЮ
ПРОКУРОР
" " 1940г.

ПОСТАНОВЛЕНИЕ
/ На арест /

Город Надворна "28" сентября 1940 года.

Я, ст. помощник начальника 5 отделения Власов

рассмотрев материалы следственного дела по обвинению гр.
Видер Ернест [illegible] 1922 года рождения [illegible] Качево,
Еврей, авто-механик

НАШЕЛ:

что [illegible] сентябре 1940 года нелегально перешел
границу из Венгрии в СССР.

ПОСТАНОВИЛ:

Гр. Видер Ернест [illegible]
Подвергнуть аресту и обыску.
Пом начальника 5 отд. [signature]

Ernest Vider's arrest warrant was a mere formality. He had already been in an NKVD prison for several days. *DAZO*

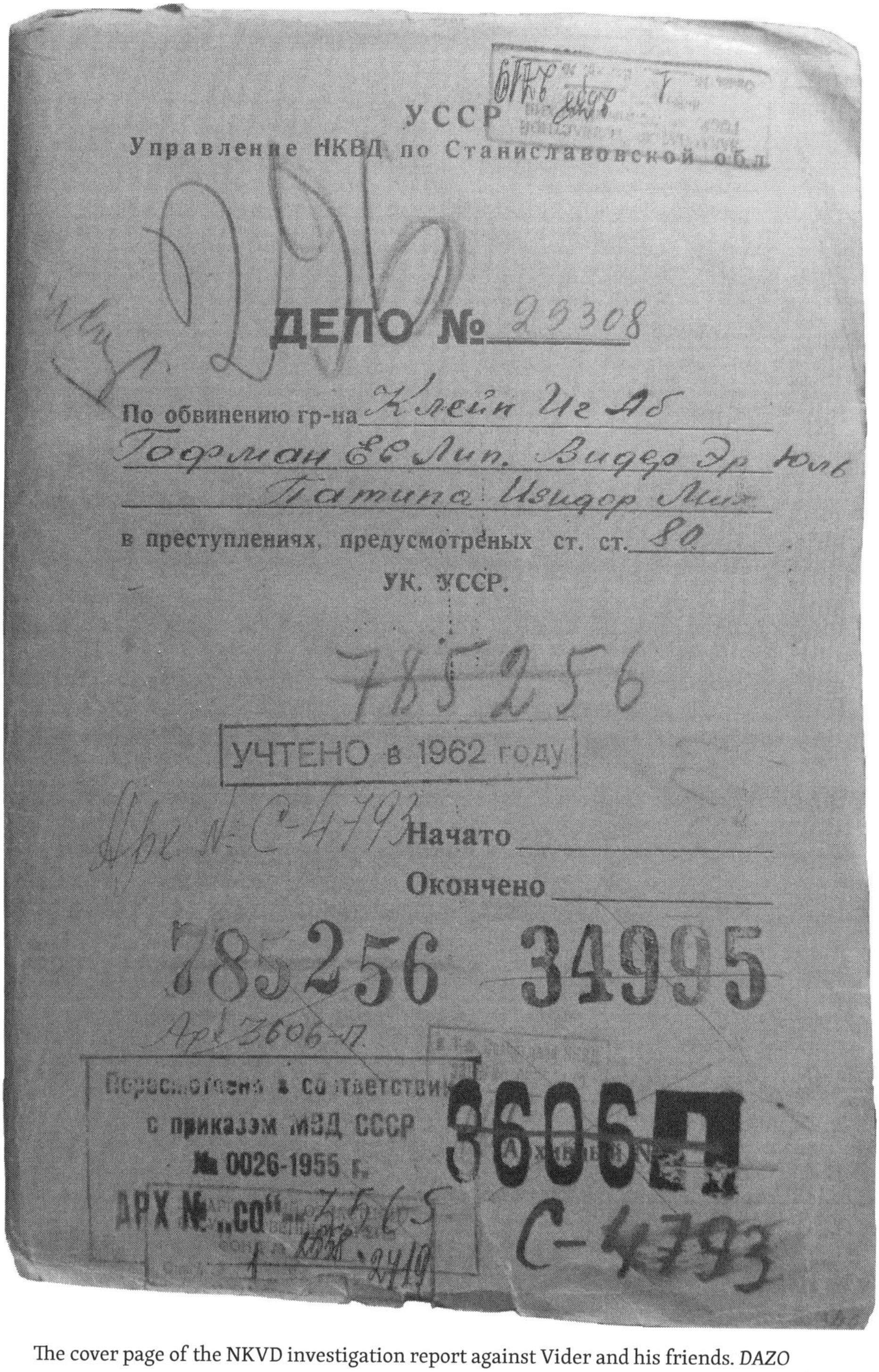
УССР
Управление НКВД по Станиславовской обл

ДЕЛО № 25308

По обвинению гр-на Клейн Иг Аб
Гофман Ев Лип. Видер Эр Юль
Патина Исидор Мих
в преступлениях, предусмотреных ст. ст. 80
УК. УССР.

785256

УЧТЕНО в 1962 году

Арх № С-4793

Начато
Окончено

785256 34995

Арх 3606-П

Пересмотрено в соответствии
с приказом МВД СССР
№ 0026-1955 г.
АРХ № „СО“-

3606п

С-4793

The cover page of the NKVD investigation report against Vider and his friends. *DAZO*

Part of the report from the interrogation of Ernest Vider at the NKVD prison in Nadvirna. *DAZO*

The remains of the transit camp, a so-called *peresylka*, in Pechora, from which the prisoners were transported on to the individual camps. *ÚSTR / Adam Hradilek*

been expelled from school. The opportunity came in September, when I went to visit my aunt in the village of Vyshkovo. There I met two lads from Khust while playing football – Hofmann and Klein, the third was Potipa from Vyshkovo. They were determined to flee across the border. So I sent home word that I was leaving and set off with them.

Why did you go to the Soviet Union in particular?
At that time I was more or less a leftist. Czechoslovakia was a very democratic country, in which there was plenty of discussion and various cultural and political resources were available. They even showed Soviet films in the cinema such as Circus, Chapaev, Jolly Fellows, and others. I also read lots of literature from foreign left-leaning writers such as Sinclair Lewis, Upton Sinclair, Egon Erwin Kisch, Lion Feuchtwanger, even Ilya Ehrenburg, and I adored their books. All this inspired me to leave for the Soviet Union. At the same time, none of us knew what things really looked like in that country, what was going on there, that it was a dictatorial state and not a socialist one. None of us had any clue, for example, that the Ukrainian Famine, in which a million and a half people had died, was provoked deliberately. We thought the Soviet Union was a beautiful country that was moving towards a just society.

Detention Centre No. 1 at Pechorlag, one of the last period testaments of political repression in Pechora. *ÚSTR / Adam Hradilek*

Did the information about what was happening to the Jews in German-occupied Poland play any role in your decision to leave for the Soviet Union?
No, we didn't know anything about it. Even the Jews they carted off to Auschwitz a few years later didn't know what was happening and where they were going.

How did you manage to cross the border?
Many refugees from Mukachevo crossed by the Volovec pass in the northern part of Subcarpathian Rus. From Vyshkovo, however, it was closer to Yasinya and Rakhiv in the east of the country. We had a Jewish acquaintance there, who knew a local Ruthenian, who smuggled people across the border for money. Three days we lived with the Jewish acquaintance in the hayloft of his barn. On September twenty-fourth, the smuggler arrived. It was a dark night, cloudy, even drizzling a bit, and he said: "Now is the right time." He took us to the border on the ridge of the mountains, where we said goodbye to him. We climbed under the barbed wire and headed down the hill. Day was starting to dawn and suddenly there were two soldiers standing before us, shouting in Russian: "Halt! Where are you going!" They immediately arrested us and drove us to the station in Nadvirna for interrogation.

Did you understand Russian?
At that time I didn't know Russian at all. I only spoke Hungarian and Czech. But Czech and Russian are both Slavic languages, so I understood something. At the interrogation, where they drew up the report, we had an interpreter. He was also a refugee. His name was Ernest like me, surname Neiman, from Rakhiv.

What did they charge you with?
As they say, when they want to put a man in jail, they'll always find an article. They suspected us of espionage. What can I say?

How did they treat you?
The same as the other prisoners. There must have been a hundred of us in a single cell in the prison in Stanyslaviv. We were crammed in there, huddled together on the concrete floor for months. Then they transported us to the prison in Starobilsk, where there was a great number of people. There an NKVD troika, or special session, judged us. It was a trial where they had say ten people called forward at once: "Ernest Vider, Ivan Schwarz and others are hereby convicted of crossing the border illegally." They called it NPG. I got three years. Luckily I wasn't in the Party. Those who were got five or even eight years. The Soviets chided them for fleeing: "You're in the Party, how could you abandon your people and seek refuge under our wings?"

What followed such a trial?
Transport to the Urals. They crammed us like sardines into the wagons. Not heated, just ordinary livestock wagons. The transport was rough. There was very little food and they gave it to us in stages. There was even less water, which was crazy. We had a single cup with a string tied to it. As soon as the train stopped somewhere, we let it down through the barred window and tried to get some water from, say, a puddle. It was muddy, black or yellow, but everyone took a drink anyhow. We spent some twenty days travelling to Pechora like that. There they unloaded us and we continued on, two days on foot. It was April, but in the north it's still cold in April. At a spot in the wilderness they stopped us and said, "This is where you're going to live. All around is taiga, forest, so get building somewhere to live." They brought us shovels, picks, saws and axes on horseback. And we started building the camp right away. They didn't give us much time to do it, however, because most of all they needed the railway built. Everyone worked in order to have a roof over their head.

Did they give you any clothing?
At the start we had our own clothing, that is, what everyone had come to the Soviet Union in. But over time it all wore out, got torn, plus, as is common

in prison, things got stolen. So later they did give us some clothing. In the summer simpler clothes, meaning trousers and a shirt and "get to work". For winter we got padded jackets, trousers, some got *valenki*, others *kochuny*. You know what those are? These kind of padded socks. We also wore *chuny*, shoes we made ourselves out of car tyres, they at least didn't let in water.

What kind of work did the Soviets use you for?
After the camp was built, it was building the railway from Pechora to Vorkuta. In the second half of 1941, the Germans had already occupied the Donbas, the main source of coal in the Soviet Union. All of Leningrad's industry and the North Sea fleet ran on coal from Vorkuta. At that time, coal was black gold. They sent an enormous number of prisoners to build the railway and mine coal, maybe as many as a hundred thousand. The work was very important for them, strategically critical.

What were the conditions like at the site?
Work on the railroad was extremely physically demanding, plus we worked twelve to fourteen hours a day. Food was given based on performance. The minimum ration was 300 grams of bread. If you met the quota, you got 600 grams. If you exceeded the norm, 900 grams. Bread was the foundation because the other food, say porridge, was good for nothing. In short, we worked more than enough. In the winter during the cold of the north it was horrible. Up to minus 40 they'd send us to work; if the temperature dropped below minus 40, we'd stay in the barracks. Naturally a lot of people died there. They didn't even bury them. Where and how could they have in that eternal frost? When someone died, they'd just leave them lying there. Then we'd go work on the next kilometre of railway and the dead stayed there. No one ever learned whether or where they were buried.

What exactly did you do?
First the railway embankment was made, then logs and sleepers were placed on it, then the rails were laid. I worked as a hook-man, hammering in the hooks that attached the rails to the sleepers.

What was the ethnicity of the prisoners and where were they from?
There were Russians, Ukrainians, Georgians, Uzbeks, Jews, Tatars, all kinds of nations from the whole Soviet Union and the surrounding countries: from Poland, Hungary, former Czechoslovakia. A kind of strange situation emerged at the camp, uncommon at home, where Jews were friends with Jews, Russians with Russians, Uzbeks with Uzbeks, Tatars with Tatars. I'd never considered myself someone of a certain ethnicity, but the camp kind of forced us to. Jews helped out other Jews and so on. There are still people

Laying of tracks by the Sevzeldorlag subcamp no. 4. *Komi Republic National Archives*

in Transcarpathia and even in Mukachevo that were with me at the camp. In Mukachevo there's Natan Landau (see interview on p. 151), he's older than me, he's already turned 81. In Uzhhorod lives Samuel Friedman (see interview on p. 177), he was also at the camp with me. Then in Budapest there's Sándor Weiss, he was in the camp with me too. Landau had a good job as a store-keeper, carting food from one place to another in a wagon. As soon as he came to Kochmes[124], where I was staying at one time, he always knew what section I was working on and always gave me something. One time it was a kilo of bread, another a few fish, another time buckwheat or oats, depending on what he had. We always helped each other out. Plus we were refugees and nobody was sending us care packages. The Uzbeks got packages. Other ethnicities from the Soviet Union were also allowed, some once a month, others once every three months, depending in part on their performance. But we were foreigners and we didn't have that option. So we helped each other out as much as we could.

124 Kochmes – a settlement between Inta and Vorkuta in Komi Republic.

There were quite a few Jews at the camp. Were religious holidays celebrated, was Shabbos observed?
Don't be naive. Observing religious customs in the Soviet Union, when atheism was considered the only worldview at that time? It wasn't just about Judaism, no religions were allowed. State holidays, yes, we did know those, because that was the one time we didn't work. That's why we looked forward to 7 November or 1 May, because we didn't have to work. But religious holidays, please. We were just trying to live or rather survive from one day to the next. And hoping we'd one day return home.

Did the officials and guards treat people differently based on their ethnicity?
I wouldn't say so. The important thing was to meet the basic obligation – the work quota. The most important thing was to build the railroad. At that time it was one of the most important structures in the Soviet Union. Therefore, there were no differences based on ethnicity. Everything depended on your work, which they rewarded with food. Nothing else, just food. We didn't get any money, just food. And then clothes. If you worked well, you got *valenki*. If you didn't work well, you walked around in just *chuny*. There was no distinction by ethnicity. But there were also various criminals there, murderers, thieves and others. For example *blatnye*, which is a special caste of thieves, *vor v zakone* we called them. They didn't work, you worked for them. The whole time they sat by the fire and kept warm, playing cards. They were connected to the commander and the guards, with whom they traded. In 1943, they brought in soldiers from the Vlasov army, with leather coats, boots, watches and other such accoutrements. The criminals robbed them of everything, literally stripping them naked, and sold the stolen things, primarily for cigarettes and alcohol, to the guards, the camp commanders, and the civilian employees as well.

Did you try to get your case reviewed? To get released?
Even in the camp, we still hoped and believed in the Soviet Union back then. In the justice of the Soviet Union. We were blind. We thought Stalin and the Soviet government didn't know what was really going on, what had happened to us. Not just me, but many others also wrote letters. They never made it anywhere though, as we learned later. As late as 1942, I wrote to the Czechoslovak embassy in Moscow asking whether I could join the Czechoslovak army as a volunteer. My older brother had been fighting in the Czechoslovak army since 1940 in France against the Germans, and then in Africa as well, though of course I didn't know that at the time. I even wrote to the Supreme Soviet, to Kalinin,[125] but the letter probably never even left the camp.

125 Mikhail Ivanovich Kalinin – until 1946 the Chairman of the Presidium of the Supreme Soviet of the USSR.

Did you have any information about events on the front?
We only started to get news in 1943. Before Stalingrad, we didn't know anything at all. Just that there was a war going on, but we had no idea what the situation on the fronts was. Only when the Soviet troops went on the offensive did the famous announcer Levitan[126] inform us from the radio: "Today our troops crossed the front line, destroying this and that..." But what was happening, say, at home in Mukachevo, we knew absolutely nothing about that.

Did you have any news about the situation of Jews in Europe?
None at all. We didn't have the slightest clue. We even hoped that when we got home, everything would be like before. That I would meet my parents, my brothers, friends, neighbours. We had no idea.

When did you get free?
As soon as my three-year sentence had ended, they summoned me to the "other part" of the camp, to the headquarters, where they informed me: "Since you are a Hungarian citizen, and Hungarians are at war with the Soviet Union, you will be detained until a special decree is issued. Sign it." Which I of course refused to do, but do you think it made any difference? They just said, "All right, goodbye." I wasn't released until December 1946. Six and a half years after my arrest. My friend Natan Landau was released in August. Weiss from Budapest was freed in October. When they finally let me go, I got several days of rations – several fish, a few hunks of sugar and two loaves of bread. Plus a train ticket, but it was only valid to Nadvirna. The officer that was processing my release claimed that Mukachevo isn't in the Soviet Union. Even he didn't know that Transcarpathia was already part of the Soviet Union. That's why he didn't let me go to Mukachevo, but just to Nadvirna, where they had first interrogated me after arresting me on the border. I got to Moscow without any problems. It was December 1946, trains were scarce and tickets were not available. People would wait at the stations, lying there for whole weeks until they got a ticket. When I saw the situation, it occurred to me to go to the police commander of Kiyevsky railway station in Moscow. I said to him, "Comrade commander, excuse me," and pulled out my release documents, "I can't get home, I have nothing to eat, I already ate my rations, I don't want to steal anything and commit a crime, help me." He called one of the lieutenants; it was evening and the station ticket counter was opening in the morning. The lieutenant put me at the front of the queue. And so I got a ticket. I even helped out a family that was going home to Kyiv after being

126 Yuri Letivan – an announcer on Soviet state radio.

evacuated from Central Asia. I bought them tickets too. Then they hosted me all the way to Kyiv. I ate, drank and was very content. In Kyiv I thought I'd repeat the approach. Again I went to the station manager with the same song: "Am I to steal or what?" And he said, "Sure, go ahead and steal something, we'll lock you up again." You see the difference between people? From Kyiv I rode to Lviv on the roof of the wagon, lots of people rode on the roofs of wagons in those days. It was winter, cold, but somehow I endured it, after all I was still young. I got from Lviv to Mukachevo by side roads. Transcarpathia was a no-go zone at the time, officially off-limits to people from the rest of the Soviet Union, but I managed to do it.

Did you find any relatives in Mukachevo?
When I got home, I got off the train and first I went to our house. Except I didn't know that my father had sold it long ago and they'd moved into a flat. I never found any of my relatives. My father and mother died in Auschwitz. Witnesses had survived who were deported with them and saw them take my father and mother into the gas chamber. After a time, I ran into my mother's cousin Kahan in the centre of Mukachevo, who had left for Spain in 1936 to fight against Franco and whom I hadn't seen since. I lived with him for five months before I found a job and place to live. My other four brothers were abroad. I didn't know that though. Only after Stalin died, sometime in 1953 or 1954, they tracked me down and we wrote. My second-oldest brother Mikuláš left home 1939 and crossed the border to Yugoslavia. When the war started, he left for Prague and then to France. After the Czechoslovak unit was formed, he joined the army and fought in France and then in Great Britain and Africa. After the war, he returned to England, got married and went to Canada. My oldest brother Meli hid in Budapest when the deportations in Mukachevo started in 1944. After the war, he went to Prague, then to Israel. My younger brothers, Andor and Kálmán, survived Auschwitz – they were liberated at the end of January 1945. After that, they went to Israel, where they fought against the Arabs and the English. Aside from Andor, who is living in Belgium until today, all three brothers moved to Canada, where I first met them after all those years in 1968.

NATAN LANDAU

Born 21 November 1916 in Khust into a strongly religious family. They spoke Yiddish at home. His mother, Toberivka Segal, came from the village of Maidan (today Mizhhiria). According to some versions, Natan was born during the move from Maidan to Khust, right on the market square. His father Haimayer (Chaim) Landau had a small print shop and a weaving workshop where he produced *tallit* prayer shawls. From five years old, Natan competed in sports. His physical prowess later helped him survive the hardships of World War II. After primary school, he entered a Ruthenian grammar school. At fifteen, he started working on a handloom. There were eleven children in the family – seven boys and four girls. Some brothers died before the war, some in Auschwitz. One of his four sisters also died in Auschwitz along with her two young children, three survived the war. After the Hungarian occupation of Subcarpathian Rus, Natan wanted to flee to the West, but after the German and Soviet attacks on Poland, he decided for the USSR. After crossing the border on 6 August 1940, he was arrested by an NKVD border patrol. Among other places, he was imprisoned in Skole and Stryi and subsequently sentenced to three years of forced labour along the Kotlas–Vorkuta route being built in the territory of today's Komi Republic. He went through several Gulag camps on this route. He didn't see release until after the war. Upon returning to Khust, he couldn't find suitable work at first, working as storekeeper at a restaurant and a furniture factory, and for a short time as chairman of the national committee. In 1951, he married a girl whose father Josip Schwarz had died in the 1930s at a Gulag camp. He first applied for rehabilitation in 1957, but only received it six years later, in 1963. For the last 39 years of his life, he worked in tourism.[127]

— — —

Why did you decide to flee Subcarpathian Rus?
When the Nazis invaded Poland on 1 September 1939, I was not quite twenty-three. I didn't understand it at all politically, but what I did understand was that we were completely surrounded by fascists. Communist propaganda was spreading uncontrollably, so people started fleeing to the Soviet Union in the thousands. It wasn't just Jews, but also Ruthenians, whole families. When the Czechoslovak army withdrew from Transcarpathia and left part of Subcarpathian Rus to the Sich and the Hungarians, lawlessness and anarchy prevailed. Those were horrible days for us. There was shooting in the streets. The young people were thrilled someone had given them guns. Father wouldn't let us outside and we hid in the attic.

127 *Archive of USC Shoah Foundation*, interview with Natan Landau recorded 25 September 1997 by Julij Sternberg, translated from Russian by Jiřina Dvořáková.

Who was the Sich?
My high school principal, Baleckiy, I remember him to this day, was one of the leaders, actually even a minister in the Sich government. I can't say they were putting out anti-Semitic propaganda, no. But they did do anti-communist propaganda. I can see it like it was yesterday: there was a demonstration in the city centre. About five thousand people came. A Russian émigré former general was giving a speech on a balcony. He would've been around eighty, hardly able to stand. He pointed: "To the east against the Bolsheviks!" I remember that the Sich were staunchly anti-communist. When the Hungarians started the occupation, they gave them 24 hours: if you surrender your weapons, no one will touch you. But that didn't happen. Avgustyn Voloshyn[128] gave the order to defend ourselves. The Hungarians got the order to shoot everyone and the same day they were all shot. They died for Ukraine. And over the following days, almost a week, they carted off the bodies and buried them in mass graves. If you drove from Kopan to Khust today, you'd encounter a large memorial inscribed with the names of those who are known to have died fighting for a free Transcarpathia, for Transcarpathian Ukraine.

Did the Jews not have any armed groups of their own?
They did. One such group was formed in Khust, led by a guy named Hartstein, I remember him to this day. When they started attacking the synagogue with rocks and breaking the windows, the group put up resistance.

Did they have weapons?
They only had truncheons, the kind Czechoslovak and Hungarian gendarmes used. But the attackers didn't have guns either, just rocks, which they threw at the synagogue, at local residents. The Jewish group was able to fight back. Once they beat one of the attackers so bad, he had to go to the hospital. Then things calmed down a bit. But it was more the calm before the storm.

What followed?
Complete disaster followed soon after. My brother Moshe was the first to end up in a Hungarian work camp. I wanted to flee to the West, I wanted to go to Palestine like my brother, but I had no choice but to flee to Russia. So on 6 August 1940, without even saying goodbye to my parents, my siblings, my friends, anybody, I left for Maidan, where my mother was born. From there, there was a bus to Kolochava. That was close to the border.

---

128 Avgustyn Voloshyn – a former Czechoslovak MP and from 15 to 18 March 1939 the president and prime minister of Carpathian Ukraine. Arrested 15 May 1945 in Prague by the NKVD and taken to Moscow, where he died after a month of interrogation of a heart attack in Butyrka prison.

The former NKVD prison in Stryi. Part of the building holds a home for the elderly today. In the foreground is a monument to the victims of political repression. *ÚSTR / Adam Hradilek*

What led you to go to the Soviet Union?

I could see that disaster was inexorably approaching and that the Germans would occupy us. I was also influenced by Soviet propaganda and their "heaven on earth", where everyone had a job, was equal and was well off. Thus I decided to flee to the Soviet Union on 6 August 1940 to avoid the Nazi occupation of Transcarpathia. It was summer, all I took with me was photos of my parents and my girl, a good-quality Doxa watch, and three medals I'd won for sports in high school. Otherwise I was lightly dressed. I was wearing some light shoes, a jacket, I didn't even take a cap. There was an old Jew living in Kolochava who knew my father well. Not far from the border was a factory where they planed shingles, and he would drive them there. When I set out for the border at 5 in the morning, he advised me: "You'll go up about half an hour and there you'll see a stone. On one side will be ČSR and on the other PPLS – Pospolita Polska." It used to be Poland, but now it was the Soviet Union. I was supposed to come out somewhere near Nadvirna, but I couldn't see anything anywhere. I was exhausted. In the last house at the edge of the village of Verkhovynka, they gave me something to eat and packed me half a loaf of cornbread and sent a boy with me, who led me to the border and then went back. I sat on the border stone and thought about what to do next. After a while I noticed some smoke and headed for it. There were some people sitting around a fire. When I approached, dogs started barking. Two soldiers came at me with rifles. I told them, "Put away your weapons, I came to the Soviet Union voluntarily." They sat me down and I saw dark black bread for the first time. They cut me a slice, cut a slice of lard and said, "Here, take it." I had cigarettes with me, good ones, Egyptian, Vlasta brand, and I offered them one. The solider tossed it in the fire, took his tobacco, rolled a cigarette and said, "Here, smoke." It was embarrassing for me, but I took it, lit it, but as soon as I inhaled, I had a coughing fit and gave up. After about twenty minutes, one of them fired into the air and a commander with stripes rode up on a white horse. He circled the fire several times while looking at me. Then they told me, "Get up." One went in front with a rifle, me in the middle, and two in the back. I explained that I was a political emigrant, that I had fled fascism to the Soviet Union. I got nowhere though. The only answer was: "*Nichego*, all will be explained." That evening they locked me up in a horse stables with two other refugees. The horses were tied up on one side, we were on the other. There was a bit of hay, but of course we didn't sleep. I was thinking about how to get back, but it was already too late for that. They held us there three days. The next day they brought in another six people. They tossed us one big loaf of bread and two fish. One was full of larvae. I didn't eat the fish. I had some bread and water and was already hungry again. The body was young, it needed food.

What happened next?
They took us by narrow gauge to Skole, to a collection camp. There must have been about a thousand people there. There were huge barracks built there, with three- to four-level bunks. It was a breeding ground for lice. Two nights I sat on the doorstep and couldn't go inside. The third day I gave in, went inside, and immediately made friends with all of them. At first the lice bit a lot, it was horrible, I couldn't fall asleep for a second. But in three days I got used to it. They held us in Skole for three months. Sometime in November, they drove us by car to the prison in Stryi.

They didn't question you at all that whole time?
There was only one interrogation session, where I repeated that I was a political emigrant. The interrogations only started at the Stryi prison. They shut us up in the former prison church. There were a hundred and six of us there, which I remember exactly because every day they gave us one hundred and six rations of food. We slept on the bare floor. Once a day they took us on a twenty-minute walk. If you found half a brick on the walk, you'd have a pillow under your head for the night. At night we could only roll over on the other

side if we all did it at once. There were so many of us there that we were lying next to each other like sardines. They held us there until 21 May 1941, when they started carting off the prisoners from that area. I say prisoners even though no one tried us. Only later did the NKVD troika give me a piece of paper to sign saying: "Sentenced to three years for illegally crossing the border."

And how did they move you?
It lasted from midnight to the early morning. We went to the train along a path lined with soldiers with dogs on each side every five steps. They would count out forty people at each livestock wagon, have them board and then close it. They were these tiny wagons with pallets along the sides on which about half the people being transported could sit. We rode for a whole month. I could go on about it for a long time, but there's one particular story I want to tell. Naturally we were terribly hungry and somewhere in Belarus the train stopped at a station. Just like in the horse stable where the border guards were holding me, they tossed in one big loaf of bread, about four kilos, and one fish each. The fish were crawling with larvae. I implored the others: "Don't eat it, just eat the bread." We had a bit of water, two buckets full actually. One served as a *parasha*[129], the other was for drinking water. But once people had eaten, the water was gone in nothing flat. Three or four days they didn't give us a drop. The thirst is hard to describe. When you're hungry, you get weak, you fall down, but you can manage it. Being without water is something different though, it's horrible. Everyone had red eyes and looked like they had rabies. How fortunate I didn't eat the fish! Those who did, their eyes... It was a dreadful sight! The suffering when you're thirsty, hunger can't compare. We pounded on the wagon doors so hard that an NKVD officer came. I say, "Be so kind as to give us a few buckets of water. People are dying of thirst here. It's going to take us another hundred kilometres and half of them will be dead." And he responded, "It's water you want, is it?" And he stomped on my foot with his felt boot so hard that I fell to the ground in pain. One day we noticed that it wasn't dark. I had a friend there, his name was Spiegel, he ended up going to Israel. He woke me up at night one time and said, "Natan, look, it's still not getting dark!" We were approaching the north.

Where were they taking you?
After a month of suffering, we arrived at the river Pechora on 20 June 1941. There they unloaded us. We crossed the Pechora on foot. It was still frozen, so even in June tractors were driving along it. The guards took everything the people had. They said, "They'll give you the things when you get there,

129 Parasha – a bucket used as a toilet.

you'll get them there." My summer clothes were completely tattered. By the calendar it was summer, but I got a frostbitten toe there. Then came one of the worst experiences from Russia. Based on the transport wagons, they divided us into fourteen or eighteen groups, I don't remember exactly. My group was somewhere in the middle. At that point they finally gave us some water to drink. That was at Kozhva[130]. The water was ice-cold, I guess they took it from the river. Then the march started. They'd given us a drink, but we couldn't quench the mad thirst we'd suffered from a good two weeks. I don't understand how we managed to walk. I didn't even have a sweater or a real coat, just a summer jacket, torn trousers and light shoes. And dressed like that I walked thirty kilometres a day. Through the taiga where no one had been before us, through the snowdrifts. What's more, surrounded by guards who told us bluntly at the outset: "You make one step to the right, one step to the left, we'll shoot." My friend Spiegel said to me, "Natan, I can't go on." – "Sure you can, you'll make it." I don't know where I found the optimism in myself, but I infected everyone with it. I pulled Spiegel on, even though I could feel my own legs not working anymore; that I was losing my strength. We walked for eight days like that until we reached a place where there was nothing other than lots of snow. "This is where you're going to live," our commander told us. It was us against the taiga and our only tools were shovels, axes and crowbars. So I grab an axe and a shovel and say, "Anyone who wants to come with me, grab some tools. Nobody's going to help you with anything here." I had already figured out that we had to help each other ourselves, otherwise we were lost. About twelve or fifteen people joined me. "All right, friends, first we'll clear an area and make a fire. Then we'll build a dwelling." It was evening by the time we arrived, you see. I can't even describe what that first night was like. Those who couldn't go on during the journey and fell behind, we never saw again. It was said they were shot. In the morning we cleared a space and cut three big poles. There were these kind of skinny pines in the taiga, so we cut off the branches and laid them on the poles, forming a kind of shelter, a *zemlyanka*. How happy we were when we first entered it! Some fifty of us crammed inside, we covered the entrance with a coat, huddled together and massaged each other's feet. The next days we built more *zemlyankas*, in the end there were around ten of them. We lived there – I don't remember exactly – for a little over half a year.

Where was the camp roughly located?
About two hundred kilometres from Kozhva, to the north. As I found out, our task was to prepare the base for the workers who were supposed to come and

130 Kozhva – an important transport (rail and boat) hub on the river Pechora, which separates it from the town of Pechora, in the north of Russia.

Gulag prisoners while working on building the railroad. *Komi Republic National Archives*

build the railroad. Although we also ended up working on the railroad. It was called the NKVD Severo-Pechorskaya zheleznaya doroga.[131]

Had you been convicted at that time?
No. No one had told us anything yet. We knew we were prisoners. We still thought and dreamt about it just being temporary, that it was some kind of misunderstanding. And then they brought us this little piece of paper, this was at the colony, which was the ruling.

We'll get to the colony...
For a time we lived in those *zemlyankas*. In July and August, it started to get warmer and the snow ended up melting. But then another scourge arrived: the insects. They tortured us beyond belief, it was insane! Only the guards and high commanders had mosquito nets, they didn't give us anything. We took shelter as best we could. The constant attacks of mosquitoes were truly

131 Severo-Pechorskaya zheleznaya doroga – one of the largest construction works by the NKVD, falling under Sevzheldorlag, the Northern Railway Corrective Labour Camp in the north of Russia in the territory of today's Komi Republic.

dreadful. But you can get used to anything. Still, we were always scratching. Once we were at the colony, we worked on laying the railroad. It was awful work. The ground was frozen to two metres down, the rails sometimes cracked at night from the frost, so we had to replace them at temperatures of forty below. That was between Oshper and Amshor or Abez and Bugry.[132] We worked eighteen hours a day. Wake-up call was at four in the morning and at five, after counting the prisoners, they led us to work. Every brigade was accompanied by two guards. In the morning we got our food rations based on how each had worked, which was determined by the group leader. At that time, the largest ration was 600 grams per day and the smallest for what were called the *filons*, who worked poorly, was 300 grams. In the morning they gave us *balanda*, a porridge made of a bit of barley or wheat. They also gave us frozen turnip. That's a beet for livestock. And sometimes they'd make a soup out of it. In the morning we also got boiling water. Because of the lack of vitamins, scurvy broke out, which is a disease of the gums, which start to bleed. Then people couldn't eat, bite. And from the lack of food they came down with pellagra.[133] I remember those two camp diseases to date. Pellagra is also an illness where you literally dry up. You dry up like a rusk and then you don't even need to eat. You completely dry up and die.

Were you ever in the hospital?
Once I ended up at the *lagpom*, that was like a kind of hospital. It was run by a former prisoner, one Ivan Yakolevich. He was a good and decent man. We became friends, so he took me in at the infirmary so I could rest a bit and get something to eat. They'd carry five or six dead bodies out of the infirmary every night. I remember how one night the man to my left died, he was lying right next to me. By morning my neighbour to the right was dead too.

How did you feel about people dying right next to you?
Today I'd take it tragically, but there, you looked at things differently than in the normal world. He just died, he got it over with, I had to keep living. People did have problems after death, though, too. The ground was frozen solid and they couldn't have a proper burial, so what they did was take five or six bodies and make a pyre out of them. Then in the spring, when the ground thawed a bit, they led our whole brigade to a completely different spot and said, "So, dig a hole for us here, we're going to have a fridge here." That's what they told us. Then they threw the dead bodies in, sprinkled some lime or chlorine on

132 Oshper, Amshor, Abez, Bugry – settlements between today's cities of Pechora and Vorkuta in the Komi Republic.

133 Pellagra – a form of avitaminosis, the accompanying symptoms of which include extensive skin deformation and diarrhoea.

them and covered them with dirt. Thus they buried them all at once. They didn't even lay them in, just tossed them there. They made about three or four rows of five. For the guards we were numbers. Everyone tried to survive, to make their life at least a bit easier in any way. Sometimes they were helped by happenstance, other times you couldn't be afraid and had to accept an offer of a job you didn't even know how to do. For example, once this guy came to us prisoners and said: "Who here can write Russian?" I volunteered. "Come with me then." So for about two months I ended up delivering groceries from Kozhva to Vorkuta.

What kind of things?
For example, barrels that were supposed to contain fish. Instead they stank of horse guts though. They would make soup out of it in the kitchen. The only part of beef we got was the horns and tails. That's what they fed us. I don't remember ever eating potatoes. There were barley groats, a few groats in the *balanda*, wheat, frozen turnip, they would sometimes give us that as a kind of second meal. To fight scurvy we'd tear off branches with pine needles, put them in a barrel, pour boiling water on them and let it steep. That helped a bit against scurvy. But there was nothing against pellagra. People just died. I'd say that only those who really wanted to live survived.

What kind of people did you meet there, who were you friends with?
Of the prisoners there was a guy named Stambler, the former secretary of General Tukhachevsky[134]. A very smart man. At that time, he was thirty-five, but he looked sixty. At first he got the death sentence, they had taken him to be executed twice, but then they changed the sentence to twenty-five years in the Gulag. You know what for? When they arrested Tukhachevsky, Stambler said he couldn't be an enemy of the people. I also met the editor-in-chief of the magazine of the Jewish social democratic party Bund from Warsaw. He was a very interesting man. He taught me a bit of English. Aside from Polish, he knew German and French very well. Once he told me: "Natan, I know you're going to get out of here, you're going to live. I have one request of you. When you get free, go to Lviv, there's a street Kollontaja 10, where my family lived. If you find anyone there, tell them you saw me on this and this day in 1943, that I was still alive." When I returned home in 1946, thanks to my job I often travelled to Lviv with tourist expeditions. So I went to the address. But I didn't find anyone and no one around knew anything about his family. There was a Polish boy with us too, everyone considered him a nutcase because he would tell us things we couldn't believe. He described how members of the

134 Mikhail Tukhachevsky – a prominent commander of the Soviet army who was executed during the Great Terror in 1937.

The Sevzheldorlag headquarters responsible for building the railroad to Vorkuta and thus for running the individual camps located along the track being built. *CVG collection*

NKVD would rape the locked-up girls and women. After the war, it turned out to be true. You can't imagine what happened after the war. They started bringing in children from the occupied areas, that is to say girls, fourteen, fifteen, sixteen. At that time, I was at the last camp in Abez. Today it's a kind of largish village. They turned all those girls into prostitutes. Why? Because they'd sleep with anyone for a bit of bread. Such children were taken... Stalin ordered: "They're from the occupied areas and they have no place in our society, they must live separately." A lot more could be said about that camp...

When did they finally inform you of your verdict?
Not until Abez. As I already mentioned, they gave us a little piece of paper stating we are sentenced to three years for illegally crossing the Soviet border. We said to ourselves, "OK, but three years is already up, it's 1943 now. They should let us out already." Some went to ask about it. "So it's freedom you want!" was the response they got and they immediately sent them to a penal colony. I suppose to avoid unnecessary fuss and false hopes, they brought us another strip piece of paper. On it was written: "You are detained until the end of the war." But in 1945, the war had already ended. Thus I went to what was called the "third ward", which everyone was afraid of, they called it the

"Beria ward". There I got my release, and so I managed to survive the last year. All day I could walk around Abez freely, but at six in the evening I had to return to the *zona*[135]. It wasn't quite that I could go wherever I wanted. They decided where I could go. I couldn't take a step outside of Abez, and definitely not leave for somewhere else. I took courage and went to see the commander again. "What do you want?" I say, "Citizen Commander, the war ended half a year ago. I finished my three-year sentence and then spent another three years in the camp. I'd like to know what's going to happen with my release." – "So you want to be free?" And he waved his hand. "Fine, then." He pressed a button and in came an NKVD officer with a rifle. "This man wants to be free, so set him free." All I could think of was that they were going to shoot me. But no, they took me to a penal colony for asking about my release.

What did the penal colony look like?
It was ruled by *zhuliks*[136] and *urkas*[137]. It was horrible there. But somehow I managed to adapt there too. There were five hundred people at the colony, of which two hundred didn't work. They were in league with the guards and helped the shift leaders to herd out all the weak people to work for them. That was the penal colony. Plus there were special rules there. For example, at six in the evening you had to be in bed in the barracks or a tent. Overall the regime was stricter than at the labour camp. They held me there three months. Then they sent me back to the camp. It turned out that the head of the infirmary, Ivan Yakovlevich, had interceded for me to be released from there. But the real bosses were the crooks and criminals. They could do anything. They didn't go to work and at night they'd rob the people who were sleeping like rocks after eighteen hours of hard labour. To help you understand what kind of power they had, I'll tell you a story. There were four-level bunks in the camp, and one time at night, when everyone was asleep, one *zhulik* starts snooping around. I open my eyes and he shows me his blade, like if I let out a peep, he'll slit my throat. I didn't make a sound. He rummaged through everyone's things. The people were fast asleep. After eighteen hours of work, of course they were tired. And these guys didn't go to work. They ran the joint. Once time I found myself in the midst of a group of those criminals. One of them says to me, "Son, you're not going to work today, you're going to guard something for us." – "What do you mean, not going to work? The shift leader will kill me." He says, "Don't worry about that." So I stayed. The shift leader came, took a look at me and didn't say anything. I understood they were in league.

135 Zona – the area managed by the camp.
136 Zhulik – swindler, petty thief.
137 Urka – criminal prisoner.

Gulag prisoners cart trailings out of a coal mine in one of the Vorkutlag camps beyond the Arctic Circle, 1940s. *Komi Republic National Museum*

To be honest, I was so busy with work at the camp and so tired after work that I don't remember much of it. Just details. For example, there was this Tatar sleeping on the pallet next to me. Once he got a kettle of oats. He cooked it and ate it overnight. In the morning it was time to go to work and he says to me, "Natan, take my cap." He couldn't move. And that day he died. That evening they buried him. A big, strong man he was. That whole six years I couldn't figure it out. I was hungry the whole time too, there was no way not to be hungry. You couldn't live off that 300, 400 or 600 grams. No vitamins, no fats – we didn't get any of that. I was hungry and weak the whole time too. Some would go to the trash heap and pick out the potato skins or herring heads, then they'd cook it and eat it. Hunger will make a man do anything. I never dug through the trash looking for rotten or frozen peels from beets or turnips like the other prisoners. At the camp I also never believed anything they told us, promised us. When they were on the run and the Germans were knocking at Moscow's door, heading for the Caucasus, and Leningrad was under siege, they reduced our already humble food rations. They said it had to be sacrificed for the army, but in the future it would be better. I knew they were lying. That they didn't care in the least, and if we died of hunger, they wouldn't give a damn. They cut back the bread rations even more. And people started dropping. It was around minus 26 degrees, we were working sixteen, eighteen hour days, and we worked under such conditions constantly, even after the Germans were defeated at Stalingrad and the Soviets were driving them back west.

Where did you get the strength?
From the age of five, I was involved in all kinds of sports, other than boxing. And that sports training helped me. I was prepared for the camp. For example, while carrying the logs, the snow was up to our waists. I knew I had to have the load once on the left and once on the right. So the strain was spread. And I was always trying to move, even though I was very weak. Even in the prison I would crawl to the window every morning to breathe in the fresh air and exercise a bit. The same at the camp in my quarters, otherwise you would start to slip, not just physically but also mentally. Which I could see around me. Lots of prisoners were thinking about chopping off their hand or otherwise injuring themselves, crippling themselves. I never considered it. I wanted to survive and, if possible, remain myself.

You didn't sign up for the Czechoslovak army?
Oh no, we did apply to join to the army. That was in 1943, when word came to the camp that there was a representative of President Beneš[138] in the Soviet

138 Most likely Colonel Heliodor Píka – from 1941 the head of the Czechoslovak Military Mission to the Soviet Union. This former legionnaire and supporter of the democratic regime was executed after returning home and the communist coup on 21 June 1949.

Union recruiting men from Subcarpathia into the Czechoslovak army. I was overjoyed that I would be getting out of the camp. I thought, better to die on the front lines than rot here! That's why we all immediately wrote up an application. They didn't take a single Jew though. Not that the Czechs wouldn't take Jews, but the NKVD didn't want to let us go. They needed us to work for them.

You were still in the Gulag in the first post-war years?
They released us, but it wasn't that simple. The commander called me in and said: "You're free. But, Natan, where will you go now? You've got a record here now, that you were in a camp. You can't wash that clean. But we'll help you out. You'll get married, we'll give you some land and you'll live here. You know civilians don't have such a bad life here." To that I responded: "I want to go home. I haven't seen my siblings in years. I know I don't have a father and mother anymore, but I want to go home." They spent three months persuading me. Finally they said: "Fine then..." At that time, I had no idea my brother Filip was submitting requests for my release all the way to state prosecutor Vishinsky, who was a big deal in the party. So they invited me to the third ward. Shivers went down your spine when they invited you to that feared section. There was some senior officer there and he pointed to a map of the Soviet Union with the words, "Choose where you want to go." I took courage and responded: "Where? I want to go home, to Transcarpathia." – "You can't go there." – "Why not?" – "Just because. We don't release prisoners to the areas where they were sentenced. Pick something else." So I said: "Give me the Lviv Oblast." – "You can't go there either. That's on the border with Transcarpathia, it's impossible." – "But why not, I want to be close to my family." – "Cool it," he quipped and I knew I had to be quiet. In the end, I said: "Well then put me wherever you want." – "No, no, you have to choose yourself." I looked at the map again and said: "Then give me the Chernihiv Oblast, put me in Chernihiv." – "What? You want to go to the regional capital?" – "Then put me in Nizhyn, that's in the Chernihiv Oblast too." – "That's the district capital, you can't go there either. Pick some village." They offered me a phone list of the villages in the Chernihiv Oblast. I flipped through it for a bit and then said: "Zarichchya then. Put me in Zarichchya." – "Fine." So I arrived in Zarichchya. And I go into the party office. There's a few propaganda posters on the wall there on the topic "What will be in five years?" A new post-war five-year plan was starting in 1946. They asked me what I knew how to do. I responded, anything you need. "We need new posters painted." I said, "Do you have brushes and paint?" – "If we had brushes and paint, we'd paint it ourselves!" Which reminded me of an experience from the camp. In Abez our unit leader once said: "I need you to reap a stack of hay." There were six of us, so I responded: "Fine, but give us at least one scythe." – "If we had a scythe, we'd cut it ourselves!" They gave us some rusty rings from a barrel. So we

wrapped some rags around our hands cut the hay. In Zarichchya I told them: "Give me a tuft of horse mane or tail and I'll paint." I attached the horsehair to a stick by some threads and made a brush. In a month I'd painted the party office up par excellence. I picked the subject matter out of the newspaper. So, there'll be millions of tonnes of coal, steel too, three times as much gold as today, just the promises and visions of the Soviet five-year plan.

What did a post-war Soviet village look like?
It was mostly just girls and women living there. If you met a man, he was a disabled veteran, a cripple. The rest of the men either worked for the NKVD or the Communist Party. As a painter of ideological topics, I got a little card from the head of the Party office that allowed me to go to a special canteen, where they cooked better and had bigger portions as well. I lived in the home of an older widow, where I had a room for myself. Once on a Sunday, she invited me for lunch. She slaughtered a hen and made a proper lunch. The soup pot sat in the middle of the table and around it wooden spoons. They didn't use cutlery. Whenever I didn't finish something, say bread, or left a bit of meat on the bone, she would take it and finish it after me, or give the rest to the children. The people there lived in great poverty, but they accepted me among them. They didn't care that I was a former *zek*, a Gulag prisoner, an enemy of the people.

What was it like with women at the camp actually?
In terms of the camp, in my whole six years there I only saw one woman, the commander's wife. Sometimes she would secretly give me a piece of bread or bit of liver. Maybe they put something in our food, I don't know, but at the camp I had no need for women, I didn't even think about it. But when I was delivering groceries for two months and had a full belly, that's when I desired women. And there was one! One night, we stopped somewhere in Bugry or in Oshper, some smaller station, and my superior says: "Natan, go and bring us two girls." I found two Lithuanian girls there. One was very pretty and young, maybe eighteen. The other was roughly the same age, but a bit heavy-set. I brought them to our wagon, where we had a *teplushka*, a room to sleep in. The young and slim one sat on my bed and the other went to the commander. The poor girls were terribly hungry and so we gave them herring, bread, onion. I felt bad when I saw how hungry they were, remembering that I had been the exact same way just a few weeks before. Then we turned off the lamp and did the deed. Then the commander said: "Turn on the light! Now we'll switch." The other one didn't appeal to me anymore though, so I told her: "I'll let you be, I can't anymore."

Let's go back to Zarichchya. How did you end up getting out?
The Party leader was pretty kind. He also appreciated me for the nice political painting I'd done. So after some time he wrote me a letter of recommendation to Chernihiv, where the district leadership of the Communist Party was based. I arrived there and said to some high-ranking Bolshevik: "Listen, I came to the Soviet Union voluntarily. You've been convinced that I'm not a spy. I've done nothing wrong. I served six years in the Gulag, and I worked well after my release in Zarichchya as well. But now I want to go home." He looked me up and down for a moment and then said: "We don't usually let people go home. But for once... Ah, fine!" And he gave me a pass. A kind of form with a red stripe. I couldn't believe my eyes! I immediately ran to the main post office and sent my brother a telegram. On my way home, they stole all my things on the train. I had one tattered officer's coat, old boots, and three days' worth of bread. They stole it all. I returned from the Soviet Union without any belongings. Well, from the Soviet Union... Transcarpathia was now part of the Soviet Union. I got home 25 April 1946. I'd been away for three months short of six years. Today I remember it fondly. I guess I needed the Gulag, because it hardened me. I'm eighty-one years old and I'm still working.

MIKULÁŠ (ZVI) FAERBER

Born 28 May 1916 in Khust. His father died in 1925 and his mother raised eight children by herself. Before the war, he worked in Moravian Ostrava as a lathe operator, also graduating from a technical trade school there. When the Hungarians started to occupy Subcarpathian Rus in 1939, he decided to flee to the Soviet Union. This saved him from serving in the work units of the Hungarian army, or from a potential transport to Auschwitz, where his mother, one of his brothers, his sister and two nephews were taken. He crossed the border along with communist Alexander Velichko on 18 October 1939. Both were immediately arrested by an NKVD border patrol. They were imprisoned in Skole and Stanyslaviv and subsequently convicted to three years in the Gulag for illegally crossing the border. They transported him to the Kandalakshlag camp beyond the northern Arctic Circle in the Murmansk Oblast on the Kola Peninsula, then to a labour camp near Kotlas after his sentence ended. After being released from the Gulag, he was sent to the Czechoslovak military unit in Sadhora. On 10 November 1944 he was enlisted and assigned to the reserve regiment. Later they sent him for accounting sergeant training. He did not take part in direct fighting. He was demobilised in Levoča shortly after the war ended – 15 May 1945. In the same year he married his pre-war girlfriend, who survived Auschwitz. They settled in Teplice-Šanov, where he worked as a national administrator in commercial shipping. In 1949, he left with his

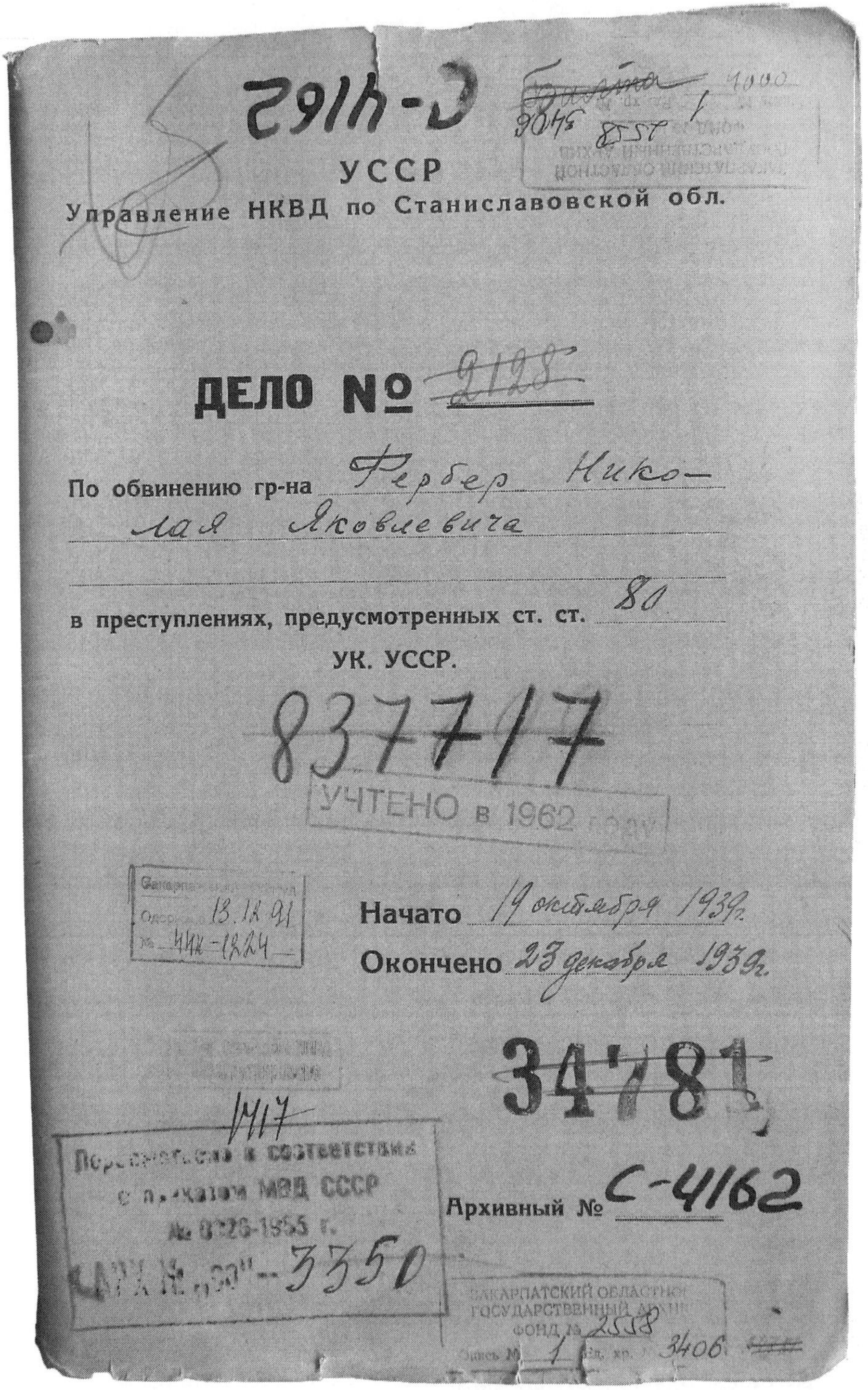

С-4162

УССР

Управление НКВД по Станиславовской обл.

ДЕЛО № ~~2128~~

По обвинению гр-на Фербер Николая Яковлевича

в преступлениях, предусмотренных ст. ст. 80

УК. УССР.

~~837717~~

УЧТЕНО в 1962 году

Начато 19 октября 1939 г.

Окончено 23 декабря 1939 г.

~~34781~~

Архивный № С-4162

Пересмотрено в соответствии с приказом МВД СССР № 0026-1955 г.

АРХ. № „ОО"—3350

ЗАКАРПАТСКИЙ ОБЛАСТНОЙ ГОСУДАРСТВЕННЫЙ АРХИВ
ФОНД № 2558
Опись № 1 Ед. хр. 3406

The cover page of the NKVD investigation file for Mikuláš Faerber. *DAZO*

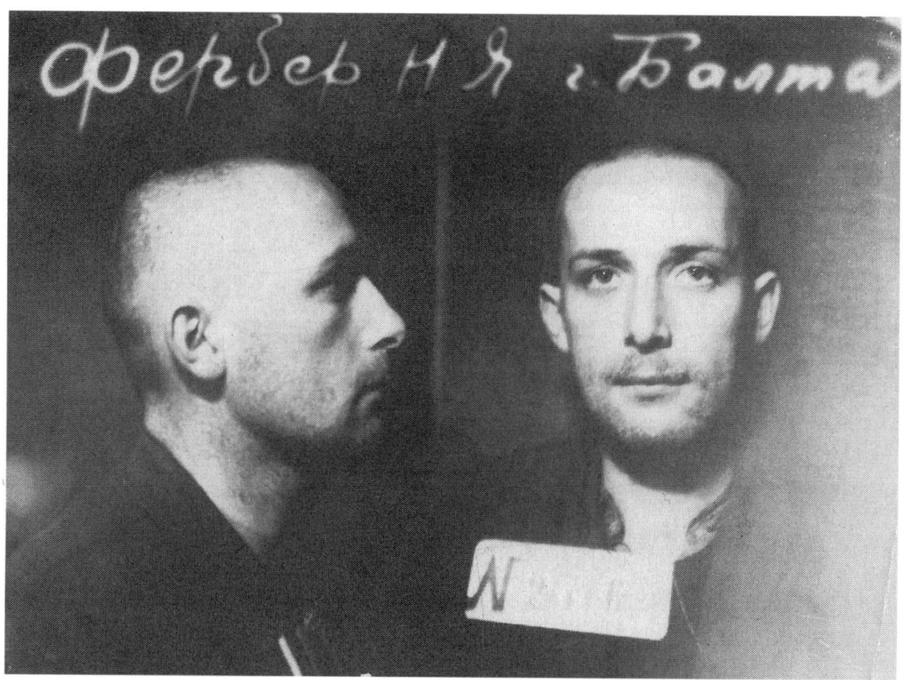

A photograph of Mikuláš Faerber made shortly after being arrested in Soviet territory. *DAZO*

wife, two brothers and sister to Israel, where he worked as a labourer and driver.[139]

— — —

When and where did you cross the border?

It was 18 October 1939. I travelled to the border with Poland, at that time already western Ukraine, and there I ran into Alexander Velichko from Khust, whose father was the secretary of the Communist Party. He told me that as a Jew I could ask another Jew and they would surely advise us on how to get to the other side. So I asked an acquaintance and he told us to go to a village about five kilometres away. It was called Prislop and there was supposed to be a Jewish family living there that would allegedly help us across the border. We set out in that direction and on the way we met some girls, also Jewish, who were returning home to Prislop. We asked them how far it was. The girls were afraid to talk to us, however. I told them I was a Jew and that we wanted to go to this and that family that was supposed to help us cross the border. But they were afraid and claimed I wasn't a Jew. So I told them they

139 *Yad Vashem Archive*, interview with Mikuláš (Zvi) Faerber recorded 7 March 1970 by Erich Kulka.

could see for themselves that I knew a few words of Hebrew because I went to a Jewish school. Then I said a few words in Hebrew, which one of the girls understood and thus believed me that I was a Jew. She said that there were Hungarian troops outside the village, which was a short distance from the border. And that no one could get through without a pass. I had a little piece of paper with me that had various words in Hungarian on it. I decided to use it. There really were troops outside the village. When they asked where we were going, I responded: "This is my assistant and we're supposed to re-write the signs from Ukrainian to Hungarian." They said, "That's good, we've been sitting here a long time and we can't read anything." We got to the family with no problem. They sent for some guy named Ivan who was supposed to take us across the border. We didn't sleep at all that night and when Ivan arrived at two in the morning, we set out. Before that I wrote a few words of goodbye to my mother, saying they should only send it if we managed to cross the border.

Did you pay this Ivan anything?
I gave him ten pengő.[140] At the first settlement, some Ukrainian women showed us where the mayor lived. We went to report ourselves to him. The mayor naturally asked where we were from. Velichko said from Khust. He was also interested in what religion we were. Velichko declared he did not subscribe to any religion, that he was a communist and wasn't baptised. I said I was a Jew. He started shouting that they don't need Jews. I was afraid of him, plus I wasn't a communist like Velichko. Then the mayor called two police officers to take us to the NKVD station. We thought we were free but a soldier on horseback guarded us the whole way. So we reached Skole on foot, where they locked us up. People from the NKVD were in charge there. In the room sat a single man, about fifty. I think his rank was major. He asked my name. Then he started asking where I was from, what nation I belonged to. I told him I was a Jew. He responded in Jewish that I should go back. I thought he considered me a spy and that's why he was telling me to go home. Then it occurred to me that he wanted to send me back with some material for the communists. I told him I was afraid the Hungarians would catch me on the border and then kill my mother, brothers and me. And also that I came to Russia to work there and then join the army. That I wanted to fight against the Germans. He responded that he could get me across the border and I had no need to fear. He could see I was hesitating, so he called in his subordinate. When I was leaving his office, I wanted to say something else, but he didn't want to talk to me anymore. By December 1939 I was already in prison in Stanyslaviv, where they interrogated me again.

140 Pengő – the Hungarian currency in 1927–1946.

Форма № 2.

ПОЛ М

Фамилия Фербер Д. форм.

Имя Николай

Отчество Якубович Год рождения 1916

Место рождения г. Хуст [illegible] Венгрия

ПРАВАЯ РУКА

1. Большой	2. Указательный	3. Средний	4 Безымянный	5. Мизинец
	16		8	

Линия 16 перегиба 8 4

ЛЕВАЯ РУКА

6. Большой	7. Указательный	8. Средний	9. Безымянный	10 Мизинец
4		2		1

Линия перегиба 2 1

КОНТРОЛЬНЫЙ ОТТИСК

Левой руки	Правой руки

Подпись зарегистрированного Фербер

Карта заполнена „27" января 1940 г.

В тюрьме НКВД г. Балта

— (указать где и в каком органе НКВД)

Карту составил дактилоскопист (должность и подпись)

Проверил

ПРИМЕЧАНИЕ: В верхней половине карты, на лицевой стороне, в каждом квадратике должны быть прокатаны пальцы. В нижней половине — в квадратах под надписью „Контрольный оттиск" помещаются не прокатанные оттиски 4-х пальцев каждой руки без большого.

сестры Амалия живет в Нью-Йорке, Франчишка – в Румынии [illegible]

Fingerprints taken from Mikuláš Faerber following his arrest. *DAZO*

3 .- 13

ОТВЕТ :
Нет, я был только в коммунистической партии и билет у меня был коммунистической партии в других партиях я не был.

ВОПРОС:
Выше вы указали, что безвыездно проживали в м.Хусты до дня перехода границы. А теперь говорите, что вы работали на фабрике Ваверка в м.Дипник в 1937 году и там-же вступили в коммунистическую партию. Кроме того раз"езжали по городам с какой-то труппой артистов около семи месяцев.
Уточните это обстоятельство ?

ОТВЕТ :
Мать моя проживает в м.Хусти безвыездно, я-же периодически, не на длительное время выезжал на работу в другие города, например: До 1931 г. я жил в м.Хусти, а с 1931 по 1934г. занимался в фабричной школе в м.Севркш, с 1934 по 1935г. жил в м.Хусти, с 1935г. пять-шесть месяцев я работал в г.Бырна, в 1936г. работал около 5-ти мес. в г.Моравска - острова. В 1937 году работал на фабрике в м.Липник, около 7 мес, в 1938г. месяцев 7 ездил с трупой артистов. В 1939 году по день перехода границы проживал в м.Хусти.

ВОПРОС:
Когда и при каких обстоятельствах Вы перешли границу из Венгрии на территорию Западной Украины?

ОТВЕТ :
В 1939 году я работал у кустаря маляра, который устанавливал указатели на трактовых дорогах. 16 октября 1939 года я выехал велосипедом из м.Хусти по направлению к границе Западной Украины с целью подправить указатели на дороге. 17 октября 1939 года я прибыл в пограничное село Торунь, где встретился со своим знакомым ВЕЛИЧКО Александром, я спросил его почему он здесь, последний рассказал мне, что он прибыл в пограничное село с целью уйти нелегально на территорию Западной Украины и предложил мне итти вместе с ним, на что я дал согласие. После чего мы отправились в соседнее село тоже пограничное, там переночевали у одной еврейки - Суры , фамилии ее я не знаю, последняя дала нам проводника и в 2 часа ночи 18 октября 1939 года мы перешли границу на территорию Западной Украины.

ВОПРОС:
С какой целью Вы прибыли в советский союз и какие причины послужили Вашему переходу границы ?

ОТВЕТ :
Причиной моего перехода в Советский Союз является то, что евреев в Венгрии преследуют,

A page of the transcript from the interrogation of Mikuláš Faerber with questions about the circumstances of crossing the border into the USSR. *DAZO*

Were there Czechoslovaks among the prisoners?
I only ran into a Czechoslovak once. It was the Komsomol member Iza Feldman of Khust. The Russians had tasked him with monitoring the prisoners and reporting whether there were any Polish officers hidden among them. For that, he got more bread. Then they transported us by train from Stanyslaviv to Balta[141]. I had serious health problems at the time, my stomach ached something awful and I couldn't eat anything for a week. When I had recovered somewhat, they transported me to Dnepropetrovsk, where I was tried. The trial went as follows: To start with, the judge asked my name. Then he said: "You are sentenced to three years of labour in a penal camp for illegally crossing the border. Do you understand? Sign it!" That was the whole trial. He didn't ask about anything else, didn't offer the option of appealing, nothing. As soon as I had signed the verdict, they put me in a car and it was off to Kharkiv. From Kharkiv I was transported by train to Kandalaksha in the south of the Kola Peninsula. There were one to two thousand of us.

Where there any Czechoslovaks on the transport?
There was one, his name was Levička, he got five years. He declared himself a Komsomol member, so they gave him a higher sentence. The thing where they say: "Why'd you come here, you should've kept working away at home." Factory owners and merchants got even higher sentences, eight years. Like one older man from Moravian Ostrava by the name of Halzer. He was a capitalist, so they sentenced him to eight years. He also went to Kandalaksha.

How long did the trip take?
We travelled for three to five days in closed wagons, guarded by soldiers. We went through Moscow and also past Leningrad. For food they gave us pickled herring. We got to Kandalaksha I think in August 1941. Only about half the camp had been built, just wooden barracks with around two thousand prisoners living in them.

Where there multiple such camps in the area?
I heard about others, but I didn't see them. The first week after arriving, we were in quarantine. There they taught us that we had to abide by Stalin's slogan: "He who does not work, neither shall he eat." During quarantine they also explained to us the work quotas, which were related to the rationing of food. The size of the daily ration was governed by the work done. Each barrack housed thirty people, who made up a brigade. There was one brigadier for those thirty people.

141 Balta – a city in Ukraine 200 km north of Odessa.

Выписка из протокола № 64

Особого Совещания при Народном Комиссаре Внутренних Дел СССР

от „10" июля 1940 г.

СЛУШАЛИ	ПОСТАНОВИЛИ
65. Дело № 2128/УНКВД Станислав. обл., по обвин. ФЕРБЕР Николая Яковлевича, 1916 г.р., ур. с. Хуст (Венгрия), еврей, [illegible] подданства, со слов был чл. компартии, токарь.	ФЕРБЕР Николая Яковлевича за нелегальный переход госграницы – заключить в исправительно-трудовой лагерь сроком на ТРИ года сч. срок с [illegible] декабря [illegible]

Нач. Секретариата Особого Совещания
при Народном Комиссаре Внутренних Дел СССР

Excerpt from the verdict report, with the transport destination handwritten as Sevzheldorlag – place of internment. *DAZO*

They were chosen from among the prisoners?

Yes. Our brigadier was a Jew form Poland. We walked to work under the supervision of a guard. We were building a factory there. The Russians said they were going to make planes in it. The work was very hard and the food pitiful. I knew several Jews there, one was from Subcarpathian Rus, his name was Jakubovitz. There were also doctors there, for example Doctor Neuer (see p. 94). I didn't know him, but I heard that he spoke Rusyn like me, which indicated he could be from Czechoslovakia. I went to him and told him that I didn't have a fever, but I felt awful, I had no strength, and asked whether he could let me stay home. When someone had a high temperature, they didn't have to go to work the next day and could stay in the barracks. He asked me where I was from. I answered from Czechoslovakia, from Khust. That saved me. He took me into the hospital and made me an orderly.

Was the work manageable?

The cruel winter was terrible. We went to work all the way down to minus 45. We could only stay home when the temperature fell to minus 46. The work was highly physically demanding. Lots of people died, mostly from breathing problems. The food rations were not sufficient for such heavy work. But whoever didn't meet the quota or didn't work due to illness, got even less – just

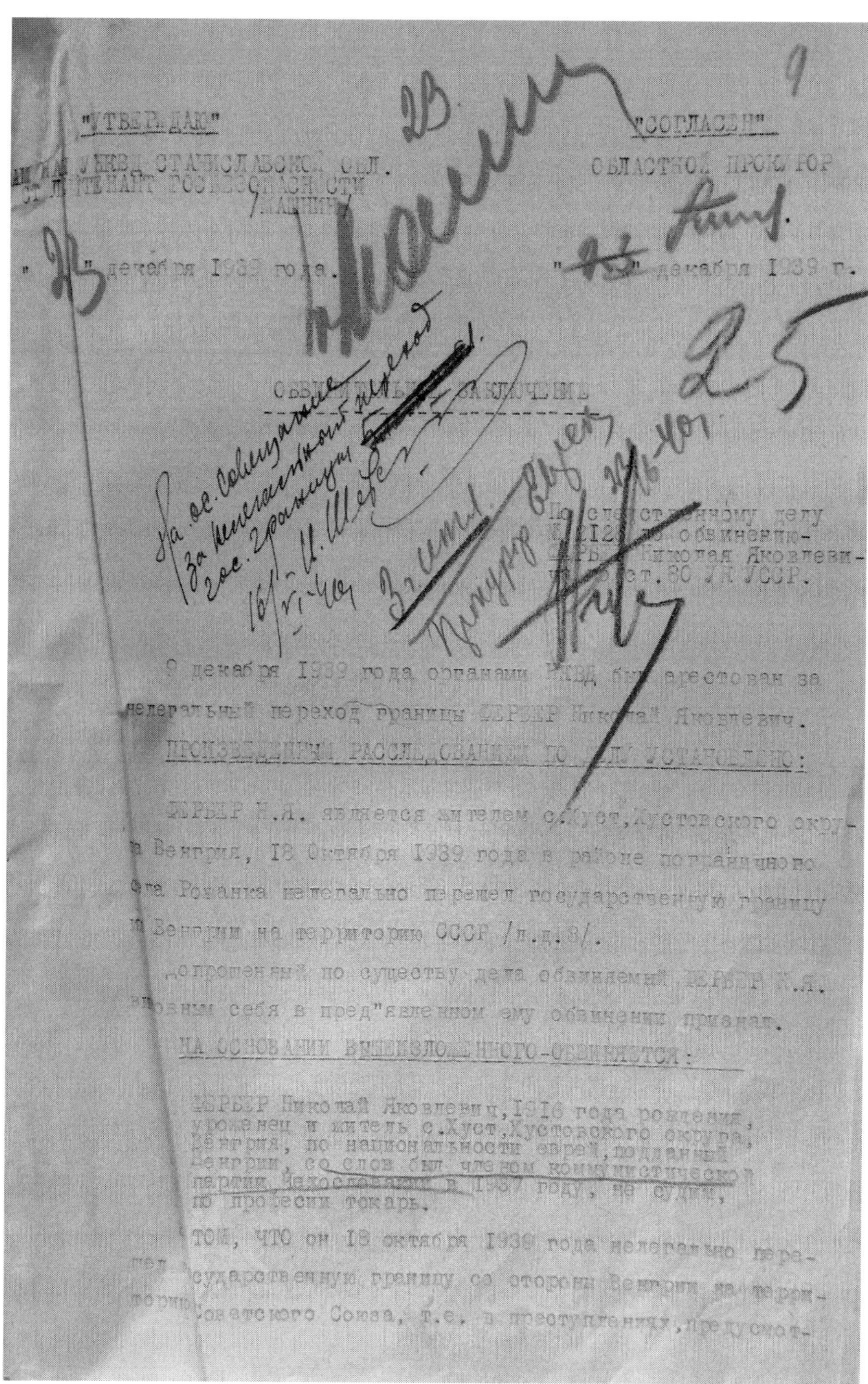

"УТВЕРЖДАЮ"
НАЧ. УНКВД СТАНИСЛАВСКОЙ ОБЛ.
СТ. ЛЕЙТЕНАНТ ГОСБЕЗОПАСНОСТИ
[illegible]

"23" декабря 1939 года.

"СОГЛАСЕН"
ОБЛАСТНОЙ ПРОКУРОР

"23" декабря 1939 г.

ОБВИНИТЕЛЬНОЕ ЗАКЛЮЧЕНИЕ

По следственному делу
№ [illegible] по обвинению
ФЕРБЕР Николая Яковлевича по ст. 80 УК УССР.

9 декабря 1939 года органами НКВД был арестован за нелегальный переход границы ФЕРБЕР Николай Яковлевич.

ПРОИЗВЕДЕННЫМ РАССЛЕДОВАНИЕМ ПО ДЕЛУ УСТАНОВЛЕНО:

ФЕРБЕР Н.Я. является жителем с.Хуст, Хустовского округа Венгрия, 18 Октября 1939 года в районе пограничного [illegible]а Роганка нелегально перешел государственную границу из Венгрии на территорию СССР /л.д.8/.

Допрошенный по существу дела обвиняемый ФЕРБЕР Н.Я. виновным себя в пред"явленном ему обвинении признал.

НА ОСНОВАНИИ ВЫШЕИЗЛОЖЕННОГО-ОБВИНЯЕТСЯ:

ФЕРБЕР Николай Яковлевич, 1916 года рождения, уроженец и житель с.Хуст, Хустовского округа, Венгрия, по национальности еврей, подданный Венгрии, со слов был членом коммунистической партии Чехословакии в 1937 году, не судим, по професии токарь.

В ТОМ, ЧТО он 18 октября 1939 года нелегально перешел государственную границу со стороны Венгрии на территорию Советского Союза, т.е. в преступлениях, предусмот-

The sentence giving Mikuláš Faerber three years of forced labour in Gulag camps. *DAZO*

300 grams of bread a day, and then they didn't have any strength at all. The Poles tried to run away. But usually they caught them and returned them to camp. Some made it to the Finnish border, which was about eighty kilometres from the work camp. They told us they were almost at the border, but they were so frozen they weren't able to keep walking. They saw a kind of cottage nearby, where they met an old man, his son and grandson. The grandfather and son helped them, but apparently the grandson reported them to the NKVD. So they brought them back with frostbite on all their toes and added another eight years to their sentence.

And how did you get out of the camp?
When the Germans started bombing the camp, we had to leave it. The Germans ended up occupying it. They evacuated some of the prisoners to Central Asia and the rest, including me, to Kotlas in the Arkhangelsk Oblast. There we were building the railway to Vorkuta beyond the Arctic Circle by the White Sea. The work was even worse than before. There were thousands of people working there from Lithuania, from Romania, from Hungary, plus a lot of Russians as well. There was a camp every five kilometres there. Either on the right or on the left of the tracks.

Vorkuta was known for its harsh living conditions. When someone died, did they notify their relatives?
As far as I know, none of the relatives ever received such a letter. Though there were doctors in every camp, when someone fell ill, got weak and couldn't work, they'd lock them up in the camp prison, where they only got 300 grams of bread a day and *kipyatok*, hot water. And when they saw the prisoner was dying, they no longer gave them any food at all, just *kipyatok*. Even so, they'd load those poor wretches on a sleigh, tie them on like a parcel, and drive them to the work site. But they didn't have any strength left whatsoever, so they just sat there. And everyone waited for them to die. Then they'd cart them back in the evening, dead. The camp commander couldn't afford to have prisoners staying at the camp. Everything was recorded, so it was in his interest there be as few prisoners as possible staying behind at the camp. He had to show that everyone was working. If a prisoner was out of the camp, it meant they were working.

Why didn't they send such cases to the hospital? You said they had them at the big camps.
Sometimes they really did cart them off. But that meant they would kill the weak and ill somewhere along the way. Outwardly it looked like they were sending them for treatment. But it never happened they would take someone away from the camp and that person would come back. I never experienced such a case, and I was at several camps.

How did you even endure?
They kept saying we had to work, so I worked and I got fed. And again, I got a bit lucky. I got to know one Ukrainian prisoner. He'd been sentenced to twenty years as a kulak and was afraid of the Russian prisoners, those kind of ordinary thieves and black marketeers who didn't like kulaks or political prisoners and beat them up. This Ukrainian was a brigadier and was interested in Czechoslovakia, so he assigned me lighter work. In the end, my sentence ended and on 9 December 1942 they released me. I was one of maybe a hundred or a thousand who they actually released. Foreigners who were done their sentence and didn't have anywhere to go were given a document to sign saying they were staying at the camp voluntarily.

What happened then?
They sent me to a railroad camp in Kotlas, because I didn't want to accept Soviet citizenship. They didn't give me another choice. I also had to report in every six months, even though I was allegedly a free man. I could leave the camp, but I couldn't leave the designated zone, which was a radius of about fifty or sixty kilometres. I did various jobs at the camp, and even got a wage. I found out about Svoboda's Army from some prisoners who came from Subcarpathian Rus like me. So I went to the Red Army draft committee, but I told them right off the bat that I want to join the Czechoslovak army. They looked at my papers and said it wasn't possible and I should go back to the camp. This repeated every six months. Only in 1944 did I find out that there was a mistake in my documents and I was listed as a Hungarian, which is why they didn't believe I was a Czechoslovak. Then they finally took me, but first into the Red Army. I spent about five weeks somewhere south of Moscow along with eleven Poles. Then they sent me via Kyiv to Sadhora,[142] where I joined the Czechoslovak formation.

SAMUEL FRIEDMANN

Born 3 August 1913 in Uzhhorod. His father Jakob Friedmann came from Romania, but he moved to Uzhhorod, where he met his future wife Gizel Fajermon and opened a small shop. His father and grandparents went to synagogue every Saturday; his mother was not practising. Samuel attended a Jewish primary school. After secondary school, he trained as a tailor. In the years 1932–1933, he worked in Košice. Then he lived in Uzhhorod up until the Hungarian occupation. Four days after the Hungarian seizure of the

142 Sadhora – a small town in south-western Ukraine. A former important Hasidic centre.

western part of Subcarpathian Rus, he decided to go to Czechoslovak Khust, as the Hungarians had arrested a number of his friends. There were Ukrainian nationalists operating in Khust, however, and it was not safe for Jews there. Thus he went even farther east to Rakhiv and Yasinia, where the occupation of the rest of Subcarpathian Rus caught up to him. In 1939, he went to Uzhhorod for Passover to see his mother, but by that time he was afraid to go out on the street. When he got a summons to enter the paramilitary youth organisation Levente, where he knew that Jews were being victimised, he and his friend Zikmund Grossman decided to flee to the USSR. Shortly after crossing the border, they were arrested by border guards and handed over to the NKVD. After being investigated by the NKVD in Stanyslaviv and Starobilsk, he was sentenced to three years of hard labour in the Gulag and transported to Kolyma. He first worked in the port, then mining gold and in the end earned a job as a tailor. Even after his sentence ended, he had to stay at the camp, where he worked as a civilian employee. He was not released until 1947. Of his family, only his brother survived, and he moved to Israel. His mother died in 1943, his father and grandmother were murdered in Auschwitz. Samuel then moved to Vynohradiv, where he met his future wife Helena, who had survived Buchenwald and Auschwitz. They were married in 1950 and received a flat from the sovkhoz where Samuel was working. In 1951, they had a daughter. Their next two children died a few weeks after being born. He lived to be rehabilitated for being imprisoned in the USSR in 1991.[143]

— — —

When did you decide to cross the Soviet border?
When I was working in Yasinia, they took several of my Jewish co-workers away to Mukachevo, to a camp set up there at the chateau. One of them returned to Yasinia and told me about the horrible conditions there. The chateau was being run by Levente and the Hungarian commander there tormented them – for example he took them to a place where there was water or mud and ordered them to lay down in it and so on. In September, I received a summons that on 10 October I was to join the same company he had told me about. My friend Zikmund Grossman told me he had a Jewish acquaintance on the border who would take us to Russia. And so it was. On 30 September 1940, a Jewish forester took us across the border near Yasinia. I don't remember how much we gave him. We spent the night at his place and agreed how we'd do it. He would take a saw, me the wedges and Grossman an axe, as if we were going to work in the woods. He said we were to walk five steps apart and not say a word. At the river he suddenly stopped and pointed the way. We

143 *Archive of USC Shoah Foundation*, interview with Samuel Friedmann recorded 12 January 1998 by Boris Timur, translated from Russian by Jiřina Dvořáková.

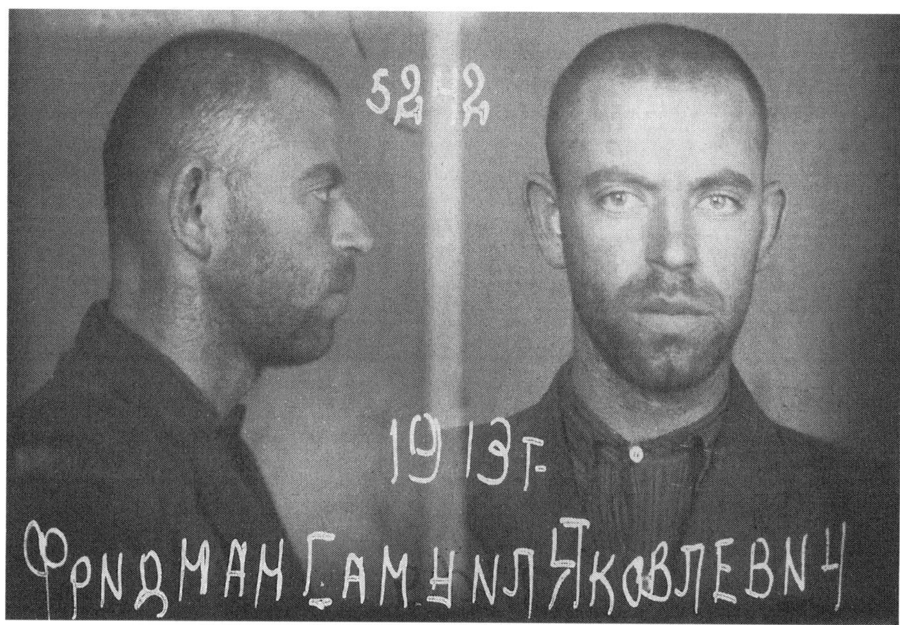

Samuel Friedmann following his arrest by the NKVD. *DAZO*

dropped everything and set out down along the path that led alongside the river. We met some girl. She figured we'd crossed the border and told us we were going the right way. After several kilometres we reached a village. For a while we debated whether to go to the local office or look for a Jew. In the end we went to report ourselves. First we ended up spending two days with the border guards. Then they took us to Vorokhta.[144] There we spent a week or ten days. They interrogated us, mostly wanting to know how we got across the border. When it was over, we were transferred to Nadvirna.

Did they ask you why you came to the Soviet Union?
Not until Nadvirna. We were interrogated by a captain who admitted he was a Jew. He said: "Samuel Jakobovich, I am like you, but in such a position that I can't even believe my own father. So I don't believe you." I explained to him what had happened back home. He didn't respond to that at all, just said we should sign our testimony. The next day, not until night, they took me to another interrogation. I asked why, I was there yesterday. They brought me back to the captain and he told me, "I felt so bad for you, I brought bread and butter, salami, tea. Here, eat!" And that happened every evening.

144 Vorokhta – a town in western Ukraine in the Ivano-Frankivsk Oblast.

Zikmund Grossman, who fled with Samuel Friedmann to the USSR, on the NKVD prison photograph. *DAZO*

Were you and your friend still together?
Yes. He also went to interrogation sessions, even though he had a different investigating officer. Then they took us to Stanyslaviv, where the trial took place. That meant they had five to ten people called forward, read off our surnames and sentenced us to three years for violating Soviet borders. Then they asked if we were satisfied! This was followed by a transport to Starobilsk. There were tens of thousands of cases like ours. From Transcarpathia, from Hungary, from Yugoslavia, from Poland, all refugees who were deported. Well, not everyone. If they found anything suspicious on someone, they'd get five or ten years for espionage. We were in Starobilsk when the Germans attacked the Soviet Union. Thus the first large transport of around seven thousand people left by freight train to Siberia.

What did you do in Starobilsk up until 1941?
Nothing! We ate well, three times a day. Every day they'd even take us on walks and once a week they took us to the river to wash.

Where did you live?
In a former convent from the time of Tsarist Russia, surrounded by a tall wooden fence. When the war broke out, they turned it into a prison. I slept in the church on the third level of a wooden bunk. But we weren't there long and they started taking us to camps.

What was the trip like?
At every station they would come around with a hammer and bang it to check whether we were taking the wagon apart. Our transport went via Aktyubinsk, Novosibirsk and Khabarovsk to Vladivostok, from there taking us on to Nakhodka Bay. On the way they fed us herring and bread. Once, before we got to Nakhodka, I don't know what town it was, they herded us out of the wagon. But then they found out there was no one to guard us there, so we continued on to Kolyma. When we got to Nakhodka, we were all bathed, shaved and fed well at a transit prison. The boat to Kolyma took several days. When someone died, they'd take them above deck and simply throw them in the water. We got to Magadan sometime in July or August 1941.

What kind of work did they assign you?
They immediately divided us up. Grossmann and I were lucky because we were assigned with a few other prisoners to the fishermen. We loaded up fish and drove them to the factory. We worked with civilian employees who took good care of us. After about a month, however, the trip north continued. They took us by car to the town of Susuman, about six hundred kilometres away, and then even farther to site of Udarnik.[145] There we panned for gold. It was September or October, but the temperature was already falling below minus fifteen, twenty degrees and we only had summer clothes and shoes. Plus it was hard work. Lots of people died there, froze there. That lasted about three months, then the chief started probing whether there were any tailors, carpenters and other tradesmen. We spoke up, so then we travelled back to Susuman, where I worked as a tailor from the end of 1941 until 1946. Night shifts the whole time, from ten at night until six in the morning.

Did you have any news about the war?
We had a rough idea of how the war was going. But they didn't tell us anything about what was happening to the Jews. It was only in 1943, when they brought in sixteen-, eighteen-year-old girls with ten-year sentences that we learned something from them. Meaning what had happened to the Jews in Ukraine. When our three-year sentence was up, we became civilian employees. There was a captain in charge of us who filled out our food rations.

Where did you live as civilians?
In a kind of camp.

145 Udarnik – a camp falling under Sevvostlag at a gold-bearing deposit on the Zaobolochenny stream in the north-west of the Magadan Oblast in what is today the Susuman district.

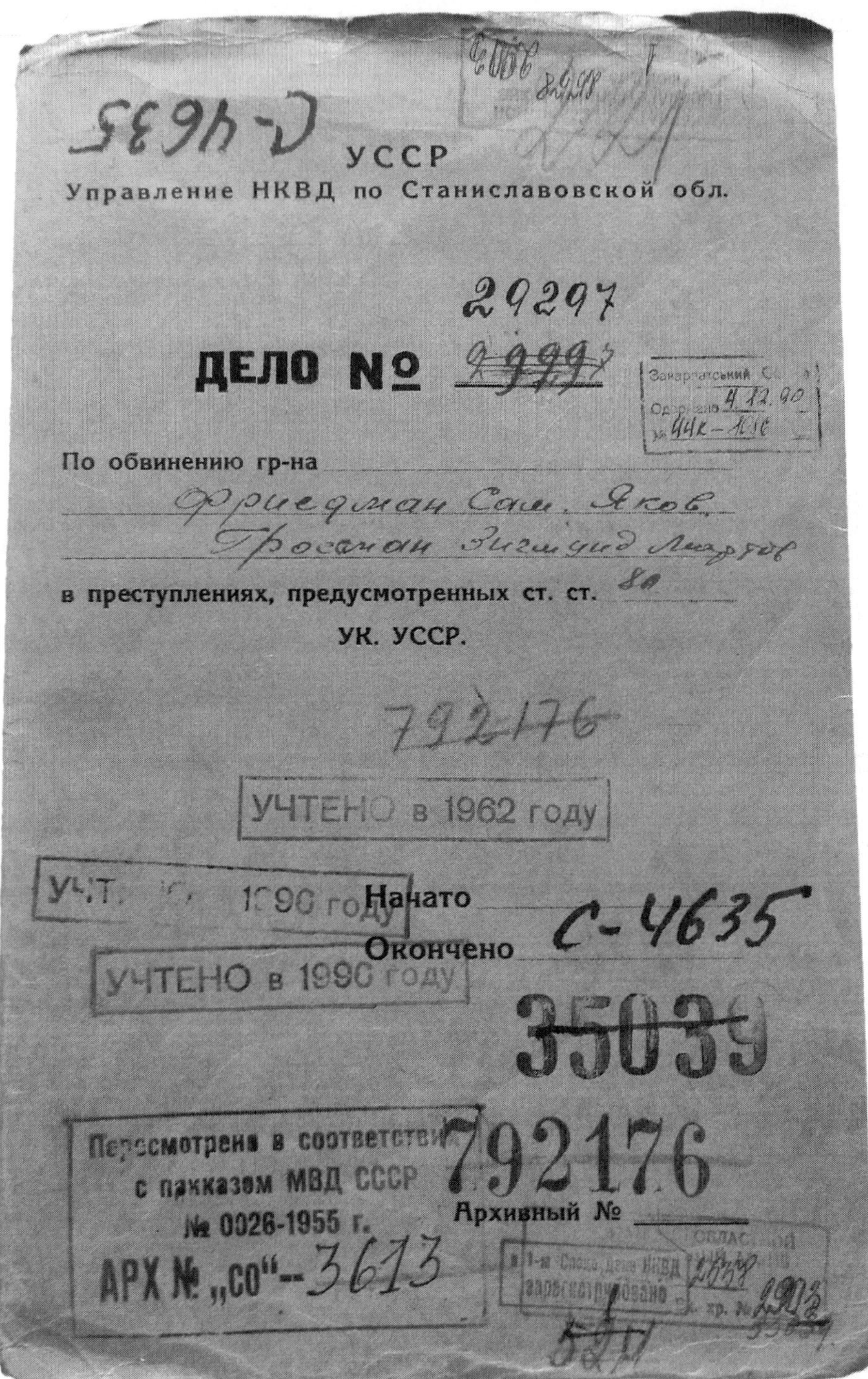

С-4635

УССР

Управление НКВД по Станиславовской обл.

29297

ДЕЛО № ~~9999~~

Закарпатський ...
Одержано 4.12.90
№ 44к-1016

По обвинению гр-на

Фриедман Сам. Яков.

Гросман Зигмунд Мардков

в преступлениях, предусмотренных ст. ст. 80

УК. УССР.

~~792176~~

УЧТЕНО в 1962 году

УЧТ... 1990 году

Начато

Окончено С-4635

УЧТЕНО в 1990 году

~~35039~~

Пересмотрена в соответствии
с приказом МВД СССР
№ 0026-1955 г.
АРХ № „СО“-3613

792176

Архивный №

в 1-м Спец. деле НКВД
зарегистрировано

хр. № 2903

The NKVD investigation file on Samuel Friedmann and Zikmund Grossman. *DAZO*

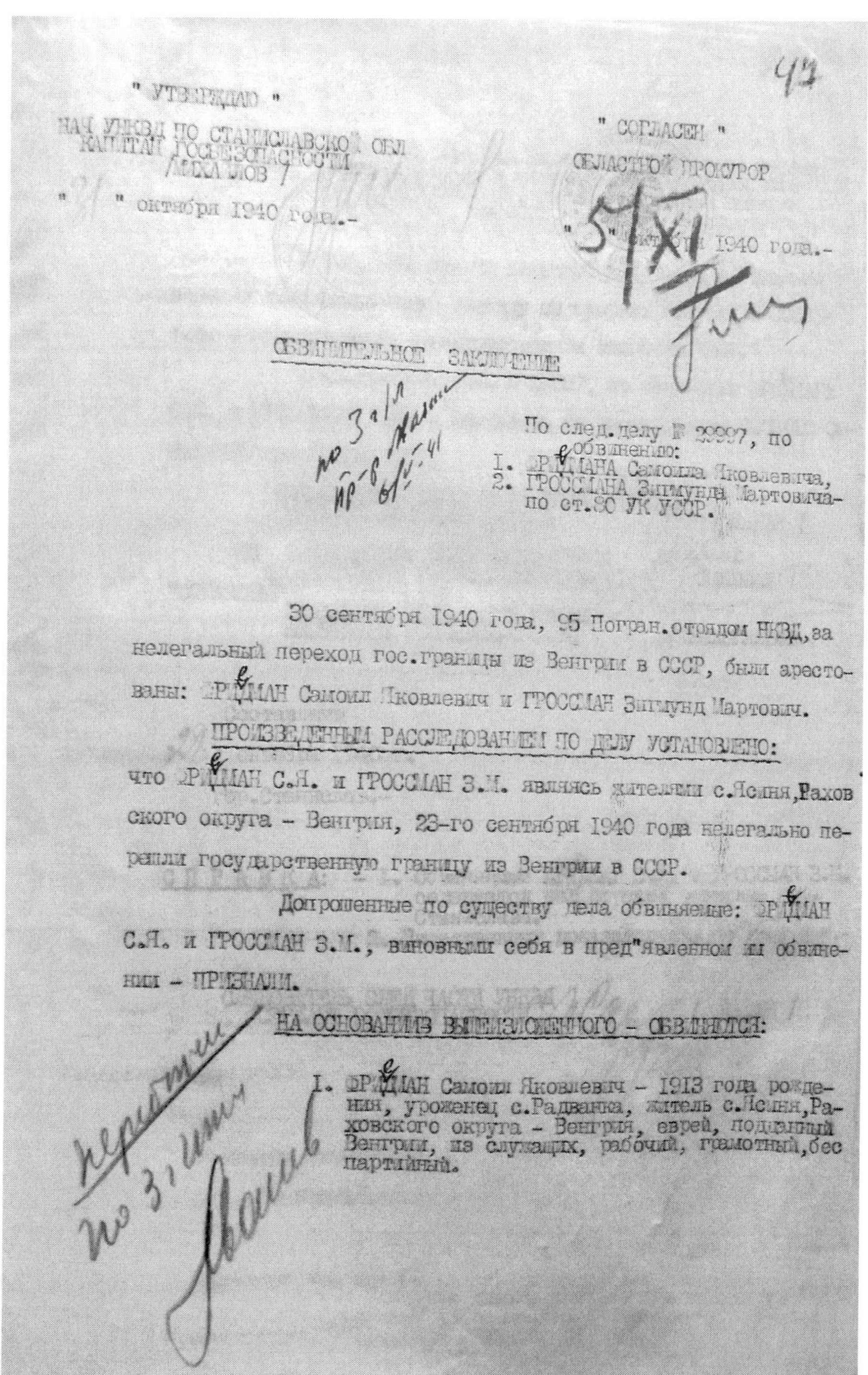

" УТВЕРЖДАЮ "
НАЧ УНКВД ПО СТАНИСЛАВСКОЙ ОБЛ
КАПИТАН ГОСБЕЗОПАСНОСТИ
/МИХАЙЛОВ/
" " октября 1940 года.-

" СОГЛАСЕН "
ОБЛАСТНОЙ ПРОКУРОР
"5" XI 1940 года.-

ОБВИНИТЕЛЬНОЕ ЗАКЛЮЧЕНИЕ

По след.делу № 29997, по обвинению:
1. ФРИДМАНА Самоила Яковлевича,
2. ГРОССМАНА Зигмунда Мартовича-
по ст.80 УК УССР.

30 сентября 1940 года, 95 Погран.отрядом НКВД, за нелегальный переход гос.границы из Венгрии в СССР, были арестованы: ФРИДМАН Самоил Яковлевич и ГРОССМАН Зигмунд Мартович.

ПРОИЗВЕДЕННЫМ РАССЛЕДОВАНИЕМ ПО ДЕЛУ УСТАНОВЛЕНО:

что ФРИДМАН С.Я. и ГРОССМАН З.М. являясь жителями с.Ясиня,Раховского округа - Венгрия, 23-го сентября 1940 года нелегально перешли государственную границу из Венгрии в СССР.

Допрошенные по существу дела обвиняемые: ФРИДМАН С.Я. и ГРОССМАН З.М., виновными себя в пред"явленном им обвинении - ПРИЗНАЛИ.

НА ОСНОВАНИИ ВЫШЕИЗЛОЖЕННОГО - ОБВИНЯЮТСЯ:

1. ФРИДМАН Самоил Яковлевич - 1913 года рождения, уроженец с.Радванка, житель с.Ясиня,Раховского округа - Венгрия, еврей, подданный Венгрии, из служащих, рабочий, грамотный,беспартийный.

The sentence laid down by the NKVD against Samuel Friedmann and Zikmund Grossman. *DAZO*

Could you move about freely?
Yes. The important thing was not to be late for work.

And what did you do outside of work?
At six o'clock in the morning, the shift ended and we went home. We had breakfast and relaxed a bit. Then we needed to go the construction site for two hours. And another two hours pan for gold. The quota for a month was several grams of gold. When we met it, things were good. They'd give us *makhorka* and even *papirosas* or candy. I don't smoke. So I'd go to the prisoners who didn't have such a strict regime at work, which you could tell by the fact they didn't have their number in the front and the back. I'd trade the pack of *makhorka* for five or ten grams of gold and thus I didn't have to keep going to the panning site. In terms of days off, during the war we had every tenth day off, after the war every Sunday. Many of us froze and died in 1941. They'd pile them up in front of the tent and cart them off to bury them once a week.

Was there any medical care at the camp? What about food?
Among the free employees, there was one doctor. When somebody needed to, they'd send them to the hospital. In terms of food, I couldn't complain. We got more than a kilogram of bread a day. If you worked above the quota, you'd get bread, *makhorka*, a piece of good soap, sugar. They'd give it out as a bonus once a month.

Were there people of different nationalities, different faiths there?
Yes, but we didn't celebrate any holidays.

Not even the Jewish ones?
Not officially, that wasn't possible, but say when it was Yom Kippur, we didn't eat. Or for the New Year we'd go to the doctor, who would give us two days' sick leave, so in that way we'd observe the holidays.

Why did you work at the same place after your sentence ended?
As soon as our sentence was over, we went to the chief, Marhuna, and asked them to let us go. He said they couldn't, he'd have to get orders from Moscow. I told him, "Fine, I'll write to Moscow and we'll see." About two months later, Marhuna came to our workshop and said, "Moscow wrote back, you'll work here until the end of the war." When the war ended, the whole thing repeated. In the end, Marhuna came and said, "Moscow decided that everyone is to go to where they came from." According to their logic, since I had crossed the Hungarian border, I belonged to Hungary. That's why they didn't even call me in when the Czechoslovak army was forming in 1942 and they took the Czechoslovak citizens from Kolyma.

How was the journey home?
There were something over fifty of us. We were not travelling as prisoners, but as free employees. In 1946, we boarded the steamship Dzhurma. Until they said the deck was closing, we walked around it freely. They took us to Vladivostok and then onwards by train. We got a ruble and a portion of food each day. The trip continued on through Novosibirsk to Aktyubinsk, where there was a collection camp for foreigners. We spent the winter there. There were a lot of us. Especially a lot of German POWs. We worked with them on a construction site. I remember they fed us poorly there. From there, they took those of us who had come from Kolyma, i.e., all the former refugees, by train to Romania, that was sometime in May, June 1947. As Hungarian nationals, we were to go to Hungary. We didn't want to, some of us had been born in Uzhhorod. So the local chief wrote to Moscow. And from Moscow came permission that those born in Transcarpathia can go there. So I got back to Uzhhorod.

ZOLTÁN ŠTERN

Born 1 September 1919 in the village of Paseka in Subcarpathian Rus as the third of eleven children into a family of petty merchants. He attended elementary school in Paseka, graduating from the Czech high school in Svalyava, eight kilometres away. In 1935, he went to Uzhhorod for business school. As a poor boy, he was helped out financially by the school's Czech principal, a Greek Catholic priest, who arranged for him to have daily board with Jewish families. He also found him free accommodation with a Jewish man named Berman. He studied for one year in Uzhhorod, then transferred to the business academy in Mukachevo. After the Hungarian takeover of Mukachevo, the business academy evacuated to Svalyava, which however also fell into Hungarian hands several months later. He completed the business academy back in Mukachevo, but as a Jew he could not get work in Hungary. He supported himself doing odd jobs, for example, picking and selling blueberries. In addition, he had to report to the gendarmerie every week. The Hungarian gendarmes also conducted home searches every two, three days and committed acts of violence. Thus in summer of 1940, Zoltán decided to flee to the USSR. He was arrested by border guards and imprisoned in Skole, Stryi and Starobilsk, from where he was sent to Kolyma. Only in 1942 did the camp commander in Susuman inform him he had been sentenced to three years' labour in the Gulag. In 1943, he and some others tried to leave the camp to join the Czechoslovak military unit, but for bureaucratic reasons he was not released until January of 1947. Even after that, he had to remain in Magadan as a civilian employee. He was only fully released in February 1948. After

Former NKVD prison in Stryi. *ÚSTR / Adam Hradilek*

returning to his native Paseka, he discovered most of his relatives had died in Auschwitz. First he worked at the prosecutor's office in Mukachevo, later he started to study law remotely at the University of Lviv. In 1952, he joined the Communist Party. In 1954, he completed his law degree. From 1966 until his retirement, he worked as a lawyer in Uzhhorod.[146]

— — —

When did you cross the Soviet border?
On the twentieth of August, not far from Uzhok. There was a smuggler living in a small village near the border. When anyone came to him, he would send them to the forest at the edge of the village and lead them across the border at night. That day, there must have been fifty of us gathered there by night. There were even women among us, as well as former soldiers. The smuggler came at night and said, "Let's go." He knew the way very well. We walked through the forest and reached the border just before morning, where he showed us which way to go not to end up back in Hungary. We gave him money, each whatever they had. We didn't need it anymore, because we were going to be

146 *Archive of the USC Shoah Foundation*, interview with Zoltán Štern recorded 15 June 1998 by Julij Sternberg, translated from Russian by Jiřina Dvořáková.

One of the cells of the NKVD prison no. 1 on Loncky Street in Lviv. *ÚSTR / Adam Hradilek*

free. We slept for about an hour and then set off for the village of Husnyi. On the way we sang in order to alert the border guards to our presence. In the village, four of them on horseback surrounded us. Their commander ordered us: "One step right or left will be taken as an escape attempt and weapons will be used." Then they led us to a kind of shack and shut us up inside. Before that, we had to surrender the contents of our pockets. They gave us a piece of sour black bread to eat. From there they then led us by foot to the village of Smozhe, then two days later to the town of Skole. There they locked us up in former horse stables, which they had turned into a camp for refugees. There were maybe a thousand defectors from Transcarpathia crammed in. After about two months, they gradually started sending us by train to the prison in Stryi.

Did they interrogate you in Skole?
Not everyone, but I did get interrogated. There was a tonne of people in Skole and the whole camp was surrounded by barbed wire. The conditions were wretched, we only got food once a day. There were also a lot of lice. One wooden dish for ten people. But a few days later, some men in leather coats showed up – we didn't know what that meant – and asked: "Who wants to work?" Of course I did, we all wanted out of there. But this one's not suitable, this one either. I finally begged them into taking me. The next day, a truck

arrived and they took everyone who wanted to work to the NKVD. They wanted to know everything about everybody, where they were from, where they'd worked and so on. This was followed by transport to Stryi. There we spent three or four months in a small cell with maybe forty of us crammed inside. We slept as commanded – first on our left side, then on our right. The food was just barely enough, but forty people in a cell, that was horrible. Then came a transport via Lviv to Starobilsk in the Poltava Oblast. On the way, they gave us pickled herring, but not bread. And when they gave bread, there was no water. In Starobilsk they locked us up in a big monastery. There were several thousand of us refugees from Transcarpathia there, as well as Poles accused of espionage, even Ukrainians. Those of us from Transcarpathia were in a separate building and they fed us a bit better. That was 1941. We didn't do anything there the whole time. Here and there they interrogated us. But then the atmosphere suddenly changed in June 1941, when they started hurriedly organising transports to Vorkuta. We left Starobilsk sometime around 10 June, just under two weeks before the German invasion of the Soviet Union. We only found out there was a war in Irkutsk.

What was the trip to the Soviet East like?
They transported us in livestock cars. From Starobilsk we travelled to the port of Nakhodka near Vladivostok forty-eight days! Here and there they gave us water or herring. And they were constantly checking to make sure no one had escaped. Then they herded us into the hold of the SS Dzhurma and we sailed another nine days to Kolyma. On the way, there was a storm somewhere near Japan, and we were afraid we would sink. We were below deck. The Poles on one floor, us from Transcarpathia on another. We couldn't see anything, only when they led us by machine gun onto the deck to go to the bathroom. In that manner we reached the Nagayev Bay near Magadan, where there was a transit camp. There they divided us into groups of thirty to forty and sent us to the goldfields. I was still in my summer clothes, by the way. I only got warmer work clothes at the Obyedinenny[147] goldfield, about 700 kilometres from Magadan to the west, towards the Indigirka.

What did it look like there?
There was a large but unfinished camp by the site intended primarily for us Czechoslovaks. Winter came. The barracks were standing, there were double bunks in them, but they weren't insulated yet. A pile of people froze there. But they didn't forget to string up barbed wire around the camp, just as they managed to build watchtowers.

---

147 Obyedinenny – a Sevvostlag camp between the basins of the rivers Berelekh and Verkhny Neksikan in the north-western Magadan Oblast in today's Susuman district north of Susuman.

Was it a surface deposit or a mineshaft?
Surface. The work went as follows: We carted dirt in a wheelbarrow over to the station, where we dumped it out and other prisoners would sluice it. The sluicing was done using old water mills. The gold was only collected after the shift was done, when they stopped the water. They always found about a kilo, kilo and a half of gold. The mills were operated by a different brigade though, I mostly worked the wheelbarrows, the carts, and in a shift I'd cart about ninety, a hundred loads. The amount was recorded, which is why I remember.

Was it hard?
Very! Cold, hunger. I'm not talking about the winter, at the start, when the water still flowed, it was fine. But in the winter, you had to wear padded trousers, *telogreikas*,[148] *fufaikas*,[149] padded gloves. When you were lying on the top bunk, your hair would freeze to the wall. We heated in barrels. Two, three, four barrels a building. You would warm up for fifteen twenty minutes, leave, another would come warm up, then in an hour or two you'd come back to warm up a bit again. And in the morning back to work.

What food did they give you?
Bread, 600 to 700 grams a day. And also soup, it was called *balanda*, they brought it into the barracks. It was mostly fish, especially "red fish", very little meat. Usually the food was the same everywhere, sometimes maybe a bit better one place, worse another. I was at several goldfields, you see. At the surface ones, you couldn't work in the winter.

Where all were you?
After several months in the Obyedinenny camp, where many Czechoslovaks froze to death, they transferred us by order from Magadan to the Maldyak camp.[150] We were without work for about a month and a half, but in May they herded us out into the goldfields again. Once again we were digging and sluicing dirt. Then I ended up at the Burkhala site. But that was preceded by an important event. In 1943, they took us, about three hundred people from Transcarpathia, to Magadan, to the transit camp where we started. We discovered they wanted to send us to the Czechoslovak unit. And in 1943, I don't know what month, a commission had met and liberated everyone, except for me. As far as I could tell, they took all the Czechoslovak Jews for the unit, just

148 Telogreika – also vatnik, a cotton wool-padded jacket.
149 Fufaika – the upper part of warm underwear.
150 Maldyak – a camp named after the eponymous tributary of the river Berelekh in north-western Magadan Oblast about 650 km from Magadan in today's Susuman district.

In the wintertime, clearing snow was one of the frequent jobs of Gulag prisoners. *Komi Republic National Archives*

not those from Kolyma. I remember it like it was yesterday: they released everyone and I was the only one left standing there. They announced that everyone was leaving and only Štern was staying. From there they took me back to Burkhala.

I'd also like to add that the chief of the camp administration in Susuman only announced our sentences to those of us evacuated from Starobilsk when the Germans were coming in 1942. They gave me a paper that I was convicted under Article 80 to three years for illegally crossing the state border. I signed it and it was done. Some people were charged with espionage. They got five years.

So everyone left and they sent me to Burkhala, where the mining was below ground. So I worked in the mineshaft. It was very hard work, words fail me.

What exactly did you do?

We mined lead there. The blasters would blast away a hunk of earth and we'd load it onto a conveyor belt with shovels. The shafts weren't all that deep, though, maybe 25 to 30 metres, in places just 15 to 20 metres. From Burkhala I wrote to everyone – Stalin, Beria, Kaganovich – that I wanted to fight for the Czechoslovak army. On the sixth of May 1944, they woke me up before dawn: "You're not going to work, at six in the morning they're taking you to the hospital in the next camp over for observation." The morning of 7 May 1944, they took me to the polyclinic. There the camp doctors examined me. They praised me: "My boy, you took care of yourself! You're going to the army!" Two or three weeks I didn't go to work and was waiting for a transport to Magadan and then on to the army.

Then the management came in and said I'd have to go to work again. No one explained what had happened, and so I was doing the same work again, up until January 1947, when they transferred me to Magadan as a free employee. Then I worked there as a salesman, sales assistant, and then as head of sales. And again I wrote and wrote, because they weren't letting anyone from Magadan go to the mainland. I didn't get permission to leave until January 1948. They assigned me to the Vinnytsia Oblast and arranged a plane ticket for me. From Magadan we flew via Khabarovsk. But on the day I got the documents, there were only available flights to Yakutsk. I immediately agreed. The main thing was not to be there for one hour longer!

I got to Vinnytsia with my wooden camp trunk. I was a miserable Jew. They didn't want to let me into Transcarpathia. So I wrote to Kyiv and to Moscow about it. Three months passed, I had no money. Then they decided at the militia that I could go back, but just as a vacation. I reached my home village, and picture the image, the poor Jew returning home, his house is still standing, but his father, mother, grandpa, brothers, sisters, none of them are there. No one survived the war. Then they told me about it in the village, it was hard to listen to. They incinerated mum and dad. There was a ghetto in Svalyava and from there they took them to Auschwitz. There my father, mother, two brothers and two sisters died. My younger sister lived to be freed from Auschwitz, but came down with typhus and died. It was hard to listen to details like that. Apparently, my older and younger brother had come to the village after the war. It wasn't until the fifties I found out they were in America. They'd left Transcarpathia, remained in Czechoslovakia for a bit, then got to America, where they lived in New York.

KAREL VAŠ

Born 20 March 1916 in Uzhhorod into the family of a Hungarian-speaking lawyer. In 1933, while still studying at the Uzhhorod grammar school, he secretly joined the Communist Party of Czechoslovakia. After graduating from secondary school, he enrolled in the Faculty of Law at Charles University in Prague. During his studies, he became actively involved in the activity of the communist movement, for which he was also punished. In 1936, he was sentenced to two weeks in prison for breaking shop windows during a demonstration. Shortly after graduating in February 1939, he left upon orders of the Communist Party to Uzhhorod, which had been occupied since November 1938 by the Hungarians, and joined the communist resistance. In 1940, he decided to flee the danger of arrest to the Soviet Union. Shortly after crossing the border, he was detained by the Soviet border guard and imprisoned. He spent over half a year in prisons in Nadvirna, Stanyslaviv and Poltava. It is evident from the preserved archival materials that during that time he was attempting to contact the NKVD leadership and Communist International in Moscow in an attempt to gain release. Despite the fact that he called himself an "ironclad Bolshevik" in his requests, one who had devoted his life to communism and was ready to continue to do so, on 10 February 1941 he was sentenced to three years of forced labour by special session of the NKVD. From the Poltava prison he was transported to the agricultural camp Kedrovy Shor, which produced food for Intinlag. Here he was imprisoned nearly two years. While many prisoners' experiences from the Gulag eroded their faith in the Soviet Union, for Vaš the work camp was a place where he started cooperating with the NKVD, as he himself later admitted: "Even in isolation in the USSR, I did not cease to be a communist. Not only did I think like a communist, but I also proved myself to be one with my actions. Even in isolation, I expressed my love for the USSR by helping the Soviet security authorities to expose hostile elements, anti-state criminals."[151] After two years' imprisonment, he was released from the camp under the amnesty declared for Czechoslovak citizens and travelled along with several other liberated Czechoslovaks[152] to join the Czechoslovak military unit in Buzuluk. Thanks to his cooperation with the NKVD, which continued after his release from the Gulag during his service in the Czechoslovak army, he was assigned to the 2nd (intelligence) division of the staff of the 1st Czechoslovak Army Corps in

151 HANZLÍK, František – POSPÍŠIL, Jan – POSPÍŠIL, Jaroslav: *Sluha dvou pánů* [Servant of Two Masters]. Lípa – A. J. Rychlík, Vizovice 1999, p. 339.

152 Cf. *CVG Collection of Interviews*, interview with Michal Izaj recorded 12 February 2012 by Jan Dvořák. M. Izaj was imprisoned in the same camp as K. Vaš and they were transported to Buzuluk together.

the USSR. In January 1945, he became deputy to Bedřich Reicin in the newly formed defence intelligence service. After the war, he continued to cooperate with the NKVD and participated in a number of illegal activities entailed in preparing the ground for takeover of power by the Communist Party in Czechoslovakia after 1945 and consolidating it after 1948. In February 1948 he was named deputy to the chief military prosecutor in Prague. On the basis of NKVD instructions, he requested to be transferred to the military department of the state prosecutor's office so he could interfere in the investigation of General Heliodor Píka. General Píka, who as the head of the Czechoslovak Military Mission in the USSR had played a fundamental role in achieving the release of Czechoslovaks from Soviet camps, was sentenced to death in 1949 due to Vaš's actions. Vaš himself was arrested 11 August 1951 as part of the power struggles within the ruling party. After two years in custody, he was given a life sentence for treason, espionage and accessory to murder on 31 July 1953. He was expelled from the Communist Party. In 1955, his sentence was reduced to 25 years under an amnesty. In 1956 he was acquitted and released. After his release, he studied history at the Charles University Faculty of Arts and worked at the Klement Gottwald Military Political Academy. In 1963 he was reinstated as a member of the Communist Party. He went into retirement from the position of editor at the Central Council of Trade Unions. After the fall of the communist regime, he applied for judicial rehabilitation, but this was denied by the Supreme Military Court. On 10 June 1991, the Regional Court of the Zakarpattia Oblast rehabilitated him on the matter of illegal border crossing in 1940. In 1998, he was charged with abuse of office leading to General Heliodor Píka receiving the death sentence. In February 2001, he was charged with murder and on 15 June 2001 sentenced to seven years in prison without parole. On 15 January 2002, the High Court overturned the verdict and criminal proceedings were suspended on the grounds of the statute of limitations. Karel Vaš died 8 December 2012.[153]

— — —

When did you decide to leave for the Soviet Union?

The resistance against the Hungarian occupying regime was so strong that the Hungarian authorities resorted to repression. They arrested my comrades taking part in the illegal resistance. I was in danger of arrest as well. So I fled across the Carpathians. The mountains were not foreign to me. I was careful,

153 *CVG Collection of Interviews*, interview with Karel Vaš recorded 15 January 2012 by Adam Hradilek; for more see VALIŠ, Zdeněk: Podplukovník v záloze JUDr. a PhDr. Karel Vaš, http://virtually.cz/archiv.php/ a.map?art=9342 (accessed 25 November 2017); HRADILEK, Adam: "Karel Vaš v SSSR. Vězněm a spolupracovníkem NKVD" [Karel Vaš in the USSR. Prisoner and NKVD collaborator]. *Paměť a dějiny*, 2012, no. 3, p. 72–88.

Inta, one of the sites where refugees from Nazism were interned in 1944–1945. *Inta Museum*

I knew the ABCs of illegal activity. I crossed the border into Polish territory occupied by the Soviet army.

How did the Soviets receive you?
They arrested me in the woods. Then they took me to a smallish town. I gave the Soviet authorities a decent, truthful account of everything I had done. And they, I have to tell you, they didn't lay a finger on me. They behaved decently, of course according to their regulations. But I had to play nice and do what they wanted.

Did they interrogate you a long time?
I don't know, it wasn't much. They were inexperienced young people. They were learning the ropes.

How long were you in prison?
Please, don't forget that I have Parkinson's disease. I forget some things. I know I was briefly in Kyiv. I stood out in the cold in the courtyard overnight in just my summer clothes and low-top shoes. Then they took me via Kyiv to the north to Komi. When we got off the train, we continued by foot in the snow to the camp. We walked a day or two, I don't know. I was walking in the snow in just my shoes. I didn't have anything else. Of course, at the camp, in time we got Soviet *valenki*. Felt shoes.

What did the camp look like?
It was a so-called experimental agricultural cooperative. It wasn't fenced off at all. We lived in *zemlyankas* there. I remember the sun didn't go down. It was constantly kind of dim, day and night.

How many people lived in one zemlyanka*?*
It varied. A hundred, hundred fifty, fifty, depending on the size.

Can you describe what such a zemlyanka *looked like inside?*
There was a stove and bunks, kind of wooden structures. It was bad.

How was it bad?
Because unless you had a coat or some clothes, you had nothing other than planks under you.

You didn't have mattresses or at least hay?
Don't forget one thing. Everything was in the stage of being built and in a state of war. The Soviet Union had been attacked. Everything was first and foremost for the army. The population was second in line. And they were short themselves. We were mere prisoners.

How many prisoners could there have been at the camp?
Where I was, there was probably nine hundred to a thousand prisoners, of those about a hundred women. Some were there a few months, some years and there were also people there who got ten years. I remember the worst sentences were ten, fifteen years.

Did you ever talk about who was in for what?
Please, no. But here and there you heard that it was for political reasons.

Did the women live along with the men, or did they have a separate section?
No, the women's and men's *zemlyankas* were separate. Contact between them was not prohibited however.

Did the interrogations continue at the camp?
No. At least not where I was. But the situation there was also interesting. The camp was partially run by prisoners. They were overseen by the state authorities. The highest economic authority, the head of the cooperative, was a Ukrainian nationalist. But the state authority was represented at the camp by an NKVD lieutenant.

What was the daily regime at the camp?
Work was ten to twelve hours. It depended on the time of year. Don't forget, where I was, the winter lasted a long time. There was basically no such thing

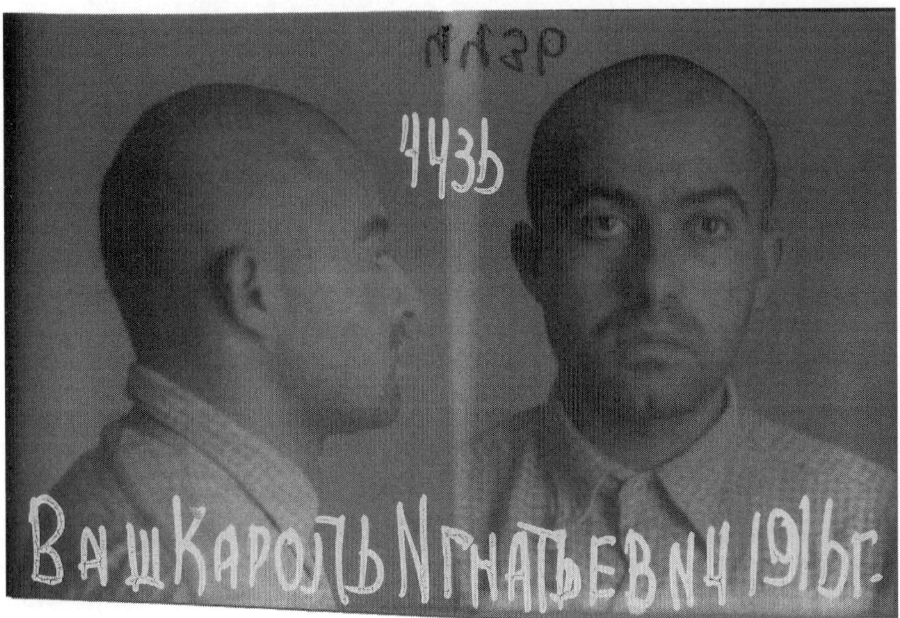

Karel Vaš shortly after being arrested in the Soviet Union. *DAZO*

as spring and autumn. We grew potatoes and other crops. It was a test of agricultural production in harsh climatic conditions. Even tobacco was grown there. The transition between summer and winter came abruptly. At six, seven o'clock in the evening, it was still warm, then at nine it was suddenly freezing. Then when the winter season started, it wasn't dark, but gloomy. We went to work either individually or in groups. The group was always supervised by a guard. But I wasn't physically insulted or abused even once. But I know there was a cell at the camp.

What did you do for work in the winter?
We chopped wood and prepared agricultural products for the warmer season. There was still frost outside and the seedlings were already sprouting in the *zemlyankas*. As soon as the weather started to change, they were planted outside.

What was done for hygiene at the camp?
There was a so-called *banya*. Naturally there was no running water. When we were ordered to bathe, everyone got a wooden bucket of hot and cold water. Every thimbleful of water was conserved. That took place three times a month.

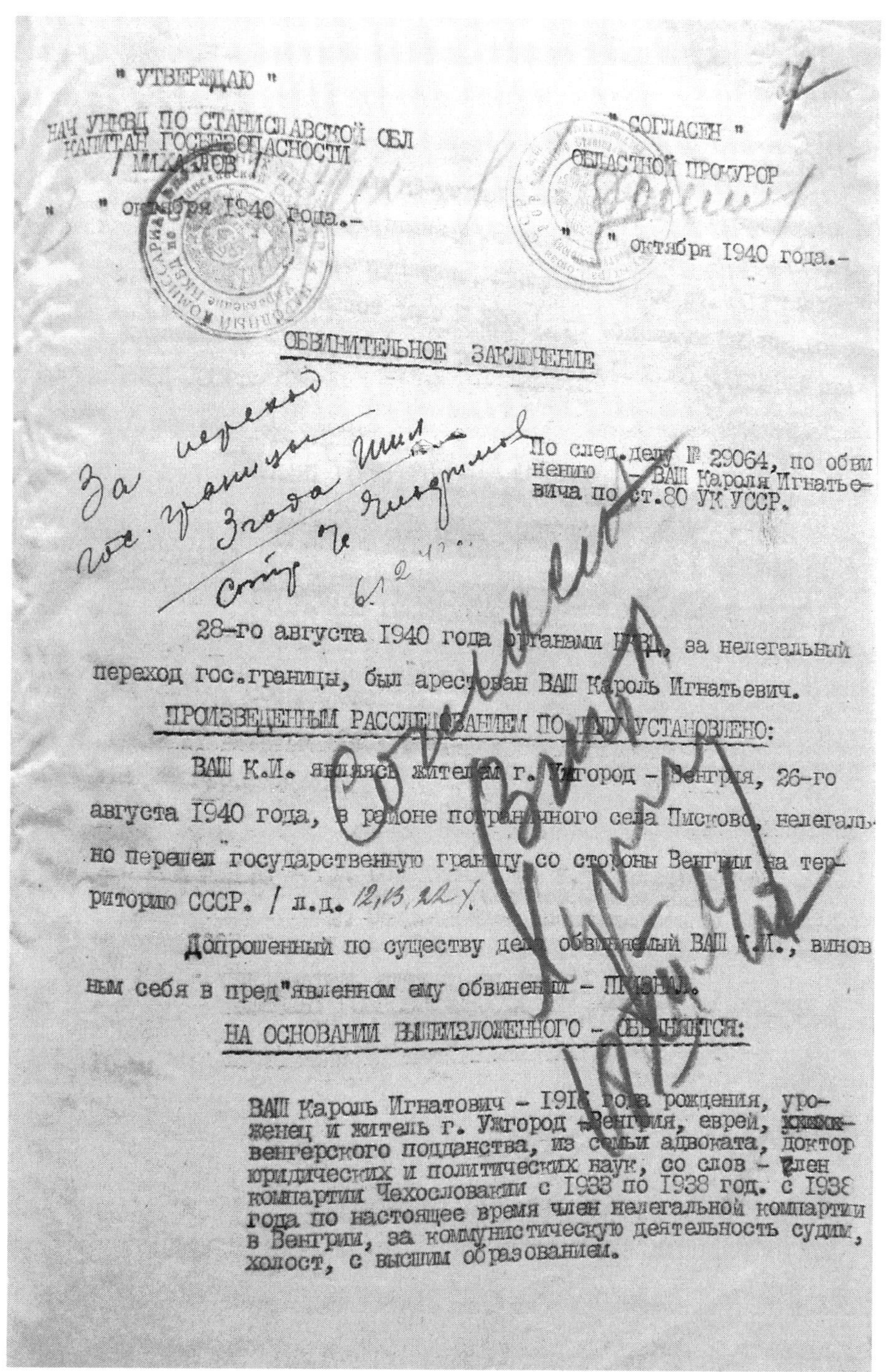

" УТВЕРЖДАЮ "

НАЧ УНКВД ПО СТАНИСЛАВСКОЙ ОБЛ
КАПИТАН ГОСБЕЗОПАСНОСТИ
/ МИХАЙЛОВ /

" " октября 1940 года.-

" СОГЛАСЕН "

ОБЛАСТНОЙ ПРОКУРОР

" " октября 1940 года.-

ОБВИНИТЕЛЬНОЕ ЗАКЛЮЧЕНИЕ

По след.делу № 29064, по обвинению - ВАШ Кароля Игнатьевича по ст.80 УК УССР.

28-го августа 1940 года органами НКВД, за нелегальный переход гос.границы, был арестован ВАШ Кароль Игнатьевич.

ПРОИЗВЕДЕННЫМ РАССЛЕДОВАНИЕМ ПО ДЕЛУ УСТАНОВЛЕНО:

ВАШ К.И. являясь жителем г. Ужгород - Венгрия, 26-го августа 1940 года, в районе пограничного села Писково, нелегально перешел государственную границу со стороны Венгрии на территорию СССР. / л.д. 12,13,22 /.

Допрошенный по существу дела обвиняемый ВАШ К.И., виновным себя в пред"явленном ему обвинении - ПРИЗНАЛ.

НА ОСНОВАНИИ ВЫШЕИЗЛОЖЕННОГО - ОБВИНЯЕТСЯ:

ВАШ Кароль Игнатович - 1916 года рождения, уроженец и житель г. Ужгород - Венгрия, еврей, венгерского подданства, из семьи адвоката, доктор юридических и политических наук, со слов - член компартии Чехословакии с 1933 по 1938 год. с 1938 года по настоящее время член нелегальной компартии в Венгрии, за коммунистическую деятельность судим, холост, с высшим образованием.

On the basis of this verdict, Karel Vaš was sentenced to three years in the Gulag. *DAZO*

Karel Vaš as deputy commander of the Defence Intelligence and NKVD collaborator in 1945. *Memory of Nations Archive*

What clothing did you wear?
It depended what time of year it was, summer or winter. In winter we wore *telogreikas* and cotton-lined trousers. The women had the exact same. There was no such thing as buttons. Instead of buttons there were just laces.

Was there a hospital at the camp?
There was something between a nurse and a doctor who practised medicine there.

Did prisoners' children live at the camp?
There were children there, but whether they were the children of convicts or the children of free citizens, I couldn't say. Some people were only sentenced to a year and a half, say. Then they were released, but they had to stay there and usually did the same work. It wasn't like normal where you can go where you want. You couldn't leave the place you had your registered address and just move. You needed a permit.

Of Selkhozlag, where Karel Vaš grew food for the Gulag camps farther north, the house of the camp commander is best preserved. *ÚSTR / Adam Hradilek*

Was it hard to get a permit like that?
Yes. It was hard getting papers.

Did you make friends with anyone at the camp?
I slept on a bunk next to a Polish colonel. He was decent, educated, a highly intelligent man. I also had a girlfriend there. She was pretty, very polite, intelligent, understanding.

What was her name?
I won't tell you that. I'll just reveal that her name started with an X.

Was she from Czechoslovakia?
No. Russian or Ukrainian, I don't know exactly. That was at a time when Ukrainian was already overrun by Russian, so to speak. So very few Ukrainian intellectuals spoke proper Ukrainian.

And do you know the name of the Polish officer, do you remember?
I don't know. I still remember his interesting four-pointed hat.

Why was he at the camp?
I don't know. But in my opinion and based on my experience, he ended up there by chance, by accident, by mistake, an oversight by the NKVD authori-

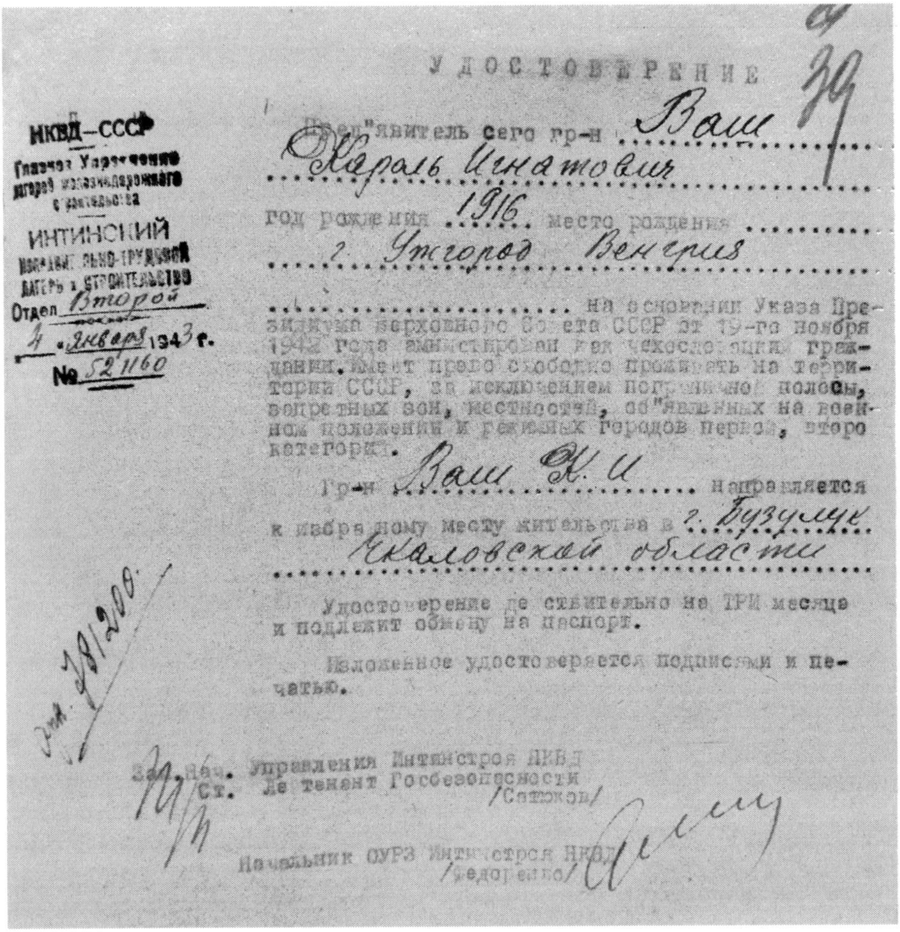

НКВД—СССР
Главное Управление лагерей …
ИНТИНСКИЙ … лагерь и строительство
Отдел Второй
4 января 1943 г.
№ 521160

УДОСТОВЕРЕНИЕ

Предъявитель сего гр-н Ваш Кароль Игнатович

год рождения 1916 место рождения г. Ужгород Венгрия

на основании Указа Президиума Верховного Совета СССР от 19-го ноября 1942 года амнистирован как чехословацкий гражданин. Имеет право свободно проживать на территории СССР, за исключением пограничной полосы, запретных зон, местностей, объявленных на военном положении и режимных городов первой, второй категории.

Гр-н Ваш К. И. направляется к избранному месту жительства в г. Бузулук Чкаловской области

Удостоверение действительно на ТРИ месяца и подлежит обмену на паспорт.

Изложенное удостоверяется подписями и печатью.

Вх. 28/200

Зам. Нач. Управления Интинстроя НКВД
Ст. Лейтенант Госбезопасности
/Сапожков/

Начальник ОУРЗ Интинстроя НКВД
/Федоренко/

Karel Vaš's release from Intinlag. *DAZO*

ties deciding his fate. What happened to the elite of the Polish army? You know the answer to that, I don't have to tell you because it's an open secret.

Do you know what happened to your girlfriend from the camp?
I don't know. I was released and I was happy I got to Buzuluk and I didn't think about it. It wasn't the first or last woman I had a relationship with in my life. Life went on.

When did you actually have time for each other? You worked ten to twelve hours every day...
She was assigned to agricultural work. Hoeing, planting. In the winter, she prepared the seedlings. But there was no work on Sunday. Later we started to have Saturday afternoon off as well. So, then we could naturally meet.

The remnants of the Kedrovy Shor Selkhozlag, where Karel Vaš was interned, 2016. *ÚSTR / Adam Hradilek*

Did it ever happen that one of the women at the camp gave birth?
There were such cases, but they were isolated in the hospitals. Of course they then received a special diet, milk, etc. Milk and select foods. We got black bread, they got white bread. They had a special milk ration. Our camp had stables for horses and for cows.

Your girlfriend never got pregnant at the camp?
Please, don't take it wrong, but your question shows you don't know some basic things. The way of life at the camp did not provide the conditions for a woman to become pregnant.

Why?
You should ask a doctor about that. I'm not a doctor. The women at the camp didn't menstruate.

How many years was your girlfriend sentenced to?
Some ten years for the fact that, according to the court, her husband committed embezzlement as an accountant and she allegedly benefitted from it. Ten years. As a lawyer I have to say it's a bit skewed.

ANDREJ ŠTERN

Born 9 May 1918 in Choňkovce in the Michalovce district into a strongly religious family as one of ten children. His father was a tailor. Like his other siblings, Andrej attended a Slovak school. After the Hungarian occupation of the south-eastern part of Slovakia, he could not study, so he joined his brother working in a bakery in Uzhhorod. Before long he was called up to the Hungarian army and subsequently, like the other Jews in his unit, transferred to a work camp in Mohács, where he had to slave away building roads. When he was transferred to work near Yasinia, he and other conscripts decided to cross the nearby border to the USSR. On the Soviet side they were captured by a border patrol. They were locked up in the basement of a temporary NKVD prison in Stanyslaviv. After the German attack on the USSR, they were evacuated to a prison in Ivanovo, about eighty kilometres past Moscow. After a year and a half of imprisonment, he was sentenced to three years in the Gulag and sent to Kotlas in the Arkhangelsk Oblast, where he worked primarily as a tailor. After his three-year sentence was up, however, he was not released. He was only liberated after he wrote an intervention request to Czechoslovak Ambassador Zdeněk Fierlinger. He reached Czechoslovakia via a transit camp in Odessa. At home he learned that practically his whole family had died in Auschwitz. All he had left was one brother, who returned from Siberia after eight years, but shortly after the war he moved to the USA. Andrej Štern opened a tailor's shop, but after 1948 the Communists nationalised it. He and his family moved to Děčín, where he worked as a shop manager. He spent the last years of his life in Prague.[154]

— — —

What was military service in the Hungarian army like?
It didn't last long. I was drafted when I was nineteen and served in Nagyatád near the Yugoslav border. At that time, the Hungarians were also occupying part of Romania, Transylvania. So for a time we fulfilled the function of occupying soldiers there, but then we went back to our barracks in Nagyatád. After about a week, they suddenly called us to form up. The commander read us an order that Hungary had adopted the Nuremberg Laws, and thus Jews could no longer serve in the regular army with weapons. They said we would be transferred to labour camps. They gave us two days off so we could go home for clothing. We had to turn in our uniforms and all our other military things. I went home and that was the last time I saw my mother and father. When I came back, they sent us to Mohács to work.

154 *Archive of the Jewish Museum in Prague*, interview with Andrej Štern recorded 28 August 1991 by Anna Lorencová.

What did you do there?
We were fixing things up there, because there had been floods that had done a lot of damage. One of the managers took a liking to me and put me in the storeroom. The others had to work hard. The living conditions were very tough. Then we had to build a road in the county of Bistrița-Năsăud in Romania, which was very hard work. People weren't used to that kind of work and the food was very bad. Eventually they took us to Subcarpathian Rus, to Yasinia, which the Hungarians had already occupied. There we were only just building the barracks we were supposed to live in. They still didn't have roofs and when it rained, it was very bad. At night we got wet and couldn't get undressed. There was eighty of us in one building. It was February 1941 and it was very cold. I worked in the storeroom. It was a bit better there, I could take an extra blanket.

Was it just Jews there?
Just Jews – from Hungary, from Romania, from the part of Czechoslovakia occupied by the Hungarians. There was one guy with us there who knew Russian, his name was Gross, he used to work at a printing house in Uzhhorod and he could communicate with the locals, with the Ukrainians. I overheard him asking how far away the border is and how to get there. He learned from the local Jews that there was a tailor there, his name was Erbst, who smuggled people across the border to the Soviet Union for twenty pengő, which was a week's wages. So I joined in and started to inquire. They told us there was no exploitation there, no unemployment, that there was a good life and justice.

So I decided I would go to. We agreed that we'd set out once we got paid. They gave us a few coins for toothpaste and shoe polish, it wasn't enough for more, but the officers got paid and after they got their pay they would go into town to have fun. We decided this would be the best time to escape. We slept in our clothes and covered ourselves with just a blanket. We all got together, there were thirty-five of us. We had made a plan that two would always leave to go to the bathroom, so it wasn't conspicuous, and the two leaving would wake up another two. We had agreed to meet at a certain spot. When we had met there, it was already midnight, but one was missing, he didn't show up. We were afraid he would rat us out, so one of us went back. The lad broke out crying, saying he'd changed his mind, that he was an only son and his mother was incredibly attached to him and she wouldn't be able to bear it. He was a boy from Hungary, from a rich family, his parents had a butcher's shop. So we left without him. We walked over the Carpathian hills, it was 30 May 1941, but it was still quite cold, lots of snow. We passed the border stone. On one side was the symbol of the no longer existing Czechoslovakia, on the other Poland, which was occupied by the Soviets. When we crossed the border, a weight fell off our shoulders. We were happy that nothing had happened,

Memorial to victims of political repression in Vorkuta. *ÚSTR / Adam Hradilek*

that we'd made it. Suddenly three Russian soldiers in fur coats showed up and started yelling at us. One of us spoke Russian and explained to them who we were and why we'd come. They ordered us to hand over all our things. One soldier spread out a blanket and we had to put everything on it: watches, knives, even combs. When we'd handed over everything, the soldier shot into the air and within five minutes, some twenty border guards appeared. They ordered us to line up three by three, saying we mustn't do anything except what they order us to. And that we can't talk amongst ourselves. They led us like that for about twelve kilometres. We still thought everything was fine. Eventually we reached wooden buildings where there were NKVD officers. They shoved us into the basement and brought us food in a bucket. It was smelly fish soup and everyone who tasted it almost vomited. But we still had some of our own food, some cans. When the soldier came and saw we hadn't eaten hardly anything out of the bucket, he declared that in time we would remember this and regret not taking it. The next night, they came for us and we had to go be interrogated. They were interested in what our parents did for a living, what we had done for work, whether we were homeowners and so forth. They filled out a report and then we could go back. The interrogations continued for about four days, always at night.

Did they interrogate each of you separately?
Yes. We asked what was going to happen to us. They said they'd see. When the interrogations ended, they took us by train to Stanyslaviv. There was a large NKVD complex full of people of all sorts of nationalities: from Yugoslavia, Belgium and many others. Their hair was overgrown and they looked quite pitiful. It was only there we started to fear what we had done, where we had gone. There was an officer there with a Jewish name, I could speak Yiddish with him. He said openly that war was imminent and they didn't know what would become of us. He said it depended what happened next. Even when they were interrogating us, they told those from the wealthy families that they were spies and could get ten years. The officers always looked at what we had handed over. If someone had a nice watch, say, they assumed they were rich. For those they didn't consider rich, after the interrogation had ended they told them that they were subject to article eighty-four for illegally crossing the border. When we asked how much we could get for it, they said from three to ten years.

As soon as Hitler attacked the Soviet Union in June 1941, they herded us into livestock cars and kept saying, "quick, quick" because the Germans were already getting close. As soon as we had left, they occupied Stanyslaviv. We knew that if we didn't board the train quickly, the Germans would shoot us. We travelled a long time, maybe a week, day and night. We had no water, only when it rained and we stopped somewhere, we could catch a bit. It was June 1941 and it was very warm. There were a lot of us in the wagon and all we got to eat was rusks. They took us to Ivanovo, about eighty kilometres past Moscow, where there was a large prison. We stayed there a year and a half. The war was raging by then and they didn't know what to do with us. Every day we got a bit of very bad food and with it a piece of black bread. Lots of people had diarrhoea from it. With the lack of hygiene, everyone's body was terribly itchy. They would take us to unload wagons or to work in the forest. Once they set up tables in the yard and we had roll call. One officer, a kind of Mongolian type, read off our names. When he called out Andrej Štern and I responded, he read off: "Statya vosemdesyatchetvertya, srok tri god," i.e., that I was sentenced to three years. The ones who got ten years went to be transported to a labour camp.

Did they try you?
There wasn't any trial, they had us come forward and read it off to us.

And did they know you were Jews fleeing from the Nazis?
Sure, but there were also non-Jews there, even in Stanyslaviv there were Gentiles with us, for example a priest, and others too. For example Ivan Matus, who lived in Děčín after the war, he was from Subcarpathian Rus, but he wasn't a Jew.

Were there ordinary criminals there too? How did they treat you?
In Ivanovo they behaved quite well, but then in the camp they took us to, it was much worse. After the sentencing, they took me and others to a sorting camp, a *peresylka*, near Kotlas in the Arkhangelsk Oblast. I had learned the tailor trade from my father and I was always bringing it up. I wasn't really built for manual work and those who worked manually were pretty poorly off. They would go down to the port to load boats with supplies for the army, which was very hard work. But there was also the Voyenpromkombinat textile factory, and they sent me there. We repaired clothes from the frontlines leftover from fallen soldiers: caps, jackets, trousers, short fur coats. There were times when there were still bits of arm in them or flesh stuck on with blood. There were a hundred and eighty of us working there, but all the employees weren't from the camp. About half of them were locals and Russians evacuated from other areas.

The plant was outside the camp?
Yes. The camp was huge, eight enormous barracks and some three hundred people crammed into each one. Those who were still strong enough were sent to hard labour in the mines all the way to Vorkuta. Because I was weaker, the doctor, Raisa Shumyanovna, a kind of humpbacked woman, recommended me as a tailor. Thus I ended up in that enterprise, and they made me the head tailor. Sewing was done by hand or on outdated machines. We tied up the repaired items in fives. Once the commander had checked the quality of the repairs, they went to expedition and were taken away by helicopter in the night.

Three years went by and we didn't know anything about the war, not even that our army was forming, no one told us anything. I got quite seriously ill, I had ulcers on my duodenum. A highly educated and pleasant Armenian operated on me. After the operation they told me I shouldn't eat the camp fare. But how was I supposed to get anything else when I didn't have any money? As a prisoner, I was still working in that military tailoring factory for free. Overhauling coats, *polushubka* they called them. We would tear off the sleeve, for example, and sew on one from another coat. We'd sew on buttons, sew up pockets. I still lived in the labour camp too, where we lay on the ground, they didn't even give us blankets, nothing at all. The camp was in the north and when a blizzard came, a *purga*, the whole building shook and it was pitch black. If we had to go somewhere in weather like that, say to work or for food, we had to hold on to a long rope and the person in front would light the way with a flashlight. That's what the conditions were like.

Who guarded you?
Members of the NKVD. They were called *dezhurny* and the lower ranked ones were *dnevalny*.

Did you have any friends there?
I had one friend from Khust, his name was Davidovich, we slept next to each other. He was a trained baker, and because I was in the tailor's shop, I asked the commander to help him get a better job. They put him in the kitchen. I was very happy about that, he didn't have to go to the forest for wood anymore. Before that he was chopping wood out of the frozen river. There were rafts that had frozen there and they would go chop them out because they needed wood for heating.

Was there any local government or other prisoner organisation?
There was nothing like that there. Even if they allowed for self-government, there wasn't the energy for it. I mean, every night, prisoners were dying of exhaustion. In the morning the nurse would come, fat Vasilievna, and in the doorway she'd shout: "Who's sick, who's got a temperature?" They'd rush towards her, but she could only take ten max. She'd take those to the infirmary, where they'd examine them and declare they couldn't do anything for them anyhow. They called exhaustion *Tsinga*,[155] it was a disease from a lack of vitamins. Stronger bodies withered the fastest. Some couldn't even get up, they just lay there. People there died very easily. They went to bed at night and in the morning they were dead. Before they distributed the bread in the morning, they'd ask: "How many dead?" We counted them, reported them, and they carried them off. Eventually we smartened up. We noticed how the Russians did it: they didn't report the dead so they'd get food for them.

Then once they told us that the war had ended. "Voina kaput, Hitler kaput." We started to celebrate. Of the original thirty-four of us that fled to the Soviet Union for freedom, twenty remained. But they told us not to rejoice yet, because the war with Japan was still going. We objected that we were sentenced to three years. "Three years, sure, but you also have indefinite written there. There's still a war with Japan and who knows how long that will last." We were still working at the plant as well. In 1946, this one Hungarian confided in me that they were sending a request to Moscow, because it seemed they'd forgotten about us. I asked him to add our group to his request as well. For a while nothing happened, then two soldiers came and said I should take all my things and go with them to the headquarters. The others were already there and some officers told us we were going to Odessa. We got three days' worth of bread, three salted herrings and a piece of chopped sugar. We boarded a train and rode and rode. More like we waited and waited, because other trains had priority. The trip to Moscow alone took eight days. We got off at the Kiyevsky train station and were supposed to wait for further orders. We

155 Tsinga – scurvy.

lay there on the platform, passengers trampling over us at night. It took several days and without food. The doctor who had operated my duodenal ulcer gave me some nutritional injections so I could get someone to inject it for me somewhere. I spoke up and they took me to the infirmary. There was a nurse there named Shura. I told her where I was from and that I had been operated on. I looked terrible, I weighed less than forty-five kilos. She went off somewhere and when she came back, she was smiling. She gave me an injection and then she took me to the seat reservation counter, where I got a special seat reservation. I immediately boarded the first train and left for Odessa.

So you were alone from your group?
Yes. In Moscow I even got some food for the trip, a brick of bread and again some dried-out and disgustingly salty fish. The journey by train took a fortnight. Odessa looked like a Babylon of nations. Everyone who was leaving the work camps was passing through. People from Czechoslovakia, Hungary, even from Holland. I remained there two weeks.

Where did they place you?
In some run-down convalescent home with broken windows.[156] There were also soldiers guarding us constantly. But we got food. Every day they sorted the people and put together transports to Romania, to Hungary. One day they called out: "To Czechoslovakia!" I immediately spoke up.

Were there many of you?
Lots, because there were also prisoners of war from the Slovak army, and Hungarian POWs too. From Odessa we walked about ten kilometres and then boarded freight wagons. We started off but soon thereafter the train stopped. We transferred onto a Czechoslovak train and rode all the way to Trebišov. I had a fever, I was not well, and so in Trebišov I ended up straight in the hospital, where the Canadian Red Cross was working. I lay there about a fortnight, then they took everyone to Malacky, where they held us until we received confirmation from our birthplace that we were really born there and that there was no trial underway against our families. For example because they were war criminals. The documents arrived in about two weeks, so they released me from Malacky. Someone advised me to go to Bratislava, where there was a repatriation centre, where they helped returnees. In Bratislava, the doctor sent me to the Jewish hospital, where I lay for some more time. Lots of people were constantly dying there. A certain Mr Berka, who I had gone to school with, gave me some money from Joint[157]. I recovered somewhat

156 Likely the repatriation camp Luisdorf.
157 Joint – short for the American Jewish Joint Distribution Committee.

and finally left for my hometown. Our home already had someone else living there. I sat in front of it, where my mother would always sit, thought about my parents and cried. There was a family with four children living in the home and the woman told me what happened when they were deporting my parents. My mother apparently grabbed hold of the door, the Arrow Crosses[158] kicked her, pulled my father by his beard and shouted at him: "You Jewish swine!" They were all drunk. When it started to get dark, the woman asked me where I was going to sleep, because I wouldn't fit at their place. I went to the neighbour's. He was a teacher at the primary school in Choňkovce, where I used to go, his name was Jan Fetkovič. He took me in and hosted me. He also told me what had happened in the village. The teacher then asked what my plan was. I replied that I'd most like to leave Europe, that I didn't want to stay there.

Did you think about Palestine, were you Zionist-oriented?
No, I wasn't a Zionist. The teacher told me that if I didn't want to stay there, I should sell the house. It was an old building, a thatched roof, tiny windows, a pen for a cow and a chicken coop. Inside a kitchen and two rooms. Under no circumstances did I want to live there and have everything staring back at me. So I sold the house. I didn't spend the money, though, and waited for my brother to return, as I had learned he had survived.

Where was he during the war?
In Siberia, in Omsk. He had also fled, but a lot sooner than me, so he spent eight years in the Soviet Union.

What do you think saved you in the Soviet camp?
For one thing, the fact that I'm small in stature and I never traded the food I got for anything. Smokers traded half their bread with civilians for tobacco. They'd meet with them, say, while working in the woods and get *makhorka* from them for half their bread. There wasn't any paper anywhere they could roll a cigarette in, not even newspaper, so they would go where the officers went to the bathroom and take the paper that the officers had, pardon my French, wiped their butts with, and they'd roll cigarettes in that. And one other thing saved me: there was a Russian officer there for desertion and he taught me to play chess. We made the figures out of bread and the board out of handkerchiefs and soot. Exhausted people who are starving and don't have anything on their mind but their own suffering, they succumbed to the horrible conditions much more easily. I remember one Romanian, he used to say

158 Arrow Cross Party – a Nazi-like, anti-Semitic political party operating in Hungary in the years 1939–1945.

he couldn't take it, that he'd commit suicide. When we went to unload the wagons and one of the sacks had burst a bit, had a little hole, we'd pour a bit out of it. One time it was barley, another oats, corn, powdered eggs. It was unloaded in the Northern Dvina port. We'd put it in our pockets, and when we got to the camp, we'd crush it up in a bottle and cook it. This thing happened to me once: it was minus forty outside and I managed to smuggle something in. Because they would pat us down, I'd made this tiny pad, stuffed it in and smuggled it under my clothes, because we had these cotton-lined coats. They usually looked in the pockets and the trousers, and when they found something, the prisoner had to strip naked and dump it out at the gate. But I got through. Except I guess some Russian prisoners saw. They were called *zhuliks*, people who had spent almost their whole lives in prisons, and as soon as they got out, they'd commit something else and go right back. They must have noticed that I smuggled it in and was cooking... There was a raid, it was dark and suddenly I discovered all I had left was a spoon, everything else was gone.

ERNEST BREINER

Born 22 November 1922 in Humenné. His father was an assistant tinsmith, his mother took care of four children. After his compulsory schooling, Ernest became an apprentice in a hardware store. There was a large Jewish community in his hometown, in whose activities he was very involved. He attended one of the local synagogues with his father, and was also a member of the left-wing Zionist youth organisation Hashomer Hatzair and several sports groups. He was not exposed to anti-Semitism until the founding of the Slovak State. Only in 1940 did he experience the Hlinka Youth militias, who several times a week forced the Jews to clean the streets, wash the toilets and perform other menial jobs in the city. Even before the war, he had attended a club where workers would meet, where he would hear words of praise for the Soviet Union and life in a socialist society. In Humenné he became acquainted with a young Jewish man who had fled the Nazis from Poland and planned to go to the USSR. In 1940, Breiner decided to go with him. At first they travelled together through German-occupied Poland. In the end, however, he made it to the Soviet-controlled eastern part on his own. After being arrested by the NKVD, he was imprisoned in Sambor, Stryi and Starobilsk, where he was sentenced to three years of forced labour for illegally crossing the border. However he ended up spending seven years in camps in Kolyma, where he mostly mined gold. He had to work additional years in the area as a civilian employee.

He could only return to his native Humenné in 1955. His parents and siblings survived the war thanks to neighbours that hid them from deportation. Ernest Breiner then worked as the manager of a grocery store and later in a restaurant. In 1956, he married, and a year later his son Peter was born, then in 1962 Pavol. Shortly after his return, he joined the Communist Party of Czechoslovakia, of which he was a member until 1988.[159]

— — —

When did you decide to flee to the Soviet Union?
We left Humenné sometime in July 1940. There were many of us young people who wanted to go to Russia. But when push came to shove, only two of us remained – me and the refugee from Poland. My parents didn't know I wanted to leave. I told them I was going to work. Except I didn't come back for fifteen years. We were heading on foot across the Lupkov Pass to Sanok in occupied Poland. The city lay on the river San, which formed the border between what was then the Soviet Union, which had taken over today's western Ukraine, and Germany, which was occupying the western part of Poland. We avoided roads and went only at night. It wasn't a problem crossing the Czechoslovak-Polish border. My guide knew Polish and twice arranged for us to spend the night on some hay in a barn. But first we watched carefully to see if there were Germans in the village. If there were, we moved on. We got to Sanok on Friday afternoon. At that time, Jews in Poland were already wearing armbands with a star. Naturally we didn't have them, so no one noticed we were Jews. In Sanok we looked for the relatives of our acquaintances from Humenné.

Did you stay with them?
No, they were afraid the Germans would do a raid and find someone there. They recommended a boarding house for young Polish Jews though. But the Gestapo raided it at night and rounded up all the lodgers. They took us to a large, empty building they were guarding. But not very carefully, plus the building wasn't locked. Anyone who wasn't afraid could escape, which one older Polish Jew and I managed to do.

And what about your Polish companion from the trip to Sanok?
We parted ways. At the Jewish Community in Sanok, they didn't want to recognise me as a Jew, I didn't have *tzitzit*[160] on, whereas he did. They asked, what kind of Jew am I then? I said: a circumcised Jew. But they said that wasn't enough. I knew Yiddish fairly well. They said, every Christian here speaks Yiddish, and they wouldn't take me. That's why I parted ways with the Pole that came with me from Humenné.

---

159 *CVG Collection of Interviews*, interview with Ernest Breiner recorded 21 October 1996 by Katarina Zavarská, translated from Slovak by Štěpán Černoušek.

160 Tzitzit – ritual tassels reminding one of God's commandments, which men of Orthodox Jewish faith must wear under their outer clothing.

Did he stay in Sanok?
He did, but I don't know what became of him. After our escape, me and the other Pole set out for Gdansk. But the Germans caught us again there at the port and sent us back to Sanok. We ended up in the same building, this time under lock and key. I spent about a month there.

Did they feed you?
Yes, but otherwise we were locked up inside the whole time, about twenty people. We slept on mattresses. It was summer, though, and it was bearable. One fine August day, I escaped from there again. I went to the people I knew, but again they didn't want to take me in, saying it was too dangerous. Again they just suggested where I could hide. In response to that, I told them I couldn't be there anymore and I didn't want to go home, so I would go to Russia. They didn't recommend that. They probably knew what was going on there. They must have had some news from the other side of the border, from Sambor, from Stryi, at that time there were Jews living in the territory taken over by the Soviet Union as well. But on the German side, the repression and night-time raids against Jews were escalating. I saw with my own eyes how the Germans surrounded a synagogue one Saturday, doused it with gasoline, and lit it on fire. Hard times were already beginning for the Jews.

So on the night of 25 August, I crossed the new border on Polish territory between what was then Germany and the Soviet Union. As I already said, it was formed by the river San, with one bank German, the other Soviet. There were patrols there, but you could cross it. I had to cross some barbed wire and then I jumped in the river wearing my clothes and shoes and a beret on my head. I had a few things underneath it. The river San is quite fierce, but I was a good swimmer and I crossed it without any major problems. On the other side I saw an enormous amount of barbed wire barriers, between which there were gaps about a metre and a half wide. Wet from head to toe, I headed for one of them and immediately I saw Russian soldiers coming towards me, calling out "Hands up!" Then they searched me.

How did the Russian soldiers treat you?
I was looking forward to them, to the fact that they're Russians, that I no longer had to have anything to do with Germans and Poles. I had bad experiences with Poles. Once they know you're a Jew, they don't treat you well, they were quite unpleasant. On the Soviet side, the first thing that quite surprised me was when I saw a rifle hanging on twine. One of the soldiers, a young lad, maybe nineteen, had it hung over his shoulder like that. Once they'd searched me, they ordered "vperyod" and led me to an enormous building of the border guard, where I ended up locked up in a room about 10 x 15 metres wide. There was a village oven there and I was wet. I had some matches under my beret, so

I made a fire in it to dry out. Sometime around five in the afternoon, the door latch lifted and a soldier brought me a piece of bread and a bowl of borscht. He bid me to eat, but I didn't really understand him. I spoke German, Hungarian, but not Russian. That same night they conducted my first interrogation, saying I was a spy. I told them: "I'm seventeen and a half years old, how can I be a spy?" Then they asked where I was from and why I came. I explained to them that I had fled from the guardsmen, that they were persecuting me. "Ty shto, komunist?" they asked. "Yes." So I spent three days there, then they took me to the prison in Sambor. There I spent a month in a cell about 4 × 1.5 metres big, where there were around twenty of us.

What nationality were your cellmates?
Ukrainians, Jews, Poles, one Romanian. They concentrated everyone they detained in the Sambor prison. From Sambor they took us to Stryi, where I spent another month. Sometime in October 1940, this was followed by transport by freight train to Starobilsk in Ukraine. There was a former monastery there with five churches, where there were about twenty-two thousand of us. The vast majority were Poles, mostly officers.

Don't forget that Starobilsk is close to the Katyn Forest. Maybe the Russians took them from that camp straight to Katyn? Otherwise there were a lot of guys there from Bessarabia, from Bucovina, Romanians, but also Slovaks, people from Subcarpathian Rus. As a teenager I worked delivering food. There were around one hundred fifty of us doing that, younger people. No one else of the twenty-two thousand prisoners worked. Only the Russian prisoners, who cooked or helped out in the kitchen. Basically, no one was allowed to leave the monastery churches other than those carrying food. Each church was divided into three floors. Mine was maybe twenty metres high and I slept on a pallet on the top floor. We washed on the ground floor, where you'd wait as much as an hour before you could wash yourself in cold water.

How did the guards treat you?
They weren't that crude yet there. We also barely had any contact with them. They didn't enter the churches much. They came once a day to count us, which was the top priority. Nobody better be missing! I didn't even go to interrogations. Once I turned 18, some NKVD officials came to me and read me my verdict, saying I'd been sentenced to three years in a corrective labour camp for illegally crossing the border. In other words in a concentration labour camp. We were in Starobilsk from autumn 1940 until spring 1941. The last transport left Starobilsk on 4 May 1941. They crammed us in freight wagons, eighty people in each. Inside the wagon was a single large receptacle for water containing about thirty to forty litres and then another one for going to the bathroom. During the transport, in Irkutsk, we received word of the

war breaking out. They took us to Vladivostok, to what was called a collection camp. There were already around seventy, eighty thousand of us. Women on one side, men on the other. From that amount of people, they decided who would go where. Some time at the start of August they took us to Nakhodka, which is a big port from which ocean liners leave for Magadan. The voyage lasted six days across the Sea of Okhotsk. At that time, Magadan had a population of around forty thousand. And it was a big port too.

Did they tell you at the start of the transport where they were taking you?
Nobody told us anything, absolutely nothing. Just to go back to the transport from Starobilsk to Vladivostok: I was sleeping next to an old Russian who had experience from work camps. They gave us rusks and salted fish to eat, cod. And the Russian told me not to eat the fish, that I'd die from it, because I'd be thirsty and drink cold unsafe water. They refilled the water where the train happened to stop, at these hand pumps. There were eighty of us in the wagon at the start of the trip. By the time we reached Vladivostok, a third of us had died. They got ill, maybe from the bad water? I didn't eat the fish and I didn't get sick. Even though I was very hungry, I threw out the salt cod like that old Russian. So on 22 June 1941, the war caught up with us at Irkutsk. They moved the train to a siding there and we waited forty or fifty hours. No water, no anything. So the desperate prisoners started rocking the wagons and shouting. The train had around fifty, sixty wagons, eighty people in each, some five thousand people total. The collective shouting was basically so loud, and reached so far, that a military train stopped next to us. The wagon doors opened and we saw Russian soldiers travelling from Vladivostok to the front. We were being taken in the opposite direction. We shouted that they hadn't given us any water. So their officer ordered them to give us some. We sat there another two or three days before they let us move on. We spent about two months travelling like that. Unwashed, filthy, louse-ridden, smelly, and on top of that people were dying. They didn't mess around with the dead bodies, just tossed them outside. They didn't bury anyone. In contrast, they did a check every evening. The guards tapped the panelling on the wagon to make sure no one had loosened the boards in preparation for escape, then they counted us. It was rough. At the collection camp in Vladivostok, everyone found a place to lie down in the barracks. At least they gave us something to eat there. In the morning tea, five hundred grams of bread a day and a hunk of sugar. During the day there was soup or porridge, in the evening porridge. We were constantly hungry even so. It wasn't enough for a young man.

Did food get stolen?
No. They killed you for stealing food. Not the guards, the other prisoners. If they caught anyone stealing someone's bread, that was the end. You could

steal anything – shoes, clothes, personal items, but not bread, that was a necessity of life. A thief like that just got hung or stabbed in the barracks. They'd have a sign around their neck: For stealing bread! The guards didn't say a word about it.

You were talking about Nakhodka...
They took us to Nakhodka from Vladivostok, but we were only there a couple of days, not long. Then they loaded us on a cargo ship named the Dzhurma, which set out for Magadan. It was a large cargo ship, with around five thousand of us crammed aboard, everyone in the hold. The cargo space had four floors. Two thirds was for men, one third for women. Most people were seasick and vomited. It was at least ten metres up a ladder to get to the toilet above deck. When the weather was bad and someone was weak, they'd totter and fall. Nobody reacted. The deck mates would just ask: "Where's Mišo? Where's Jano?" You know what it's like to climb a ladder weak and tormented from the previous journey? Moreover without water – sometimes they didn't give us any water, or just a cupful a day. The food was cold, rusks and fish. I ate the rusks and was constantly hungry. At Magadan they unloaded us and took us by truck to the next collection camp. It was big, thousands of people. They took the women somewhere else. I saw them being unloaded from the hold – weak, dirty, wet – using a net. And then they dumped them on the truck beds like some kind of raw material. It wasn't a pleasant sight. Then they took them somewhere else.

You didn't know where?
Nobody knew anything about our own next destination, let alone the women's. At the Magadan camp they washed us, cut our hair and shaved us. All our hair and body hair. Until then we had had our own clothes, which were pretty dirty and torn by then. There we got camp clothes.

Anyone who was sick had to report it. Aside from lice, I wasn't suffering from anything. Then they locked us up in the barracks, where we slept on the concrete floor, only leaving to go to the dining hall, a kind of wooden building with hundreds and thousands of people pushing and shoving. In the morning they gave out tea and a piece of bread. I had already learned how to manage bread in Sambor. When the prisoners got their bread in the morning, usually they ate it all right away. But what then? They didn't get more until the next day. So I sewed a little pouch where I'd store the bread until evening. In the morning I'd eat half, and the rest in the evening. It required a lot of self-control because I was constantly hungry. But I had to get used to the regimen if I wanted something to eat in the evening. Sometime in early September 1941, they loaded us onto American heavy Diamond-brand trucks that also had trailers. It worked out to a wagon and a half of cargo, but it didn't go faster than fifty kilometres an hour. Two drivers took turns driving, with a mechanic riding along. They drove us about twenty-five, thirty hours, we completely lost our sense of time. There was a lot of dust everywhere, there was no asphalt, just dirt roads. Eventually we reached the Svetly[161] goldfield, which was about five hundred kilometres from Magadan. There was an old half-ruined work camp, buildings without roofs and so on. 1200 people were supposed to live there. We got axes and went to the forest for wood. In five days we had more or less repaired the buildings. Mostly the roofs and windows. It was just in time, because on 14 September the first snow fell. The barracks had bunk beds for four people, everything made of wood. Two hundred prisoners slept in each building. The guards divided us up into brigades of thirty, forty people. The guard also decided who would be the brigadier. He didn't care if they were a political prisoner or a criminal. He'd just look and say: "You're going to be the brigadier." And that was that.

What kind of work did they use you for at the camp?
For mining gold.

What was the mining method?
In the summer, the ground thawed down to half a metre. It was gravelly, stony soil. Blasting holes were drilled by hand, about fifty, sixty centimetres deep. We had to make about ten such openings a day. We used a rounded iron rod, called a *lom*, and with that we dug or drilled the holes, about eight centimetres in diameter. Then an explosive was placed inside and the blasting was carried out. Civilians did that part. We loaded up the ore and carted it to a facility about twenty metres tall. The ore travelled up along conveyor belts and then fell down, getting rinsed with water. Waste by-products such as dirt, sand and gravel were collected on metal mats, or more like metal plates. In 1943, they started to form smaller, five- to ten-member brigades. I ended up in one such brigade. It mined gold in a different manner. We'd heat up a boiler with coal until the water inside started boiling and became steam. The steam then travelled along a fifteen-metre hose, at the end of which was an iron bar with a hole about half a centimetre in diameter, a kind of protuberance for punching the ground. Thanks to the steam, even the permafrost would loosen up a bit, so you could hammer away as much as it was possible. In that manner we got as deep as a metre and a half and in a day we would remove about four cubic metres of soil. In the winter we worked in underground adits. There we also blasted and the gold-bearing ore was carted out onto huge heaps.

---

161 Svetly – the name for the camps on the river Armani in the Tenkinsky District north of Magadan, where the prisoners lived who worked in the mine Svetly, also called Stalinsky.

Did you find a lot of gold?
A massive amount.

Did anyone keep some gold for themselves?
Not that I know of, maybe at other goldfields. But everyone knew that a gram of hidden gold meant another ten years in the Gulag, ten grams execution. No one wanted to risk that. Don't forget, there were snitches and informants among us. We hid gold so that we could meet the daily quota. You see there were days when we didn't find anything. And then there were days when we mined up as much as ten kilos. So then we took some of the withheld gold, which was hidden somewhere outside at the work site, to meet the daily quota. Which was 150 to 200 grams for each brigade.

What were the relationships among prisoners like?
It depended on what company you ended up in. When a plebe like me ended up among criminals, it was miserable, because political prisoners tended to be servants to the criminals. That was an unwritten law and there was no one to complain to. They never went to work, and their brigadier couldn't get them to. Politicals always went, criminals would rather sit in solitary. It was beneath them to work. That was another unwritten law. They also dealt with any major problems amongst one another or with other prisoners quickly and simply, by murdering the person in question. No one ever found out who did it. We ourselves didn't know where someone got hung in the night, even though we lived there. The criminals had their own silent technique. You never heard anything, not a rustle.

Did they inform on you?
No, criminals didn't usually inform. More so the politicals. For a piece of bread, for a bit of tobacco. The criminals always figured out who it was and then murdered them. They had no love for informants. Even though there were informants among the criminals as well. But they had major benefits for it, a certain status they achieved by informing.

So you were constantly mining gold?
Not always. In the winter, I ended up on a logging campaign. With an axe in hand, in Russian "s toporikom", and snow up to my chest. Under such conditions, everyone had to log three cubic metres of wood a day.

Did you have any special clothing?
Yes, for underclothes we got long johns and shirts. Those kind of Russian shirts, *fufaikas*, with no collar. Then we wore a warm coat, called a *bushlag*, and cotton-lined trousers. *Valenki* instead of leather boots. They were made of

coarse felt, like you put under a horse's saddle. Leather would soak through. The felt on the *valenki* was roughly a centimetre thick, that didn't soak through. When a prisoner got back to the barracks from work, they would knock the snow off well, then hang them up and they'd dry out nicely. The barracks were heated, ours had two stoves made of petrol barrels. We cut a door in the front, made a chimney hole in the back, then fitted on metal pipes leading the smoke out through the roof. The weaker ones, who didn't go to work and stayed home because the doctor had found them unfit to work, took care of the fire during the day. When we came back from work in the evening, everyone still had to go into the forest and bring some wood. When a thousand people do that, you get a good supply. If we didn't bring back enough, they'd chase us back into the forest several kilometres so there was enough for the kitchen and the guards. Sometimes coal was delivered if there were coal mines near the camp.

Did you try to make any contact outside the camp? Were you curious what was going on the world?
Contact with whom? There were just a few buildings beside the camp where the guards and chief lived. We didn't have information about anything. No newspapers, books, nothing. None of the guards told us anything about any events. Each of us prisoners also only worried about ourselves first and foremost; the main thing was to survive.

What followed after the logging campaign?
In 1943, I ended up at the Maldyak goldfield. Like the other camps, it was also part of Sevvostlag, the commander of which was the infamous Garanin.[162] There were three camps there. One of them was a penal camp. During the Great Terror, the largest purges, it served as an extermination camp. They eliminated political prisoners they didn't manage to shoot in Russia there. I didn't see it with my own eyes, but the old prisoners told us stories about it, and showed us the places where the mass executions took place. When we arrived at that camp, it was all scrubbed clean, which was a difference from the other camps. It was also enormous, there were eighty barracks at the camp, each for two hundred people. In total there were sixteen thousand of us! Of that a large part comprised auxiliary personnel. After all, there were at least twenty kitchens for cooking there and another twenty buildings served

162 Stepan Nikolaevich Garanin (1898–1950), in the years 1937–1938 the commander of Sevvostlag, the main administration of camps in the Kolyma district, according to a number of witnesses (among them the writer Varlam Shalamov) he participated personally in the execution of prisoners (the largest mass execution in Maldyak took place on 15 August 1938, when 159 prisoners were shot). At the end of 1938, Garanin was arrested and imprisoned at Pechorlag, where he died on 3 July 1950.

Stepan Garanin, the infamous commander of Sevvostlag in the years 1937–1938, who himself died in the gulag in 1950. *Repro ÚSTR*

as dining halls in the winter. In the summer people ate outside in the grass or on the pavement. At night, the barracks were closed up after nine and nothing happened till five in the morning.

How did Maldyak function with such a large number of prisoners?
They had the camp divided into zones. Every zone numbered 1000 to 1200 people. The zones weren't fenced off though, just marked out. Each had its own head guard. And watching over them was the camp chief, Captain Pisirov. I don't know if he was Uzbek or Kazakh, but he was a devil.

Why a devil?
He was both God and Tsar. The camp was a republic where he ruled. Even Stalin couldn't give him orders.

And what kind of work did you do there?
Again we were mining gold. The gold-mining area was as big as the whole Humenné district. I probably would've stayed there longer if they hadn't shot me and I didn't end up in the hospital. We were walking to work in rows of five, accompanied by two soldiers. Before leaving they always warned us: "One step left or right and we'll shoot!" So, we'd just left the gates and I tripped

and fell out of line, and a shot rang out. They shot one of my ribs, so I ended up in the hospital in Susuman. There I got purulent pleurisy and they had to operate on me and cut out another rib. I was treated from winter 1943 till the start of winter 1944, ten months.

What did the hospital look like?
The staff, including medical staff, was made up of prisoners. That meant they behaved decently. Especially the doctors, they provided me with all the help and care they could manage there. It was a Jew that operated on me. In the barracks by oil lamp and without narcosis, just local anaesthesia and I watched what they were doing. He must have been an excellent surgeon, from 1943 to date I've never had any problems, it never got infected, never hurt. I still do have consequences because the pus that accumulated after being hit by the bullet pushed down on my lungs, which is why they had to take another rib as well, so the pus could get out. One lung never regained its original size. It's a few centimetres smaller than the other one. But until fifty I couldn't feel it. Then it started making itself known when I was walking fast or going up stairs. But there's no pain.

When they let you out of the hospital, did you go back to Maldyak?
No, they took me to what was called a "forest camp", 23 kilometres from Magadan. There we didn't go logging in the forest, but we cut wood for the central prison hospital for the area, which was right next door. It was a big hospital, for approximately a thousand people, and they did everything imaginable there – amputating mutilated limbs, operations, treatment. Everything in ground-floor buildings where the doctors and staff also lived.

And what were the conditions like at the forest camp?
Pretty normal, there were about sixty of us, all former patients who had recovered. They cooked fairly well for us. Plus, the cook chose me as an assistant and so I found myself at a food source and after three months I quickly got back on my feet. We also didn't sleep on bare pallets covered with a coat, but we had straw and blankets. My convalescence ended, however, and they took me back to Maldyak, where my sentence soon ended and I was supposed to be let free. But they summoned me and informed me that I would be detained until the end of the war. Which happened. Some people finished a ten-year sentence, say, and they added on another five years even though they hadn't done anything.

This took place in front of a court?
No, there was no trial. The chief simply pulled out a piece of paper and read off that I was detained until the end of the war. So I came to terms with it. At

that time we already had some information about the course of the war from imprisoned soldiers coming from the front.

Were you mining gold again like before being shot?
Yes, but now in a brigade without an armed convoy, unaccompanied by guards. There were ten of us and we went to work on our own. They knew we weren't going to run away when our sentences were over and we were just "doing extra time". That meant things were a bit looser, not just the walk to the work site. We were looking for gold on our own and many of us already had the experience necessary to find it. Thus we often found a good spot and turned up a lot of gold. But when we found more gold than the quota stipulated, we left it right at the work site for a rainy day. Because we didn't always find enough to meet the daily quota. Then they transferred us to the Chkalov goldfield.

What was it like there?
We did the same, but the work and personal conditions were many times worse. Yet it wasn't even a particularly big camp, around 1200 prisoners. But there were young guards there, that was the worst. Older supervisors and guards were used to convicts. The memories of the young ones are not pleasant.

Did they beat you?
That happened too. There we worked under supervision again, accompanied by soldiers. They would mark out where we could go and where we couldn't. When someone crossed the invisible line, they fired immediately. I also remember that there was one Russian who wasn't doing very well, and nevertheless he had to carry these long eight-sided steel rods used to drill into the ground to the blacksmith for sharpening. Long story short, he wanted to warm up at the blacksmith's fire a bit, but the guard quickly and aggressively shooed him away. When the guard turned around, satisfied, the Russian immediately rushed up to him and stabbed him from the back. The other soldier shot him immediately. They dragged both the dead bodies away and life went on.

Were the quotas at Chkalov higher than before?
We worked from six in the morning to six in the evening. The only technical convenience used was blasting, everything else was done by hand. In four months my situation got even worse, as they transferred me to Chaurya, to an area known as the Valley of Death.[163]

---

163 In connection with the Gulag camps in Kolyma, the term Valley of Death was most frequently used for the Butugychag camp, where uranium was mined. It was located 200 km to the north of Magadan.

Why was it called that?
The Valley of Death had the highest death rate, which was because of the inhumane treatment, the working and living conditions, the poor and irregular diet. When they named an area like that that was already in the Russian Far East, it had to really earn it compared to other camp complexes. There were terrible conditions everywhere. Consider that 1200 of us came on the transport to the Svetly goldfield, and by spring there were only 180 of us left.

That many prisoners died?
Yes, people died of exhaustion, hunger, from the unbearable cold. It wasn't possible to bury people in the winter, so we would put the dead in these kind of sacks with a tag attached by wire to the leg. In the spring, as soon as the soil allowed, they herded almost all the prisoners outside and a mass grave was dug, approximately two metres wide, two metres deep and a kilometre long. Then dirt was thrown on the dead bodies and that was that. No one knew exactly where who was buried. I only experienced an exhumation once, which was after the war at the end of 1945. It was some Latvian whose father had become a high-ranking official in Soviet Latvia. The poor dead man had served with the Germans as a pilot. The Soviets captured him, but didn't shoot him, and he got fifteen years. His name was Kriske, I'll never forget it. There was great pressure from above at the time that we should find him at any cost. Luckily, one of the prisoners knew him and remembered where they'd buried him.

And did you find him?
We did, but exhuming his body from the frozen ground was tough.

Did you establish any close contact with any fellow prisoners, friendship?
At the camp it was essential to know how to deal with that terrible situation, to get out of work. I gradually learned as well. Others helped too. As soon as there was a Jew in the kitchen, making bread or in the infirmary, another five Jews turned up around them. There was never as much solidarity among them as there, in the camp. It was different with the Polish Jews. They weren't pleasant, friendly, congenial, none of that. They were people who didn't wish anyone anything good, they only envied others. When I got to the aforementioned Chkalov, there was a man named Blokh there, a Jew, a military veterinarian. He worked as the camp doctor. He was a former Russian officer from the Kyiv District. He was supposed to be promoted to general, but in 1937 they picked him up in the night and gave him ten years. Some distant aunt of his in America had remembered him and sent him a greeting by post. Under Article 58, this was "contact with foreigners", with America. As a doctor, he saved himself though. That was a privileged position in the camp too, as there were

never enough doctors and they were needed everywhere. Before his sentence ended, I met with him a lot and he helped me out. When I then also left the labour camp, I immediately sought him out. He was conducting his profession at a nearby livestock farm. Later they let him go home. He couldn't go all the way to Moscow, so he lived at the "101st kilometre".[164] He couldn't return to the city until 1954. When I was going back to Czechoslovakia, I visited him in Moscow.

How did you find out about the end of the war?
The guards were the first to tell us the war had ended. Then they turned on the radio: "The Great Patriotic War has ended with victory over fascism, Berlin has been conquered," and so on. For me, with my sentence having been extended until the end of the war, it meant liberation. The governor really did call me in, but only to tell me I'd be staying at the camp until further orders. I signed a declaration acknowledging this, and the next day I was already travelling from Chaurya to Karbulyakh and Kalaybit, which were two camps next to each other.

What awaited you there?
They weren't large camps, each holding about four hundred people. We were building a road. There aren't any trains in the Magadan Oblast. There's constant permafrost, then in the summer it's swampy, so you can't build a solid foundation there. So people and material could only be transported by road. These were built as follows: the surface of the ground was dug out down to about half a metre in the width of the road, then stones, bits of wood and beams were put in the holes. Then a layer of dirt and crushed stone was put on top and packed down. I was in a brigade there too. The brigadier was a criminal, but a very decent man, Zolotukhin, a kind of petty thief. But otherwise a prince among men, he never slept at the camp. He was always on the road. He would go rescue cars carrying loads of flour, canned goods, anything, that had got stuck somewhere. He would take people from the brigade with him and they never came back empty-handed. For that reason, we even cooked in the barracks, because we had ingredients. I spent the second half of 1945 there and the years 1946 and 1947. Later as a nurse, I didn't have to build roads anymore.

164 101st kilometre – for USSR citizens inconvenient to the regime (exiles, families of political prisoners, dissidents, etc.), a complete ban was applied on living within a hundred kilometres of major cities.

A group of prisoners building the Kotlas–Vorkuta railway. *Komi Republic National Museum*

Did you undergo any nursing course?
There was no course. I just had to learn everything myself. To clean out and bandage wounds and the like.

Did you ever have to deal with a difficult injury?
Serious injuries got taken to the hospital. Where we worked, there weren't many of those. But it did occur that someone deliberately chopped their leg with an axe, we called those *samorubs*, or they'd chop off three fingers so they didn't have to work. Or they ask someone else to do it: "Otrubi mne nogu!" But it wasn't really worth it, they'd have a five-year sentence and get another ten for deliberate mutilation. There were even those who had thirty-year sentences. For example, attempting escape was rewarded with ten extra years. But where could such desperate cases flee? A few kilometres and then they'd come back or get caught. They didn't have anything with them and no one lived anywhere far and wide. Only after I left the camp did I end up in the area where natives lived, Yakuts, Evens, Chukchi. They didn't help out much though and were more likely to turn a fugitive in, because they got a financial reward for doing so. So where could you flee? Through the frozen taiga with snow up to your chest? Or in the summer through the swamps among billions of mosquitoes? You couldn't take the road, there were patrols there. There was no hope associated with escape.

On 23 February 1947, they unexpectedly told me I could pack my things and go. A telegram had come to the camp and they gave it to me and so long. Luckily I was relatively well dressed; it was very cold outside. But I was surprised nonetheless. Release was always uncertain, Taixler from Humenné could tell you about that.

What happened to him?
He was a communist and in 1939 he went to the Soviet Union. There he got an eight-year sentence. At home he'd played football and the camp governor was a football fan. When Taixler's sentence was about to end, the governor told him: "If Dynamo wins, you'll go home to Czechoslovakia. But if they don't, you'll never see Czechoslovakia again." Dynamo won and in 1947 they let him go.

Did you know about him?
I didn't. We were five hundred kilometres away from each other. I just suspected he'd be somewhere in Russia. He must have found out about me somehow though, because as soon as he got home, he told my parents I was somewhere in Russia. My parents started searching, but they didn't find out anything, even though I had written lots of letters and even sent some telegrams after I was released. They didn't get any of it.

Where did you go when they set you free?
My first trip led from Kalaybit to Adygalakh,[165] where there was something like the HR department of the Road Administration, where they had summoned me by telegram. I got there on the back of a truck. Sitting in that HR department were comrades wearing medals on their chests, one had a prosthesis, no leg. They asked where I wanted to go to work. I told them I was a Czechoslovak citizen and I want to go home. They answered: "No, no, we need you here." And they gave me a paper that I would go be a stoker at a power plant. I also got a document for a boarding house and a bill of exchange for two hundred rubles and the tickets needed to buy clothes. I paid for that myself. I was accommodated in a relatively clean room where there were ten of us and each had their own bed. And then I started working at the power plant.

How long did you last there?
Not very long. I left to do security. Every food and industrial enterprise had its own security guards. It was clean and easy work. I needed to rest after the hard work of the labour camps. I didn't make much, about six hundred rubles, but it was enough for food and some clothes. I worked in security until the end of 1948. In 1949 I transferred to a bakery, where I spent about half a year, then I signed up for a three-month chef's course. I aced the exam, so I became a cook for a boarding school cafeteria. There were about one hundred fifty youths from the surrounding settlements at the boarding school that took care of road and truck maintenance. There were teenage girls among them too, which is dangerous for a single guy, so I moved to a nursery school and cooked there for the rest of 1949. Then I transferred to another camp, where I was a freight forwarder. At that time, every truck had a guide that supervised the transported food and industrial goods. I worked the route from Magadan to Adygalakh, which was eight hundred kilometres. There and back, winter and summer. We had around one hundred fifty vehicles. The drivers were former prisoners and knew the local roads perfectly. It was fairly well-paid work, if dull. You would sit for twenty, sometimes even thirty hours in a truck. I lasted there a year and a half.

Did you try to make any contact with home?
I was in Magadan about five times a month. And every time I either sent a letter or a telegram to the Czechoslovak consulate in Moscow. No response ever came. I also sent telegrams, I paid two hundred rubles for one, which was a lot of money. I always filled in the old address we'd lived at before the war. And nothing, nothing. Then another job change came along. The military

165 Adygalakh – a camp in the basin of the eponymous river Ayan-Yuryakh, sixty kilometres from Susuman.

chief for the district was Major Koroyov. He summoned me and said: "You're going to be a store manager. It's not far from Adygalakh, do you agree?" It really was a settlement a mere five kilometres away, inhabited by road workers, lumberjacks, around five hundred people. I went to take a look at the place. It was a fairly large shop and the manager got their own flat. I took the job. There I also got to know normal people, not former prisoners, and I slowly started to feel like them. They came there to work and had signed a contract for say three years. At that time, normal people would make pretty good money like that in the Soviet East. In Moscow, a standard wage was say a thousand rubles, in the East they'd get two thousand. And every six months, your salary would increase ten percent. After two and a half years, such an employee would be entitled to a vacation of half a year. With the trip by plane home and back covered. So I worked at the shop and only walked to Adygalakh to go to the cinema. In the settlement they only showed films twice a week. Or I'd get a ride. Often a driver would recognise me and take me the five kilometres. In 1953 or at the start of 1954 they made me the manager of an industrial kitchen. It was a large kitchen for five thousand people that worked in two shifts. I lasted there until the impending end of my Russian adventure. You see, sometime in the spring of 1955, they summoned me to come to Kadykchan about sixty kilometres away, where the main post office was. There I was in for a big surprise. They gave me the replies to my letters and telegrams to the consulate. Apparently the post office couldn't find me!? So I filled out what the consulate wanted from me, and soon I received confirmation of Czechoslovak citizenship as well as a passport. Thus I started running around getting the permits to leave and other formalities. Eventually I had arranged everything, including the appropriate stamps in my new passport, and in August I flew from Magadan via Yakutsk and Irkutsk to Moscow. But I already knew how difficult travelling around the Soviet Union was. In 1953 I had been on vacation and also flown by plane.

Where'd you go?
To Crimea, to Sochi. But instead of six months, I had only got a month of vacation, plus ten days for travel. In all that fifteen years it was my only vacation. They didn't even give me a dime for the labour camp, where I spent seven years. Nothing. We worked for them for lousy clothes, room and board. Despite the hard physical labour and its enormous utilitarian value. Just take the amount of gold, coal and wood we harvested for them.

Did you ever get rehabilitated?
No. The only thing I got from my time spent in the camp was knowledge of Russian. There was an engineer named Pap from Czechoslovakia that helped me with that. I met him in the hospital in 1943. He built bridges and went to

Russia as an expert at the invitation of the Soviet government along with his wife and child even before World War II. In 1937 they arrested him and sentenced him to ten years.

For what?
For contact with foreigners. His wife had returned to Czechoslovakia and he was writing letters with her. So he got ten years for writing letters with the outside world. He was working as a paramedic at the camp hospital and he pressured me to learn Russian. He had some Russian books, from which I slowly learned to read and then also write. It took me a year and a half. Otherwise there weren't any books or libraries at the camps in Kolyma.

By the way, I also met an American at the camp. He was a sailor and in 1939 his boat had docked in Odessa. He went for a walk, got lost and the boat left without him. The militia found him and naturally immediately labelled him an American spy. He got ten years. We met at the camp in 1944 and spent two years together. In the end he didn't last and died. That American was the only one I buried normally. Not in the mass grave.

How many people could have died during your time in Kolyma?
I don't know the exact numbers, but thousands. The number of prisoners was constantly being replenished. Otherwise work in Kolyma would have stopped; the exhausted and ill people there were dropping like flies. The people were mostly replenished in the summer, when fresh transports would come. Including at the time when I was already long out of the camp. I'm also only talking about the camps I know personally. There were many more camps though. In the Seymchan Valley, for example, there were women's labour camps. That was by the sea, vegetables grew there. They grew potatoes, cabbage.

Let's return to your definitive departure from Magadan. What did you do in Moscow?
I lived with the mother of an accountant from the industrial kitchen. He wasn't in Kolyma as a prisoner, but came to work there. I also had a good deal of money, about fourteen thousand rubles. During my whole period of normal employment, they deducted a hundred rubles from my salary for a government loan in exchange for paper bonds. I never lost or threw out those bonds, and at the advice of an official from the Czechoslovak embassy, I went to the state savings bank and told them I'm a Czech and going home. They checked the bonds and my passport and then without a single word paid me out those fourteen thousand rubles. That was really a lot of money.

So you could at least afford a plane ticket to Czechoslovakia...
No, I went home on the Moscow–Prague train. But I didn't leave until November, and spent the end of summer and autumn in Moscow. I finally reached Humenné on 5 November 1955. From the train station I went by foot carrying my suitcases and came to the corner of the street where we used to live. There was an old but familiar man standing there. So I asked him in Hungarian if he knows where the Breiners live. He looked at me and blurted out, "Ernest, is that you?" We used to live in the same building. His son had also been planning to travel to Russia, but ended up not going. The former neighbour led me to our door and called out: "I have a guest for you!" The door opened and there stood my mum, she immediately recognised me. So tears, crying and so on.

Who all was at home?
Just mum and another lady. Dad was at work and my brothers were at military service, the youngest in his first year and the middle one in his second. The guy who led me there went to a nearby workshop to get my father. He came home right away. He hadn't changed much, just got a bit balder. He cried too. I told them not to cry, that they should laugh and rejoice that I was home. Myself, I didn't feel any emotions though. After that hard fight for life, you were made of stone. Eventually my sister came home as well. We sent a telegram to my younger brother, who got three days' leave and came. The middle brother also came from the barracks and so we got together as a whole family. The celebrations lasted quite a while. Acquaintances, relatives, a few schoolmates that had survived. But they were few as saffron. Of the three thousand Jews in Humenné, a mere hundred fifty had survived the war.

How did your family save itself?
I didn't ask for a long time. I didn't know anything about the hardships they went through. Good people helped them a lot. We had neighbours, the Maďarik family, who hid them and saved them from transport to extermination camps like Auschwitz. The most gratifying thing for me was that they were alive, that they'd remained healthy and nothing had happened to anyone.

What did you do after your return?
First I waited for the money from Moscow. I had transferred the rest of the fourteen thousand rubles in my name to the bank in Humenné. It took a while, but at the end of November the money came. By the standards of the time, it was a nice sum. Then I started working and in 1956 I got married. My wife's family didn't agree with the marriage for a long time though. They said I was from the East, from Russia. In a way, they were right, that Russian camp behaviour stayed with me for a long time and it took years before I got used to civilisation.

IV.
DESERTERS FROM AUXILIARY LABOUR UNITS OF THE HUNGARIAN ARMY AND PRISONERS OF WAR IN INTERNMENT CAMPS

ZIGMUND WEISS (b. 1918 in Dunajská Streda), in May 1941, he deserted a Hungarian army labour unit to Soviet territory, sentenced to three years of forced labour. Died 13 March 1944 in Oneglag. *DAZO* ▶

изович 1918 г.

Deserters from the Hungarian army and people who fell into captivity during war operations within the Soviet Union comprise a specific group of Czechoslovak Jews who ended up in Soviet internment during World War II.

Military service was compulsory for all men within the territories annexed by the Hungarians, and Jews in Subcarpathia and south-eastern Slovakia were no exception. Initially everyone served in regular armed units, with only the unfit, regardless of their ethnicity, to be assigned to the auxiliary labour units established in the spring of 1939. With the growing restrictive measures against Jews, however, their position in the army also started to shift. In autumn 1939, they stopped being promoted to officer status. After the Second Vienna Award in August 1940, all new Jewish recruits were automatically assigned to labour units, and in August 1941 the remaining soldiers of Jewish origin were also transferred to these.[166] Today the number of Jews that served in these is estimated at roughly 100 thousand.[167] After the attack by Nazi Germany and its allies on the Soviet Union, approximately half of these were transferred to the front, with the rest being used for slave labour within Hungary.

As anti-Semitism grew, the conditions in labour units became worse, gradually becoming eradicative in nature. The men were used for hard labour, for example building roads, railroads and bridges. After the war with the Soviet Union broke out, the units were deployed to clear mines and unexploded ordnance, and to build and remove trenches and fortifications on the front lines. There was heavy loss of life here, further compounded by the insufficient food rations, denial of medical care and cruel treatment. There are known cases where the company commanders competed with each other to see who could kill more Jews, and those unfit to work were beaten to death or shot. Escapees were punished by mass executions. In one case, hundreds of labour unit members infected with typhus were herded into a barn and burned alive.[168]

It is very difficult to reconstruct the final number of victims of the labour unit system, but partial statistics can give us an idea of the scale of the tragedy. Of a total of about 40,000 people of predominantly Jewish origin deployed on the Eastern Front in labour units, eighty percent died as a result of hardship, war operations or Soviet captivity.[169] Captivity, which thousands

166 ROZETT, Robert: *Conscripted Slaves. Hungarian Jewish Forced Laborers on the Eastern Front during the Second World War.* Yad Vashem, Jerusalem 2013, p. 48.

167 Aside from Jews, tens of thousands of "politically unreliable" persons and members of ethnic minorities – Romanians, Serbs, Croats and Ruthenians – were placed in the labour units.

168 ROZETT, Robert: *Conscripted Slaves. Hungarian Jewish Forced Laborers on the Eastern Front during the Second World War*, p. 161.

169 Ibid, p. 62.

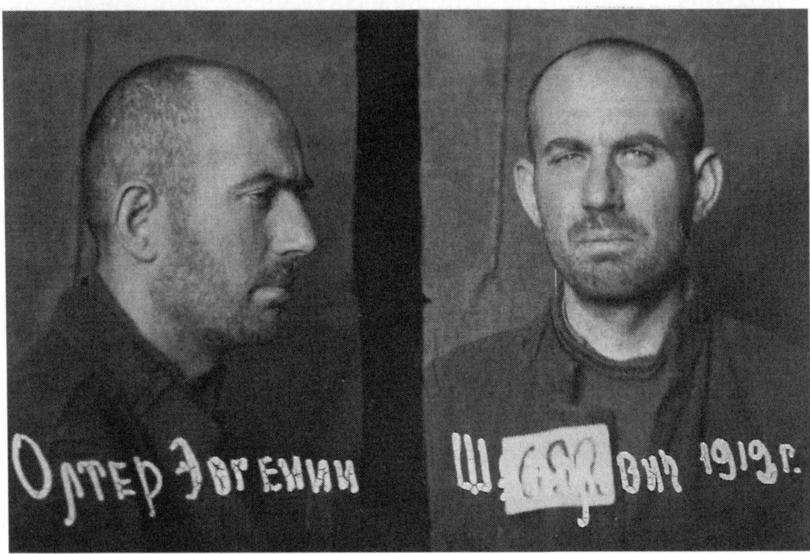

Košice native EVŽEN ALTER (1912) deserted from a Hungarian army labour unit on 7 September 1940 while digging anti-tank trenches near the Soviet border. By 10 September he had been arrested by NKVD authorities and imprisoned in Skole, Zhytomyr and Novocherkassk, from which he was transported to NKVD Prison No. 3 in Tomsk in the Novosibirsk Oblast. During evacuation of the Bogayevskaya station in the Rostov Oblast on 4 October 1941, he died. Likely as a result of the confusion caused by the invasion of the USSR, this fact escaped the NKVD authorities, as on 5 January 1942, three months after his death, Alter was sentenced to 10 years of labour in the Gulag for alleged espionage.

DAZO, f. 2558 (1939–1993), vol. no. 4391.

of Jewish conscripts sought out voluntarily in hope of rescue and a warm reception, completed this work of devastation.

In connection with the outbreak of World War II and the Soviet attack on Poland, on 19 September 1939, the People's Commissioner for Internal Affairs Lavrentiy Beria ordered the creation of an Administration for Affairs of Prisoners of War and Internees (abbreviated UPVI) run by the NKVD much like the Gulag. As part of the reorganisation of camp administration in 1945, it was renamed the Main Administration for Affairs of Prisoners of War and Internees, today known under the abbreviation GUPVI.[170] At its height, the administration consisted of approximately four thousand units – camps,

170 Ibid, p. 225.

prisons, hospitals and work squads scattered throughout the USSR, often at the same locations as Gulag camps. The individual systems were so interwoven, that it is often not possible to separate them. Camps were formed in some Gulag complexes, termed *lagpunkts*, that were intended for prisoners of war, who worked alongside the other prisoners and whose fate was very similar.[171]

In the years 1939–1955, more than 4 million people passed through these – prisoners of war captured during military operations as well as civilians captured by Soviet authorities in conquered territory and taken to the USSR for forced labour.[172] Especially during wartime, but also after the war had ended, there was a huge mortality rate at (G)UPVI facilities. Due to hunger, cold, epidemics and violence on the part of the Soviets, more than a million prisoners died. Particularly the frontline POW camps such as Davidovka, Morshansk and Khrenovoye[173] went down in history as places where absolute anarchy reigned and the starving and dying prisoners were deprived of all human dignity.

Here it must be said that, at the same time, millions of civilians in the USSR died as a result of the hardships of war brought on by the attack of Nazi Germany, and the mortality rate of Soviet soldiers in German captivity reached sixty percent.

Tens of thousands of Jews also passed through (G)UPVI camps. These were not only deserters from labour units or prisoners of war from the Soviet counter-offensive at Voronezh in January 1943 (who constituted the majority), but also Jewish civilians, often having freshly returned from Nazi concentration camps, who were arrested along with other inhabitants of Hungary in the final phase of the war and even afterwards and sent to slave labour camps in the USSR. In Budapest alone, over 100,000 civilians were arrested and sent to Soviet internment. Among these was, for example, Swedish diplomat Raoul Wallenberg, arrested 17 January 1945, who just a few months prior had saved tens of thousands of Hungarian Jews from deportation to Auschwitz.[174]

---

171 APPLEBAUM, Anne: *Gulag. Historie* [The Gulag. A History]. Beta-Dobrovský, Prague 2014, p. 381. In the original: *Gulag: A History*, Doubleday, 2003.

172 KARNER, Stefan: "In Stalin's Custody. The Soviet Camp System for Prisoners of War During and After World War II". In: BISCHOFF, Günter – PLASSER, Fritz – STELTZ-MARX, Barbara (eds): *New Perspectives on Austrians and World War II. Contemporary Austrian Studies*, Vol. 17. New Brunswick 2009, p. 122.

173 E.g., Khreovoye POW Camp No. 81 was established on 20 January 1943 not 30 km east of Voronezh by the village of Khreovoye in order to concentrate soldiers captured during combat operations on the Southern Front. It was originally intended for 10,000 prisoners, but this limit soon more than doubled. Due to organisational confusion resulting in the starvation of the internees, 13,796 people died here in two and a half months of the camp's existence. See BYSTROV, Vladimír: *Průvodce říší zla* [Guide to the Realm of Evil], p. 179.

174 Raoul Wallenberg (1912–1947), a Swedish diplomat and part of Righteous Among the Nations. After arrest on suspicion of espionage, he was transferred to the central NKVD prison Lubyanka in Moscow, where he was most likely executed in 1947. His fate has however still not been fully clarified by Russian authorities to date.

Лагерь № 3171

Национальность Чехословак В какой армии противника состоял Венгерской

1. Фамилия Мермельштайн
2. Имя Герман 3. Отчество Лидель
4. Год и место рождения 1903 д. Тростеница у гор. Мукач – Чехословакия
5. Адрес до призыва тоже
6. Подданство или гражданство Чехословацкое
7. Партийность б/п 8. Вероисповедание еврейская
9. Образование:
   а) общее 6 кл. нар. шк.
   б) специальное —
   в) военное —
10. Профессия крестьянин

Учетное дело № 4484

Арх. №

The Russian State Military Archive in Moscow contains a database of 39,000 of the total 70,000 POWs originally from Czechoslovakia, which include Jews forced to serve in the Hungarian army labour units. One of these was HERMANN MURMELSTEIN (1903) of Mukachevo, who fell into Soviet captivity as a member of work squad 108/51 on 14 February 1943. While he did survive to see the end of the war at GUPVI Camp No. 3171, he died on 10 August 1945 of pulmonary tuberculosis.

RGVA, f. 465, index card for Murmelstein Hermann.

Desertion from labour units did not only take place on the front lines, but ever since they were established in 1939. Among the hundreds of files on Jewish refugees from Subcarpathia preserved in the State Archive of the Uzhhorod District, 81 of them concern persons who had fled to Soviet territory in order to avoid this service. Research in the aforementioned archive shows that especially those who fled to the USSR before the German attack in 1941 were placed in Gulag camps.

The Soviets did not generally distinguish forced conscripts from members of the regular army. Deserters from labour units were thus subjected to the same ruthless treatment as their tormentors from the ranks of Hungarian or German soldiers. Not infrequently they were shot with other POWs shortly after being captured, or sent to POW camps, where the majority died before the end of the war as a result of hunger, illness and violence.[175]

175 ROZETT, Robert: *Conscripted Slaves. Hungarian Jewish Forced Laborers on the Eastern Front during World War II*. Yad Vashem e-newsletter, see http://www.yadvashem.org/yv/en/education/newslet-ter/31/conscripted_slaves.asp (accessed 25 November 2017).

Some deserters from the Hungarian army labour units avoided repression on the part of Soviet authorities, which was the case of JOSEF MÜLLER (1920) of Chop, who fled to the Soviet side on 1 December 1943 during fighting near the Don. "The Soviet officer ordered the soldiers to bring bread. They placed it on the ground in front of us and asked me if I was hungry. When I affirmed, he continued: 'Before I give you the bread, tell me the blessing that Jews say before consuming it.' Before I could finish 'Blessed art Thou, Lord our God, King of the universe who brings forth bread from the earth,' I had the feeling that tears were glistening in the captain's eyes. He was a Jew!" The sympathetic Soviet officer gave him a letter of introduction to work at the hospital in Kursk before he enlisted in the Czechoslovak army.

Memory of Nations archive, interview with Josef Müller conducted in 2007 by Adam Hradilek; quoted in: MÜLLER, Josef: Fighting for All That I Loved. A Story of Love and War. 1st Books Library, 2002, p. 50.

In isolated cases, members of labour units even had a worse position in captivity than the Hungarian officers, who enjoyed special treatment according to rank.

Some deserters managed to avoid repressive measures. Those who fell into the hands of Soviet officers of Jewish origin familiar with the tragic situation of Jews on the other side of the front were particularly fortunate.[176] As evidenced by the case of Josef Müller, sometimes they found sympathy with their Soviet captors, who helped them obtain more privileged positions in the camp or facilitated release from the POW camp.

Most of the deserters of Jewish origin that escaped racial persecution, mass extermination and the horrors of the labour units and turmoil of war were however sent to POW camps.

Among the 20,000 to 30,000 prisoners that were Jews forced to serve in Hungarian army labour units, an estimated several hundred to a thousand

176 BRAHAM, Randolph L.: *The politics of Genocide. The Holocaust in Hungary.* Wayne State University Press, Detroit 2000, p. 52.

of them were originally from the territory of Hungarian-occupied Czechoslovakia. In contrast to Hungarian and Austrian prisoners of Jewish origin, they were fortunate enough to be covered by the amnesty for Czechoslovak citizens, and were usually allowed, sooner or later, to leave the POW camps and enter the Czechoslovak army.

JAKOB FRIEDMANN

Born in 1918 in Ilnica in the Irshava District into a religious family. Studied to be a rabbi. When drafted into the Czechoslovak army, he was registered as a chaplain. On 1 March 1939, he started full-time service in Trebišov, where he remained a mere 14 days until the occupation of Bohemia and Moravia and the dissolution of Czechoslovakia. After 15 March 1939, he was demobilised and sent home to Ilnica. In the summer of 1939, the Hungarians occupied the remainder of Subcarpathian Rus and Ilnica along with it. In October 1939, he and other Jewish youth from the Hungarian-occupied parts of Slovakia and Subcarpathian Rus were drafted into the Hungarian army. In 1940, as part of anti-Jewish measures, he was released from a military warehouse in Debrecen. During the Hungarian mobilisation against Romania, he was called up once again, performing auxiliary work at barracks. Shortly thereafter, however, he and other Jewish soldiers were sent to a work camp in Solnok, where there were around 700 men. There they were stripped of all military privileges, decorations, weapons, and started to be treated as slaves. After about two months, the camp was moved to Transylvania, where the men worked in military warehouses for the German army, and then to Subcarpathian Rus. After that, he worked near Budapest. He was stationed building roads in Yasinia on the Polish-Hungarian border up until war broke out between Germany and the Soviet Union. The night after that, they sent him to Polish territory to build bridges for the advancing German army. After about two months he was demobilised and in November 1941 sent home to Ilnica. On 10 May 1942, he was again called up to Debrecen to a concentration labour camp, where there were around 300 members of the Jewish intelligentsia. On 15 May 1942, they were loaded onto a train and taken to the Russian front near Kursk. From there they marched about 500 kilometres to the Don in the Voronezh Oblast, near the village of Orodeyka. People in the labour unit were dying as a result of cruel treatment, exhaustion, cold and illness. On 18 January 1943, the Soviets attacked. The Jews from the unit remained at the site with the goal of deserting, but the Soviet soldiers captured the group and placed them in a POW camp in Krasnogorsk. Friedmann joined the Czechoslovak unit in the summer of 1944 in Kamianets-Podilskyi. He was assigned to the signalmen. During the march to Dukla, he was a liaison officer for the

3rd brigade general staff. After the war and the annexation of Subcarpathian Rus by the Soviet Union, he claimed Czechoslovak citizenship and moved to Teplice-Šanov, where he found work in a chemical plant. In 1948, he became a member of what was called the Jewish Brigade.[177] He underwent training in the barracks in Hranice na Moravě. In February 1949, he went to Israel in the third transport. The main fighting had died down in Israel by then, however, and a ceasefire was signed. He found work in an oil refinery, where he was employed as a technical clerk.[178]

— — —

How did you fall into captivity?
When the Russians attacked, the Hungarians fled and we stayed put. Thus we ended up in Soviet captivity and then the Svinovoyitel POW camp in the Voronezh Oblast. It was one of the worst. They were holding some forty-eight thousand prisoners of war there. Allegedly twenty-eight thousand of them died. There was nothing to eat there, no hygiene, no doctor, and we slept on the ground in the stables of the state stud farm.

Did they identify the dead prisoners?
No. No one cared about the dead. They tossed the bodies out in the cold, on piles. Then they took them away in cars and buried them nearby. Sometime in October 1943, there started to be rumours an International Red Cross committee was coming. So the Russians started clearing the camp. They took a small portion of the ill somewhere, but most people were deported to the Urals. Many of them never reached the destination as they died along the way. The healthy and stronger prisoners remained behind and got the camp in order. I managed to get to Butorlinovka, about sixty kilometres away, where there was supposed to be a hospital. There was a doctor there, but he didn't have any instruments or medicine, so he could barely be of any help. What we could do there though was get washed, disinfected and rid ourselves of lice. They also gave us clean underclothes. There was enough food there, but heavy and fatty, and many prisoners died after eating it. After a month, they took those that were left to the Urals to a labour camp in the Vorkov Oblast. Of the three hundred fifty prisoners that came on my transport, maybe thirty could have been Czechoslovaks, mostly Jews. The rest were Hungarians or Germans. They treated us Czechoslovaks well at the camp, but we worked hard. The political

177 The Jewish Brigade – a voluntary military unit comprised primarily of men and women of Jewish origin who had served in the Czechoslovak Army Corps in the USSR. It was primarily created in order to help the nascent State of Israel. The training of 1335 people took place from the end of August to the start of November 1948, when they left with their families for Israel.

178 *Yad Vashem Archive*, interview with Jakob Friedmann recorded 27 June 1969 by Erich Kulka.

commissars checked us several times, and they would sometimes give us Russian newspapers. From those we found out there was a Czechoslovak military unit in the Soviet Union. We learned that sometime in the summer of 1943. Until then, we'd had no idea something like that existed.

What did you have to do to be accepted?
We immediately started asking the commissar how to join the Czechoslovak army. Thus we filled out some papers, but not until October 1943 did they summon us and say our applications had been approved and we could go. There were twelve of us, of those eight Jews. They sent us to Moscow by train and placed us in the nearby Krasnogorsk POW camp. It was a political screening camp, where they were also holding high-ranking German officers and generals. This was where they were gathering volunteers joining the Czechoslovak military unit from certain areas.

What did it look like in Krasnogorsk?
Party employees came to the camp from Moscow. These *politruks* interrogated us, tested our outlook thoroughly and checked our data. There were several thousand POWs living in the camp. Around four hundred of them could have been Czechoslovak volunteers at that time. They were placed in two separate buildings. Maybe two hundred of that number were Jews, mostly from Subcarpathian Rus, who had gone through Hungarian labour camps and fallen into Russian captivity. We spent about three months at the camp. In the meantime, one transport of released prisoners went to the Czechoslovak military unit, another allegedly to the Urals. It was said that not all the volunteers were going to the army, just those who passed the screening. It was rumoured there were already a lot of Jews in the Czechoslovak army, so they didn't want any more.

Did you notice any form of anti-Semitism, mistrust of Jews?
Such reports were primarily spread by the Russian *politruks*, who said there were lots of Jewish officers in the Soviet army and that their numbers would have to be reduced. The screening took a long time and was irregular. They had us fill out various questionnaires, filled out forms, conducted endless interviews with us. It was hard to tell what they were actually looking for. Sometimes they asked about completely ordinary things, other times they wanted to know what we thought about the political and military situation. After several hours of being interviewed, we didn't know what they actually wanted and what all we had told them.

Aside from the politicians, no one interrogated you?
Only the Russian *politruks* carried out the screening. I think they had their people in the camp and they watched us and provided information about us that was likely the basis for the interviews and screening. The *politruks* let us speak freely, not avoiding any topics and if we had questions, they'd answer them. In January 1944, they took us to another, much smaller POW camp. There were about thirty Czechoslovaks there, the rest Lithuanians, Spaniards, Italians and other nationalities. Even though there was less food there, it was orderly and clean. There was a toy factory near the camp where we worked in the winter. When it got warmer, they took us to work in agriculture, in the fields.

Did the Soviets treat all foreigners the same?
We Czechoslovak volunteers had much more freedom than the other prisoners. For example, we could freely leave the camp to the surrounding area. The members of other nationalities, especially prisoners from Russia, weren't even allowed to approach the barbed wire. There were also other *politruks* at the camp who interrogated us again. Our *politruk* was a Polish Jew and he assured us that we were all right, that they had approved us in all respects and that we would soon be going to the army. One day they took us to the main camp and there the *politruks* started interrogating us again. Then they sent us before a military commission, where there were six Russian officers, by their appearance five of them Jewish. One of them, with the rank of colonel, started speaking Yiddish with us. He had us re-tell our life stories, whether we were in any Zionist organisations, whether we were adherents of Betar.[179] He just wanted to know everything concerning Jewish politics. When talking about Israel, I mentioned that the kibbutz movement there was implementing the true idea of communism. He evidently didn't like my words, because he declared that communism could only be realised in the Soviet Union through collective farms. Then he persuaded us that there is no social system more perfect than communism. Eventually he let us go, assuring us that we would soon be able to join the Czechoslovak army. He sent us back to the main camp, where we soon really were provided with documents and sent to the Czechoslovaks. There were twenty of us, the other ten stayed at the camp. Some didn't want to join the army, others didn't have the proper documents or hadn't been screened. I don't know what happened to them afterwards.

179 Betar – a Zionist youth movement whose main ideologue was Vladimir Jabotinsky.

MICHAEL LAVI (LEBOVIČ)

Michael Lavi in the interwar period as a student in Uzhhorod. *CVG collection*

Born in 1913 in Velyka Dobron as Michael Alexander Lebovič. He had seven siblings. After completing grammar school in Berehove, he started studying at the Charles University Faculty of Medicine in Prague in 1934. After the signing of the Munich Agreement, however, he was expelled like most of the students from the occupied Czechoslovak areas. Thus he returned to his home village, where he worked on his parents' farm, and after the occupation of Subcarpathian Rus by Hungary in March 1939 at a friend's electrical goods shop. In 1940, he was married and had a son the same year. At the end of October 1940, he was called up for military service in the Hungarian army along with other Jewish men. About two hundred Jews were concentrated in a labour camp in Mukachevo at that time, from which they travelled to a camp near Oradea, where they worked building roads until its dissolution in February 1941. Though Lebovič was allowed to return for several months to Velyka Dobron, in September 1941 he was once again called up to the labour unit. At that time, the Hungarians were gathering all able-bodied Jews in the old cavalry barracks in Košice, where they remained until spring 1942. Several weeks later, he was once again called to the labour camp headquarters in Abaújszántó, where they loaded the Jews onto wagons and transported them via Komárno, Hodonín, Ostrava and Krakow to Minsk. From there, they were sent to the Hungarian units right on the front line near the city of Voronezh. On 25 December 1942, they reached a spot about nine kilometres away from the Soviet battle lines. Lebovič volunteered along with another seven men to carry ammunition to the firing positions. Before that happened, however, one of the gendarmes recommended him as an assistant to the Hungarian military physician. That saved his life, as almost none of the Jews that volunteered to carry ammunition survived. When heavy Soviet bombing began one day and the Hungarian units were ordered to retreat, he and other Jews hid in a bunker, where they were captured by the Russians. He and the other POWs then had to march to the enormous Davidovka POW camp in the Voronezh Oblast, which was packed with some hundred thousand prisoners. At the camp, where epidemics such as louse-borne typhus were raging and many prisoners had severe frostbite, hundreds of prisoners were dying

Michael Lavi with his son in front of the synagogue in Uzhhorod in 1941. His son was taken along with Lavi's wife Zuzana to Auschwitz, where the Nazis murdered him immediately upon arrival. *CVG collection*

daily without medical care. Thanks to his medical skills, Lebovič soon became the camp doctor. He, too, however soon contracted typhus and only recovered thanks to the help of two Jewish female doctors. At the end of March 1943, he was transported to another camp near the town of Usman,[180] where he once again worked as the camp doctor. Here he also heard about the recruitment for the Czechoslovak military unit. However instead of going to the army, he was transported in July 1943 via Moscow to another camp for prisoners of war in Krasnogorsk.[181] This camp was also home to high-ranking enemy officers, including General Paulus. Here Lebovič soon got into a dispute with a German prisoner, and was sentenced to six months of forced labour for beating him. He was fortunate, however, because they assigned him to a group of Yugoslav and Finnish prisoners, where he once again worked as a physician. Because the group met the work quotas, they got much better food than ordinary prisoners. Eventually he was released and then reached the Czechoslovak military unit in Novokhopyorsk.[182] As a physician of the 2nd artillery regiment, he participated in the military campaign all the way to Czechoslovak territory. In 1948, he left for Israel, where he adopted the name Lavi. There he worked as a physician until his retirement. He died on 25 October 2015. His parents and four sisters died in the Auschwitz extermination camp.[183]

— — —

180 Usman – a town not far from Voronezh in Russia.

181 Krasnogorsk – a city on the western edge of Moscow.

182 Novokhopyorsk – a town in the Voronezh Oblast in Russia.

183 *Yad Vashem Archive*, interview with Michael Lavi recorded 19 December 1970 by Erich Kulka;

Michael Lavi (standing on the right) in the Hungarian army work unit before being sent to the front. *CVG collection*

How did you end up in captivity?

On 13 January 1943, the Hungarian doctor I was assisting ordered me to go to the front to vaccinate soldiers. I got food from the kitchen and prepared to make my escape. But heavy Soviet bombardment began and the Hungarian troops were ordered to retreat. Me and my friend Kleinmann from Mukachevo didn't listen though and hid in a bunker. The shooting stopped and we heard the Russian command, "Rubay!" The Russians set up a machine gun on the roof of the bunker and shot at the fleeing Hungarians. So we ended up prisoners of the Russians along with about twenty soldiers. They took all our things and after a short interrogation they sent us to the rear with the other prisoners of war. It wasn't a very pleasant journey, we walked for two days and they were constantly shouting insults at us: "Fritzes!" After a long march, we arrived at the enormous Davidovka POW camp in the Voronezh Oblast, through which tens and tens of thousands of prisoners from all possible armies passed. There were Germans, Hungarians, us. I even saw a few German generals there. Our whole group of about twenty Czechoslovak Jews

---

Memory of Nations Archive, interview with Michael Lavi recorded 7 June 2006 by Adam Hradilek; Czechoslovaks in the Gulag project collection (CVG collection), handwritten memoirs of Michael Lavi "The Story of My Life By Dr. Michael Lavi".

After being released from the GUPVI camps, Michael Lavi served as a physician in the Czechoslovak army. In this picture from a documentary film, he is treating a wounded comrade on the front line. *Repro ÚSTR*

ended up in a barrack together. The Russians came and registered and interrogated us. There was a Jewish Russian physician among them. When she found out I was a medic, she made me the head physician for the POW camp, where there could have been a hundred thousand miserable people concentrated. Epidemics were raging in the camp, in particular louse-borne typhus. Plenty of prisoners were also suffering from severe frostbite. Yet there was no medicine, nor the conditions for treatment and recovery. Nor of course any possibility of personal hygiene. In short, it was horrible. To this day I don't understand how I survived. Hundreds of people were dying every day and no one was taking care of the dead, identifying them. The dead bodies were piling up, but the ground was frozen solid and it wasn't even possible to bury them. It was awful and lots of prisoners started to lose their minds from it as well.

How many prisoners do you think died at Davidovka?
I can't say, but thousands, people were dying like flies.

Did you have at least a bit of food?
At first we got a kind of porridgey soup, but then nothing. Many of the captives ate human flesh. It was mainly the Corsicans who killed people to get

A group of new ensigns of the Czechoslovak army after the battle at Zhytomyr. Michael Lavi is seated in the middle. *CVG collection*

fresh blood. As a physician, I had the opportunity to get more porridge and thus I could at least help a few friends. The Soviet physician also had no means for alleviating the catastrophic situation. Once, I proposed that I could go to Moscow and try to contact representatives of Joint there and get help for the POWs. She was horrified by my suggestion and told me to put it right out of my mind. From that time, I also never saw her again. To stop the epidemic, they sent five young female Soviet physicians without any experience to the camp, but the situation did not improve whatsoever. I myself caught typhus and was afraid to go to the hospital, because it was louse-ridden and you could catch something else there. Of the new doctors, two were Jews, and they set me up at a peasant woman's place, where I got milk and recovered. Then I would go to the train station to help with the medical service for arriving transports. There I heard that during transport, prisoners had seen Czechoslovak soldiers going to the front.

Did you have to apply in some way to be transferred to the Czechoslovak military unit?
Various political workers would come to the Davidovka camp and interrogate the prisoners, fill out forms, register them and take photographs. One time they interrogated our whole Czechoslovak group. During the interrogation I said that, as a Czechoslovak, I wanted to fight with the other Czechoslovak soldiers on the front against the Germans. The interrogating officer declared: "Sit down and write a letter to Stalin." Which I did. At the same time, I knew

there was a Czechoslovak government-in-exile in London, so on a dirty piece of paper I also wrote to President Beneš in London.

Who knows where those letters ended up...
I don't know about the letter to Stalin, but the one for Beneš did end up in Czechoslovak hands. After the war in 1946, when I was applying for recognition of military service in the Czechoslovak army since January 1943, I was received at the General Staff in Dejvice by General Heliodor Píka, the one the Communists later executed. We talked about my joining of Svoboda's Army and he suddenly pulled out that piece of dirty paper I had written the letter to Beneš on back then at Davidovka, and he said that for him that was the date I joined the army.

Let's go back to the camp. Did the living conditions change?
The conditions there did not improve, the number of ill increased, so I got some friends to help me treat people as best we could. Thanks to that, we got some food, but otherwise we were working in tough, primitive conditions. Our activity caught the attention of a *politruk* and he gave us a building we could use as an infirmary. Of the roughly hundred thousand prisoners of war, probably ninety-five thousand were deported to other camps, and of the five thousand that remained at Davidovka, about five hundred remained alive. From time to time, they would take a group of captives away from that hell. It was rumoured they were shooting them somewhere by the train station. Once I accompanied such a transport as the physician and I saw them loading prisoners onto livestock wagons and taking them away. At the end of March, our group also left by a similar transport to the Kursk Oblast. The train that was carrying the POWs, that was something awful, everyone did what they could to survive. We arrived at penal camp number 82 in Uman. There I once again worked as a doctor. Political interrogations and checks were conducted once again at the camp.

After a time at Usman, they again led us to the train station under guard and took us to another camp. At night, the bed bugs came out. It was horrible how they bit us. So we ended up at the Krasnogorsk camp not far from Moscow. As I learned later, it was intended for political education. They wanted me to go work in a hospital, but I said no, that I wanted to join the army. Screening was taking place at the camp. At night they would call us in to the *politruk* to fill out forms. The same thing repeated the next night and then several more times, with them posing questions. They were particularly interested if we were in any political party, whether we subscribed to any Jewish organisations and the like. The *politruk* would check over every discrepancy in the forms or provision of information. For example, I wrote "Jewish nationality"

After the war, Michael Lavi left for Israel, where he became a well-known physician and head of the main hospital in Ashkelon. In the photo (in the foreground) with then Prime Minister Ben-Gurion (middle) during his visit to the hospital in 1961. *CVG collection*

on the questionnaire. Which the *politruk* wouldn't accept. They wanted us to declare as Czech, Hungarian, Slovak or Carpatho-Ruthenian Jews.

Did you have any information about the Czechoslovak unit?
Once an officer from the political department showed me a copy of the Russian magazine Krasnaya Zvezda, where there was an article by Colonel Svoboda. He wrote about the fact that Jews had also fought bravely in his unit in the Battle of Sokolovo. There were eighty Czechoslovaks in the camp, of those sixty Jews. We all signed up for Svoboda's Army.

Did you experience any anti-Semitism at the camp?
One German who was working as a storekeeper there addressed me with a provocative anti-Semitic insult. So I beat him up. They put me in jail and I waited for my trial. The judge accused me of trying to kill a prisoner of war. My defence was that I had been upset and agitated, as I was to go fight against the Germans, and here a German fascist was publicly insulting me on Soviet soil. Despite this, they sentenced me to six weeks of forced labour. I ended up in a group of Yugoslav and Finnish prisoners, where I once again worked as

Michael Lavi during the interview in 2014. *ÚSTR / Adam Hradilek*

a physician. They cut wood in the forest and were very good with axes because they had worked in the forest their whole lives. When they saw me, they said you sit down here and we'll chop. Our group met the quotas par excellence, so we got great food, even Canadian milk and chocolate. After my experiences from Davidovka and being ill, I finally recovered a bit there physically.

They sent you to the Czechoslovak army after your sentence had been served?
One day a guard came to me and at gunpoint put me in a car with bars in the windows. I thought it was the end of me, as I had taken a couple of carrots from a garden on the way home from work. As soon as we reached the Moscow suburbs, however, a Soviet officer got in and told me I was going to the Czechoslovak army. We reached the Moscow train station, where a transport had been prepared for around a thousand Czechoslovaks, brought in from various camps from Siberia and elsewhere, many Jews among them. We set off in livestock wagons for Novokhopersk to reinforce the Czechoslovak combat units.

LADISLAV (LES) MAGET

Born 15 March 1916 in Košice as one of seven children to Lipold and Berta Maget. His father farmed and traded in furs, his mother took care of the children and household. The Magets observed kosher customs, attended synagogue service on Saturdays, and the children attended religious school, a *cheder*. In 1933, Ladislav graduated from secondary school, and after an apprenticeship worked as a fabric salesman in a department store. After the dissolution of Czechoslovakia, Košice was occupied by the Hungarians and in 1940, Maget and the other Jews from Košice and its surroundings were drafted into Hungarian labour units, which were deployed for the heavy labour associated with the advance of the Hungarian and German armies. In October 1942, they sent him to the front in the Soviet Union. There he managed to survive in the horrid conditions until the Soviet breakthrough on the Don in 1943, when he crossed over to the Soviets with a group of deserting Jews during the retreat of Axis troops with the goal of joining the Red Army and fighting against Nazism. They were however captured and after harsh interrogation imprisoned with the Germans, Hungarians, Romanians and Spanish captured on the front. Along with these, they were packed into freight wagons and taken to a camp in Morshansk.[184] There they survived in rough-hewn barracks, sleeping on the bare ground, or on a pile of conifer branches they dragged in from the surrounding woods. For a short time, Maget ended up in the camp infirmary, but when he discovered it only served as a dumping ground for hopeless cases, he mustered enough strength to return to work. He managed to survive until he and the other Czechoslovak Jews were transferred to a camp in Gubash, where the conditions were much more tolerable. There they were finally allowed to join the army and were sent to camp 241/1 near Solimansk to recuperate so they would not arrive at the Czechoslovak military unit in such a miserable state. There, Maget served as the house elder and also as a cook, so after several years he could finally eat his fill. He was enlisted 19 April 1944 in Yefremov and took part in the military campaign in the Soviet Union, Poland and Czechoslovakia. Only one sister of his large family survived until the end of the war, the rest were murdered during pogroms in Poland, in Nazi concentration camps, or they did not survive serving in the Hungarian labour units. In October 1945, he left the army and settled down in Ústí nad Labem in a textile shop left behind by a deported Austrian citizen. In 1946, he married a girl who had been through the camps in Poland. In 1949, the Magets went to Israel, and in 1952 from there to Australia, where they successfully operated several restaurants.[185]

— — —

184 Morshansk – a town in the northern part of the Tambov Oblast.

185 *Archive of the USC Shoah Foundation*, interview with Ladislav (Les) Maget recorded 20 October 1996 by Peter Seller, translated from English by Štěpán Hlavsa.

How did you get to the Soviet side?

In 1943, when the Russians managed to break through on the Don and we – meaning the Hungarian army – were to retreat. Myself and some other Jewish soldiers agreed that we would cross over to the Russians. It was at the village Novo-Uspenka. The Germans and Hungarians were fleeing in trucks, which the Russians were constantly shelling, bombarding. We hid inside a house, there were eighteen of us, and waited for the Russian soldiers. Then they showed up. One of our group was so happy that our escape was successful and that we were with the Russians, he wanted to hug one of the soldiers. As soon as he threw wide his arms, I guess the Russian though he wanted to do something to him, and he shot him on the spot. So it didn't start out so well. Even though we weren't wearing military uniforms, but tattered civilian clothes, they yelled at us: "You killed my mother! You killed my brother!" It was hard to explain to someone that we hadn't done anything.

They took you prisoner?

Yes, we were captives. And something I'll never forget happened. We were speaking Yiddish and a Russian officer overheard us. He came to us and said, "So you're Jews!" We quickly explained our situation and that the Russians were mistreating us so that we could hardly walk. So the officer told the soldiers leading us: "These aren't enemies, these are ours. Try to make sure

After being arrested, several months of imprisonment and exhausting transport to the forced labour sites, the refugees, like the other prisoners, often had to first build makeshift shelters. *Komi Republic National Archives*

they arrive safely." Which certainly saved our lives, because we continued on and sometime before dawn, around six, we suddenly heard a *garmoshka* and we see a group of completely drunk soldiers dancing around a musician. We were the first POWs they'd seen, so they wanted to shoot us straight away. Luckily our escort wouldn't let them. Then other prisoners started to turn up, thousands of Germans, Hungarians, Romanians, Spaniards. We then passed through a village, and again us Jews were sticking together and speaking Yiddish. This Russian man noticed us, he must have been of Jewish heritage himself, and when he saw what we looked like, he ran home and brought us lots of bread. I immediately realised that he needed that bread for his children, but he gave it to us anyway. I'll never forget that. After about four days, they loaded us into wagons. They crammed a hundred and twenty people in a single wagon! Us Jewish lads, there were about eighteen of us, we all stuck together, but it was hard. We had agreed on a call-out, so we could always find each other, otherwise we'd lose each other. So we travelled like that in a single wagon three days without them opening the door once. In January, with no food, no water, packed together like sardines. After three days, the doors opened and they gave us herring to eat. Then they let us outside to have a drink. The water was ice cold, but everyone drank it like mad. You don't want to know what went on in the wagon after that.

When you defected to the Soviets, were you planning to join the Red Army?
That's what we wanted, to fight against the Germans, the Hungarians, with weapons in our hands. But the Russians didn't believe a word we said. They asked us our names maybe twenty times, also the names of our mother, our father, why we came, it was unbearable. Only at the last camp, where there were about two hundred or three hundred Jews from Czechoslovakia, they finally let us into the army.

What were the living conditions in the camps like?
The first camp I ended up at was Morshansk. It was horrible, the worst of all of them. Then came Gubakha[186] and Solikamsk. You wouldn't believe it, but in the first camp, there wasn't even water, just snow. For shelter and sleeping we had these kind of bunkers[187] made of beams covered with dirt, with as many as a hundred people crammed into a single one. I remember that in one of those bunkers, they tried to make a fire, and everyone burned to death inside. That didn't happen to our group of Jews because I told the lads right away that we were going to sleep in something smaller. We were in a barrack where there were thirty or forty of us, and we all took care of each other.

186 Gubakha – a town 400 km north-east of Perm in the Perm Krai.
187 Meaning *zemlyankas*.

I went to the village to work, they didn't want to permit it, but somehow I got there, and there I stole food for the lads at the camp. One day, something happened: I was working outside the camp and I saw some frozen fish there. For a minute I thought, what can I do with frozen fish, but then I put one in each trouser leg. But as I was working, the fish started to thaw and I was suddenly wet, with water coming out of my trouser legs. I got sick from it and got terribly weak. They put me in hospital, which meant lying on the bare ground, there was no doctor and of course I didn't get any medicine. In the woods we chopped some branches and at least lay on those. It was just terrible. And after four or five days, they sent us away. I was so weak that I couldn't walk. The Russian was hurrying me but I told him that if he wanted to shoot me then go ahead. In the end I got there, but really slowly. When we were still in those bunkers, every morning they would come and ask: "How many dead?" We carried them outside and that was the end of it. Later it was better, but that first camp, that was a disaster.

Did you work at the camps?
Yes, everyone had to work. But at Morshansk, almost no one could even walk, that's how bad the conditions were there. I don't understand how I survived, I was convinced I couldn't take it, but I survived. At the next camp, everyone had to work, but I was always a smart aleck, I tried to not go to work. I always said there was something wrong with me and would wander around the kitchen, trying to get inside. And when they took me to peel potatoes in the evening, that was lucky! And then in the third camp, I was a cook, that was amazing. By then I was on my way to the army.

How did they transport you from camp to camp? Did you walk?
For the Morshansk camp, we walked there from the train. To Gubakha we walked the whole way. From Gubakha to Solikamsk by train again, it took six days. After our previous experiences, in Solikamsk we felt like we were on holiday. There were barracks there with ordinary beds. As well as sheets, blankets, luxury. We really liked it there. This Russian told us he needed a team of about eleven people. I don't know why, but I raised my hand. I always raised my hand. By then I already knew Russian, so he asked if I want to be the leader. I agreed, he gave me ten people and I was responsible for the whole building, for cleaning, for food, for everything. That was naturally a great job. You could walk into the kitchen and get an extra potato or some soup.

Did they give you any special clothing at the camps?
No. We still had our tattered clothes – Hungarian or German uniforms. We just had a number sewed to the back. That's how they checked us. When we were going to work outside the camp, they checked us maybe ten times.

You mentioned potatoes. What did you get to eat?
It depends on what camp we're talking about. The first one was awful, we barely ate there. In the second it was better. For example they gave ten people a can of condensed milk. I remember we got two little teaspoons and I thought: "This is it! This will save my life!" At the third camp we got fed five times a day, but tiny portions. They said if we ate any more, we'd be dead in half an hour. Your stomach gets so contracted that you have to start slow.

In order to survive, I tried to either get in the kitchen, or get work in people's homes. That's why I always volunteered when a different opportunity arose than hard labour in the woods. Once some Russian said he needed someone who knows how to build ovens. So I raised my hand. One Hungarian also volunteered. Then when we were walking together, I asked him: "And you know how to build an oven?" – "No, I thought you did." Then we came into a room where there was nothing. No cement, no water, just a few bricks lying around. So we stacked the bricks on each other and stuck them together with mud. In the end, the oven somehow came together and you got a bit of bread or a few potatoes, which was the most important thing, finding some food. At the first camp, say, we went into the forest for wood, it was already chopped, we just had to bring it. But we were terribly weak, completely undernourished, we only ate like once a week. When the Germans didn't want something because it was rotten, they'd give it to us. We could barely keep on our feet. And then you had to go into the woods and carry logs on your shoulder. One time I was walking through the woods and I saw nothing but dead frozen people along the path. If you fell down, no one would come back for you. We tried to convince the Russians that we couldn't do such hard work, that we were too weak. But they said that if others can do it, we must be able to handle it too. But us Jews in the labour units hadn't eaten properly in months, unlike the Germans or Hungarians. The Russians were utterly stupid. They couldn't understand that someone who hasn't eaten properly in many months is not in the same condition as someone fed.

Did you get any news of developments on the front?
In the third camp there was a radio, so we could listen to how far the Red Army had gotten. There were Germans with us there, Nazis. When the radio announced how many enemy cannons, artillery and other military material the Russians had taken, the Germans joked: "Und hundert Nachtgeschirr!", "And a hundred potties!"

What was your relationship with the Germans like?
At the camps they ignored us, there was no anti-Semitism on their part. At the last camp though, where there were thousands of people, we found this one Hungarian sergeant. The lads that had served under him in the labour

unit found him. So we treated him the way he'd treated us. They'd told me about him, saying he was a murderer, that he was able to just kill a man for nothing. But we didn't kill him. One night, he climbed out of the barracks and tried to pinch something somewhere. And I caught him. I was a cook in the kitchen by then. The lad that was with me recognised him and said, "Ah, look, sergeant. How are you doing?" We shut him up in the storeroom behind the kitchen, where it was incredibly cold. He shouted like mad, but we didn't let him freeze to death. Because he had beaten our people before, he also got a fine beating.

How did you get to the Czechoslovak army?
We signed up as volunteers. All the Jewish lads signed up. Nobody forced us. The Russians took us to the city, where we got nice uniforms taken from the Germans with the Czech coat of arms on them. And when people wanted to beat us up, they were told: "Leave them alone, these are ours! They're going to the front." And suddenly everything changed, suddenly we were friends.

SALOMON DESIDER

Born in 1918 in Khust into an Orthodox family as one of seven children of the owner of a local printing house. He attended a school that taught in Czech and Ukrainian. He trained as a printer. After the Hungarian occupation, he was drafted into a military labour unit, which was deployed on the Eastern Front in 1941. After the Soviet counter-offensive on the Don in 1943, he fell into Soviet captivity by the village of Chernyanka. Subsequently he was interned in the POW camps Davidovka, Khrenovoye and GUPVI Camp No. 101. In the Davidovka and Khrenovoye camps he witnessed cannibalism. In 1944, he found out about the Czechoslovak military unit in the USSR from some Soviet officers. He immediately applied, but due to his missing fingers, they refused him. He did end up getting out of the POW camps to a less extreme camp in Moscow. After returning to Czechoslovakia, he learned that practically his entire family had died in Auschwitz. He settled down in Prague, where he got a newsagent's shop on Bělehradská. After the Communist coup in 1948, however, he had to give it up due to nationalisation. He went to live with his sister in Los Angeles, but after three years he returned to Czechoslovakia.[188]

— — —

188 *Archive of the Jewish Museum in Prague,* interview with Salomon Desider recorded 6 September 1991 by Anna Lorencová.

What were the conditions in the Hungarian labour unit like?
There were about two hundred of us Jewish lads, twenty to twenty-two years old. The Hungarian lieutenant welcomed us with the words: "Beat the Jews, stinking Jews. I brought you here so that as few of you as possible would return home. If you don't meet the plan for digging trenches, I'll shoot you myself." And that's what he did. The Don was frozen, everything was frozen, we couldn't work normally. And the Hungarian soldiers started killing us.

So you had to work under all circumstances?
Yes, but the ground was so frozen that it was impossible to carry out the plan. And from the other side of the front line, the Soviets were enticing us to come over to them.

How did they entice you?
They could see that we were Jews, so they called to us through a megaphone to run across the frozen Don, that we would be free with them. About ten percent of the prisoners managed it, even though the Hungarians were shooting at them. But the ones who really did cross over ended up in Siberia. The Stalinist camps were worse than the Jewish concentration camps. Hitler sent people to the gas chamber, but at least he didn't torture them. Surviving Khrenovoye, Chernyanka and Davidovka was horrible. At the Khrenovoye camp in 1943 for example, we ate dead people. The Spanish taught us that. They'd pull out a corpse, cut off what they could and then roast it on the fire.

Was it just Jews in the camps?
Mostly, but then Spaniards and Germans arrived. The Germans were better off than us. In 1943 and at the start of 1944, the Soviets started picking out the engineers and technicians in their ranks in the interest of their military production. Of course they were most interested in those who worked on the V2 rockets.

Let's go back to the time you were in the Hungarian army. Did you ever get into the fighting with the Soviet army?
No. My hands were so frostbitten, it wouldn't have even been possible. There was still a Jewish Religious Community in Budapest at that time and it arranged for the wounded and frostbitten to be taken to hospital in Budapest. The Red Cross sent a train for such people. I was among them. At every station, we dumped out dead bodies.

You were among them because you had frostbitten hands?
Yes. But in the village of Chernyanka, they had us get off the train. They said the Soviets had cut the line, so it wasn't possible to go on. Of course the rest

of the train with the injured Hungarian and German soldiers continued on. It was only us Jews they kicked out. Sick, dirty, tattered, hungry and louse-ridden.

That was in 1943?
Yes, in the year 1943 when I fell into Soviet captivity.

What happened after that?
There the Soviets captured us and housed us in a former mill. They called it the Krasnaya militsiya, the Red Militia. We lay on straw, there was almost nothing to eat, or drink, so we drank our own urine or other people's. This was all described in the book *From the Danube to the Don*, which was written by the Hungarian Jew István Kossa[189] and which came out after the war. In Chernyanka they herded us off the train and then the madness started – hunger, misery, corpses. We became prisoners without any trial and more or less for eternity.

Did you have to work at Chernyanka?
Yes, we went to work outside the camp, mostly at night. It wasn't until the Khrenovoye camp that we didn't work, we got there after two months in Chernyanka. Khrenovoye was an even worse camp, where there was no medicine, there wasn't anything there at all. There we were just frozen. Then they took us to Camp 101 about two hundred kilometres from Moscow, where luckily they were looking for Czechoslovak citizens for our foreign army in June 1944. The Soviet officers announced that Czechoslovaks could apply, if healthy, including Jews. But various Hlinka Guard members also joined up, who had fought on the side of the Germans and especially Hungarians. The condition was being in good health. I looked strong, I was fat because I was all bloated from drinking urine, so the recruiters took me. But when I was leaving the commission and took hold of the door handle, the Soviet physician saw my hand. He told me I couldn't fight. I had tears in my eyes. In the end they did end up taking me. We were waiting to be transported to the Czechoslovak unit, so we were no longer viewed as POWs. I didn't work. I couldn't have managed it physically. So I was a medic and interpreter in the infirmary. Eventually they took us by normal train to Moscow, where I remained until the end of the war. They gave us soup and rusks with it, which they distributed twice a day. Most of us couldn't even eat anymore though, we were skin

189 István Kossa – a prominent member of the Hungarian Social Democratic Party who fell into Soviet captivity as a member of the penal unit of the Hungarian army, to which he was assigned on political grounds. After being released, he joined the anti-fascist resistance. From the end of the war until the 1960s, he held high government positions in communist Hungary.

and bones, plus louse-borne typhus had broken out again. I caught it too, but I survived. But for my parents, brothers and sisters, before they took them to Auschwitz, I was dead. Whenever any of us got to the Soviet side, into captivity, the Hungarians sent the relatives a telegram that they had died or been killed. So all my loved ones went to the concentration camp thinking I was no longer alive.

Were you free at the Moscow camp?
Yes. We got food, but we didn't have to do anything. There wasn't even anyone to write. I was ninety percent sure the Germans had taken my whole family away.

How did you find out?
We knew it from some Hungarians who got captured and had served in Subcarpathian Rus under German and Hungarian command. They told us: "You won't have anyone at all at home." And the Soviets told us the same: "Where are you going? You don't have anyone at home." That the Germans had killed us all.

How long did you stay in Moscow?
About four, five months, until the end of the war. Anyone who wanted to could stay longer.

How did you get back to Czechoslovakia?
I arrived in Khust, which was Soviet by then. There I learned that my sister had come back from Auschwitz and my brother-in-law had survived the war in the Czechoslovak army. But they were in Prague, where they lived before they moved to America. So in Khust I took my documents, my birth certificate, my work certificate and other things, and went to them.

LUDVÍK KELLNER

Born 23 August 1920 in Dubovica in the Rimavská Sobota district as the fifth child in an Orthodox family. His family made a living by farming on leased land. After primary school, he studied at the grammar school in Rimavská Sobota, but after the Hungarian occupation of south-eastern Slovakia, he was forced to leave Slovakia. First he worked in Budapest as a textile worker, then in autumn 1940 he had to return home and supported himself by knitting stockings on a manual machine. In spring of 1941, he worked on regulating the river Rimava. At the end of the year, he was drafted into the Hungarian army labour unit. His brother Josef was a journalist, International Brigadista, and

Ludvík Kellner while recovering from an injury he incurred in the fight for Dukla. *Archive of Josef Kellner*

soldier of the Czechoslovak army. In 1942 he was captured and taken to Majdanek, where he was murdered. His parents and three sisters met a similar fate, being transported to Auschwitz in 1944, where they all died. Ludvík Kellner's work squad was deployed on the Soviet front in 1942. He and the other members were forced to carry out the hardest work, from digging trenches to clearing dead bodies as well as mine fields. The gruelling slave labour involved constant beating, kicking, and hits with rifle butts or a bullwhip. He made several attempts at self-mutilation and was considering escape. But the armed guards and increasingly frequent unsuccessful escape attempts, the torture and murder of unsuccessful escapees, and decimation of the units the deserters had come from dissuaded Kellner from this plan. In desperation and utter exhaustion he deliberately injured himself with a pickaxe. The wound became infected and he had high fevers. He was taken to a hospital in Goncharovka roughly thirty kilometres from the front, where he became a nurse after recovering. In January 1943, the Soviets re-took the area where the hospital was located, and its personnel fell into Soviet captivity. He was taken to the Khrenovoye POW camp along with several thousand others, not just Hungarian and German soldiers, but also many Jews from the labour units. There was almost no supply of food at the camp and many prisoners thus resorted to cannibalism. In March 1943, the camp was evacuated. Kellner then spent time at POW hospitals and other camps, where he signed up for the Czechoslovak army. After enlisting, he was assigned to the tank brigade. He was seriously injured in the Battle of Dukla Pass. Shortly after the war he married and remained in the army, rotating through different crews all over Bohemia. In 1954, he moved to Prague and studied history at Charles University. In 1956 he published an autobiographical description of the journey of the Czechoslovak military unit alongside the Soviet army under the title *Jediná cesta* [The Only Way].[190] He devoted a mere several lines to his prior captivity. Only during the Prague Spring in 1968 did he elect to write the "omitted" chapter on his memories concerning the

190 KELLNER, Ludvík: *Jediná cesta* [The Only Way]. Naše vojsko, Prague 1956.

Ludvík Kellner in the pre-war period and by a tank, 1945. *Archiv Josefa Kellnera*

POW camp. It had to wait another twenty years to be published however. In 1968 he was discharged from the army and he worked in the Tesla Hloubětín technical library. In 1982, he went into retirement and pursued his hobby – electronics (often publishing about it under pseudonyms). The year after the fall of communism, he could finally publish his memoirs of the Soviet POW camp, suppressed for several decades. It was printed under the name *I Went Through the Hell of a Soviet POW Camp.*[191] He died in 1995.[192]

— — —

When did you reach the front?

In June 1942. We got off the train near Kursk and walked to the Don, which is some three hundred kilometres. It was a terrible journey, even the horses were dropping, so they hooked us up to the wagons. At first it was still OK, because you could find something to eat in the fields. But the conditions rapidly declined in the frontline zone and by the Don near the village of Belogorye was where hell began. We worked day and night building trenches, shelters, firing positions. The Russians were on the opposite bank of the river. It's interesting that almost no one shot at us. We were in civvies, marked with a yellow ribbon. As soon as one of the uniformed guards showed up though, they immediately opened fire. The workday began at five in the morning and ended at eleven at night. The food varied, sometimes nothing, other times

---

191 KELLNER, Ludvík: Prošel jsem peklem sovětského lágru [I Went Through the Hell of a Soviet POW Camp]. *Reportér*, 1990, no. 8, Supplement, p. I–V.

192 *Archive of the Jewish Museum in Prague*, interview with Ludvík Kellner recorded 17 February 1991 by Anna Hyndráková.

Ludvík Kellner's memoirs, which came out during Communist rule, left out his experiences from the POW camp in the Soviet Union. *ÚSTR copy*

dried vegetables soaked in water or some beans. I couldn't take any more, so I decided to do something. I tried to chop off a finger with a spade, but my arm automatically stopped the blow. So I stuck my leg under my neighbour's pick-axe and he didn't notice and the tip of his tool pierced my left knee. My leg swelled up and they couldn't force me to work. At that time we were in the village of Bashlayevka, where we were sleeping in collective farm stables. The village was empty, I guess the locals had fled, so during the day I would wander the abandoned gardens and dig up potatoes or pick tomatoes. The leg wasn't healing well and I got a high fever. I ended up in Goncharovka in a Hungarian field hospital. They fed us there and didn't make us work, so the leg healed and the fever went away.

Did they send you back to the work detail?

No. A Hungarian doctor came to see me and said they were opening a Jewish hospital and that me and others would be nurses there. Me, a nurse?

I thought. I had hated the sight of blood my whole life. That's what happened with my first case too. They brought in some poor soul who had stepped on a landmine and they hadn't changed his bandage in ten days. Of course it had started to fester. When I took off the paper bandage, the pus shot all the way to the ceiling and I smelt an awful stench. I let go of the leg and ran outside to throw up. It was clear to me that I had two options: either go back to the front to the detail, which meant death sooner or later, or stay in the hospital. So I stayed. I should clarify the term "hospital". It consisted of several huts, with about a hundred and fifty patients lying on straw. Most of them had frostbite, typhus, dystrophy or starvation sickness. Operating worked that you'd take a knife and say chop off a blackened leg.

Was it only members of the work units you treated?
Yes. The Hungarian soldiers were in a normal field hospital not far from us. The only thing we shared was the kitchen we got food from. There was also a lot of stealing and trading in everything imaginable in order to survive. Soon thereafter, the horrible Russian winter started, and we only had summer clothes. The Jewish Communities did send us winter clothing, but everything was stolen on the way. We didn't have any news from the front, but we felt that something wasn't right. The Hungarians were quite nervous and the officers that went on leave didn't come back. We couldn't write home, so we didn't know what was happening there either. After New Year's, the front started moving closer, artillery could be heard more and more. On 14 January 1943, we woke up and discovered that the military field hospital was gone. They had only left the worst cases to their fate. We had remained behind in no man's land. On 20 January 1943, the Russians came and we were liberated. I wrote about what that liberation and the next two months looked like in *Reportér*; I won't go into it here.

At least briefly...
The Soviets rounded up those of us who could walk. About a hundred and fifty patients remained there, I never heard about them again. They put us with other Jews found hiding in the villages, among them the rest of my former work squad. Then there were around thirty Hungarian soldiers there, Germans, a few Italians. The next day, when they were gathering us up, the Soviets separated them from the prisoners in civilian clothes and shot them. Then we marched seven days without food. We were joined from various sides by more and more, thousands and thousands of people, Hungarians, Germans, Italians, here and there a Romanian. You couldn't see the beginning or the end of the procession.

In polar regions, the roads had to be reinforced with wood so vehicles and people wouldn't fall through into the thawing ground in the summer. *CVG collection*

Where were you going?

No one knew, just straight ahead. To the east. We crossed the Don and just walked and walked. In a day we made maybe five kilometres, maybe more. There was lots of snow, no path, nothing. Around us thousands of dead that had died in battle, but especially who had frozen. They were completely black. Anyone who fell was just left there. On 27 January, we arrived at a large village, its name was Khrenovoye. There were huge horse stables there, supposedly they used to raise horses for the Tsar's family there. The manure was probably still there from that time and they gradually crammed thousands of people into the stables, without counting them, nothing. People lying on top of each other, nothing to eat, nothing to drink. On top of that lice, typhus, dystrophy and all sorts of other diseases. I'm not going to describe the camp, I've already described it, but just to say that human flesh was eaten there. Every day there were hundreds of dead bodies, piled up like a pyre. Some they carted off to mass graves, assuming they could even dig one, because it was at least twenty degrees below zero. And when the camp finally started to thin out in this manner, sometime around 10 March, the Soviets started to evacuate it. I'd estimate that of the tens of thousands of prisoners, maybe a thousand survived.

What happened to you next?
They took us by train east to Uren, which is somewhere between Gorky and Kazan. There were fifty of us in the wagon and when we reached the last stop, the nurses carried out seventeen alive. In Uren I ended up in a POW hospital. Quite a decent one by Russian standards. The bunks had white sheets and a blanket. They bathed us, cut our hair and deloused us for a time. Of course the lice always came back, but not to the same extent as before. I weighed forty-five kilos and my liver was swelled up by about three or four fingers. On top of that malaria, dystrophy, enlarged heart and who knows what else. In that state they transferred me from one hospital to another. Sometime in May I learned, really quite by accident, that there was a Czechoslovak army. I read it on a used scrap of newspaper that was flying around the hospital courtyard. So three or four of us went to the commissar, saying we are enlisting in the Czechoslovak army. Of course he didn't know anything about it, so I showed him that shit-covered piece of newspaper, where there was an article about the Battle of Sokolovo. He nodded his head and let us be.

Hunger reigned at the hospital. While we did get food regularly, the portions were minimal because the nurses and staff were stealing food. As it happened, an inspection came and I complained about the shortage. When the inspection left, my reward was being sent on the first transport to the labour camp in Vakhtan, which is past Gorky. From Gorky you continued on through the marshes along this kind of twenty-kilometre wooden bridge. I walked about three kilometres and fell to the ground. My feet were swollen like an elephant's. They took me to the infirmary of some forest camp, the number of which I don't remember, where the healthy prisoners went to work in the woods. In the infirmary I saw bed bugs for the first time, but not the last. They had settled in that infirmary in the millions and billions and at night they raided us from the ceiling. I was there about three weeks. Then they sent me to the hospital in Vakhtan. That was another POW hospital for all possible nations. Again there were Jews, Hungarians, Germans, Romanians, Italians. By Russian standards, they took fairly good care of us. The food wasn't too bad, but very scarce, though in line with the standard. The main doctor was time. In all the hospitals I was at, the first thing I did was go with the others to the commissar saying we wanted to join the Czechoslovak army. The same answer always followed: "Da, da, seychas, zavtra, podozhdi."

At that hospital, because the hours were long, I became a watchmaker. I set up a workshop and with handmade tools I repaired watches and clocks from a radius of at least fifty kilometres. I fixed one Russian captain's gold

Ludvík Kellner in 1994. *Archive of Josef Kellner*

watch. I stuck it in my pocket and when I bent over, it fell out and broke definitively. I knew Hungarian and Russian swear words, but what that captain spurted out, I never heard before or after. I went straight by the first transport to another camp, unhealed of course. But that saved me, otherwise I'd probably still be sitting there today. They transferred me to Oranki, a former monastery, where Ludvík Svoboda's Czechoslovak group had also been interned for a time. It was all Romanians there and one of the Romanian engineers took me on as a technician. The camp commander was missing four fingers on one hand. We made him a good prosthesis and so we were fairly well off there. I kept insisting I wanted to join the Czechoslovak army. Sometime in June 1944, the wheels started turning and they sent me along with fifteen other Czechoslovaks via Moscow to Kamianets-Podilskyi and then by car to Sadagura where, following proper enlistment, I became a Czechoslovak soldier on 1 August 1944.

PROŠEL JSEM PEKLEM SOVĚTSKÉHO LÁGRU

LUDVÍK KELLNER

Tato historka žila ve mně už od války, kdy jsem to všechno prožíval. Občas jsem z toho někomu něco vyprávěl, mnozí tomu stejně nevěřili, dokonce při prověrce r. 1970 mi to otloukl o hlavu i podplukovník Kabrhel, manžel nechvalně známé Marie. Na papír jsem se bál povídku napsat.

Jaro 1968 tento strach odehnalo a v červenci jsem povídku napsal. Byl jsem domluven s paní Faktorovou z Listů, že 21. srpna, ve středu dopoledne v 10 hodin, jí povídku odevzdám, ale v té době už v redakci bylo okupační osazenstvo, které neumělo ani číst, ani psát po našem...

Schůze se uskutečnila až někdy v říjnu, kdy „hosté" z redakce už odešli do Milovic a přilehlých posádek od Aše ke Košicím. Paní Faktorová dala povídku přečíst lektorům, kteří ji do týdne vrátili a byli z toho celí vyšinutí. Nastalo dohadování, může se to ještě vytisknout, nebo ne? Snad by to ještě šlo, ale já jsem začal couvat a myslím, že jsem to odhadl správně... neměl jsem pojištění... a měl jsem toho dost, i bez povídky... A tak povídka odpočívala až do nového jara 1990, kdy doufám, že v redakci Reportéra nebudou hosté, které tam nikdo nikdy nezval...

* * *

Kohn horlivě obhajoval svou pravdu:

„Rusové vědí, že jsme tady a co jsme zač. Nikdy na nás nestříleli, když jsme pracovali před liniemi, přestože nás viděli. Máme žluté pásky, jsme v civilu, nejsme vojáci, čeho se máme bát?"

Jeden z odvážnějších členů myší rodinky se nenechal rušit naší debatou a klidně šplhal po kolmé stěně ještě teplé pece v bláhové naději, že tam najde něco na zub.

„Nemyslíš, že Rusům je úplně jedno, kdo jsme? Kopeme zákopy, stavíme drátěné zátarasy, nosíme miny pro Maďary a Němce, tak proč by nás měli očekávat s otevřenou náručí?"

A diskuse, která neměla ani konce, ani výsledky, pokračovala dále, jako každý den. Ošetřující personál židovské nemocnice v Gončarovce se hádal o to, jak to bude, až přijde očekávaný den, kdy se Rusové dají na pochod a smetou německou a maďarskou armádu, pro které nás přinutili nejen otrocky pracovat, ale i umírat jako mouchy na podzim. Že ten den přijde, o tom nikdo neměl pochybnosti, jen otázkou bylo, kdy a jestli se toho ještě dožijeme. Budou nás vítat s otevřenou náručí, nebo nás pošlou na Sibiř, do lágrů, jak o tom povídali vojáci z předešlé války a psaly válečné romány? Pro nás ale není jiného východiska než při první příležitosti přejít k Rusům. Ti, co jsou z Československa, sní o československých legiích...

Venku fičí vítr od Donu, mrzne, zanáší cesty sněhem. Nevíme, co je doma, nevíme, kde je fronta, o Stalingradu jsme ještě neslyšeli, ač jsme o pouhých pár set kilometrů severněji, jen ti, kteří se k nám šťastně dostanou z pekla nucených prací, vykládají, že mezi vojáky v první linii, asi dvacet kilometrů od nás, panuje nervozita a bojí se nejbližších dnů. Něco visí ve vzduchu. Ale co? Co bude s námi? Měli bychom se na události příštích dnů, týdnů nějak připravit.

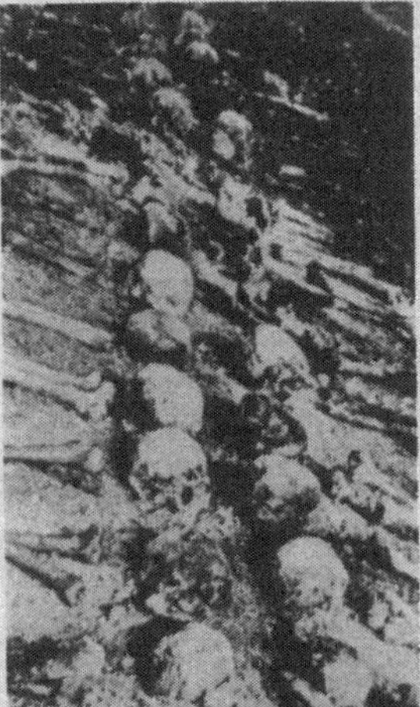

Ale co máme dělat? Naše věčné spory k tomu nedávají žádné návody, žádné východisko.

Už je po vánocích, přišel nový rok a neklid zachvátil i dosud klidnou maďarskou nemocnici, ke které jsme přifařeni. Už občas slýcháváme z dálky děla, hřmění se pomalu blíží. Naše stráže spolu s posádkou a nemocnicí do rána nás jedné noci bez rozloučení opustily, zůstali jsme sami. Na památku nám nechaly těžce nemocné z vojenského špitálu. Ujímáme se moci v zemi nikoho. Posbíráme několik zahozených pušek, obsadíme sklad potravin, několikrát bláznivě střílíme — z bezpečné vzdálenosti — i po ustupujícím vojsku, které naštěstí nemá čas, aby se námi důkladněji zabývalo, ale několik kulometných dávek přece jen vystřelí, a jeden kamarád to má za sebou. Několik dní je kolem nás velký zmatek, stovky a tisíce vojáků ustupují jednou tam, potom zpátky, vozy, koně, auta, tanky zapadají do sněhu a pak zase kamsi jedou. Domníváme se, že bude lepší stáhnout se dál od toho všeho, zahodíme zbraně a zalezeme do svých baráků. Najednou všechno zmizelo a zůstali jsme sami. Asi dvě stě nemocných, většinou neschopných pohybu, a my, deset ošetřovatelů, lékař. Osud sem zanesl i mou bývalou rotu, lépe řečeno její zdecimovaný zbytek, k němuž se přidali další uprchlíci z jiných pracovních táborů, ale ve vesnici se najdou i vojáci beze zbraní z maďarské, italské i německé armády, kteří už toho měli dost.

A tak čekáme na svůj osud v tom mrazivém a nadějném lednu léta páně 1943.

Na okraji Gončarovky v rozházených chalupách, na slámě, rozestřené na většinou hliněné podlaze, leží na dvě stě Židů z takzvaných pracovních táborů. Ještě nedávno pracovali v hadrech v první linii v třeskutých mrazech. Nyní leží zde, na rukách, na nohách namrzlé hnědé prsty, které mokvají a samy odpadávají, omrzlé uši, nosy. Zranění od střepin nášlapných min, se svrabem, oslabení podvýživou, vy-

Příloha **REPORTÉRA**
ČÍSLO 8/1990 STRANA I

Ludvík Kellner could only publish his experience from the POW camp after the fall of the Communist regime. *Repro ÚSTR*

I WENT THROUGH THE HELL OF A SOVIET POW CAMP[193]

LUDVÍK KELLNER

Suddenly everything disappeared and we were left alone. About two hundred patients, most of them immobile, and us, ten nurses and a doctor. Fate had brought my former work squad here as well, or rather its decimated remnants, joined by additional refugees from other labour camps, though unarmed soldiers from the Hungarian, Italian and German armies who had already had enough could also be found in the village.

And so we awaited our fate in that frosty and hopeful January in the year of our Lord 1943.

In scattered cottages on the outskirts of Goncharovka, on straw strewn out on mostly dirt floors, lie two hundred Jews from so-called labour camps. Not long ago they were dressed in rags working on the front line in the freezing cold. Now they lie here, frozen brown fingers and toes oozing and falling off, frostbitten ears, noses. Wounded by landmine shrapnel, with scabies, weakened by malnutrition, emaciated to the bone, with louse-borne typhus, malaria, with wounds from canes and the butts of old Mannlichers. Together we wait for tomorrow. Today still in no man's land.

It is night, but the land already belongs to its rightful owners. The cottages on the outskirts of the village are awakening. Those of us able to walk are taken by Russian soldiers to a kind of gathering point. A truly international society has gathered here, with even a few German soldiers peppered among the Hungarian and Italian ones, but the majority comprises Jews from the labour camps. Day slowly breaks. We move out of the overcrowded building, our new commander standing in the doorway. He tears off my yellow armband, pulls the horse blanket I brought from home out of my backpack and throws it on a pile already full of such things. Dr Várady's armband with the red cross on it also goes on the pile. "Vsyo rovno..."

We wait on the street. Among all the ragged civilians, the military uniforms of various armies cry out their presence. The cold stings. We hop in place and wait. The Russian commander is dressed almost like a paramilitary, but the soldiers follow his orders. There are ten, fifteen of them. The commander tells them something and they explain to us in gestures that the

193 Text was first printed in 1990 in the magazine *Reportér*.

soldiers are to step out of our ranks. Anyone who doesn't understand, they pull out of the crowd themselves. We consider it just that they are separating the soldiers from us. We don't want anything more to do with them, we've had more than enough. The soldiers check once more to make sure there's no more uniforms among us (I'm lucky I didn't take that military fur coat yesterday despite the fact that I was dressed in just a pitiful jacket). They herd the soldiers onto the other side of the road and line them up four abreast. They remove their coats, place them in a row with their backpacks in military style and march off to the nearby yard led by the Russian soldiers, their things remaining behind. There are about thirty of them. We wait on.

The silence is broken by bursts of machine-gun fire. Another few bursts from several machine guns. Heartrending screams. Another few shots and silence falls again. The village inhabitants, who have been watching us from a safe distance, quickly divvy up the soldiers' belongings when the word is given. The commander is the last to return, fastening his pistol holster. He gives the order: "Nu davai!"

I look around me wondering whether it's not a fever dream, what I just heard. Whether it's not just a game of strained nerves, but no one is after us anymore. Past a bend in the road I see the yard where the soldiers lie, half-naked, the villagers quickly stripping off their clothes.

We walk through the village. To the left are the houses with our patients, about whom I never heard anything again and whom I never saw again.

We leave the path. Tanks are barrelling towards us in a whirlwind of snow. Ten, twenty, fifty. Soldiers sit on the machines. Some wave to us in greeting, some shake a fist. One throws a pack of cigarettes. We can choose whichever we want. The treads have thoroughly broken up the frozen snow and we sink deep with every step. I walk with Kohn. I have to help him, he still has great trouble walking. He didn't want to stay in Goncharovka. He wanted to get to the other side at all costs, saying they know about us and are expecting us. The others slowly pass us and we're getting left behind. We're already about twenty metres behind the group and the commander has caught up to us. He shouts something and all I understand is the word "davai", but when he shouts some more, I understand another word: "yevrey". That explains everything. Whenever I'd heard that word, whether it was Jude, zsído or now yevrey, it never sounded flattering. But I didn't expect it here. At any rate, I know where we stand. Kohn is trying, but he can't walk any faster. I try with all my might to pull him, perhaps I've already got a bad feeling, but it's no good. The commander is still on our heels, shouting, and in the chilly air I catch the smell of rum as he pokes me with the barrel of a machine gun. I start to understand that I'm supposed to leave Kohn behind and get forward. I desperately try to explain to him in some language that I can't leave him behind. He can't walk and he'll freeze, but a painful poke in the ribs from the machine-gun barrel and a long curse laced with the epithet "yevrey", capped off with a kick, forces me to leave Kohn. Another kick for the road and the machine gun pointed at me were finally strong enough arguments to compel me to start running and catch up to the rest. Occasionally I look back. Kohn's efforts are in vain, he is merely staggering. A short burst from the machine gun. Kohn lies on the ground, his head buried in the snow. The commander doesn't even turn around and quickly catches up to us. I want to scream, kick at the world around me in boundless rage and pain, but the tears just freeze on my cheeks. I march with the others over the white plains of snow above Goncharovka. I don't want to fall behind, I don't want to see anything, hear anything. I still want to live. I try to remain in the crowd, I'm afraid of being alone. Kohn was right: they knew about us and were expecting us.

Twice during the morning, a short burst of machine-gun fire is heard from the back of the group. No one speaks, we walk with our heads down, resigned to our fate.

It was already long past noon when we reached Saguny. They herded us into a big hall, which was already full without us. We sit, lying on top of each other on the dirty floor and whoever has something in their backpack eats. Most of the inhabitants here are now Hungarian, German and Italian soldiers. The noise is awful. Suddenly the door opens and our commander appears. The machine gun is on his back, he pulls his pistol out of the holster. Without aiming he fires several shots into the swarming crowd. Indescribable panic follows. People scream, cry, tussle. I lie under a pile of people half-mad with fear. I scream as well. I try to move and I manage to raise my head. The commander is still standing in the doorway. He is still holding the pistol. A second might have passed or it might've been a few minutes. The panic continues. Suddenly a soldier appears behind him. He is wearing a proper uniform, officer's straps on his breast, some markings on his collar. With his left hand he grabs the commander's collar and pulls him away from the doorway. I see him holding the commander in front of him, a pistol in his right hand. A shot and our former commander falls down the stairs into the snow. The door closes.

Towards evening we set out. The body of the former commander is lying in the snow beneath the stairs. It's getting dark, the cold is setting in and only the snow lights our way. We walk hours and hours, then get some rest in some large empty barns by the road. We make a fire, but I'm afraid to fall asleep because I'm sure to freeze to death in that dreadful cold. My teeth chatter. The clothes I left home with in the summer are not made for this cold. The old, already broken ski trousers and jacket with the three-quarter-length loden coat that served my father and brother twenty years were not made for Russia. It's a good thing at least my boots are good. In order not to freeze I jump up and down and run to and fro in the open barn. A pack of Italian soldiers is sleeping by a burnt-out fire, an overcoat lies nearby. It is lined with lambswool. I can't resist – I'm terribly cold – and steal the coat. I quickly return to my group and they can't even recognise me. The coat reaches to the ground and is wonderfully warm. It's possible its former owner is dead or froze without the coat – I don't know. One thing is sure, and that's that that coat saved my life, not just then but many times more. For a coat that meant my life to me, I became a thief, perhaps even a murderer.

I walked on in my Italian coat. That seven-day march, or more like crawl, all runs together in my memory. I can't tell the events of the individual days apart. Seven days in a horde constantly moving ahead without knowing where. Like a wide river, boundless and endless, black and roiling ahead and behind me, no end in sight, with smaller rivers, streams, being swallowed into it and swelling it further. Thousands and thousands of people. And like a swollen wild river that furiously tosses its unnecessary burdens upon the shore, so too did this human river cast off and leave behind its unneeded cargo: dead bodies. Ever more and more of them.

We walk by day, stagger by night. I don't even think they were guarding us, there's nowhere to run. Sometimes I'd stop at some deserted spot, at the edge of an abandoned village or in a bare snowfield. It's possible I slept occasionally, I don't know. But I definitely must have slept, maybe just while walking. But lying down to sleep? There was no awakening from that.

We walked through the former front lines. The soldiers hadn't left the trenches, they were still there. Forever. Some had managed to jump out, but they didn't get more than few metres. The rest met death where they stood. Hundreds of dead everywhere. At first we would walk around or step over the dead bodies, later we no longer had the strength for this show of respect.

Across the Don we pass through villages that didn't see war. Without a word, without protest, we tolerate the inhabitants taking whatever they want from us. I don't even thank the old woman that comes up to me, presses what is surely her last piece of dry bread into my hand and blesses me with the cross. They pull my neighbour's shoe off his foot and toss him a rag from an old sack. They are particularly fond of shoes.

We walk like a poorly-oiled machine whose last cog is about to break.

We are starving. The whole time, I got a handful of rusks twice. While resting we boil snow and drink the hot water. With millions of lice, we carry our present and future death. Beyond the Don there are no longer trenches of dead. It is our river producing dead bodies en masse. The human flow is ever slower, but corpses ever more. They remain behind after resting or simply fall out of the herd while marching, or sometimes lie down. We are so free that no one is forced to go on. We can't even see anyone around in charge of such a thing. Instead of kilometre markers, our path is lined with the dead, but much more densely. Sometimes you still look to see whether it's someone you knew or whether they're wearing anything that could be useful. But usually the dead bodies no longer have anything. They are completely naked in no time.

You don't have to die lying down. I saw a man frozen solid in the position of moving his bowels. I saw a soldier in a crawling position. I saw a dead body standing leaned up against a tree. I saw one on his knees, his hands folded in prayer. There are all kinds of ways to die.

If only there were some kind of destination before us! When a Russian soldier does happen by, the response to our queries is always the same: you'll see, "budyet, zavtra".

We crawl towards the Great Uknown...

During the march, no one is surprised when his neighbour starts talking nonsense, or talking to someone who is thousands of kilometres away. They just state the unmistakable diagnosis: louse-borne typhus. There can be no mistake. The diagnosis is more certain than from a council of the most famous professors. I myself discover that I'm starting to have a fever, and I can see in the faces of my friends that I'm occasionally saying strange things to them.

On the afternoon of the seventh day, we are approaching a large village. The guards herd us into a pack, all they're missing are the sheepdogs. We don't yet know, and many never will, that the village is called Khrenovoye. Its name was once famous, but not for khren – horseradish, but for the horses they bred here for the Tsar's family. We do not yet know that those who survive – it will be one twentieth – will still wake up in a sweat twenty years hence, in deathly fear, with chattering teeth, when they dream of Khrenovoye. We don't know this place yet.

We're there. We stand before an enormous gate. There is no sign on it. Dante was not here. He didn't see it. His later fellow countrymen are waiting with us to be let in. There is a cluster of Russian soldiers by the entrance. We walk in through the gate four abreast – they keep saying: "pochetyre" – so they can do a rough count. They're not meticulous about it. Four abreast becomes three to six abreast or a throng, a hundred here, a hundred there, who really cares. There are a lot of us. It doesn't even occur to anyone to write down the names. What would be the point?

We enter the former stables. There could've been thousands of horses here, all that's left of them is manure. A whole Himalayas' worth. I don't know how many yards, with long rows of stables all around them. To the left and right of the entrance is a long corridor, on both sides stalls for probably two horses each. They are separated by 1.5 m wooden partitions, with iron bars above them. The brick floor is covered in a half-metre or more layer of horse manure, frozen solid. Up high are little windows with no glass – it's as cold inside as outside. They herd about fifty of us into each stall, body to body, legs, arms twisted together, darkness, curses, blows. We try to lie down somehow. Only Várady ended up in the same stall as me, my other friends are somewhere in the corridor, in a different stall. I've been pushed into the furthest corner, wrapped in my Italian overcoat. I've got a fever, I think I'm sleeping, fever dreams passing before my eyes, not even sure where I am and what is going on. Sometimes I cry out in my sleep, but it doesn't bother anyone, because half of the occupants are in the same state. Night is a good friend, covering everything, even quieting the fever dreams. The shouts, the wailing and the crying slowly die down, thousands of people having fled with me and their misery into salvation, into sleep.

The cruel morning shows in the dim light what was covered in darkness last night. The endless stables corridor. The huge overflowing latrines in the courtyard with yellow snow all around, because everyone has diarrhoea. There's no water. We're thirsty, so we eat the reeking yellow snow. Before I get back to my stall, I'm already stepping over the first corpses in the corridor.

There's a lot of traffic in the corridors. Everyone is looking for something, trading. Everything, even the most worthless, has its value. I'm hungry and cold. I wrap myself back in my overcoat and sleep. The more I sleep, the less I am aware of our bleak situation.

Some people have found some planks and old doors and built a bunk in the stall, where they have also moved in. More space is left in the manure on the ground. I have kept my old spot. The fever has risen and I have slept more than been awake, living in a state resembling delirium. Only occasionally do I return to cruel reality, the difference between day and night and sleep and wakefulness slowly disappearing. We wait for them to give us something to eat. In vain. In several days, in an unbelievable tumult and battle of man against man, we receive – if one manages to get hold of one – a glass of hot water with several pieces of bran floating in it. Two days later, they hand out bread, about three or four mouthfuls. This order then stabilises. One day water with bran, the next day we fast, the third day bread, then nothing again, and so on. People are going mad with hunger, despite the fact that theoretically, with typhoid fever and a dozen other illnesses, we shouldn't even have an appetite. We would only drink water – if there was any. But all we have an excess of is yellow snow.

People have become walking ghosts. Wandering the halls in rags like lost spirits, while the bodies pile up around the latrines. Every morning we drag several corpses out of the stall, where they lie for a while in the corridor, naked of course. During the day they're carted off somewhere. Poor Várady didn't even last a week. We'd talked just the evening before, then in the morning he was dead, his lips all black, his shoes already missing.

We have lice everywhere. There's no point picking them out. For every one killed, another ten move in. Our hair, beards, clothes, everything is full of them. There are eating us to the bone. There's enough space at night now, we can lie comfortably on the manure, because many of us have involuntarily moved to the corridor. Permanently and irrevocably. When the fever abates and I can't sleep, I wander the corridors and courtyard, looking for my friends. We live in a state where we don't care about anything. I don't find many people I know, they've died. Gabi died too, his brother Dini sits next to the corpse, not wanting to leave it. He doesn't have a fever. I want him to move in with me, but he just shakes his head. By evening he is lying next to his brother in the corridor. I couldn't find Miki, my cousin, either. A few days ago I gave him the fountain pen I had miraculous hung on to so he could trade it for potatoes. Then I don't look for anyone anymore. I lie and wait for my turn to come, for my last spark of will to live to leave me. I don't resist. I no longer have the strength to get up, to participate in the tussles during food distribution, so I don't get anything at all. I await the inevitable end. It's as if the whole world, my whole twenty-something years, everything I experienced, my family, my life had just dissolved into nothingness. I can't think of anything specific. Individual images just appear before me as if on a movie screen, only to disappear again. Most of the time, I no longer have any real thoughts, just fever dreams. I rise up somewhere between heaven and earth. Perhaps children before being born or old people at death's door live in such a state. I don't know.

In several days, the fever dreams start to subside and I start to become aware of what is going on around. Very little has changed. There are less than half of us in the stall, the other stalls are the same. The corridors are still full of corpses. Their clothes and shoes have become "hard currency" because – who knows how – they bring in potatoes, onions and even bread from the village for them.

Sometimes I'd see a corpse with its head split in half. Ever more frequently. My brain was only working at its most basic level, so I couldn't find an explanation. My hunger started to get worse, even though I was managing to get distributed food.

One evening, my neighbour brought me something in his Italian dinner bowl. It wasn't customary to give someone anything, but to my surprise, my neighbour fished something out of the bowl and gave it to me. I couldn't see what it was because it was dark. In my mouth I tasted something salty, soft and raw, and I rolled it over my tongue. It tasted like the blood I sucked out of a wounded finger. At that moment a light lit up in my head! I knew what I had in my mouth and I spit it out immediately. It was raw human brain! That's why the heads of the dead bodies were split open, empty. The neighbour said nothing, just took his spoon and left. I'm not going to do that! I'd rather die. The atavistic instincts inherited from our ancient ancestors did not awaken in me. Even though I was living outside civilisation and outside human life, there was still something left in me that Khrenovoye couldn't wash away. No, even Khrenovoye couldn't force me to cannibalism.

I think that was the shock that brought me back to real life. As if awoken from a coma or a deep hypnotic sleep, I opened my eyes, listened to what was being talked about, looked at what was going on around me. I also asked. I discover that everyone already knows about the cannibalism. They've taken it under advisement like the cold, the hunger, the lice, and death. It's a reality, a fact you cannot escape, save death set you free. There's naught to be done. It's fate. Most do not participate in the cannibalism. But everyone knows the technique. You crack open the head of an as yet unfrozen corpse with an iron rod taken from the stalls. In some cases they even cut open the belly and take out the heart and liver, and it also happens that they cut a piece of meat off the thigh as well – if anything is left on the skin-covered bones. They say people also get killed at night by the latrines so they can get warm meat. At first no one wants to believe, but the pile of mutilated corpses in the corridors every day provides compelling testimony.

There's no more than fifteen of us left in the stall.

Some Hungarian staff sergeant starts putting things in order. Despite our resistance, stemming from our passive awaiting of our fate – a slap or two was also needed – he forced us to carry out handfuls of the manure we'd been lying on. He has the floor swept and institutes rapid removal of bodies into the corridor. I'm terribly weak, I can barely stand on my own two legs, taking ten steps requires superhuman effort. At least twice a day, the staff sergeant shoos us out of the stall and forces us to do something, thereby perhaps saving our lives. Otherwise we would have kept lying idly on the manure until the others carried us out into the corridor as well.

We are unbelievable dirty, louse-ridden, shaggy, our feet are swollen like an elephant's, but our bodies are just skin and bone, covered with ulcers, open festering sores. We suffer from constant diarrhoea but I don't know what else we can put in the latrines but blood, because the food is still the same, perhaps with an extra spoonful of hot water or a centimetre of bread in place of those who no longer need it.

We carry the dead, or rather drag them, two and two a single corpse along the frozen paths across the whole camp. We tie a rope to their foot or hand and tow them with superhuman effort. At the other end of the camp by one of the entrances stands a former church made of red brick, which has become a mortuary. The frozen-solid corpses are piled into a pyre like logs in the forest. The pyres are several metres high, thousands of corpses, every one of them naked. Head to head, the next row perpendicular. Many of them have their heads split open, some their bellies ripped open, here and there a piece of meat sliced off. For unknown reasons, sometimes a hand or leg has been separated from the body and stuck in the opened belly. The pyre is erected by a group of strong, well-fed prisoners who, aware of their importance, have perfectly mastered the art of building pyres out of corpses so the authorities can be satisfied with a perfect job.

The church is packed, there's no more room.

Soldiers enter the camp, randomly pick out the strongest-looking individuals and take them somewhere to the edge of the village, where they dig shallow pits in the frozen ground for mass graves. They start taking the dead there from the church.

One day, word comes to the stall that the Hungarians are to gather in some yard somewhere, because Rákosi has come to the camp. I don't think anyone even knew who that was supposed to be and no one even moved. After many years I learned that it wasn't Rákosi, but another leading Hungarian communist, Zoltán Vas (who also recalled it in his memoirs). After the war, a friend told me he was present at that meeting. He recalled how Vas smelled of cologne after a fresh shave, how he backed off to a safe distance from the louse-ridden, reeking, dirty ghosts that had gathered. But for us just lying on the brick floor – now free of manure – unheard-of things started to happen over time. A rumour was going around that the whole camp *nachalstvo* – of whom we'd never seen a one – had been executed and a new commander had come. This news was confirmed when the food-bearers started coming every day and bringing real soup, bread and some sort of porridge. Meals finally started working. At first there was still a scuffle around the distribution of food, but it soon stopped. People even started offering food because there were already so few of us and lots of us couldn't even eat. We often vomited up the food or put it straight in the latrine a thousand times in unimaginable agony. Even the smell of food could evoke vomiting. All we wanted was onion and sugar – but there was no such thing in the whole world. Soldiers started visiting the camp more frequently. They'd herd us out of the stalls, have us line up and spend a long time counting us. Sometimes they'd take some of us away, but most of them slinked off on the way and came back to the stalls. Some didn't manage to disappear and they generally had to dig graves. It also happened that some didn't return at all. It seemed the camp was starting to empty out.

One time I, too, could not escape fate, there was no getting out of it. We went out the gate, it was terribly cold. We trudged through the deep snow for several hours before we'd covered two or three kilometres. There was some straw beneath a metre of snow on an immense field. Each of us was to dig out as much as we could. So like the others I dug out a handful of black, rotten, stinking straw that we carried back the same way like the holy eucharist. The long and tiring journey completely exhausted me, and somewhere halfway back I collapsed and couldn't get back up. One of the guard soldiers stood over me holding a rifle with a long bayonet wantonly cursing the Germans, Hungarians and Italians with a rich vocabulary. He made sure to include their mothers, God and all the saints and he managed to elegantly repeat it in all sorts of variations. For I while I listened to it, but then I had to set the record straight. I was wearing my Italian overcoat, so I foolishly wanted to explain to him that appearances are deceiving if he considers me a member of the nations mentioned, because I am merely from the "rabochiy batalyon". But my soldier's reaction was quite different than I expected. He became even more incensed and was evidently sufficiently acquainted with the organisation of the enemy armies because he thwacked me with the butt of his rifle with the words "yob tvoyu yevreyskuyu mať" and pointed the barrel at me in an unequivocal gesture. He no longer had to explain anything to me, it was all clear. With superhuman effort I managed to stand up and, accompanied by terse curses all including the word "yevrey", we caught up to the group.

There weren't even ten of us left in the stall. We'd all been for straw, which we'd laid out on the ground – about a handful per square metre. But we couldn't even enjoy the luxury of that rotten and wet straw. That same evening a pack of soldiers showed up, among them – judging by her insignia – an officer, a doctor. We'd never seen anything like that in Khrenovoye before. With a loud shout she ordered me to gather up our precious collected straw and throw it out because, she said, lice live in straw. When we had collected and thrown out the straw in front of her, she and her suite left, satisfied. And so we were once again without straw, but the lice didn't abandon us because of it. I guess they didn't miss it all that much.

Several days later they shooed us out of the stall again. Some soldier promised that they were taking us to the hospital, but based on our previous experience, whoever could, slipped away. I stayed. So we're walking through the camp, through several yards towards a big building that at first glance looks like a riding school. A guard with a rifle stands by the entrance. Inside are huge mountains of manure and there are hundreds of dead and dying lying on those hills and valleys. I quickly turn around and want to leave, but the guard won't let me. You can only go in, not out. Luckily I have the presence of mind that I point to one of the dying, saying I just brought him in to the "hospital" and that I'm going back for another, so the guard lets me out. I quickly return to the safety of the stall.

Roll calls are every day. February has passed and the first days of March are arriving. People are still dying. Once after roll call there is no escape. We leave the gate, no one even counts us, and there is a row of freight wagons on the nearby train tracks. They count us off in fifties and we board the freight wagons. I meet my old classmate Lazar and together we climb on a bunk by the window. They give us a few loaves of bread, a barrel of porridge, water and close the doors.

At night the train starts moving. When it stops somewhere, they give us some more food, but no one can eat. We suffer from constant diarrhoea, fever.

It's cold, people are freezing, crying, moaning, praying and dying in their own excrement. The lice travel with us. When the train is moving, we don't even know about them, but as soon as it stops, it's as if they want to make up for the time travelled and eat us alive. I think some scholar among us could write an academic paper on this interesting fact – if they survived.

The trip takes a week. We can't tell from the signs at the stations where we are or what direction we're travelling. When the doors open after a week, we see a little train station with the name Uren. We don't know where that might be.

None of us can stand and leave the wagon themselves. Women dressed in white coats come and carry us out, or rather just the live ones. There's seventeen of us. They pile thirty-three right on the ground next to the wagon. The ratio is roughly the same by the other wagons, but the score is worse for the one right next to us: only three have survived. The soldiers count it all and it seems the numbers add up. No one escaped – except from life. But that can all be counted up to state – the numbers add up.

A small, young slender nurse climbs on the bunk and collects me along with my Italian coat. She is not afraid of me – I must look inhuman – or my lice. She scoops me up like a newborn and carries me out of the wagon. She places me on a low sleigh tied to a little hairy horse. My mind is somehow still boggled by how easily the girl carried me, since I'm not that small.

The sleigh stands in front of a low building with steam pouring out of it. The girl explains something, but I don't understand, so she scoops me up again and carries me inside. She takes off my Italian overcoat – that was the last time I saw it – pulls off my other dirty and louse-ridden clothes as well and sits me on a low bench. She shaves my head clean, then shaves me from head to foot, I didn't even have time to be ashamed, then takes a bucket of hot water and soap and uses some kind of whisk to remove two months of filth from me. It takes some work. Then she smears me with some kind of smelly liquid – she explains that it's against lice – dries me with a sheet, wraps me in a blanket and carries me like an infant into a nearby building. I can't believe my eyes. In the room are bunk beds with white sheets and a blanket. She lays me on a bunk.

I feel like I've come back to the world from the other side of the Styx. My eyes close. When they wake me, they feed me like a baby. Then, finally, they asked me for my personal information. And wrote it down. For the first time.

LIST OF ABBREVIATIONS

CVG	Czechoslovaks in The Gulag project
DALO	Derzhavnyy arkhiv Lvivskoyi Oblasti, State Archive of Lviv Region
DAZO	Derzhavnyy arkhiv Zakarpatskoyi oblasti, State Archive of Transcarpathian Region
f.	fond
Gestapo	Geheime Staatspolizei, Secret State Police
Gulag	Glavnoye Upravleniye ispravitel'no-trudovykh LAGerey, Main Directorate of Correctional Labour Camps
GUPVI	Glavnoye upravleniye po delam voyennoplennykh i internirovannykh, Main Administration for Affairs of Prisoners of War and Internees
HDA SBU	Haluzevyy derzhavnyy arkhiv Sluzhby bezpeky Ukrainy, State Archives Department of the Security Service of Ukraine
KSČ	Communist Party of Czechoslovakia
lagpunkt	lagernyy punkt, camp site
NKVD	Narodny komissariat vnutrennih del, People's Commissariat for Internal Affairs
RGVA	Rossiskii Gosudarstvennyi Voennyi Arkhiv, Russian State Military Archive
USSR	Union of Soviet Socialist Republics
UPVI	Upravleniye po delam voyennoplennykh i internirovannykh, Administration for Affaiirs of Prisoners of War and Internees
USC	University of Southern California
ÚSTR	Institute for the Study of Totalitarian Regimes

ABBREVIATIONS OF GULAG CAMPS

Belbaltlag	Belomoro-Baltiyskiy ispravitelno-trudovoy lager, White Sea-Baltic Corrective Labour Camp
Intinlag	Intinskiy ispravitelno-trudovoy lager, Inta Corrective Labour Camp
Ivdellag	Ivdelskiy ispravitelno-trudovoy lager, Ivdel Corrective Labour Camp
Kandalakshlag	Kandalaksha ispravitelno-trudovoy lager, Kandalaksha Corrective Labour Camp
Kargopollag	Kargopolskiy ispravitelno-trudovoy lager, Kargopol Corrective Labour Camp
Karlag	Karagandinskiy ispravitelno-trudovoy lager, Karaganda Corrective Labour Camp
Oneglag	Onezhskiy ispravitelno-trudovoy lager, Oneg Corrective Labour Camp
Pechorlag	Pechorskiy ispravitelno-trudovoy lager, Pechora Corrective Labour Camp
Sevpechlag	Severo-Pechorskiy ispravitelno-trudovoy lager, North Pechora Corrective Labour Camp
Sevvostlag	Severo-Vostochnyy ispravitelno-trudovoy lager, North-East Corrective Labour Camp
Sevzheldorlag	Severnyy zheleznodorozhnyy ispravitelno-trudovoy lager, Northern Railway Corrective Labour Camp
Siblag	Sibirskiy ispravitelno-trudovoy lager, Siberian Corrective Labour Camp
Solikamlag	Solikamskiy ispravitelno-trudovoy lager, Solikamsk Corrective Labour Camp
Unzhlag	Unzhenskiy ispravitelno-trudovoy lager, Unzha Corrective Labour Camp
Ustvymlag	Ustvymskiy ispravitelno-trudovoy lager, Ust-Vym Corrective Labour Camp
Volgolag	Volzhskiy ispravitelno-trudovoy lager i Stroitelstvo gidrotekhnicheskikh uzlov, Volga Corrective Labour Camp and Hydrosystem Construction
Vorkutlag	Vorkutinskiy ispravitelno-trudovoy lager, Vorkuta Corrective Labour Camp

LIST OF SOURCES AND LITERATURE USED

ARCHIVAL SOURCES

Czech archives

Security Services Archive

f. Main Administration of Intelligence Service (1st administration)

f. Main Administration of Military Counterintelligence (302)

f. Jewish Organisations (425)

Central Military Archive

registration files, qualification files, personal files

Foreign archives

State Archive of Lviv Region (Derzhavnyy arkhiv Lvivskoyi Oblasti)

f. Criminal Files R-3258 (1939–1950)

State Archive of Transcarpathian Region (Derzhavnyy arkhiv Zakarpatskoyi oblasti)

f. Criminal Files 2558 (1939–1993)

State Archives Department of the Security Service of Ukraine (Haluzevyy derzhavnyy arkhiv Sluzhby bezpeky Ukrainy)

f. Criminal Files (1939–1994)

State Archives Department of the Security Service of Ukraine (Haluzevyy derzhavnyy arkhiv Sluzhby bezpeky Ukrainy) – Lviv

f. Jewish Files (1939–1941)

State Archives Department of the Security Service of Ukraine (Haluzevyy derzhavnyy arkhiv Sluzhby bezpeky Ukrainy) – Uzhhorod

f. Criminal Files (1939–1950)

Russian State Military Archive (Rossiskii Gosudarstvennyi Voennyi Arkhiv) – Moscow

f. 465 (prisoners of war)

UNPUBLISHED MEMOIRS, INTERVIEWS

Yad Vashem Archives Jerusalem

f. P25 – Erich Kulka Archive. Testimonies collected by Erich Kulka regarding the war period. Record Group 0-59, Collection of Testimonies and Documents on the Participation of Czechoslovak Jews in the War against the Nazi-Germany:

interviews with Mikuláš (Zvi) Faerber, Jakob Friedmann, Moritz (Moshe) Friedner, Michael Lavi (Lebovič), Chana Nagel, Marek (Mordechai) Neuer

Archive of the Jewish Museum in Prague – Shoah Documentation Department

f. Oral History Collection:

interviews with Salomon Desider, Ludvík Kellner, Andrej Štern

USC Shoah Foundation Visual History Archive, accessed at the Malach Centre for Visual History at Charles University

Holocaust Collection:

interviews with Karel Borský (Kurt Biheller), ID: 19560; Samuel Friedmann, ID: 24462; Alice Salamon Kupferman, ID: 8622; Natan Landau, ID: 36701; Ladislav (Les) Maget, ID: 22369; Bedřich (Fred) Morgenstern, ID: 14673; Zoltán Štern, ID: 45090; Ernest Vider ID: 35817

Institute for the Study of Totalitarian Regimes
Czechoslovaks in the Gulag project collection (CVG collection): interviews with Ernest Breiner, Sigmund Hladík, Michael Lavi (Lebovič), Egon Morgenstern, Yehuda Parma (Leopold Presser), Hanan Ron (Hanuš Rosenbaum), Karel Vaš
Memory of Nations Archive
interviews with Michael Lavi (Lebovič)

PUBLISHED MEMOIRS

GLIKSMAN, Jerzy G.: *Tell the West.* Gresham Press, New York 1948
GOLIAT-GOROVSKÝ, Karel: *Zápisky ze stalinských koncentráků* [Notes from the Stalinist Concentration Camps]. Index, Köln, 1986
HERLING-GRUDZIŃSKI, Gustaw: *A World Apart.* Heinemann, London 1951
IZAJ, Michal: *Příběhy mého života* [Stories of My Life]. Československá obec legionářská, Prague 2011
KELLNER, Ludvík: *Jediná cesta* [The Only Way]. Naše vojsko, Prague 1956
KELLNER, Ludvík: Prošel jsem peklem sovětského lágru [I Went Through the Hell of a Soviet POW Camp]. *Reportér*, 1990, no. 8, Supplement, p. I–V
LEVORA, Vladimír: *Ze stalinských gulagů do československého vojska* [From Stalin's Gulags to the Czechoslovak Army]. Organised by Zora Dvořáková. Nakl. Josef Hříbal, Plzeň 1993
MARGOLINE, Jules: *La condition inhumaine. Cinq ans dans les camps de con centration sovietiques.* Traduit par N. Berberova & Mina Journot. Calmann-Levi Editeurs, Paris 1949
POLÁK, František: *Otroci sovětských koncentračních táborů* [Slaves of the Soviet Concentration Camps]. Self-published, New York 1955
POLÁK, František: *Cestou ze sovětských koncentráků* [On the Way from a Soviet Concentration Camp]. Self-published, New York 1959
POLÁK, František: *Sedm let v Gulagu. Vzpomínky pražského advokáta na sovětské pracovní tábory* [Seven Years in the Gulag. A Prague Attorney's Memories of Soviet Labour Camps] (eds. Adam Hradilek – Zdeněk Vališ). Institute for the Study of Totalitarian Regimes, Prague 2015
FRISCHEROVÁ, Helena: *Dny mého života. Vzpomínky na gulag* [Days of My Life. Memories of the Gulag]. Academia, Prague 2017
WIESENTHAL, Simon: *Justice, not Vengeance: Recollections.* Grove Weidenfeld, New York 1989

MANUSCRIPTS

HRADILEK, Adam: *Perzekuce uprchlíků z Podkarpatské Rusi do SSSR v letech 1939–1945* [Persecution of refugees from Subcarpathian Rus to the USSR in 1939–1945]. Thesis. Technical University of Liberec, 2017
LAVI, Michael: *The Story of My Life.* CVG collection

STATISTICS, DIRECTORIES, OVERVIEWS

Reabilitovani istoriiu. Zakarpatska oblast I–II. Uzhhorod: VAT "Vydavnytstvo 'Zakarpattia'", 2003.

INTERNET LINKS

ROZETT, Robert: *Conscripted Slaves. Hungarian Jewish Forced Laborers on the Eastern Front during World War II. The international School for Holocaust Studies.* Yad Vashem Newsletter, 2013: http://www.yadvashem.org/yv/en/education/newsletter/31/conscripted_slaves.asp
VALIŠ, Zdeněk: *Podplukovník v záloze JUDr. a PhDr. Karel Vaš:* http://virtually.cz/archiv.php?art=9342

LITERATURE USED

ADLER, Eliyana R.: "Crossing Over Exploring the Borders of Holocaust Testimony". *Yad Vashem Studies*, Vol. 43, n. 2, 2015, p. 83–108

APPLEBAUM, Anne: *Gulag. Historie* [The Gulag. A History]. Beta-Dobrovský, Prague 2004

BENDA, Jan: *Útěky a vyhánění z pohraničí českých zemí 1938–1939* [Escapes and Expulsions from the Czech Borderlands 1938–1939]. Karolinum. Prague 2013

BORÁK, Mečislav: *České stopy v Gulagu. Z výzkumu perzekuce Čechů a občanů ČSR v Sovětském svazu* [Czech Traces in the Gulag. From Research on the Persecution of Czechs and Czechoslovak Citizens in the Soviet Union]. Silesian Museum, Opava 2003

BORÁK, Mečislav: Českoslovenští Židé – oběti gulagů a popravišť v Sovětském svazu [Czechoslovak Jews – Victims of Gulags and Execution Centres in the Soviet Union]. In: MACHÁČKOVÁ, Helena (ed.): *První pražský seminář. Dopady holocaustu na českou a slovenskou společnost ve druhé polovině 20. století* [First Prague Seminar. The Impact of the Holocaust on Czech and Slovak Society in the Second Half of the 20th Century]. Varius Praha – Spolek akademiků Židů, Prague 2008, p. 97–110

BORÁK, Mečislav (ed.): *Perzekuce československých občanů v Sovětském svazu (1918–1956). Sborník studií. Část 1. Vězni a popravení* [Persecution of Czechoslovak Citizens in the Soviet Union (1918–1956). Collection of Studies. Part 1. Prisoners and Executees]. Silesian Museum – Silesian University in Opava, Opava 2007

BORÁK, Mečislav: *První deportace evropských Židů. Transporty do Niska nad Sanem (1939–1940)* [First Deportations of European Jews. Transports to Nisko (1939–1945)]. 2nd revised edition. Český svaz bojovníků za svobodu, Ostrava 2009

BORÁK, Mečislav: Příprava a průběh niských transportů [Preparation and Implementation of the Nisko Transports]. In: *Akce Nisko v historii „konečného řešení židovské otázky" – k 55. výročí první deportace evropských Židů. Mezinárodní vědecká konference. Sborník referátů* [The Nisko Plan in the History of the "Final Solution to the Jewish Question". On the 55th Anniversary of the First Deportation of European Jews. International Academic Conference. Collection of papers]. Responsible ed. Ludmila Nesládková. Rondo, Ostrava 1995, p. 100–105

BORÁK, Mečislav: Z nacistického koncentračního tábora do sovětských gulagů. Osudy ostravských Židů z transportů do Niska nad Sanem [From Nazi Concentration Camp to Soviet Gulag. Fates of Ostrava Jews from the Transports to Nisko]. In: *Příspěvky k dějinám a současnosti Ostravy a Ostravska 25* [Contributions on the History and Present of Ostrava and the Ostrava Region 25]. Ostrava University, Ostrava 2011, p. 97–135

BRAHAM, Randolph L.: *The Politics of Genocide: The Holocaust in Hungary.* Wayne State University Press, Detroit 2000

BROŽ, Miroslav: *Hrdinové od Sokolova. 1. čs. samostatný polní prapor v SSSR: seznam příslušníků praporu a účastníků bitvy u Sokolova 8. března 1943* [Heroes of Sokolovo. The First Independent Czechoslovak Field Battalion in the USSR: A List of Battalion Members and Participants in the Battle of Sokolovo 8 March 1943]. Ministry of Defence of the Czech Republic, Prague 2005

BYSTROV, Vladimir: *Průvodce říší zla* [Guide to the Realm of Evil]. Academia, Prague 2006

CONQUEST, Robert: *The Great Terror: A Reassessment.* Oxford University Press, Oxford 1991

Dějiny Ruska 20. století. Díl II. Ed. Andrej B. Zubov, Argo, Praha 2015

DOVHANICH Omelan: Repressii uhors'koho okupatsiĭnoho rezhimu proty hromadian kraiu. In: *Reabilitovani istoriiu. Zakarpatska oblast I. Uzhhorod: VAT "Vydavnytstvo 'Zakarpattia'"*, 2003, p. 21–38

DOVHANICH, Omelan: Peresliduvannia hromadian radyans'kym totalitarnym rezhymom u peredvoienni ta povoienni roky. In: *Reabilitovani istoriiu. Zakarpatska oblast I. Uzhhorod: VAT "Vydavnytstvo 'Zakarpattia'"*, 2003, p. 39–56

DVOŘÁK, Jan: Směr Nisko nad Sanem. První organizované deportace Židů z Vídně [Destination Nisko. The First Organised Deportations of Jews from Vienna]. *Historica. Revue pro historii a příbuzné vědy*, 2012, vol. 3, no. 1, p. 44–57

DVOŘÁK, Jan – FORMÁNEK, Jaroslav – HRADILEK, Adam: *Čechoslováci v Gulagu* [Czechoslovaks in the Gulag]. Czech Television – Institute for the Study of Totalitarian Regimes, Prague 2017

DVOŘÁK, Jan – HRADILEK, Adam: Perzekuce československých Židů v Sovětském svazu za druhé světové války [Persecution of Czechoslovak Jews in the Soviet Union in World War II]. In: *Historie – Otázky – Problémy* [History – Questions – Problems], 2013, vol. 5, no. 1, p. 105–120

HANZLÍK, František – POSPÍŠIL, Jan – POSPÍŠIL, Jaroslav: *Sluha dvou pánů* [Servant of Two Masters]. Lípa – A. J. Rychlík, Vizovice 1999

HORVATH, Attila: "War and Peace: The Effects of World War II on Hungarian Education". In: LOWE, Roy (ed.): *Education & the Second World War: Studies in Schooling & Social Change.* Falmer Press, London 1992, p. 139–150

HRADILEK, Adam: Karel Vaš v SSSR. Vězněm a spolupracovníkem NKVD [Karel Vaš in the USSR. Prisoner and NKVD Collaborator]. *Paměť a dějiny*, 2012, vol. VI, no. 3, p. 72–88

KHLEVNIUK, Oleg Vitalyevich: *Historie gulagu. Od kolektivizace do „velkého teroru"* [History of the Gulag. From Collectivisation to the "Great Terror"]. BB/art, Prague 2008

JELINEK, Yeshayahu A. – MAGOCSI, R. Paul: *The Carpathian Diaspora. The Jews of Subcarpathian Rus´ and Mukachevo, 1848–1948.* Columbia University Press, New York 2007

KARNER, Stefan: "In Stalin's Custody. The Soviet Camp System for Prisoners of War during and after the World War II". In: BISCHOFF, Günter – PLASSER, Fritz – STELTZ-MARX, Barbara (eds): *New Perspectives on Austrians and World War II, Contemporary Austrian Studies,* vol. 17, Transaction Publishers, New Brunswick 2009, p. 121–134

KREJČOVÁ, Helena – BEDNAŘÍK, Petr: Emigrace do Československa a z něj po Mnichovské dohodě [Emigration after the Munich Agreement]. In: *Exil v Praze a v Československu 1918–1938 / Exile in Prague and Czechoslovakia 1918–1938.* Pražská edice, Prague 2005, p. 206–207

KULKA, Erich: *Židé v československé Svobodově armádě* [Jews in the Czechoslovak Svoboda's Army]. Naše vojsko, Prague 1990

LÁŠEK, Radan: Obrana Podkarpatské Rusi [The Defence of Subcarpathian Rus]. *Paměť a dějiny*, 2009, vol. III, no. 1, p. 21–29

MOSER, Jonny: "Nisko. Ein geplantes Judenreservat in Polen". In: *Das Jüdische Echo*, Bd. 120, Nr. 36. Verein zur Herausgabe der Zeitschrift „Das Jüdische Echo", Wien 1989, p. 118–122

OFICYNSKYJ, Roman: Nelehalnyj perekhid uhorsko-radyanskoho kordonu v 1939–1941 rokakh. Studia Carpatica – Karpatoznavchi studii: specialnyj vypusk. Uzhorodskyj derzhavnyj universitet; Naukovo-doslidnyj instytut karpatoznavstva, Uzhhorod 1993.

POLONSKY, Antony: *The Jews in Poland and Russia. Volume III: 1914 to 2008.* The Littman Library of Jewish Civilization, Oxford – Portland, Oregon 2012

POSKOČIL, Stanislav: *Egon Morgenstern. Přežil jsem peklo gulagu* [Egon Morgenstern. I Survived the Hell of the Gulag]. Nakladatelství P3K, Prague 2015

PRZYBYLOVÁ, Blažena: "Emigrace ostravského židovského obyvatelstva ve 30. a 40. letech 20. Století" [Emigration of Ostrava Jewish population in the 1930s and 40s]. In: *Sborník prací Filozofické fakulty Ostravské univerzity – Historie/Historica 153* [Collection of Works of the Ostrava University Faculty of Arts – History/Historica], 1995, p. 63–65

PŘIBYL, Lukáš: "Osud třetího protektorátního transportu do Niska". In: KÁRNÝ, Miroslav – LORENCOVÁ, Eva (eds.): *Terezínské studie a dokumenty* [Terezín Studies and Documents]. Academia, Prague 2000, p. 309–346

PŘIBYL, Lukáš – PLZÁK, Michal: *Zapomenuté transporty* [Forgotten Transports]. Kalich, Prague 2013

ROTHKIRCHENOVÁ, Livie: Osud Židů v Čechách a na Moravě v letech 1938–1945 [The Fate of Jews in Bohemia and Moravia in 1938–1945]. In: ROTHKIRCHENOVÁ, Livie – SCHMIDTOVÁ-HART-MANNOVÁ, Eva – DAGAN, Avigdor (eds.): *Osud Židů v Protektorátu 1939–1945* [The Fate of Jews in the Protectorate 1939–1945]. Trizonia, Prague 1991

ROZZET, R.: *Conscripted Slaves. Hungarian Jewish Forced Laborers on the Eastern Front during the Second World War.* Yad Vashem, Jerusalem, 2013

RYCHLÍK, Jan – RYCHLÍKOVÁ, Magdaléna: *Podkarpatská Rus v dějinách Československa 1918–1946* [Subcarpathian Rus in the History of Czechoslovakia 1918–1946]. Vyšehrad, Prague 2016

SOLZHENITSYN, Alexander Isayevich: *Dvě stě let pospolu. Dějiny rusko-židovských vztahů v letech 1917–1995*. Academia, Prague 2005

ŠVORC, Peter: *Zakletá zem. Podkarpatská Rus 1918–1946* [Cursed Land. Subcarpathian Rus 1918–1946]. Nakladatelství Lidové noviny, Prague 2007

VALIŠ, Zdeněk: Heliodor Píka v boji za životy Podkarpatorusů. Ze sovětských gulagů do Československé armády" [Heliodor Píka in the Fight for the Lives of Subcarpathians. From the Soviet Gulags to the Czechoslovak Army]. *Časopis Slezského zemského muzea. Série B – vědy historické*. 2008, vol. 57, no. 1, p. 22–59

VALIŠ, Zdeněk: "Ze sovětských gulagů do československé armády. Heliodor Píka v boji za životy Podkarpatorusů" [From the Soviet Gulags to the Czechoslovak Army. Heliodor Píka in the fight for the lives of Subcarpathians]. *Historie a vojenství. Časopis Vojenského historického ústavu*. 2008, vol. 57, no. 1, p. 43–58.

ZEMSKOV, Viktor N.: K voprosu o masshtabakh represiy v SSSR. *Sociologicheskie issledovania*, no. 9, Moscow 1995, p. 118–127

EDITORIAL NOTE

Preparation of the interviews for publication required significant editing. Some had to be translated from the language in which they were conducted. All of them had to be arranged according to the chronology of events for the best possible comprehensibility and edited in line with the standards of printed text, as well as for grammar, syntax and style. All modifications were however carried out with careful efforts not to distort the content. (Those interested in the authentic form of the interviews can find the original version in the respective archives and collections.) Aside from removing clear errors, especially those of a statistical nature, the editing did not affect the content. For example, if the interviewee recalled that *"thousands of people died"* at a given place, but it is known from other sources that there were demonstrably fewer of them, such information was corrected in the sense of *"many people died"*. The value of personal testimony from direct witnesses is not however in the exact factual description of the experienced events. Their significance lies precisely in the conveying of a personal subjective experience of historical events that would otherwise be lost in the flood of data and phrases. Despite this, it is necessary to keep in mind this subjectivity, this lack of objectivity, and treat their testimony not as historical fact, but more as a reflection of reality in the mind of the given person, influenced both by the internal mechanisms of human memory and from without (the memories of others, other personal experiences, literature, media, etc.).[194]

Interviews conducted by: Barbara Appelbaum, Eva Benešová, Jan Dvořák, Renee Hecht, Adam Hradilek, Anna Hyndráková, Erich Kulka, Anna Lorencová, Peter Seller, Julij Sternberg, Boris Timur, Katarina Zavarská.

194 Cf. the issue of Holocaust memories, e.g. in: PŘIBYL, Lukáš – PLZÁK, Michal: *Zapomenuté transporty [Forgotten transports]*. Kalich, Prague 2013, p. 53—54.

ACKNOWLEDGEMENTS

This book would not have been possible without the help and support of many people and institutions. Special thanks go to the Foundation for Holocaust Victims for financial support; Mečislav Borák and Zdeněk Vališ for valuable comments and consultation; Jaroslav Formánek for helping edit the interviews; Martin Šmok and Jakub Mlynář of the Malach Centre for procuring the interviews stored at the USC Shoah Foundation; Pavla Neuner for providing the interviews from the Jewish Museum in Prague; Andrej Kohut for providing the documents from HDA SBU; the employees of the State Archives in Uzhhorod, Lviv and the employees of Yad Vashem and the Hebrew University in Jerusalem for assistance finding and kindly providing archival materials; Štěpán Černoušek, Jiřina Dvořáková, Štěpán Hlavsa and Jan Horník for assistance in procuring and processing these.